Involved

Writing for College, Writing for Your Self

Charles Bazerman

University of California — Santa Barbara

D1518567

Houghton Mifflin Company   Boston   New York

Sponsoring Editor: Jayne Fargnoli
Basic Book Editor: Martha Bustin
Senior Project Editor: Susan Westendorf
Senior Production/Design Coordinator: Jill Haber
Senior Manufacturing Coordinator: Priscilla Bailey
Marketing Manager: Nancy Lyman

Cover design: Mark Caleb
Cover image: Words superimposed over writing paper; envelopes and pen, Tony Stone images.

Text and Photo Credits begin on page 365.

 As part of Houghton Mifflin's ongoing commitment to the environment, this text has been printed on recycled paper.

Printed in the U.S.A.
Library of Congress Catalog Card Number: 96-76862
Student Edition ISBN: 0-395-67182-5
Exam Copy ISBN: 0-395-67183-3

1 2 3 4 5 6 7 8 9—BH—00 99 98 97 96

BRIEF TABLE OF CONTENTS

TABLE OF CONTENTS

3 Writing Processes   44

4 Journals and Reflective Writing   72

5 Notes and Summaries: Writing to Remember   94

6 Exam Writing: Displaying Knowledge 123

PART THREE
Using Concepts to View the World 151

7 Illustrative Writing: Connecting Concepts and Real Examples 152

8 Autobiographical Writing: Connecting Concepts and Experience 166

For most students, college is a new world. Students meet new kinds of people, engage in new kinds of discussions, read new kinds of books, and are asked to write new kinds of essays. Those who are drawn into this new world, who find questions and knowledge that excite them, who relate to the readings, who express their thoughts and learning—they succeed at college and get the most out of it. Those who have trouble communicating within this academic world and cannot connect its goals with their own—they often struggle and do not get from college all that they had hoped.

Whether college becomes an exciting environment or an alien one depends to a great extent on the mastering of college-level reading and writing, because texts are central to the life of the university. In college, students must absorb information of increasing sophistication from a range of reading materials. They are expected to think about, synthesize, and critique these materials and to use their knowledge to understand and investigate the world. Students, ultimately, are in college to become complex and knowledgeable participants in the world, able to articulate and argue their insights in effective writing.

These are tough demands that depend on students becoming deeply involved with their subject matters. Only that personal involvement can provide sufficient motivation to do the kind of disciplined work that allows one to get the most from college. Involvement is not a matter of luck, as many students may think. It is built through every act of reading and writing. Involvement increases every time a student finds some personally valuable meaning in a reading assignment, finds a class assignment stimulating, or a writing assignment to be an opportunity to develop thought. Involvement increases every time a student states his or her ideas forcefully enough to get a serious response from teachers and other students. Involvement increases whenever a student notices his or her reading, writing, and thinking going to a new level.

Involved: Writing for College, Writing for Your Self helps students to understand their college experience as a way of advancing their own personal concerns and to draw substance from their reading and writing assignments. By enabling students to understand what it is they are being asked to write—from basic to complex communications—and how they can go about fulfilling those tasks meaningfully and successfully, *Involved: Writing for College, Writing for Your Self* helps students to develop themselves in all the ways the university offers.

❦ Distinctive Features of *Involved: Writing for College, Writing for Your Self*

- **The Involvement theme helps students to be active participants in their college education.** *Involved* encourages students to take responsibility for learning, to connect college and college writing to their personal concerns and development, and to recognize their own stakes and local opportunities. It approaches involvement, a key component in success, as something one builds through acts of careful reading and writing, through the finding of personal meaning in assigned work, and through the sharing of ideas with teachers and others.

- **Many examples of student writing appear in the book.** Student writing is carefully built into the chapters, exemplifying and reinforcing the writing tasks taught in the book. Questions entitled "Thinking About Student Writing" follow each example; they create a context in which student writing is taken seriously and foster analytical skills that the student then applies to his or her own writing.

- **Realistic readings and assignments teach critical thinking and college-level reading skills.** *Involved* approaches college as a unique rhetorical context, with distinctive agendas and expectations. The readings and assignments are intensely practical, directly tailored to the types of reading, writing, and class styles that students actually encounter. Integrated readings are drawn from a range of disciplines and from accessible, yet college-level articles, books, and textbooks.

- **The writing process is presented in an innovative way.** While speaking to the recognized needs of students and the familiar concerns of first-year writing, *Involved* presents the writing process not as a monolithic one-style-fits-all entity, but as a series of personal and social processes relating to the situation, the task, and the writer. It explores both how writing processes vary according to the situation and how some parts often recur.

- **Instruction focuses on writing tasks typical of the academy.** *Involved* aims to be highly practical for the college student, and thus concentrates on reading journals, summaries, essay exams, illustrative writing, autobiographical and reflective writing, analytical writing, investigative writing (library, field, and lab research), case studies, and argument.

- **A unique final part on "Dealing with Complexity" addresses a crucial need.** Chapters in this part treat "Writing About Complex Worlds," "Writing About Problem Cases," and "Arguing Your Case."

- **Sidebars integrate rhetorical concepts, research findings, and localized examination of the writing process into the discussion.** The text features three types of sidebars: (1) Useful Concepts from Rhetoric; (2) News from the Field; and (3) Reviewing Writing Processes.

- *Involved* **covers relevant, up-to-date topics such as electronic discussion groups, the Web, memory techniques, and privacy issues.** Activities entitled "Getting Involved Electronically" also appear at the end of the chapters.

- *Involved* **incorporates the best of current research and theory.** Many people in the composition field recognize that freshman textbooks have lagged behind the latest developments of composition theory and research. This book combines a concern for process with a sociocultural perspective, which helps students understand their personal position, stake, and goals in writing. Its goal is to help students develop a reflexive understanding of their college situation and their activity in college so that they can become more focused agents. *Involved* provides students with a reflective frame for their college experience so they can understand the communicative situations they are in. Students learn to see the classroom and the disciplines as "discourse communities" in which they can become active participants for their own benefit.

- *Instructor's Resource Manual* **provides a wealth of supporting material.** The 150-page manual moves chapter-by-chapter with

  Chapter Goals

  Some Potential Student Difficulties and How to Address Them

  Some Useful Roles for the Instructor

  Changing Classroom Relations

  Providing Support for and Responding to Assignments

  Further Related Activities and Discussion Topics

  Working with the "Getting Involved Electronically" Activities

  It also contains five essays:

  What's Interesting?

  Where Is the Classroom?

  The Life of Genre and the Life of the Classroom (a review of the literature)

  Students Being Disciplined (a review of the literature)

  The Classroom as a Communication System

- **The Dictionary Deal is offered with** *Involved. The American Heritage Dictionary* **(complete/concise)** can be shrinkwrapped with the text at a substantial savings.

Acknowledgments

First and most profoundly, I must thank the many students I have had the privilege of teaching over the years. In their struggles to write with meaning in their lives, they have shown me how difficult and how important writing is to living in the modern world. I also thank the many teachers of writing whose dedication has buoyed me and whose insights have opened my eyes. Finally, I thank the editors and sales representatives for Houghton Mifflin who for twenty years have taught me how to reach the classroom with books that serve the needs of students.

For this particular book, I have enjoyed the perceptive criticism of my consultants: Carol Berkenkotter of Michigan Technological University, Susan MacLeod of Washington State University, David Russell of Iowa State University, and Barbara Walvoord of the University of Cincinnati. In addition, the following colleagues served as valuable reviewers, offering helpful advice, ideas, and suggestions:

Marshall Alcorn, George Washington University (DC)

Wendy Bishop, Florida State University

Jo Ann Bomze, Beaver College (PA)

Patsy Callaghan, Central Washington University (WA)

Elaine P. Maimon, Queens College, CUNY (NY)

Douglas Richards, Keuka College (NY)

Duane H. Roen, Arizona State University

Lucille Schultz, University of Cincinnati

Kristin Snoddy, Indiana University, Kokomo

Molly Travis, Tulane University

Arthur Walzer, University of Minnesota, Twin Cities

Steven Weisenburger, University of Kentucky

Irwin Weiser, Purdue University (IN)

I have also enjoyed the help and constructive wrangling of my editor, Martha Bustin, and the efficient and skillful help of my assistant, Michael Austin.

My son, Gershom Bazerman, I thank for his wisecracks, and my partner, Shirley Geoklin Lim, I thank for her wise comments.

Charles Bazerman
University of California—Santa Barbara

Writing
Your Self
into
College

P A R T

One

1 Strategic Writing

AIMS OF THE CHAPTER

This chapter introduces a rhetorical approach to college writing. Rhetoric is the study of effective communication in specific situations. A rhetorical approach emphasizes that writing is a way of acting in situations. In college, most of your activity is communicative; you learn by listening and talking, by reading and writing. Becoming more skillful in these activities will help you become more involved and give your efforts more personal meaning. The concepts presented in this and the next chapter should help you develop terms to describe the rhetorical situations in which you find yourself and the goals you may wish to accomplish in those situations.

KEY POINTS

1. Writing is rhetorical: an action you take when you participate in a specific situation.

2. Rhetoric has its origins in the classical world, but two cultural changes since then affect your current rhetorical situation in college:

   - The rise of schooling and literacy
   - The specialization of knowledge and professions

3. In school and life we learn many strategies of minimizing our own feelings to please others. However, your success as a writer in college and elsewhere depends on your overcoming these strategies of disengagement so that you become more involved in your activities.

4. Involvement comes from finding out what is important to you and then acting on what you have found.

QUESTIONS TO THINK ABOUT

- How is writing different in different situations? How might college writing differ from the writing you did in high school? How do the goals differ? How do the styles differ?

- When have you felt most involved in learning? When have you felt least involved? Has the chance to discuss and write about what you are learning and thinking made a difference in how involved you feel?

- What do you hope to get out of your education? What does writing have to do with accomplishing those goals?

A First-Day Assignment

On the first day in writing courses, students are often asked to write some variation of the following assignment. You might take fifteen minutes and try it.

> Write a paragraph introducing yourself to your instructor and your classmates. Tell about your previous experience in this subject, what you enjoy doing in school and out, what concerns you, and what your ambitions and goals are.

Although you know many things about yourself, this may not be an easy assignment to write. It raises questions about which you have little information on the first day of the term, perhaps even on your first day of college classes. Who are the people you are writing to? How will these strangers respond to what you write? What will this class be like? What will college be like? What impression will people get from your writing? What impression would you like to give in this class? What role and identity would you like to establish in college? This assignment asks to give a picture of yourself, but until you know more about the situation, you may not feel at all sure about what kind of picture you want to draw. So writing this assignment is not just a matter of simple description but rather a matter of self-presentation in a social situation.

One way to handle this assignment is to take no risks and just remain friendly.

> Hi. I'm Bill Stanley, an eighteen-year-old freshman at State University. I graduated last year from Franklin Roosevelt High School, where I most enjoyed my courses in math and science. I also played trombone in band. I have always gotten good grades in English, although I find writing difficult. Teachers tell me I ought to be more descriptive, but I say why waste words once you get your idea across. I hope to major in biology and go on to medical school.

This does what is asked, gives some details, and leaves Bill Stanley's options open. But it does not announce that Bill will be an enthusiastic and memorable participant in this course. In order to take a more emphatic place in the class, another student might take a more challenging stance, but still give no important facts.

> Yes, here I am. Writing again. In another English class. Telling you who I am. I love writing, but I sure am tired of this assignment. Sure I came from some high school. Sure I like some subjects, and didn't like others. I got good enough grades to get into college, so I could do the work. But this isn't what is important about me. What is important is that I am looking — looking for new ideas, looking for a style. I listen to music that's at the edge, I read stuff you'll never find in school, I live in cyberia. Will I find what I am looking for here or will this be just one more dull English class?
> *Rachel "Razzti" Rasmussen*

Do you think either of these responses gives a full or revealing picture of the students who write them? What kind of response do you think might start someone off well in an unknown situation? Are there any things about the situation that might help you decide how to represent yourself?

There is no right or wrong way to handle this assignment, but any way you choose starts to establish your identity in the conversations, written and spoken, that will take place in the class throughout the term. What makes this assignment difficult and makes any response likely to look a little bit foolish is that the conversation hasn't yet taken place, so you are writing as part of a relationship that is only beginning. This is as tough as introducing yourself to a stranger at a party.

Writing for people you don't know in a situation you don't understand is the hardest writing to do. Every time you learn more about a situation and the people you are writing to, you understand better what you want to accomplish, what you want to say, and what will work. Writing is not an abstract skill that is always the same; it is strategic communication to fit the circumstances. How can you know your strategy until you know the circumstances?

✇ Writing as Rhetoric

Each of you making it to a college classroom has succeeded in many situations where you have needed to write. You wrote well enough to complete the tasks required of you. Even more, you expressed yourself, your knowledge, and your ideas in ways that helped you develop and interact with others. You wrote in high school for your teachers, in letters to your friends, on shopping lists to take with you to the store, or in diaries to yourself. You found ways of getting by, meeting your needs in each of those situations — sometimes spectacularly, sometimes just adequately. But you did find a way.

Why then must you study writing one more time? Why does learning to write never end? Why isn't it enough to say, "Now I know how to write, and I'm done with it"?

Learning to write never ends because you keep encountering new kinds of situations. Whereas in high school you may have used materials from your American history textbook to write an exam question about Lincoln's actions in the Civil War, in college you may be asked to argue, using evidence from personal letters, that Lincoln issued the Emancipation Proclamation for political motives rather than as an act of moral leadership. If you then become a publishing historian, you may argue in a book that Lincoln was more a politician than a statesman. These examples are all just within one field of history. Legal briefs or management reports or chemistry research articles will be done for totally different situations requiring different skills, resources, and motives. As situations change, so must writing; in other words, writing is rhetorical. Writing must speak to each situation, to the particular local circumstances, to be successful.

Abraham Lincoln's 1858 debates with Stephen Douglas spoke to the politically and morally charged atmosphere in the United States just before the Civil War.

Writing for Reflection

This is the first of a series of Writing for Reflection assignments that appear throughout the textbook. These assignments are intended as informal ways to think through your own experience of writing and learning in relation to the ideas presented in this book. They need not be formal essays. Here is the first assignment:

To gain a clearer picture of your writing experiences before coming to college, describe in a few paragraphs the various kinds of writing you have had to do in school and out. In each case describe the situation you wrote for (for example, at the end of a term in a world history class, for a community newspaper, or as part of a political campaign), the kind of writing you did (for example, a biography of a writer, a sports news story, or a sales brochure), and how that kind of writing fulfilled the needs, demands, or opportunities of the circumstances.

Rhetorical Situations

As the preceding discussion has made clear, rhetoric is the practical art of making successful statements in specific situations. If the purpose of communication is to interact with others — to influence, to cooperate with, to oppose, to control, to comply with, to negotiate — then you have a greater chance of success if you think about the following points:

- What the situation is
- Who you are communicating with
- What you want to happen
- What ways you might achieve that end

How can we use language in purposeful, practical ways to achieve our goals? That question is the heart of rhetoric.

Successful communication varies from person to person and situation to situation. There is no simple, single "good rhetoric," no one way to write. You must always think about the specifics of the situation: what you want to accomplish, with whom, and through what available means.

In college you will find yourself writing in a variety of new situations, and you will need to think through how you want to respond to them. That is, you will need to develop a "rhetoric for college" — a way of thinking about your writing for the next few years that will help you get what you want out of college and also satisfy the writing demands college places upon you. At other points in your life you may need to develop a rhetoric for your profession, a rhetoric for sales, a rhetoric for managing people, a rhetoric for city politics, a rhetoric for talking to your children, or a rhetoric for talking to your loved one. Right now, however, your most pressing need is likely to be a rhetoric for college writing.

Writing for Reflection

Make a list of the kinds of situations where people have to speak or write to carry out their part in an activity, such as chatting as part of a pleasant dinner with friends, making a statement at a public meeting, filling out a form to apply for a job, or writing a letter to publicize the work of your organization. Then in a few phrases for each, characterize how people might use language in each situation and what strategies might be successful. For example, at a dinner people might try to be pleasant and humorous while sharing stories about themselves and mutual friends.

The Origins of Rhetoric

Many societies around the world have recognized that how people use language is related to who they become, how they are viewed, and what they accomplish. Traditional sayings in many cultures offer advice about how to speak in public and private. Hindi traditional lore, for example, counsels, "Write like the learned; speak like the masses." Thai wisdom advises, "To speak well one must reflect, and to hit the mark one must aim." Turkish lore, however, warns that people are not always happy when you tell them the truth: "He that speaks the truth must have his foot in the stirrup."

As literacy developed in various cultures, treatises on education often included language education as an important part of the training of leaders. For example, the Chinese scholar Liu Xie wrote "The Cultivating of the Mind and the Carving of the Dragon" (*Wen Xin Diao Long* — literally, "pattern mind carve dragon") around 500 A.D. To become a dragon — that is, a wise and powerful leader — one needs to carve out a patterned mind by learning how to use the written language. (For more information, see H. Zhao, "Rhetorical Invention in *Wen Xin Diao Long*," *Rhetoric Society Quarterly* 24 (1994), pp. 1–15.)

Ancient Greece and Rome developed an extensive and organized body of thought about how to communicate successfully and how to help people represent their interests within the new political institutions of democracy and republic. Since reading and writing were not widespread in this period, even among the elite class of citizens, rhetoric first developed in relation to public speaking.

In public speeches, people accused of crimes needed to defend themselves; members of the consul needed to persuade others of their proposed policies and laws; and people needed to be brought together with common beliefs and values. These three forms of talk, all having their origins in the *agora* — or marketplace where citizens came to meet and talk — were tasks of argument and persuasion. Most of classical rhetoric's concepts and guidelines are especially applicable to the forums of democratic government. Today, our courts, legislatures, and politics are similar to, and even patterned after, classical models. It is no accident that courthouses, legislatures, and governor's mansions look like Greek and Roman buildings.

The speeches of
Marcus Tullius Cicero
(106–43 B.C.E.) were a
powerful influence on
the Roman Senate and
public.

To highlight some of the most useful concepts that have developed in the
rhetorical tradition, throughout this book there will appear definitions and
explanations of key rhetorical terms in places where they are most relevant to
the topic or activity being discussed (see the list below). The last chapter in
the book on argument will draw together many of these concepts.

⟲⟳ USEFUL CONCEPTS FROM RHETORIC

The Types of Rhetoric

C lassical rhetoric was developed to help in three kinds of public speech situations common in the classical world, all of which still continue in the modern world.

Courtroom or forensic rhetoric — the strategic use of language to accuse or defend a person concerning misdeeds or crimes. It is practiced today in court cases.

Legislative or deliberative rhetoric — the strategic use of language to persuade people to take particular actions or adopt particular laws. It is practiced today in legislatures, editorials, and debates.

Political or epideictic rhetoric — the strategic use of language to praise and blame people in order to encourage and discourage behaviors and beliefs or to reinforce values in the community. It is practiced today in sermons and political rallies.

Writing for Reflection

To explore how well the three traditional categories of rhetoric — forensic, deliberative, and epideictic — cover the range of public and personal speaking and writing today, identify one place where people communicate frequently (such as a classroom, a coffee shop, a church or temple, an office, a newspaper, or a talk radio channel). Either from memory or by revisiting the location, make a list of the different kinds of messages people present. Then develop categories for the different kinds of language used. Do the three categories of traditional rhetoric fit, or do you need to develop other categories? Describe your findings in a few paragraphs. Then in a class discussion compare your findings and thoughts about the location you examined to the findings and thoughts of other class members who examined different locations.

Courtroom lawyers engage in forensic rhetoric as they argue for the guilt or innocence of the accused. Here Johnny Cochran argues for the innocence of O.J. Simpson.

⌒⌒ Rhetoric in a Changing World: Literacy, Specialization, and Technology

Although aspects of modern American life are deeply influenced by Greek and Roman models, life today has also changed from classical times. Thus although we may find that many concepts of traditional rhetoric help us understand contemporary situations, we also need new concepts to fit our new ways of communicating. One major change especially relevant to college is the rise of literacy. Reading and writing have joined listening and speaking as major forms of communication. Today, although talk certainly takes place at all levels of education, much of schooling is defined by the books you read and the papers and tests you write.

Whereas the spoken word tends to be more personal, the written word can travel through time and space and can be multiplied in many copies, influencing more people over a greater distance in a more enduring way. For these reasons, the written language has become central to major institutions of society. Religions are based on holy books, and legal systems are based on written codes, contracts, and records. Governments rely on regulations, orders, and information. Sciences formulate in writing knowledge about the world we live in. Journalism records news and trends. Literature offers books for entertainment and enlightenment.

The development of printing five hundred years ago has made books and other printed material cheap and readily available. In turn, literacy — the ability to read and write — has become more necessary for all aspects of life. Schooling developed to meet that need for literacy. Reading and writing became not only subjects of instruction but central activities in all courses of instruction. The basic 3Rs — reading, 'riting, and 'rithmetic — are all fundamentally literate practices — paper and ink operations. All school courses are structured through written syllabi, plans, guidelines, and catalogues. Even classes that emphasize physical skills such as flight training or laboratory technique have lesson plans, textbooks, manuals, and written exams. So doing well and getting what you want from college is very much a matter of reading and writing.

Although electronic communication technologies, starting with the telegraph and telephone over a century ago, have changed our life, they have not displaced literacy. In fact, the latest tools of the electronic revolution, computers and computer networks, seem to have led to a proliferation of the written word, as word processing has made composing and revision easier, electronic databases have increased access to written information, and online networks have increased the rapid exchange of text. Written communication flows across the Internet, from the most informal e-mail jottings to the complete texts of literary masterpieces and scholarly essays. The most recent developments in computer technology are supporting the combination of written word, sound, and picture. Reading and writing are becoming seamlessly integrated with other modes of communication. Even the programs that direct electronic representation are written, in the specialized languages of programming.

A second change has been the development of specialized professions and disciplines (that is, specific areas of study such as biology, sociology, and history of art), especially in the nineteenth and twentieth centuries. Each of these communities has developed specialized ways of using the written language to carry out its work. A medical doctor writing a patient's case record writes differently than a literary critic evaluating a novel. A lawyer writing a contract writes differently than an engineer writing a technical report. Whatever your chosen career, you will notice that people in that field have special ways of communicating with each other using particular styles and vocabularies. At college your education is likely to be organized by disciplines, in which you learn the information and the ways of communicating appropriate to each. Most probably you will have to declare a major, identifying a specific discipline that you will study more intensively and adopt more fully as a mode of communication.

These two changes, the rise of literacy as a school-taught skill and increasing specialization, influence the kind of rhetoric that you will need to develop for college — a rhetoric for written language as used in schools of higher education, organized along disciplinary lines. Your reading and writing, influenced by the disciplines of the courses, are framed within the structure and practices of a classroom. Although you may read about biology and may even read articles from biology journals, much of what you read is in textbooks, much of what you write is for assigned papers and examinations, and usually your goal is to demonstrate your knowledge and share your developing thoughts with your instructors. Thus a rhetoric for college is as much attuned to the work of the classroom as it is to the work of the professions and disciplines.

Writing for Reflection

Write several informal paragraphs on the various technologies you use for communication (from speech and pencil and paper through the latest electronic tool), on what occasions you use them, and how you use them. Be as specific as possible. For what kinds of communications do you use the telephone? What kinds of documents do you write on word processors? What interactions do you carry out only by face-to-face talk? Have you ever made a video, or do you just watch commercially produced television? Then, in class discussion, compare your observations with those of your classmates.

Rhetoric and Decorum in Daily Life

All of us already know a great deal about rhetoric because we learn and use language to interact with each other. From earliest childhood we assess the effect our words and actions have on others. We learn who answers our requests by doing something for us, who tells us to do it for ourselves, who ignores us, and who gets angry. We adjust our behavior accordingly, learning how to talk to different people. We also learn at what times our parents will listen to us, when we will be told to hush up, or when we will be put off with an absent-minded nod. On the basis of this knowledge, we often consciously judge what to say. We learn what kind of comments may meet with approval, rejection, and irritation. Thus we start to learn about audience, timing, and goals within various situations.

We also have learned about forms and styles appropriate to different situations — when to say "please" and when telling a joke fits the situation, when to be precise, and when to be informal. We learn how to talk in the

Calvin and Hobbes   by Bill Watterson

classroom, or the schoolyard, how to write a history exam, or a literature essay, and how to write a letter to our aunt. Communication and behavior appropriate to a situation is known as *decorum* (for more on decorum, see below).

For each of these situations you have developed a strategy for maximizing the results for yourself. Sometimes it may have been to keep a low profile, to stay out of trouble, and to not upset anyone. You may even have been rewarded for passivity with praise for seeming cooperative. In other situations you may have found the most pleasure from fitting in, trying to talk or write like everyone else around you so you feel accepted. Sometimes your strategy may have been to follow the explicit instructions of an authority and even to anticipate the authority's desires, saying or writing whatever you think will please the authority. All these are strategies of going along on a path laid out by others.

On the other hand, sometimes you may have created your own path and have sought strategies that defined your individuality. You may have taken risks to define your own point of view, reveal your own observations, question something others believe, request something you really want, or oppose something that you dislike. In doing so, you have brought a difference into the situation that sets your statement apart. This is known as saying something.

USEFUL CONCEPTS FROM RHETORIC

Decorum

Decorum, or the use of language and behavior that fits a situation, is a much richer concept in rhetoric than the usual use of the word. Today we usually associate decorum with polite, serious, respectful behavior, such as authorities would like to maintain in classrooms or courtrooms. Sometimes we associate decorum with etiquette, which is a formal set of rules for polite behavior in formal social circumstances. However, in rhetoric decorum can be any behavior that fits the circumstances, so one can also speak of the decorum appropriate to a loud dance party, a football game, or a raucous political argument.

Decorum is attuning yourself to the circumstances. It can include everything from learning to write a history paper that sounds like it comes from a skilled history student to learning how to write a script that sounds like it belongs on the evening news. Decorum doesn't limit what you can say or do, but just helps you find a tone, style, and vocabulary that will be recognized, acceptable, and effective as part of the unfolding situation.

✐ ✐ The Strategy of Growth

Every student who has gotten as far as college has developed automatic ways of adjusting to the decorum of the classroom, of getting through each school day without too much risk and with a moderate amount of success. For many students, this strategy of getting by may have become so habitual that it no longer seems like a strategy — it just seems a natural response to the situation.

It is worth thinking through this position within each college classroom. Paying attention to spelling, grammar, and well-organized paragraphs will keep you from losing points for making a mistake, but if that is all you are paying attention to, you have not yet begun to communicate. If you listen carefully to the teacher's statements only to repeat them, you may be marked correct, but you have not yet begun to grapple with the ideas and information. If you give the teacher exactly what you think the teacher wants, the teacher may be pleased with what you say, but there is no dialogue. The teacher cannot respond to what you are really thinking and cannot speak to your real questions, concerns, and differences of opinion.

As you grow older and have more experiences, your understanding of yourself becomes richer, your skills and knowledge increase, and your interests become deeper. At this point superficial cooperation becomes less satisfying. You naturally want something more involving and challenging.

In your relations with your friends and classmates you are all discovering new facts, encountering new ideas, confronting new problems, and finding new directions. Although you may want to be accepted in a crowd where you can relax, tell jokes, and go to the movies, you may also want to develop relationships where you can share the changes in your life. Sharing what you are going through demands a greater involvement and investment of yourself and your own concerns than just telling jokes and making pleasant comments. With certain close friends you may develop a more honest and involving kind of communication based on a trust that they will respect what you say, no matter how different and personal.

Just as you are demanding more from your life, teachers look for more from you. Their expectations are higher. Although college teachers may continue to pass students who follow orders and do little else, such students do not catch their personal attention or get the best grades. Teachers start asking you for original thinking, novel problem solving, and honest engagement, asking you to go beyond the safe minimum. They will be starting to prepare you for professional life, where you will have to make confident, personal judgments on difficult cases, judgments that must hold their own before other professionals.

Because of this, both your own needs and the demands of the situation suggest that you put more of yourself on the line, but in a way appropriate to each situation. Putting yourself on the line does not always mean being conflictual or oppositional but rather identifying where you stand, elaborating your position, and offering reasons. At times learning the power of the concepts and approaches offered by a discipline and instructor may provide the greatest growth and excitement, with you feeling you have little to add; even then, however, you still need to identify how you are perceiving the material and what you are getting from it.

To get the most out of college, you need to set your own directions. After all, although you were required to attend high school, you have chosen to be at college, and you have chosen the particular college you are in, and that college has chosen you. You choose your classes (often there are options even within course requirements), and you choose your major. So lying low no longer makes sense. What makes sense is taking the risk to become who you are becoming, to become personally involved in your learning.

Writing for Reflection

To help you identify the kinds of independent stances you have created through language, describe one or more incidents where you took a stand contrary to what other people in the group expressed or approved. This could be with parents, peers, community groups, or teachers; in classes or clubs; or in any other situation where you used language to identify where you stood apart. Describe the particular tactics you used to express your individual position and the reaction others had to your statement.

Becoming Involved Through Writing

Research indicates that student success in college is directly correlated with involvement. According to these researchers, involvement includes such activities as talking to teachers, spending time in the library and on your courses, discussing your work with other students, thinking about what you are hearing and reading, developing your own opinions and positions, and asserting your ideas and goals in talk and writing. Involvement is a much higher predictor of success in college than high school grades, achievement and aptitude tests, IQ scores, or any other indicator researchers have found. As we have already discussed, in a very basic way the strategy for success in college is involvement — being high profile and not low profile.

However, involvement is not just a general impulse; it must be made real through specific actions. Every time you find a more successful way to communicate about what you are learning and what you are thinking, you become more involved in your learning and classes. Nothing is more involving than writing a paper you believe in, that is well received by your teacher, and that leads to further discussions among you, your teacher, and your classmates.

However, finding involving directions for our work, discovering areas we are interested in exploring, identifying what we have to say — these things often do not come easily. We don't always know ourselves and who we are becoming well enough to make simple choices about what we want to do. Our memory of our past is limited and changeable from moment to moment. Our vision of who we are is influenced by every event in which we take part. The present has far too many possibilities for us to notice as we pass through it, and the future . . . well, who knows. The best we can do is follow what vague hunches we have about what might engage us and maybe interesting things may develop.

Precisely because so much is unknown, learning to write means trying something new. If an assignment seems to ask for more than you are used to, excites new ideas that you don't quite know how to put together, or suggests some research you think may be too hard, you will not learn if you depend on an old strategy that worked for less challenging situations. It is important to see what you can do in a new way, what ideas you can present for the teacher to respond to. See what kinds of claims you can justify, once you put yourself on the line.

As you take risks, what seemed dull and unrewarding may hold far more than you imagined. The best way to discover what the real value of an idea or a subject is, is to challenge it and to ask what it means. Even the act of defining those subjects or approaches or courses that seem empty will help you identify other areas that fit better with what you want to explore and learn. When you find something that excites you, follow it. Conversely, when you find something that holds nothing for you, no matter how much and energetically you explore it, then move past it as rapidly as you can to get into something that will involve you. Don't try to cover your lack of interest by inflating the subject, pretending an enthusiasm where you have none, or making up empty phrases to cover a lack of things to say. Decide to get through the dull work or uninteresting topic as efficiently and directly as possible so you can spend more time on what interests you.

What has just been described is a strategy to increase your involvement and concentration. In sports, concentration and involvement are also necessary to notice and respond to moment-by-moment opportunities. Coaches advise, "Keep your eye on the ball." "Watch the position." "Bear down, concentrate." Learning is also being responsive to moment-by-moment circumstances. Your learning is in all the problems you have to solve, all the information you need to absorb, all the ideas you puzzle over, all the skills you have to develop, and all the statements you make in order to become part of those situations which you pass through.

The analogy with sports, however, is limited in at least one very important sense. In sports you are driven to outdo an opponent; a tough opponent may drive you harder, improve your skill, and get you more involved. Competition is a driving force in most sports. Education, however, is driven only by your desire to extend yourself and learn new things. Tough material and rewarding projects may lend new challenges, exciting teachers and classmates may increase your attention, but your own sense of growth is the only thing that will carry you through every day. Whereas it is easy to be challenged by a tough opponent, your own personal growth is a more elusive target, a challenge that can get lost in discouragement or vagueness. If you are lucky, teachers and others will notice your growth, point out directions for you, and reflect your development back to you. But ultimately you have to pull the picture together to locate your own motivation to face continued challenge and growth.

One of the ways to keep an eye on yourself and your own growth is to watch your writing. If you keep a file of your papers as you go from year to year and course to course, you can get a sense of where you have been, where you are going, and how far you have come. By seeing who you are becoming as a writer, you can reflect on who you are becoming through your education.

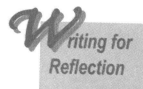

Writing for Reflection

1. Describe one occasion when you got caught up in a writing assignment for a course. What was the assignment? What specifically did you choose to write about? What did you say in the paper? What made the assignment so engaging? What did you think about as you wrote the paper? What did you learn from writing it? What were you proudest about in the paper? Who read the paper? How did they respond?

2. Interview several friends about one time they became involved in their writing for school. Ask them about the assignments, what they wrote, what made their work interesting for them, and what they felt they accomplished. Then write a paragraph about each of the engaging assignments to share and discuss with your classmates.

NEWS FROM THE FIELD

What Difference Does College Make?

Most students hope that college will make a difference — not only in income, but in the kind of life they lead. Is this just a hope, or does research confirm that college does make a difference?

Ernest Pascarella and Patrick Terenzini's book *How College Affects Students* (San Francisco: Jossey-Bass, 1991) presents a comprehensive survey of the extensive research on this subject. It reviews hundreds of studies of students in colleges of all sizes and kinds and in all regions of the country — making comparisons among them and with students who have not attended college. The authors report that college indeed has a marked effect.

1. Seniors usually have better verbal and quantitative skills than freshmen. Moreover, seniors reason better abstractly, solve problems bet-

ter, use evidence more effectively to reason through issues that have no certain answers, are more flexible in seeing multiple sides to issues, and can organize and manipulate more complex ideas. In short, college tends to make you smarter.

2. Most seniors have greater self-understanding, self-definition, and personal commitment than freshmen. They also have a better self-image and more self-esteem, as well as more independence from their parents. In short, college helps you become a reflective, confident, self-directed adult.

3. Seniors tend to have an increased openness to and tolerance of diversity. Moreover, they tend to reason about moral issues in principled ways more than freshmen. In short, college can help make you a more tolerant and reasonable person.

4. Seniors have more interest in art, culture, and ideas than freshmen. They tend to believe more in the value of a liberal education and less in college as a form of vocational training. In short, college helps you value education and culture.

5. Completing college has strong socioeconomic benefits over one's whole career, but when you complete college you tend to care less about money and more about the intrinsic value of education than when you entered. Moreover, upon completing college you are more likely to enter challenging careers and engage in lifelong learning. In short, you are likely to earn more money if you finish college, but the money won't seem as important.

Of course, statistics never tell you what will happen in any particular case. There are no guarantees that upon graduation you will play the violin, be on your way to a Nobel Peace Prize, earn a six-figure salary, or not care whether you earn a six-figure salary. Your personal situation, motivation, and activity affect how you are influenced by your college experience. But research does confirm that the changes are almost always positive.

As you engage in the college activities that lead to these personal changes, you often need to think about what you should say, what you should write. By learning to articulate your thoughts, experiences, and learning through writing, you are learning to articulate yourself as a person. That is a theme that runs throughout this book.

Writing for Reflection

Write a few paragraphs looking forward to the next few years. How do you think or hope that college will affect you? In what ways would you like to grow or change? What parts of yourself do you hope or expect will not change? What do you think you will be most involved in; and what not?

Getting Involved Electronically

Find the procedures for getting an e-mail account at your school, and establish an account. Learn the procedures for writing, editing, and sending a message. Send a short message to your instructor. Send another to a classmate introducing yourself.

2 The Classroom Situation

AIMS OF THE CHAPTER

This chapter views each class as an organized system of communications —
those you receive and those you create. Each statement you speak or write
in a course fits within a web of statements and can be shaped to be most effective for the situation. Seeing the classroom in this way will help you recognize the rhetorical situations the class presents.

KEY POINTS

1. Your writing in any class is part of the way you participate in its learning activities. Your writing will become more effective as you understand the communication structure of the course.

2. College courses can be seen as communication systems in which the
   teacher initiates reading assignments, lectures, and discussion questions and students respond in discussions and assignments. However,
   each class is also a unique system that you must evaluate in order to
   understand your own opportunities.

3. Although all students learn to get by in classrooms by trying to understand what the teacher wants, you will gain more from defining your
   own goals and activities.

4. Writing is open-ended, requiring you to frame your own goals and motives appropriate to the situation for which you are writing.

QUESTIONS TO THINK ABOUT

■ Have you ever written a paper or said something in a class that you felt
was "not yourself"? Have you ever not spoken up in class or not written something because you felt those parts of yourself you would be ex-

pressing would not be well received? Have you ever felt you had to silence yourself to get by in a class? What made you feel that way? What kinds of things would you have written or said if you were being more honest to "your self"? What does being "yourself" in class really mean?

- Compare two classes, one where you felt involved and one where you did not. What made for the difference?

- How do classrooms set up different situations for your writing? How do you write differently in different classes?

Writing in any course, not just a writing class, joins together what you bring with what the course and other people have to offer. Participating in the unfolding discussions of a class challenges you to confront the new ideas, information, and skills presented by your textbook, your teacher, and the other students. As you address new intellectual challenges, learning becomes an active search for useful and meaningful knowledge.

To participate in any class, you must obviously engage in certain activities, such as listening to the teacher reading the assignments, participating in class discussions, writing papers of the assigned length, turning in assignments on time, and taking exams. But what does it mean to do these things? How do they fit together? How specifically should you do them? There are many ways to listen, many ways to read, and many ways to write papers. What do all these activities, moreover, add up for you, your goals, your interests, and your commitments? How do all these activities come together when you are on the spot to write a paper or exam essay?

To answer these questions you need to determine what is going on in the classroom, what the teacher is asking you to do, and what kinds of responses will be received well and rewarded. Then you need to line up the situation as you see it with your own goals. Once you take this last step, the classroom turns from a set of obligations into a set of opportunities.

Calvin and Hobbes   by Bill Watterson

☾∕◯ Sizing Up a Class Instead of Psyching Out the Teacher

Sizing up a class and what you do in it is, at one level, easy. You have done it all your life. Some teachers make it even easier by laying out exactly what is expected of students. When the teacher does not explicitly tell students exactly what to do, students have learned a classroom etiquette that, no matter how much minds may wander, keeps them in their seats doing the teacher-identified task. Some students create active places for themselves by aggressively seeking information from the teacher and maximizing their participation. Other students take more passive roles, never testing the limits, never seeking individual conferences, and rarely participating in discussions. Still others are confrontational, looking for weaknesses in the teacher's position in order to rise in the esteem of classmates, who are amused at the disruption of classroom power.

Whatever stance a student takes, however, the teacher takes a central role in the classroom. Students always make choices by scrutinizing the teacher's expectations, demands, and behavior, even when the teacher encourages individualized student activity or reorganizes the class into peer work groups. This control is exerted by assignments, grades, minute-by-minute praise and correction, responses to different student behaviors, or particular questions. Students, recognizing this fact, frequently talk of "psyching out" the teacher — figuring out what's in the teacher's mind.

"Psyching out" a teacher, however, is not a very satisfactory way of dealing with your own participation in the classroom, for it leaves your own needs, motivations, and ideas out of the picture. To draw on all your resources and to make the classroom as satisfying as it can be, you must put yourself into the picture. Rather than "psyching out" the teacher, you must "size up" the situation as an opportunity for your own participation. This is often difficult for freshmen because of the many differences students find among their college classes (see below).

☾∕◯   N E W S   F R O M   T H E   F I E L D

One Freshman's Struggle

In a field study on the experience of college writers, Lucille Parkinson McCarthy spent three semesters in three separate classes with Dave Garrison, a beginning student at a private liberal arts college in the Northeast. McCarthy conducted extensive interviews with Dave, his peers, and his professors, and she attended classes with him and read all drafts of his writing assignments. The three courses included in the study were freshman English, poetry, and cell biology. McCarthy selected the first two for their emphasis on writing, and the last because Dave was a biology major. The study gives us a revealing inside view of college writing that may remind you of what you are experiencing as you try to make sense of the demands of your classes. Where those demands matched Dave's own interests and needs, he did best.

McCarthy observed that Dave viewed each new writing situation as something completely new and unfamiliar — even when the same skills had been covered in previous courses. For example, even though the freshman English course had covered summary writing, Dave saw the summary writing required by the biology class as fundamentally different than anything he had ever done before. As a result, he felt lost. McCarthy commented that students in introductory-level classes are often so overwhelmed by the vocabulary and analytical style that they must learn for a given discipline that they cannot access their own past experiences productively — even when those past experiences would be helpful.

McCarthy also observed that Dave's success or failure in the classes depended on how he valued the writing assignments. In both the freshman English class and the biology class, Dave was able to identify a number of personal benefits he could get from the assignments. For example, he saw the papers he wrote as helping him prepare both for a career and for future college classes. Consequently, he was motivated and did well in both classes. In the poetry class, however, Dave saw only one function of the writing assignments: to demonstrate academic competence to his professor. He received the lowest grades in this class.

McCarthy finally observed that Dave had to figure out on his own what constituted an appropriate response to an assignment. He used six different strategies for, as he put it, "figuring out what the teacher wanted": These six strategies were: (1) the teachers' comments about writing in class; (2) model texts provided by the teachers; (3) discussion with other students; (4) teachers' written comments on earlier papers; (5) his own previous experience; and (6) personal talks with teachers.

McCarthy's study led her to describe college students as "strangers in strange lands." Each new class presents, not only a new subject matter, but new ways of talking, reading, writing, and understanding the world. Students often go from class to class unsure of what to expect and unable to use the specialized language that each discipline demands of them. Ideally, instructors should act as guides to the conventions and communication styles of the new discipline. However, they are often unable to recognize — or unwilling to assist — students who are struggling with an unfamiliar language. Ultimately, then, the responsibility for mastering the rules of the "strange lands" falls to individual students. Dave recognized this responsibility when, at the end of the 21-month study, he was asked what advice he would give to an incoming freshman about college writing. "I'd tell them," he said, "first you've got to figure out what your teachers want. And then you've got to give it to them if you're gonna' get the grade. . . . And that's not always so easy."

From L. P. McCarthy, "A Stranger in Strange Lands: A College Student Writing Across the Curriculum," *Research in the Teaching of English* 21 (1987) 233-35.

When assigned writing in your courses, have you ever felt as Dave felt? In what way? How did you deal with the situation? Did you follow similar strategies as Dave, or did you go down a different path? What was the outcome? In retrospect, did you have any more effective options? Is there anything the instructor might have done or said that would have made the experience more useful or successful?

Writing Is Open-Ended

As we have seen, an overly narrow focus on a teacher's signals creates an obstacle to self-motivated learning, the kind of learning that becomes increasingly important at higher levels of education. When your choices are limited to only how to respond to each question or direction presented by the teacher, you never have to think about the underlying meaning of the activity or what you might gain from it. If you feel that all the serious decision making of the classroom is totally in the teacher's hands, you never have to take responsibility for your own education.

Writing, however, almost always involves taking responsibility. You make your own statements in an open-ended situation. No one can say ahead of time exactly what you should write, what you will think, or what ideas you should express. To come up with something interesting, important, and challenging to write, you must think about the meaning and possibilities of the situation.

No matter how narrow a writing assignment appears, it contains many possibilities of going beyond the minimal adequate response. Even assignments that ask you to summarize a textbook give you options in phrasing, focus, detail, and depth of presentation. In the next few years you are likely to run into assignments that ask you to frame original issues in a subject area, draw on a range of sources, read widely on your own, seek new data from research, provide novel analyses, and come up with new ideas and arguments.

The most open-ended work is often a major term project submitted as a paper. Typically, as you advance in your subjects, more responsibility is put upon you to develop ambitious papers that reflect more of your own choices and judgment and rely on more of your own preliminary work, thought, and research. In such major written assignments you decide how to develop the topic, what skills and knowledges to draw on, how to organize your time and activity, how to structure the work that leads up to the completion of the assignment, and what form your final presentation will take.

Your problem in open-ended tasks is to find a way to draw on your own motivations, interests, skills, and resources to create something original. Then you will have work you can feel committed to and involved in, that will show the teacher what you can do, that will extend your own learning in ways that are important to you, and that you will be proud of.

❧ Writing Your Self into College

As you find involving and motivating ways to take part in the activities of your classes, you are more likely to elicit engaged responses from your instructors. They see you as potential professionals making original contributions to knowledge and the community. Generally, they look for and reward those students who seem to have an original drive and personal commitment. They notice students who show a knack for the subject or for addressing problems. They notice students who treat the course content not as pre-packaged knowledge to be memorized, but as a complex area to be explored and become familiar with. When you really start talking with your teachers about the ideas and problems posed by your courses, you will be involved even more deeply.

Sometimes teachers describe at length ways to approach the novel problems posed by your assignments. At other times they may leave you to your own devices, with only your experience to help you figure out what to do. No matter how informative the instructor is about the expectations of the assignment, you must determine the kinds of resources and work that need to go into the assignment and the kind of result you should aim at as your final product. That is, figuring out the assignment is part of the assignment.

The way to figure out the assignment is not to search for obscure hints about what is in the back of the teacher's mind, but to size up the organization of the class and activities. Teachers often spend much time thinking about what goes into a course, how it is structured, and what the students ought to be doing. They are setting up an experience for you to take part in. When you start to understand what they have set up, you can see more clearly what kind of part you can play in it. You can then think about what you might want to say in class and write in papers.

The remainder of this chapter focuses on understanding the dynamics of communication within the classroom structure. It provides a general way of looking at classrooms to see what kind of rhetorical situation you are in every time you are asked to write. The next chapter will examine the social and personal processes through which you write your papers and make your statements. Then the remainder of the book will examine in detail the typical activity systems that occur in classes and the kinds of writing assignments that fit within them.

Writing for Reflection

1. To help develop an understanding of the difference between psyching out the teacher and sizing up a classroom, write two short informal pieces. First, in a few paragraphs describe an incident when you or a classmate psyched out a teacher by determining what the teacher was looking for and then by providing it. Second, describe in a few paragraphs how a current class provides specific opportunities for you to learn what you want to learn, grow in directions you wish to grow in, or carry out a project you want to carry out. In class discussion, compare your various experiences.

2. Write a short description of a time when you had to put up a false front in writing or speaking for a course. Then describe another time when you could really express who you were. Using those two examples, consider what you think "integrity" consists of and how it is relevant or not to your education.

Classrooms as Communication Systems

Most classrooms in college look bare. In elementary school the teacher would decorate the room with seasonal signs and decorations, alphabets, and math problems. In high school, class projects and papers, maps, and educational posters might have given you something to look at. Once you step into most college classrooms, however, there is little else to do but look at and listen to the teacher and the other students.

It is communication that fills up the room for the hour and the many hours that go into preparing for class. The communication is centered on you, the student. Many messages are given for you to process: textbooks and other assigned reading, lectures, blackboard writings, overhead transparencies, electronic bulletin boards, questions and observations, assignment sheets and exam papers. In turn, some communications are expected from you: questions about your confusions, answers to questions posed by the teacher, discussion, homework papers, term projects, and exam answers.

For the most part, the communications directed to you transmit what you are supposed to learn, frame your assigned activities, and provoke you into communicative action. The communications that come from you help you put together what you have learned, develop your intellectual and critical skills, and show the teacher what you have learned. Most of the communications flow directly from the teacher (and teacher-assigned materials) to you and from you back to the teacher. In some classes, however, information flows as well from student to student — sometimes in ways set up and structured by the teachers, but sometimes in ways students arrange on their own.

Some classes also send you out into the world to communicate with others — perhaps through the books in the library, or through cooperative work experiences or fieldwork research.

Each class is a communication system. Your learning is at the center of each of these communicative systems. The writing assignments, in particular, are your most serious, formal, lasting, and well-thought-out contributions to the communication system in each class, and thus your most important way of participating in the learning process in each class.

The Communication Systems of Three Classes

As an example of communication systems, we might consider one course, Introduction to Psychology, taught at three neighboring colleges by different professors with different philosophies about the course. All three courses use the same textbook.

The first course, in a small liberal arts college, is taught in small discussion sections. The overall aim is to help students learn to relate the concepts and research of psychology to their own lives and to observe and reflect on psychological processes in themselves and in others. The daily textbook readings become the topic of class discussions about whether psychological concepts fit with the students' experiences and observations, where the students have seen these concepts in action, and how these concepts help clarify or make more complex their view of human behavior. Assigned papers follow directly from the connections made in class discussions. Students are expected to write about their own experiences and link them to the concepts presented in lectures and textbooks. Instructors are likely to recognize and reward deep application of concepts and discussions of their possible implications. They welcome bold thinking by the students, even if the ideas aren't fully precise or supported.

At the second college, part of a large research university, introductory psychology is taught in large lectures supplemented with a weekly small meeting led by a graduate teaching assistant. The course introduces students to the research and theory developed by research psychologists. The lectures explain experiments that support the concepts in the chapter. A major distinction is made between everyday life and psychological research. Movies supplement lectures to show what happens in controlled laboratory settings. Weekly section meetings help clear up students' uncertainties about material presented in the lectures and textbooks. Exams are a mixture of multiple-choice questions and short essays, testing students' memory of theories and research as presented in books and lectures. Several short essays are required throughout the term asking students to compare how different theories would address certain questions. In all instances students are discouraged from bringing in their own experiences from the uncontrolled messy confusion of life. On all assignments the instructor grading the work (usually the teaching assistant) is looking for knowledge of the material, precision in the use of concepts, and awareness of the specialized nature of thinking in the discipline.

The third introduction to psychology, at an engineering college with a strong emphasis on computer science, emphasizes models of human cognition and how those models relate to models of computer thinking. Students are given puzzles as to what a certain theory would mean about behavior, or how a behavior could be modeled in a robotics or artificial intelligence system. Included in the readings are descriptions of cognitive models of human behavior and artificial intelligence projects. As in the research university, classes are taught primarily in large lectures, but the weekly section meetings taught by graduate students are run as workshops where students are asked to look into their own mental operations and describe what they are doing. They are also asked to consider the logic by which computer programs work and to think of hypothetical automated systems. Writing assignments tend to be either highly speculative in terms of how various processes might be modeled or quite concrete in describing a possible artificial intelligence project. Exams consist of puzzles of human or machine behavior that are to be analyzed in terms of the models studied. On exams and essays teachers like ingenious solutions, plausible but unproven suggestions, hypothetical models, and concrete applications.

In these three cases the instructors have different views of their subject — psychology — and the uses to be made of it. Each instructor builds those views into a structured set of activities that present and apply the subject knowledge. We can even think of the three classes as three different dramas where students play different roles and learn different things (see Burke's dramatism, page 29). The student learning psychology would have a different experience depending on which institution and class he or she was in; nonetheless, in each case the student can rapidly become oriented by paying attention to the pattern of communicative activity in each of the settings. Participating in the small personal-experience course is different than participating in the large lecture or computer science courses.

Even without such extreme variants, however, differences among courses are not simply random, but rather reflect differences in faculty, departments, and colleges. In finding out these differences, you will see that each course makes a kind of sense, and you can get the most out of each if you understand that sense.

The typical parts of classroom communication systems are already familiar to you, although you may not have thought about them in this way. There are the elements brought into the classroom by the teacher and by you, there are the elements spontaneously created in the classroom interaction, and then there are those generated in response to formal requirements — the demands put upon you to say or write various sorts of things. This last is what puts the most pressure on you, what may most worry you, and what this book is aimed to help with. But this last must be understood in relation to the other parts and how they are held together in the teacher's structuring of events and activities. These elements all set the stage for your major productions. They all define the spot you are put on when you are given a writing assignment.

Writing for Reflection

1. Following the example of the descriptions of psychology courses on pages 27–28, describe a class you are taking now as a communication system. Discuss such things as what you expect to get from the course, how you believe the knowledge will be useful for you, how the professor thinks the knowledge will be useful, what actually appears to be offered in the class, and how the class is structured communicatively. What kinds of communications will you receive, from whom, and what kinds of communications will you produce, for whom and with what purpose? Then in class discussion compare the different communication systems of the courses you and your classmates are taking.

2. Imagine an alternative version of the course you described in answer 1, set in a different kind of college and based on different goals. Describe the communication structure and activities of this hypothetical course. Then consider whether this alternative course might be more or less to your liking than the version you are taking.

 USEFUL CONCEPTS FROM RHETORIC

Dramatism

In his book *A Grammar of Motives,* Kenneth Burke, one of the pioneers of twentieth-century rhetorical theory, outlined a model that can be used to tell what is happening in communication. Burke thought that acts of communication could be best understood when compared to the actions in a stage play. To understand the dialogue in a play, we must interpret the lines in their dramatic context, taking into account such factors as the type of play that it is, the actions of the other characters, the way that the play is staged, and the time and place of the action. Similarly, Burke argued, we should try to study communication between people by considering all the elements of the human drama in which the communication is situated. Thus he developed the theory of **dramatism,** which identified five dramatic components that appear in any human communication:

1. The **act** is the actual text of the communication. It is not limited to written or spoken words. Burke defines communication broadly and insists that gestures and actions, and even silences and omissions, contain a rhetorical purpose and are therefore "communications."
2. The **agent** refers to the person, people, or institutions who perform. In a play, the agents would be the actors themselves. In a communicative situation, the agents are the people who initiate, or are otherwise involved in, the communication.

The pentad of Kenneth Burke's dramatism is illustrated in the public briefing (act) delivered by General Norman Schwarzkopf (agent). Through maps, printed and spoken words, gestures, dress, and flags (agency) he explains, justifies, and maintains support for U.S. actions (purpose) to the press and through them to the American public during Operation Desert Shield in the Gulf War (setting).

3. The **scene** consists of all the background information that sets the stage for the communicative act. Scenic considerations include the physical locality as well as the social, cultural, economic, philosophical, or religious values that shape the way that communication occurs in a particular context.

4. The **agency** deals with how the act is accomplished by the agent. All of the tools of rhetoric and communication, all of the various skills of writing, speaking, debating, and denouncing, are part of what Burke labeled "agency."

5. The **purpose** refers to the reason for the communication. Although it isn't always possible to determine exactly what someone's motives may be, there are always purposes — some stated and some obscured — for every kind of speech act. Analyzing these purposes is an essential part of understanding the communication.

Burke called these five terms, taken together, the **pentad** and devoted most of his book to showing how the various relationships and ratios between these five items can explain much of the history of Western philosophy and rhetoric. Each of the parts of the pentad influences each of the others in a reciprocal fashion. If we change something about the scene of a communication, for example, then we will automatically change the act and the agents; in doing so, we also alter the agencies and the purpose. To illustrate the way that Burke's pentad works in rhetorical analysis, consider the following drama of communication:

> An elderly male professor (an **agent**) is giving a lecture on the poetry of Keats (an **act**). The professor is employed by a small, private, prestigious liberal arts college on the East Coast that caters primarily to upper-class students (a **scene**). The professor has a strong belief that poetry is its own reward, and he refuses to lecture on Keats's life or attempt to explain the poetry. He believes, instead, that, if he reads the poems with enough feeling and emphasis (the **agency**), the students will see how beautiful poetry can actually be. In this way, he hopes to instill in his students the same love of the great masters that he has always felt (a **purpose**).

If any one of these factors were different, the entire drama would change. The age, gender, status, and personal philosophy of the agent affect the entire drama. If the teacher were a young woman, or a graduate student, or a Keats hater, then everything about the lesson would change. Likewise, if the scene were an understaffed, poorly funded urban city college or a large state university, the teacher would have to do things much differently. To analyze what is happening in this communication, we must take into account all of the relevant factors and the way that they affect each other.

Dramatism provides a series of questions that takes us beyond the written or spoken text of a given conversation. The meaning of a word depends, to a very large degree, on the context in which it is used, and the elements of the pentad help us see all of the factors that go into creating that context. The five parts of the pentad were designed to answer five key questions about any rhetorical instance: who, what, where, why, and how. For Kenneth Burke, as for many contemporary students of rhetoric, these factors represent the minimum amount of information that must be known for any communication to make sense.

From Kenneth Burke, *A Grammar of Motives* (Berkeley: University of California Press, 1969).

◎╱◎ The Teacher's Role in Classroom Communications

Some of the most visible communications in the classroom system are those defined by the teacher — from assigned readings, to lectures, to handouts of statistics. The readings — frequently from textbooks, but also from other books and articles — are usually done before the class. Instructors sometimes prepare you by providing background or by focusing your attention on certain issues. Lectures and discussions also sometimes review material you have just read to help you see how it fits into the themes the professor is stressing. However, no matter how much support the professor gives you for the reading, it is up to you to understand the reading and fit it into the puzzle of the course.

◎╱◎ Textbooks

Textbooks are of various types. Some set out large bodies of information organized in an appropriate way, making connections among the various facts and ideas — such as history textbooks. Others introduce you to a range of theories, approaches, and research findings that make up the developments of a field — such as sociology textbooks. Still others identify various topics studied in the field and explain the research and concepts the field has developed to help you understand them — some experimental psychology textbooks do this. Some textbooks focus on different areas of practice or problems you will need to understand in professional work. Examples would be textbooks in nursing or management. Still others, such as mathematics or physics textbooks, introduce you to a set of skills and concepts that you will learn to manipulate through a set of sequenced exercises and problems. But all of these books are written for you, the college students taking the courses, and they provide sequences of learning appropriate to the subject.

Teachers may use the textbook as the framework of the course, working through the book chapter by chapter with explanations and discussions of the material followed by assignment of problem sets, exercises, and activities from the end of each chapter. For such textbook-driven courses it is especially important to see the position the textbook puts you in, how in a sense the textbook surrounds you in order to direct and support certain activities on your part. Other instructors may have the classes and lectures run parallel, but not overlap, with the readings, providing an alternate view or a second way into the subject. Still other instructors leave the textbooks far behind, having students use the books just as background reading or as a reference resource.

Although teachers use textbooks in different ways in the lectures, discussions, and assignments, it is also worth understanding the structure of each textbook you are assigned, the kind of information it delivers, the sequence and development of materials, and what the textbook expects students to learn and be able to do. Since teachers or departments usually choose textbooks that fit their conception of the courses and that will help students fulfill those expectations, orienting yourself to the textbook will orient you to the assumptions and expectations of the course.

Writing for Reflection

1. Describe and compare two textbooks you are currently assigned in two different courses. What kind of information does each textbook provide, in how much detail? What kinds of concepts are explained, and what are you expected to do with them? What kinds of skills or instructions are explained? What kinds of questions, problems, and activities does the book provide? How is each book related to the aims of each course?

2. After asking permission, observe a roommate or friend preparing a textbook assignment for a subject in which you have not taken a course. First ask the friend about the course and ask to look over the book for a few minutes. Then watch and take notes as your friend begins to study. Does he or she read straight through, skip around, or refer back to earlier sections? What parts does he or she take more or less time on? Does your friend take notes, underline, or highlight? Does he or she answer questions or solve problems, and how does the material of the book help in those activities? Then write a few paragraphs describing what you observed and your thoughts about how work with the textbook fits into the learning of the course.

Other Readings and Resources

Assigned readings in college often come from a wide variety of sources beyond the textbook. They might be newspaper articles, popular books, economic reports, selections from specialized professional journals, or any kind of text written for any audience. Instructors may have many different reasons for including such materials and may ask you to use them in different ways.

Clippings from newspapers and general circulation magazines may be assigned as supplements to textbooks, to provide late-breaking developments in a field, or to explain specialized concepts. Current materials could also be assigned to provide examples of how the concepts of the course, such as Economics, work their way into daily life. Articles may also provide a case study — for example, in the political process — that you will be expected to examine using the concepts and methods you have been learning. You might be asked to compare how the press treats issues with the more specialized, professional perspective you are obtaining in the course. For example, you may be asked to describe how issues of discrimination are portrayed in the popular media. If you keep in mind both the source of the articles and why they are made part of the course, you will know what kinds of attention to give to them.

Similarly, articles from the professional literature in a discipline are frequently used in college courses. Sometimes teachers use these to present the most current and advanced thinking and research in the area. Instructors may also want you to become familiar with how new findings are communicated using the specialized language, reasoning, and methods of the field. In that case you need to pay attention to how the arguments are built as well as the ideas and information presented. If the teacher wants you to become aware of the different approaches and debates in the field, you need to contrast articles, positions, and evidence with each other. Finally, the teacher may want you to learn to question the validity of some arguments and methods, and so you will need to evaluate the articles. As you advance in your fields, you will be asked to take more complex stands toward what you read.

In addition to newspaper and journal articles, you may be asked to read books written for different audiences. Some may provide specialized information (such as histories or presentations of the latest theories in science), but others may raise large issues that are of general public interest (as in books arguing for a new educational policy). You may be asked to engage in discussion with these texts, criticize the approaches they take, examine their role in the formation of public attitudes, or (as in literature or philosophy classes) interpret, analyze, place in context, and theorize about them.

Teachers may also bring in many other communications, from outside speakers to films and videos to computer programs. Some may be required; others may be supplementary or recommended, kept on library reserve, or in an audiovisual resource room; and still others may be only mentioned in a bibliography handed out for you to consult as you become interested in a topic or develop a term project.

✑✎ Interacting with the Written Material

Each of the readings or other materials presented in a class was written for a specific audience at a specific time with particular purposes. In a way the text asks you to take on the role of that original reader. A French political editorial from the eighteenth century asks you to take sides on an issue of French politics of the period, even though the dispute is long dead and from another country; a comic strip, even if it is from a World War II GI newspaper, aims to make you laugh; and a classic essay in Renaissance science still aims to persuade you of its truth, even though the science has since moved on. Even if you know enough about French politics or the situation of GIs or Renaissance science to understand the issues, you may no longer find the politics acceptable, the science convincing, or the joke funny. From the perspective of the original reader, you may not find the old texts interesting or useful. Even if you did, you still may not be getting from them what the instructor hoped for by making the assignment. These texts become useful, relevant, and interesting for the course only when taken from a special perspective that ties them into the work and thinking of the course, such as understanding the violence of emotion that overtook the French Revolution, the role of humor in American culture to mediate between beliefs in individualism and the compulsions of military life, and the changes in scientific thinking over time.

Only with textbooks (and a few other materials used in a similar direct instructional way) are you clearly in the position of the primary user and can take a natural attitude of a reader, following the cues and directions the author sets for you. Even with textbooks, as we have discussed, it helps to reflect on what the text asks you to do and how. With all other readings you need to be even more reflective, asking yourself what the text attempted to do for original readers, how the teacher is asking you to read it, and what the reading adds to the total learning of the course.

Teachers frequently give some explanation and justification for the various readings and other materials, perhaps on the first day of the course in going over the syllabus. It is easy to overlook this beginning-of-the-term information if you are focused more on how many pages you will have to read and write. Sometimes teachers may give a sentence or two of explanation at the end of a class meeting to prepare you for the next reading. Again, it is easy to ignore such orientations as you are packing your books and rushing to your next class. You will gain much, however, by paying attention to such clues about how the teacher uses these resources in class and about what questions you will be asked about them. If you have any doubt about why you are assigned any reading or other material, what kind of attention you are supposed to give it, or what you are supposed to get from it, just ask the instructor.

Writing for Reflection

Describe a recent instance when a teacher assigned nontextbook reading for one of your courses. What was the course? What was the material? What was the source? What was the original purpose of the material? For what purpose did the teacher assign it? What attitude or perspective did you need to have to the material to relate it to class activities? How did your role of reader differ from the role of the original readers? Given the difference in your perspective, what things did you see or understand about the text that might not have been evident to the original readers?

❧ How the Instructor Shapes What Happens in Class

In addition to setting materials for you to read or otherwise use, the instructor determines the plan for each day's class. If the instructor fills class hours with lectures, films, or other spectator events, your success lies in figuring out when and how to engage actively with the material. Alternatively, if the instructor structures the class around student participation, your success lies in participating most fully. In either case much is determined by what the teacher brings to the class, how he or she structures the class, and how he or she prompts student activity.

Lectures and Active Listening

Although lectures seem to hand authority totally over to the lecturer for the hour, really they call upon all your resources to be an active listener. Lectures can do many things:

- Deliver information
- Provide understandable explanations of difficult concepts
- Lead through a sequence of related information and ideas to build a sense of connections
- Apply concepts of the course to situations of interest or concern
- Explain procedures
- Provide examples and models of tasks that will be assigned
- Define the teacher's expectations

The college classroom is a complex communicative system where students' comments respond to textbooks, other readings, films, lectures, questions, and discussion in order to communicate with classmates and the instructor.

- Provide provocative arguments to get reactions from the students
- Be enriched by handouts, overheads, slides, or films

Each of these tasks and techniques requires different kinds of listening, processing, and thinking. Lectures are not undifferentiated information to be memorized, but rather complex resources and prods for activity.

Lectures are central to most courses; they identify what the teacher thinks is important and what the teacher thinks the student ought to be learning and doing. Making some record of the lecture, therefore, is essential. Whether you should take notes or record lectures, and in what format, is a personal decision based on your sense of the course and your own sense of how you work best. Everyone has his or her own style of organizing thoughts, remembering information, and taking notes. Each course has its own demands and its own relation to material in the lectures.

However, note taking has the unfortunate effect of putting the student in the position of a passive receiver of authoritative words, concerned with transcribing rather than responding or thinking about the words. When you come to study your notes, you may be simply tempted to memorize the lectures rather than working them into your own way of thinking.

Depending on how the lecture relates to what is in the textbook, how well you know the material, and how your own memory works, you may also use your notebook for your own thoughts about the lecture as it happens, for questions, or just for the major ideas covered. To encourage students to think about what is being said, lecturers sometimes provide their own set of notes, or notes may be available from a student service. There is nothing wrong with using prepared notes if you use them to free yourself to really listen and think about the lecture. If you find that you do want to spend the lecture taking notes, you can use the few minutes after the lecture, perhaps walking to the next class, to reflect about what went on and how it relates to the overall development of the course. Step out of the maze of the lecturers' words to encounter your own thoughts and reactions.

Writing for Reflection

Closely observe a lecture you are required to attend for one of your classes. Take notes on the style of delivery and presentation. Does the lecturer use anecdotes, charts, slides, videos? Is the material formally organized around an obvious outline, or does it seem to follow a flow of ideas? Is it delivered from notes, a prepared text, or apparently spontaneously? What kind of information is provided? What do you think you were supposed to get out of it? What kinds of things are you supposed to be able to do as a result of hearing the lecture?

Describe what you found and your thoughts about the lecture in several paragraphs.

Discussion

Discussion, as opposed to lecture, gives you moment-by-moment clues on what you ought to be thinking about. Teachers are constantly providing prompts for you to think about, posing problems, or asking questions. Each of these prompts defines an activity in which you can engage. Usually teachers expect that you will prepare assigned materials, readings, and exercises before the class meeting so that the prompts can build on this material. The questions may also call on other material you may have studied or skills developed in a previous class. If there is something about the questions that you don't understand, or if you don't understand where other students' replies are coming from, you can always ask the teacher to explain what he or she is looking for and what kind of knowledge would help in providing an answer.

Where and how the teacher guides the class discussion are particularly revealing about what the teacher thinks is important and what you ought to be able to do with the material. Some teachers may be open to taking discussions in directions that reflect your interests and concerns, whereas others may be more resistant. By staying tuned to teachers' questioning, you can see what skills, ideas, and assumptions the teacher relies on and note characteristic patterns or interests that develop over the term.

More deeply than simply providing clues to teacher expectations, these questions and other discussion-leading devices establish the immediate framework for your activity. The teacher's questions are like scaffolds within which you can construct your answers. By asking particular kinds of questions, the teacher prompts you to think about particular kinds of things. If the teacher asks you to locate where a character in a story first shows uncertainty about his beliefs, that question focuses your attention on what the character believes and then sets you to searching through the story for phrases that indicate uncertainty. That search through the story helps you build a view of the changing beliefs of the character.

Through many such techniques, teachers focus your attention on specific kinds of information and thoughts, helping you develop your skills and ideas. How the teacher arranges the seating in the class, whether the teacher establishes group activities and in what ways, at what point in each class the teacher shifts back and forth from lecture to discussion, whether there is a lab attached to the course and what activities are scheduled for those periods, what kinds of explicit instructions, advice, or rules govern activities — all these things and others shape how you participate in the classroom and thus what information, ideas, and skills you learn as a participant. By seeing more clearly the activities the teacher is asking you to participate in, you can see how you can extend yourself to new learning.

Writing for Reflection

In the next discussion section of another class, write down the questions and other prompts used by the teacher to get students to talk. What do you think the teacher is looking to get from the students? What is his or her strategy? Also describe how the students respond to the various prompts. How did they get a sense of what the teacher was looking for? How did different students respond? To which responses did the teacher react most favorably? Which responses did you like best? Least? To what extent did students fulfill what the teacher was hoping for, and to what extent did they go in different directions? How did the teacher deal with the new directions? Describe in several paragraphs what you found.

The Student's Role in Classroom Communications

While the teacher may provide information and frames classroom activity, all classroom communication ultimately sets the stage for your participation, what you communicate. Some of your communications will help teachers evaluate your work, such as the papers, tests, and class presentations that will be graded. Whether these will be formally graded or not, they are constant indicators of your participation, involvement, and learning, to which the teacher can respond. More than that, however, your communicative activities *are* what you learn. You learn to solve certain kinds of puzzles, answer certain kinds of questions, produce certain facts and concepts in particular circumstances, and develop and articulate certain kinds of thoughts. While you may remember a certain amount of information that you may passively listen to, the more you actively use what you have heard to carry out meaningful tasks, the more you will remember, and the more you will be able to apply that learning when you need it. How you understand what is being asked from you (see Task Representation, page 40) will shape what you do.

In developing your own communications you are involved with knowledge and ideas, trying to shape them in ways that meet the standards and interests of the class.

Especially in more extended and open-ended projects, you focus your attention and knowledge for a substantial period of time in order to build structures of thought around the subject matter and materials of the course. In this way you draw on all the communications that have occurred previously in class, whether from the textbook, discussions, lectures, lab activities, or extensions of classrooms through assigned library projects or field work. You fit together what has come before to extend it in a way appropriate to the assignment. In other words, you incorporate the entire communication system of the class in the process of creating your own communication. Those patterns then become part of you, always available for you to use in later courses and after you graduate.

✺✺ REVIEWING WRITING PROCESSES

Task Representation

Success or failure in college may depend, not on how well you compose sentences or organize ideas, but on how accurately you interpret your writing assignments. In an experimental study on task representation, Linda Flower, a composition researcher at Carnegie Mellon University, has determined that, even when given the same assignment, students may devise very different strategies for organizing information and presenting ideas.

Flower began her experiment by having a group of students read a series of comments and opinions about revising papers. The students were given a typically open-ended assignment to "make a brief (1- to 2-page) comprehensive statement about the process of revision in writing." However, instead of composing the paper as they normally would, students were instructed to think out loud while they were writing.

By examining what the students said as they wrote and comparing that to what they wrote, Flower determined that the students chose from five general strategies for responding to the assignment, depending on how they represented the task to themselves:

1. *Summary.* Some students approached the assignment as a summary. They read the information carefully, selected what they considered to be the most important ideas from each paragraph, and wrote a paper highlighting and explaining these main points.
2. *Response.* Other students used the assignment as a springboard for their own responses. Students who wrote response-type papers generally searched the text of the assignment for some point or key phrase that they could use as a reference point for their own experiences or opinions. Often the finished papers were only tangentially related to the text of the assignment.
3. *Review and comment.* Another group of students settled on a combination of summary and response. These students would either summarize a point briefly and then add their own response to it, or they would summarize in the first part of their paper and then add an "opinion paragraph" at the end.
4. *Synthesis.* A fourth group of students attempted to create a structure that connected the various statements about revision into a single controlling thesis. These students went well beyond the requirements of a summary by creating a concept Flower describes as "a substan-

tive, informative idea rather than an immediately obvious inference."

5. *Interpretation for a rhetorical purpose.* A final group of students wrote papers that were designed to set up an issue or argue a point. They interpreted the information as either supporting or refuting a general proposition about the nature of writing or revision. These students interpreted the assignment as an invitation to make or explore a controversial issue, and they organized the information accordingly.

None of these responses could be considered right or wrong, since the assignment did not give the students enough information to choose among the strategies. All five strategies represent valid types of academic writing. Many teachers give similarly open-ended assignments even though they expect students to employ (or to avoid) specific strategies. In such cases, the student has to determine the best way to organize the paper and process the information. If you have the chance to ask your teacher whether your representation of the task matches the teacher's expectations, you can approach the assignment with greater confidence.

Flower, Linda et al. Reading to Write: Exploring a Cognitive and Social Process. Oxford UP 1990.

✆✆ Being on the Spot

When you recognize a moment when you must say or write something, you may feel on the spot. You are in what is called a rhetorical situation (see page 42). In class you may place yourself on that rhetorical spot by raising your hand in a discussion, or the teacher may place you in it by assigning a paper, but in both cases the next move is yours. You feel pressure to respond, to make a statement. What do you say? What do you write?

What you say or write, however, does not need to come out of the blue. The more attention you pay to the situation, the more clues you will have to

find both what will fit the situation and what you want to say in it. For example, usually a major paper is preceded by many smaller events, such as class discussions, meetings with your professor to talk over your planned project, perhaps smaller pieces of assigned writing, or after-class discussions with classmates. These less demanding events prepare you for the bigger statements.

The school term is a series of activities developing your skill with the material and your relationship with those around you in the class. The big moments are only later points in a process of development. Teachers who are aware of this process create a sequence of activities that lead to more ambitious writing projects at the end of the term. Sometimes, however, you have to leap from a series of small-scale, limited activities, like taking notes in a lecture, to a single complex performance, as in a major analytical paper. When you are suddenly on that very big and unprepared spot, you have to build that bridge from daily activity to the larger, more independent response.

Over your education, these moments add up. Over your college career you will write many papers, each one an experience that prepares you for the next. If all goes well, by your senior year you will be writing at an entirely different level. Looking back then at the papers you wrote over your college years, you may be amazed at how far your thinking, knowledge, and ability to write effectively about difficult subjects have come.

✐✐ USEFUL CONCEPTS FROM RHETORIC

The Rhetorical Situation and Rhetorical Timing

A *rhetorical situation* is a situation that appears to ask you to make a statement. It is defined both by other people, in what they are saying and doing, and by your own motivations. For example, your friends may be discussing where to go for a snack, but since you have to run off to a class in a few minutes, you have no stake in the discussion. So this is not a rhetorical situation for you. However, another friend passes you and says that class has been canceled. Suddenly you have reason to urge the group to choose your favorite coffee bar; the situation is now a rhetorical one for you. But before you can speak, they have already agreed to go there, so the rhetorical situation has evaporated. All you have to say is, real coolly, "Whatever."

Rhetorical timing has to do with the right moment to make your statement. You may be in a situation where you have something very important to say, but if you blurt it out at the wrong moment, people won't listen, may react negatively, or may not understand what you are talking about. As you listen to your friend who is depressed over a bad grade in a frustrating class, you may be aware that the situation calls for you to oppose her plan to drop out of college. On the other hand, you realize that this is not the right moment to tell her how much she is getting from the experience. Instead it may be the right moment to help her figure out just what is so frustrating about this class. Later, once she can start to see the bigger picture again, may be a better moment to encourage her to stay in school.

Much of the art of rhetoric is in recognizing those situations in which making a statement will have some useful effect, being able to perceive what is going on, identifying your own stakes or interest in influencing the situation, and choosing the right time to make your statement most effectively. Since situations often change moment by moment, those people who recognize the opportunities of the moment and are ready to act rhetorically can make themselves heard and can accomplish things that would be impossible at other times and places.

Of course, the situation and timing of college writing is often set by the teacher through the assignment and the deadline. Still, understanding the situation of the classroom, your own interests, and exactly where the assignment fits in the unfolding of the course over time will help you write more appropriately for that moment in that course.

Writing for Reflection

Describe one situation in which you were assigned to write something to be read by the instructor or the class. How did the assignment depend on reading assignments, class lectures and discussions, or other previous communications? When was the assignment due, and how did that affect what was expected and what you were able to accomplish? How detailed was the teacher in defining the assignment and in setting specific goals and expectations? Were there specific class or group activities to help you write the paper, such as brainstorming or editing sessions? How did your own interests and knowledge influence what you chose to write and the approach you took? How did you expect the teacher would respond to your paper, and were you surprised by the actual response? In retrospect, would you have approached the assignment any differently?

Getting Involved Electronically

Find out how to log on to the World Wide Web. Visit the home page of your college. (Your instructor will provide you the URL address.) See what kind of information your college makes available and what kind of image it presents to the world. Write a few paragraphs describing how your college represents itself.

3

Writing Processes

AIMS OF THE CHAPTER

To write is to take part in many processes, personal and social, in interaction with others, inside your head, and between you and a sheet of paper. This chapter provides an overview of these processes, which will be examined in greater detail in later chapters. Understanding that writing is part of many processes helps relieve the uncertainties and anxieties of writing and helps you focus on the next relevant part of the process. Understanding the variety of processes that vary from situation to situation helps you choose how to go about writing any particular paper and helps you write more creatively, effectively, efficiently, and appropriately.

In the latter half of the chapter, an extended case study shows the processes of writing in action for one student writing a paper for a course.

KEY POINTS

1. Every piece of writing comes into being through many processes.

2. Writers progress step by step, trusting in the processes, even when they are not sure where all the steps will lead.

3. The processes of each kind of paper differ from those of every other kind, and the processes of each individual paper differ from others of its kind.

4. Several processes, however, often appear in a recognizable form. These recurring processes range from the general ways situations unfold to the detailed procedures of improving your drafts through revision and editing.

QUESTIONS TO THINK ABOUT

■ Have you ever been stuck in trying to write something? At what point did you get stuck?

- What different things do you do when you write a paper for history than when you write a paper for English? When you write an essay in an exam compared to when you write a research paper? When you write a letter to a friend compared to when you write a shopping list?

- Does writing help you to learn? What has writing any particular paper taught you? When has writing helped you understand the material better, shown you how parts of the subject fit together, increased your skill, or led you to new thoughts?

An Author's Confession

Often enough when I sit down in my familiar desk chair and turn on the computer, I have no idea what I am going to write or how I am going to write it. Not every day, not on every page, but often enough, I find myself at a loss as to what to do next. I may have a general idea for a book chapter on a certain topic, using certain materials and referring to certain ideas. Or I may need to write a handout for a class or a recommendation for a student who wants to go to law school. Beyond these general goals, however, I really have no idea what will go on the page or how I should organize my thoughts to produce those words.

This is usually the moment I go make a cup of coffee, or read my e-mail, or find out what new games my son has loaded on the computer.

I have the dreaded blank-page syndrome. I can't begin to imagine how I should begin working, how I am going to fill up the page to have something creditable to meet my deadline. Not knowing what words to start putting on the paper, I am overcome with panic and an overwhelming desire to do something else.

After almost half a century of writing and almost thirty years of teaching writing, I ought to know better — but then again I keep getting myself into new spots, so even if I figured out what to put on the page yesterday, I still don't know what I ought to put on the page today. That's what creative work means — and all writing is creative work, even if it is just creating a summary of an article you have just read. You create something new, and if it is new, how could you know before you began what it would be? Inevitably, almost all writers at one time or another face the questions of, What am I doing? Can I do this? How do I even begin thinking about this?

Trusting the Process

I have learned one thing that helps control the panic and guides me toward useful activity. Writing is always a series of processes. I have come to trust

the processes of writing. If I take first steps that seem to make sense, I will start to go down a path that will lead to a finished piece of writing. As I go down the path, I will engage in different activities that will help me figure out what I am doing, how I should go about it, and eventually what words I will use.

I can't expect a finished product to emerge the moment I turn my mind to a writing task or stretch my fingers over the keyboard. Any one of a number of rather different activities can get me going. I think about the goals I wish to accomplish. I jot down phrases or ideas I think might be relevant to the subject. I look over the writing that I have done to that point on the project, maybe even outline it, to see where the work was going. I look for some data or sources that will help develop my ideas. I freewrite about the germ of a thought in the back of my mind. I read something related to get some ideas. I ask myself where I am in the process of writing. Any of these or many other actions can help me take the next step, bring my task into clearer shape, and make my task that much easier the next time I sit down to write.

❧ The Variety of Processes

Writing is a process of responding to the statements of others, a way of acting and participating within the drama of the term. Because each kind of paper is part of a different drama, a different kind of interaction, the writing process varies from situation to situation. Thus the process of writing a summary of a chapter for study purposes (see page 107) differs somewhat from the process of writing a summary to demonstrate to a teacher that you have read and understood a difficult philosophic passage (see pages 127–130). Both of these differ substantially from the process of answering an essay exam question based on the same material (see pages 127–130). If these apparently closely related activities (covered in Chapters 5 and 6) differ, how much more would they differ from preparing an analytical essay (see Chapter 9), a laboratory report (see Chapter 12), or a persuasive argument (see Chapter 15)?

The different assignments writers in college are likely to encounter are described in various parts of this book. Their locations are listed on the chart on this page. In these sections the text identifies at least one good path that leads in the appropriate direction. You may well think of others that will also work for you.

℅⌒ PROCESSES FOR DIFFERENT KINDS OF ASSIGNMENTS

℅⌒ Some Common Processes of Writing

The following sections describe some large organizing processes that appear in some form in most writing assignments. Again, this list should not be considered a single path to be always followed. Aspects of these are discussed in the following chapters in the context of specific kinds of writing.

1. The process of unfolding situations
2. The process of putting your goals and the task in focus
3. The process of developing ideas
4. The process of finding and gathering resources
5. The process of thinking through your materials
6. The process of planning and organizing your statement
7. The process of producing text
8. The process of making your sources explicit
9. The process of examining and improving text
10. The process of receiving responses and moving on to the next statement

Unfolding Situations

Each situation in which you write is preceded by various events and interactions — things you have read, things others have said to you, and things you have said and written. Thus, as we have discussed, your writing somehow fits into a sequence of unfolding events and carries that interaction on to the next stage, even if you are not always aware of it. Sometimes this process is obvious, as when you write a letter of application for a job after reading a want ad, the company responds requesting more information, and you write back. Sometimes the unfolding situation is less obvious, as when a reflection on your life seems to pop out of nowhere when you are writing a journal. Nonetheless, if you think for a few minutes you may remember what led you to wonder about your life in this way.

By recognizing the unfolding writing situation, you can place your statement in a larger set of interactions. The writing assignment or rhetorical situation (see pages 40–41) usually grows out of easily identifiable sequences of interactions. In school writing this process of interaction evolves in discussions, lectures, and reading, as discussed in Chapter 2. This process involves many people, not only the instructor and other students, but also the authors of the books and articles you read and other people whose statements find their way into the class.

Putting Your Goals and the Task in Focus

Once you realize you are in a rhetorical situation — specifically, that you need to write something — you start to reflect and plan. In college writing this process is often set in motion by a teacher-given assignment. The assignment to some extent poses a problem, sets goals for you, and directs you toward specific tasks. But since in writing there is rarely any single correct answer, you decide on your own specific plans for completing the assignment; that is, you represent the task to yourself so you can direct your activity. (See the discussion of task representation on pages 40–41.)

Identifying your rhetorical problem, goals, and tasks helps you define your purposes in writing and focuses your energies in useful channels.

Although this process may be carried out largely on your own, discussing your understanding of your task with the instructor and other students can help you clarify your directions. If you are writing as part of a collaborative team, you need to discuss plans deeply to develop a common understanding of your goals and how the work will be divided and coordinated. Too often students on a team think they share an understanding of a project only to go off in separate directions that never wind up fitting together.

Developing Ideas

Once you know what you want to accomplish in general terms, you still need to develop the specifics of your statement. Rarely do words immediately start to flow in perfect prose to make a perfect statement. You usually first need to think through what kinds of ideas and materials will achieve your goal. If you want to persuade your parents that your desire to switch from computer science to art is not totally insane, a waste of money, and a threat to your future livelihood, you need to think about what arguments will help them to understand your reasons (see Chapter 15 on how to develop arguments). After thinking about their values, their views of life, and their hopes for you, you realize that you need to develop the idea that art and graphic design are a major sector of the new economy of the information age, that computers and electronic communication are providing major new opportunities for graphic designers, and that someone with your background in computers will have a great advantage in the job market. Moreover, you realize that to support these ideas it would be useful to get some examples of the kinds of new opportunities opening up and some economic projections of how much work is likely to be available in this area in ten years.

Similarly, imagine you have been assigned by your history professor to examine an incident that reveals something about changing attitudes toward immigration. To satisfy this assignment, not only do you have to pick a relevant incident, but you need to find out much more about the incident and develop some ideas about what the incident reveals.

The process of determining the ideas and materials you will discuss is known in classical rhetoric as *invention* (see pages 75–76 for a fuller discussion). Brainstorming and other individual and group techniques can help you find what you will write about. If you are working with others, it is especially important to share ideas with all members of the group to get the benefit of everyone's thinking and to come to a common agreement on what you will write.

Finding and Gathering Resources

The process of locating and drawing on resources can be a distinct and major part of any piece of writing. Even a letter of complaint about a defective CD player will be stronger if you can find the guarantee and sales receipt that prove the machine is still under warranty; the complaint may be even stronger if someone who knows about electronics can help you describe the difficulty you are having.

In some writing situations you already know what you need to draw on. Even in these cases, however, you may still need to prod your memory to flesh out the details of incidents or to expand on ideas you already hold (see Chapters 4 and 8). In many cases, finding resources outside your own experiences can add strength, specificity, depth, and persuasiveness to your writing. The most obvious external resources are in the library (as discussed in Chapter 11), but interviews, field observations, and laboratory experiments can provide important substance for your writing (as discussed in Chapter 12). Sometimes just reading a book or an article on a subject will help spark your own ideas. All resources you use contribute substance and strength to your writing. They draw you more deeply into the issues, and then they back you up.

Thinking Through Your Materials

Once you have gathered your ideas and materials, you need to think through how they add up, how they may be taken apart or combined in new ways, or what meaning you can find in them. (This process, called analysis, is examined in Chapters 9, 13, and 14.)

Planning and Organizing Your Statement

At times you may know quite early some aspects of what your final piece of writing will look like. If you are assigned to write a five-hundred-word analysis of a short story, for example, you know right away that the final paper will be about two double-spaced typed pages, that there will be quotations from the story, and that some sentences will explain the meaning of the story. As you read and reread the story, you may start to notice specific passages that you think are important. You may also develop specific ideas and certain phrases that you will use in your final essay. You may even identify a sequence of related thoughts that turn into the structure or backbone of your argument. However, at one point you must draw all your planning together with the thought that you will soon be writing a draft. At this moment, outlines, sketches, flow charts, or other planning notes help you see how you will fit the parts of your paper together. You may revise the plans once you start writing, but a plan at this point helps you know where you are going in your writing. (*Planning* is further discussed on pages 206–207.)

Producing Text

It is much easier to face a blank page once you have focused goals, formulated ideas, gathered resources, thought through materials, and written out a concrete plan. When you know where you are going and some of the important places you need to pass through, you don't have to pull sentences out of the blue. Instead, you need only to write the sentences that take you down your path. Your first draft marks out the things you need to say. Once you have established that basic path of words, you can flesh out, explain, qualify, sharpen, adjust, or otherwise improve that basic path, but you will have the security of knowing how to get from start to finish of your statement. You will have a text to work with.

Making Your Sources Explicit

In the course of developing your paper you may have drawn on many resources. When you finally start writing your essay, these resources work their way into the text, directly or indirectly. The resources you bring most directly into the text need to be identified so that the reader knows what you are using. In personal or autobiographical writing this may mean describing memories or experiences that you are writing about or that explain why you believe in particular ideas. (Chapters 4 and 8 suggest ways of discussing personal experiences.) When you rely on other people's writing, you need to refer to the ideas and words of those other texts (see pages 240–242) and then explicitly identify what book, magazine, or electronic source you got the words and information from. (Principles of citation are discussed on pages 242–247.) Chapter 11 on library research presents standard formats for citing books, magazines, and other research material.

Examining and Improving Text

With the text of a first draft completed, you can look it over and see how it may be improved. You can ask many different kinds of questions about it, from fundamental issues of argument to surface issues of appearance. You can ask if you have left out any necessary or useful part of your argument or evidence, whether you have explained your ideas and resources fully enough, or whether you have taken into consideration opposing views. You can ask whether you have approached the topic from the right angle or placed the parts in the most effective order, or pushed your conclusions far enough or too far. You can ask whether readers can follow your reasoning, will have the necessary knowledge to understand you precisely, or will find your examples and evidence persuasive. Nearer to the surface, you can ask questions about whether readers will find your sentences clear and easy to follow, whether your style is appropriate for the situation, or even whether you have spelled all the words correctly.

Every question you ask about the text gives you a perspective for revision and editing. Deeper questions and improvements are usually called *revision* — seeing the writing again through fresh eyes. Improving the surface features, such as sentence readability, grammatical correctness, and spelling, is usually called *editing*. Giving your text a final examination for typographic errors and other mistakes is usually called *proofreading*. All three are a part of the process of looking at your drafts to see how they might be improved.

Some writers tend to examine their drafts only for surface correctness. Proofreading, because it requires only checking out the text for such things as correct typing, spelling, and grammar, is perhaps the easiest and least painful aspect of improving a text. The questions to ask at this level are fairly clear-cut. Proofreading is necessary, but it doesn't lead to deeper improvements.

In editing, you question what you want each sentence to say and the most effective way of saying it, so it requires more complicated thinking. You consider how clearly your sentence formulates your ideas and what your different options are for putting your ideas together. You also think about how you want your ideas to connect with each other. So editing is a bit tougher and a little more painful than proofreading. But it does make for better, clearer, more readable writing.

The most difficult and sometimes most painful process is basic revision. It is difficult because it involves thinking about what the entire piece of writing is trying to say, and how to bring the parts of the writing together. It is sometimes painful because you may have to change your text in substantial ways. You may have to move parts around, throw away sections and sentences you were previously pleased with, and write new paragraphs. You have to open up issues that you had thought you had solved when you got your first draft down on paper. In your relief at having completed a draft, you may not feel very excited about asking tough questions about what you have already done. On the other hand, only after looking again at your text fully and deeply and revising can you see whether you have accomplished what you set out to do. Showing your drafts to others will often help you see your writing freshly and ask the right kinds of questions to improve it. (See pages 145–146, 184–186, and 158–159 for more on these subjects.)

Receiving Responses and Moving on to the Next Statement

The writing process continues after an assignment is handed in to the teacher or a memo is distributed to coworkers. The people who read the paper or memo will have some response to it, which they may express. These responses may be thoughts of their own counterarguments, follow-up actions, or (as in the case of teacher grading) evaluation and suggestions for improvement. You may have the opportunity and desire to answer to these responses, or you may simply think about what others have said. In either case, these responses show how others see your writing, what you have been able to convey, and what you might want to do differently the next time around.

If a piece of writing is part of an ongoing interaction, such as a continuing course, a work project, or a public dispute in, say, student government, it becomes background for the next interchange. As you discuss the next topic in class, the discussion may build on ideas and topics you examined in earlier papers, and unresolved questions may come up again for discussion. If you are working on a long-term project at work, the findings of your first report may be incorporated in a follow-up report. If you are engaged in a public debate, your opponent may quote your words back to you. Your words stay alive in an ongoing process of interaction.

REVIEWING WRITING PROCESSES

The following list identifies brief reviews of particular aspects of writing processes that appear throughout this book. Because some writing assignments focus more on certain processes, these reviews appear where they are most relevant. The review of planning, for example, although it often occurs early in the process of writing a paper, is placed in a later chapter in relation to analytical writing, which usually requires more thought about planning than other forms of writing. Proofreading, which is usually one of the last things you do with a piece of writing, comes in an early chapter in relation to answering exam questions because last-minute checks of your writing are quite useful in these situations.

Task representation (see Chapter 2)

Planning to write (see Chapter 9)

Invention (see Chapter 4)

Revision and drafting (see Chapter 7)

Referring to your sources (see Chapter 11)

Revealing your sources and avoiding plagiarism (see Chapter 5)

Editing (see Chapter 8)

Proofreading (see Chapter 6)

The Processes of One Classroom Writing Assignment: A Case Study

The best way to see how the particular processes of any piece of writing grow out of a specific situation is to look in detail at how one piece of writing developed. The following case study describes how Sandra Malowski, a first-year student in a large state university, came to write a paper for a course within her school's Communications Department.

Sandra, along with eighty other first- and second-year students in the course Communications 11: Mass Media in American Life, was assigned a three-page paper analyzing newspaper stories. The paper was due in the tenth week of the semester. It was the third of four assigned papers for the course, each one requiring some analysis of actual newspaper, magazine, movie, radio, or television stories. Throughout the term the professor and her teaching assistant explained the kinds of analysis they were looking for and the kinds of ideas the students might be exploring through the analysis. Because of this preparation, Sandra and most of the students had a good idea of what was required and how to go about it by the time the paper was assigned.

The Course Unfolds

The class met for four hours each week. Twice a week the professor lectured on how movies, television, radio, newspapers, and magazines reflected and influenced modern American society, repeatedly suggesting that the media had become central to our actions and attitudes. The lectures were illustrated with movie and video clips, radio recordings, and excerpts from news and magazine stories. The third meeting each week was a class discussion and analysis of a television show or news story. Finally the students met once a week in small groups with a graduate teaching assistant to discuss all the ideas raised in lectures, discussions, and readings. The readings were from a textbook and an anthology of articles about current controversies about the media. Thus the paper Sandra had to write was part of a process of discussion of ideas, information, and materials that went throughout the term.

The course began with a few historical lectures about how the media had moved into prominence in American society, starting with the expansion of newspapers in the late nineteenth century, continuing with the rise of Hollywood and the creation of radio networks, and ending with the growth of the cable TV industry and the start of the Internet. In these lectures, the professor emphasized how the media influenced the changing shape of American society. For example, she discussed how, starting in the 1920s, going to the movies became a major social activity and how movie stars provided models for social behavior and styles. She also discussed recurring criticisms going back to the nineteenth century that music, and later movies and television, were corrupting the morals of the youth. The first assigned paper asked students to explore how those historical controversies were still alive today.

After this historical introduction the course turned to the contemporary media — how they were organized, what roles they served in society, and what kinds of stories, images, and attitudes they communicated. For example, some classes were devoted to the social images of family, race, gender, and sexuality presented on television situation comedies. The second assigned paper asked students to look at how television represented certain groups of people or certain issues.

A few classes then examined how radio and TV talk shows were forms of political expression and influenced the political process. Next the class turned to how the news was presented; this unit culminated in an assigned paper. Thus the papers Sandra had to write were part of a process of discussion based on materials in the course.

The first paper asked students to analyze recent complaints about a particular movie, television show, or piece of music in relation to similar historical controversies. Sandra did fairly well on that paper, getting a B–. However, the teaching assistant, who marked the paper, commented that Sandra spent too much time describing the plot of the movie *Natural Born Killers.* She said that Sandra pointed out controversial aspects but did not focus on those details that made them controversial and did not discuss the exact way in which the current controversy related to the themes of previous controversies. In the second paper, in which Sandra analyzed gender roles in her favorite television drama, *E.R.* she did better, getting a B+. The grader, however, mentioned that although Sandra had collected many details on how men and women acted in gendered ways and had made some good observations about those behaviors, her analysis would have gone farther if she had organized those details into categories, such as behaviors that show deference to authority and behaviors that show aggressiveness. In the meantime, in the discussion sections, both professor and teaching assistant kept pressing students to make their claims more detailed and orderly and to identify what exactly led them to their observations. Thus each paper was part of a process of instructors defining what they wanted and of students learning to meet those requirements.

The Paper Is Assigned

With this background, the instructor handed out the assignment sheet for the third paper in late October. The assignment sheet read as follows:

```
Communications 11 — Mass Media in American Life
Writing Assignment #3
Length: about 1000 words or three typed pages
Due: November 17


    Over the next three weeks we will be studying how
news on television and radio and in the newspaper has
influenced American society. The kinds of stories news
media tell and the way they tell them frame how we view
events, particularly political events. This assignment
examines how the news media frame news stories.

    You are to read "Making Sense of the News" by W.
Russell Neuman, Marion R. Just, and Ann N. Crigler from
their book Common Knowledge: News and the Construction
of Political Meaning (University of Chicago Press,
1992). In this chapter the authors describe the five
typical ways, or frames, that people in the news media
use to write stories and that viewers tend to use to
understand news.

    Your task is to analyze one story or several closely
related stories on a political event as presented on
major network television news or in a major newspaper.
The analysis is to examine how the way the story is
told creates the meaning of the story. For your analy-
sis, try using the categories presented in the Neuman,
Just, and Crigler chapter. Show how the patterns they
present reveal how the story is being presented, and
therefore what meanings are being conveyed about the
```

political process. Be as detailed as you can in showing
how the stories are organized and given meaning within
these patterns. If you do not think that the categories
work well for your stories, explain why and develop
new, more appropriate categories.

The chapter the students were asked to read was about fifteen pages long. It defined frames as "the conceptual tools which media and individuals rely on to convey, interpret, and evaluate information." The chapter then described research based on interviews with ordinary citizens about how they perceive several current news stories and on analyses of media stories of those events. The research found that both the interviewees and the media stories most often used five frames to interpret the news: "economic themes, divisions of protagonists into 'us' and 'them,' perceptions of control by powerful others, a sense of the human impact of the issues, and the application of moral values." The chapter then discussed and gave examples of each of these five frames. Here are excerpts from the discussions of the five frames:

The Economic Frame

Both the news media and individuals apply the economic frame to a broad range of issues (Barkin and Gurevitch, 1987). The economic frame reflects the preoccupation with "the bottom line," profit and loss, and wider values of the culture of capitalism. The media tend to employ technical language for the economic frame, while people are far more likely to overlay the frame with a moral or evaluative dimension. The economic frame fits well with the media's propensity to cover news from the standpoint of official sources (Sigal, 1973). Media stories frequently covered the costs of government programs and the economic consequences of pursuing or not pursuing various policy objectives. SDI, drug abuse, and AIDS stories included dollar estimates of costs for government programs that had come from various official sources. The *Boston Globe,* for example, reported that "Reagan's $3.7 billion funding request for the 'Star Wars' program in the current fiscal year has been trimmed by approximately $1 billion."

The Conflict Frame

The communications literature is rife with references to the media's emphasis on conflict as a means of attracting attention and readership. Polarized forces — "the two sides of the issue," "horse-race politics" — are dominant themes identified with the presentation of news. The conflict frame fits well with the media's game interpretation of the political world as an ongoing series of contests, each with a new set of winners and losers (Crouse, 1973; Gans, 1979; Patterson, 1980). In fact the received definition of good journalistic practice emphasizes reporting stories in terms of experts who offer clashing interpretations (McDougall, 1968; Green, 1969; Brooks et al., 1985). In covering the South Africa story, for example, the media cited many different polarized forces including these: blacks vs. whites, blacks vs. police, the South African government vs. journalists, and South Africa vs. the rest of the world. Dan Rather's lead-in to a story typifies the latter frame: "South Africa today turned a defiant deaf ear to worldwide calls for clemency and hanged a twenty-eight-year-old black poet for killing a policeman."

The Powerlessness Frame

Powerlessness was essential to the stories about AIDS. AIDS was covered in the media as an epidemic and spreading beyond anyone's immediate control. "The NAS [National Academy of Sciences] panel's greatest worry is that the virus is being spread further every day and largely by people who may not know they have it . . . Little if anything can be done to help those who are now infected and will fall sick over the next five years." The *Time* story later quotes the Public Health Service to warn people that AIDS can infect anyone: " 'This virus does not discriminate by sex, age, race, ethnic group or sexual orientation.' "

The Human Impact Frame

The media's use of the human impact frame focuses on describing individuals and groups who are likely to be affected by an issue. The official voice of the journalist, however, avoids direct expression of compassion for the people involved. Rather, it seems that reporters put a "human face" on stories by providing human examples and exemplars (Mencher, 1984). In contrast, the individuals who employ a human impact frame express their personal concerns and compassion with a visceral directness. . . .

While the media stories used in our experiments did not explicitly frame stories in empathetic or compassionate terms, they did employ adjectives, personal vignettes, and visuals that might generate feelings of outrage, empathy, sympathy, or compassion from their audiences. For example, a television story on the effects of cocaine use during pregnancy told the story of one young child who had been taken from her mother and placed in a foster home. The video shows a view of the foster parents trying to help the little girl sit on her own in their living room. Part way through the story, the camera pans back so that we can also see another child playing and drinking milk out of a cup while she is standing in front of the cocaine-affected child.

FOSTER MOTHER: "She has no sense of balance. As you can see when we sit her up, she will fall either forwards, backwards, or to the side."

REPORTER: "She cannot crawl. A neighbor child, Miriam, is exactly the same age but normal and developing. The cocaine youngster with her bottle."

FOSTER FATHER: "She just forgets that she likes that milk. Her brain just doesn't transmit that to her. She just drops the bottle and then she'll cry."

REPORTER: "Miriam can drink from a cup. What's ahead for her playmate?"

The Morality Frame

The professional norm of "objectivity" in journalism has been with us for so many years it is taken for granted by journalist and audience member alike. Schudson's illuminating historical analysis of how that norm evolved (1978) reminds us not only that a century ago norms were very different but also that such norms are culturally and economically derived. Of all the content analyses of media framing cited above, none would dispute that cultural values are deeply embedded in modern journalistic practice. References to moral values in the media are simply more indirect. . . .

While our respondents might condemn the "sinners" who got AIDS with some vehemence, the media make reference to such a moral frame indirectly through quotation or inference. As with expressions of empathy in the human impact frame, reporters, for the most part, are not in a position to speak directly and have to find someone else to "raise the issue." For example, *Time* used the views of the Roman Catholic church to raise the question of the morality of sexual education. "In the view of the Roman Catholic Church, for example, a Government campaign to urge use of condoms would be encouraging people to commit mortal sin. The church regards condoms as artificial contraceptive devices whose use, even to avoid lethal disease, is forbidden."

Since the chapter was part of the assigned reading for the first week of the unit, Sandra read it quickly for the next class, noting the five kinds of frames and thinking briefly about them. During the class the professor illustrated these frames with some examples from the newspaper and some video clips, which the class discussed. Some students wondered whether there might not be other ways of telling news stories, but Sandra argued that since people were interested in the news to learn about money, conflict, power, human predicaments, and moral values, they were the natural categories to use.

Over the next few meetings, the class read and discussed other aspects of how the news is presented and is part of the political process: the increasing role of television in elections through debates, interviews, campaign stories, and political analysis shows; the increasing use of political ads, particularly attack ads; the increased role of fund-raising and special-interest groups in politics because of the need for money to pay for video ads; and the way candidates, and government officials work to create video images through photo opportunities and soundbites (brief quotations that will sound good on the news). Thus the paper assignment followed through on extended class examination of the topic from several angles.

While Sandra was putting off hard thinking about the paper during this period, she did watch the television news more regularly, noticing how stories were presented. Since this was a period when President Clinton and Congress, under the leadership of Senator Dole and Representative Gingrich, were engaged in a conflict over the budget, she started to pay attention to how this story was being presented. She noticed how well the story seemed to fit the frame of a conflict story, with reporters wondering who would back down first, who would stand stronger, and who would win. She thought this was a little bit odd, since at one level this seemed obviously an economic story about how we ought to balance the federal budget. It also occurred to her that, even though the government's fundamental role was at stake in this conflict, no stories really looked into those issues. This conflict seemed to Sandra a good issue to write about, even though it was quite complicated and there were far too many stories on it to cover them all.

The Writing Moves into Focus

On Monday, November 13, the professor reminded the class that the paper was due that Friday. Having definitely decided to work on the budget con-

Senate Majority Leader Dole, Vice President Gore, President Clinton, and Speaker of the House Gingrich hold a press conference during the budget crisis of 1995.

flict story, Sandra videotaped that evening's national news on two networks, reviewed the different versions of the story, and selected the one that seemed to lend itself to analysis. She then rewatched the four-minute segment she had selected several times and took notes. Her notes included the introduction to the story by the news anchor, a summary of the story, and some quotations from the reporter and public figures quoted in the story. She also took notes on the visual images that accompanied the story. As she was taking notes, she kept in mind some of the ideas the class discussed about sound-bites and presentation of political images. Because the short segment moved so rapidly and she wanted to make sure her notes were accurate, she watched the tape one more time after her notes were complete to doublecheck their accuracy.

These are her notes

Lead from show intro.

One of three top stories

"In Washington the President vetoes, The Republicans Dig in. Much of Washington could shut down."

anchor, "That running game of political chicken between the President and the Congressional Leadership."

first segment 2 minutes by Brian Williams "Brian, any late movement there tonight"

Reporter standing in front of White House.

reports "signs of movement in the game of nuances" indications that WH would give on spending cuts if Republicans would give on Medicare. "beginning of a framework of a deal"

Pres. later spoke to moderate democrats "told them what they wanted to hear." 15 second sound bite of President Clinton. "I am fighting it today, I will fight it tomorrow. I will fight it next week and next month. I will fight it until we get a budget deal that is fair to all Americans."

Reporter: "It is enough to make an anti-government cynic out of anyone. Anyone in this town will tell you this is all just driven by momentum and sheer politics. It almost takes a crash to start it back up again."

follow up question: President scheduled to leave for Japan on Wednesday, moved to Friday.

Second segment, 2 minutes reported by Lisa Myers from Capitol Hill starts with clip of "The Chaplain opening the Senate with a plea for divine intervention to avoid shutdown."

"But there are no negotiations"— quick shots of capitol dome and white house, while reporter describes conflict.

quote from Senator Domenici about how President seems to want conflict.

"Republicans are not budging either" Repubs want the president to embrace their goal. shot of senate chamber.

Quote from Gingrich, "What the Clinton Administration objects to is that we are committed to balancing the budget in seven years." Similar quote from Dole. shots of committee meetings.

Congress to stay open until midnight to allow visit from the WH, but senior republican comments "a visit from tooth fairy is more likely."

Switch to discussion of impact — multi-colored chart showing close down means 800,000 workers furloughed; passport office, monuments and national parks closed. Another chart of unaffected services: post office, social security payments, essential services such as military and air-traffic control.

Story ends with quote from another senior Republican going back tough stand on conflict: "This will not be a one- or two-day affair."

Jennings: "despite the Budget Crisis it was another good day on Wall Street."

Thinking Seriously

As Sandra kept reviewing the videotape and her notes, she started to analyze and think about how parts of the video segment matched the categories of frames she had read about. First she noticed that the story was structured in a conflict frame. The lead sentences read: "In Washington the President vetoes, The Republicans Dig in. Much of Washington could shut down." The anchor said, "That running game of political chicken between the President and the Congressional Leadership." The story was organized around conflict, with two opposing segments from the White House and Capitol Hill and contrasting video images of the White House and president versus the Capitol and congressional leaders. Sandra noticed that there were even dueling soundbites from the president and the various leaders.

Sandra also saw that each half of the story was supplemented by a brief human impact frame — how the presidential plans would be affected and what would happen to government services.

Sandra then decided to sketch out analytic notes on how the five frames applied to the story, hoping that this process might help her develop her thoughts. These are her analytic notes:

Economic Frame — the economic issues aren't here except as moves in a game. Odd, the next lead in to the stock market report suggested that the budget battle was irrelevant to the real economy, as though Wall Street didn't even pay attention. Policy issues behind economics totally invisible.

Conflict frame — most obvious. basic structure of story is of conflict of two sides. the way the story is told. conflicting soundbites. conflicting images, posturing of two sides.

Powerlessness frame — here the conflict is presented as who would have power. The powerless ones are only the by-standers — the working government and the people of America. who have to watch their needs bypassed in this battle of the leaders.

Human Impact frame — No direct stories about people stranded because they need passports — only general reports about impact.

Morality frame — interesting. Not directly but only through ironic quotations. Chaplain asking for divine intervention, cynical quotation ending each one, "just driven by politics," and "tooth fairy." Ironic stance of reporters, that this is all silly posturing.

She then reflected more on what the notes showed:

The weirdest thing is that the economic story vanished. The report has no real discussion of different ideas behind the conflict, what exactly would be the difference if either side won, what even were the exact, detailed points of disagreement. The conflict is taken only as a matter of belief, like two opposing religions or conflicting sport teams. You don't ask then why people disagree; it is just their belief or commitment.

> There is a funny cynicism of commentary. Everyone knows the politicians are staging a rigged fight for the media. Story is only become bizarre tip of a very serious iceberg, but we are never shown the iceberg. How did this happen? How did a debate over the government get turned into a personal contest?

As we look over the thoughts Sandra had about the news story, we can see that she went through a substantial process of thinking and analysis before she sat down to write a draft. That thinking process involved writing a few things down, but not in final form. Even though she may use in the final paper some phrases that she first used in these thinking notes, she did not try to come up with a formal paper at this point. She recognized that this writing was just a stage in the process of developing her thoughts.

Planning

Now that Sandra had some ideas about what she wanted to write, she spoke with the teaching assistant after class Wednesday to confirm that she was on the right track. The TA liked her topic and insights and gave her some suggestions about how to organize the paper. Immediately afterwards, Sandra sat down in a quiet corner of the cafeteria and sketched out a plan for the essay. She didn't like writing formal outlines; she preferred to sketch out ideas in a loose paragraph form.

Plan for Analysis of Political Story

Dramatic confrontation on TV.

Seemed extreme example of conflict frame for news. Two opposed parts, 2 minutes each, contrasting White House, Republican Congress.

two reporters at two locations. contrasting shots of WH, Cap buildings, and then President and Republican leaders. Fighting opposed quotes.

Impact and powerlessness frames point to citizens as victims to politicians fighting over power.

But same time as presented as a dire crisis, moral frame is presented through quotations from chaplain, unnamed people, makes the conflict appear silly, unrelated to real events. Economic frame is totally absent, even though the fight is over a budget issue. Policy questions not reported.

Conclusion — cynicism of press and public (maybe bring into intro).

Writing the Paper Up

With her thoughts well worked out and with many notes to work from, Sandra should have had an easy time writing a first draft that night. Actually, she spent a long time hanging out with friends after dinner, and then, back in her room, felt tired and overwhelmed by the task of writing. She took a nap. But finally, trusting in the process, she forced herself to get up and look at her notes. She realized everything she needed was there. It only took her about two hours to turn out a rough draft, because her plan worked well and most of the details were in her notes. Exhausted, she left the last couple of sentences to write the next day. She had no idea whether what she had done was any good, but at least she felt she had something on paper. She printed out what she had and went to bed.

The next morning she took her draft with her and looked at it during an hour break between classes. She was pleased. She noticed and marked up in pen some sentences she could write more clearly, a couple of examples that went on too long, a couple of spelling and grammar errors, some typos. Overall, however, the essay made sense, presented the conclusions she had come to, and spoke to the assignment, which she reread just to make sure. Unlike some of her other writing where she kept juggling the order of ideas, this essay seemed to have a real logical order, focused first on describing the news story through the conflict frame, and then talking about how the other frames fit in and put the conflict in perspective. Ending with the morality frame showed how the conflict frame seemed to be missing the point; she could then discuss how the economic issues that lay behind the story were totally hidden. She was still stuck on an ending, but she figured that one would come to her that night when she sat down again at the computer. She also wondered what to do with the cynicism expressed by the reporters and some people they quoted.

That afternoon she checked through the videotape one more time to make sure she had the quotations right. Then that evening she entered her revisions into the computer and made a few other changes. With everything she had written clearly in mind, her closing paragraph almost wrote itself. As she read the paper over for one final time, the title came to her. She printed the paper out and got to sleep before midnight.

We can see in Sandra's process of writing up the paper how much she relied on all the processes that came before. All of them made the actual act of coming up with and revising a text much easier. The earlier processes — carried out at many different moments, spread over a long period — gave her almost everything she needed, except for the final words, and even some of them came from earlier stages.

```
The Big Fight — over what? Oh, just the future of the
country


    Sandra Malowski
    Communications 11
    November 17, 1995
```

On the evening news on November 13, 1995, Americans saw a dramatic confrontation between Democratic President Clinton and the leaders of the Republican-controlled Congress. This confrontation would result that night in a shutdown of the government of this country. As Peter Jennings, the anchor, announced at the beginning of the ABC Nightly News, "In Washington the President Vetoes, The Republicans Dig in. Much of Washington could shut down." The story was overwhelmingly set in a conflict frame, one of the five frames Neuman, Just, and Crigler say dominate the presentation of the news in the United States. My analysis reveals that this news story was built around conflict, both by the news media and by the politicians who provided the conflicting soundbites and visual images. The human impact and morality frames are also brought in indirectly; however, the most important frame, the economic, is entirely hidden. The way these four frames fit together built a strange cynicism into the story, a cynicism that seems all too common in the way we view politics these days.

Neuman, Just, and Crigler say that conflict stories emphasize "polarized forces" in competition, related to a view of "the political world as an ongoing series of contests, each with a new set of winners and losers." Peter Jennings couldn't have been more obvious in the way he framed the story, introducing it by calling it "that running game of political chicken between the President and the Congressional leadership." Then the four-minute story was split into two two-minute segments, devoted to the two sides of the conflict.

Brian Williams reported the first segment on the President's side of the conflict. Williams was standing in front of the White House, lights burning into the night. He emphasized the gamelike strategy of the story by presenting the President's suggestion of a compromise as "signs of movement in the game of nuances." Williams then presented a fifteen-second video clip of a determined president delivering a determined soundbite: "I am fighting it today, I will fight it tomorrow. I will fight it next week and next month. I will fight it until we get a budget deal that is fair to all Americans."

Even while presenting the President's fighting words as fighting, the reporter nonetheless called attention to the fact that the fight seemed something of a show, put on for the press, saying that the President told his audience of moderate Democrats "what they wanted to hear." Williams then commented about the budget negotiations, "Anyone in this town will tell you this is all just driven by momentum and sheer politics. It almost takes a crash to start it back up again."

The second segment, on the Congressional side of the battle, was reported by Lisa Myers from Capitol Hill. This story opened with a bit of ironic commentary, showing a video clip of a chaplain opening the Senate session "with a plea for divine intervention to avoid shutdown." The story rapidly moves from the hopeful prayer to the conflict: "But there are no negotiations. The Republicans are not budging either." The summary is accompanied by quick shots of the capitol dome and the White House, followed by shots of the Senate floor, committee rooms, and Republicans being interviewed. Each video clip is accompanied by a fighting soundbite, such as the one from House Republican leader Newt Gingrich, "What the Clinton Administration objects to is that we are committed to balancing the budget in seven years." Senator Domenici, Senator Dole, and an unnamed senior Republican are also quoted. The story ends again with an ironic commentary on the staged nature of this fight show. Lisa Myers reports that Congress is planning to stay in session until midnight just in case someone from the White House comes down with an offer, but she then quotes a leading Republican as saying that "a visit from the tooth fairy is more likely."

The budget battle is presented as though it were a boxing match or a football game where we are shown the fighting mood of each side, and the opponents are putting on a big show of how psyched they are for the conflict. However, this is not just a sport; it has an effect on people. At the end of both segments there are short additions about the impact of this battle on the President's trade mission to Japan, which will be cut short, and on government operations. The story on government services is accompanied by two multicolored charts listing the major negative impacts and which essential services will remain opened. This presentation is not quite the human impact story that Neuman, Just, and Crigler suggest. It is not, for instance, the story of a family being evicted because they could not apply for social security or an angry worker laid off because a trade agreement was not reached with Japan. Yet the human impact frame is being evoked.

In light of the consequences, the conflict is presented as almost immoral and certainly silly. The moral judgment on the conflict is presented most directly through the words of others: the chaplain's futile prayer for divine intervention, the Republican's comment on the tooth fairy, and the vague "what anyone in this town will tell you." Neuman, Just, and Crigler point out that reporters rarely make the moral judgment themselves, but use quotations from others to express a judgmental attitude. That is certainly true in this case.

Strangely, the story never mentions that the conflict is about basic economic choices the country is facing. Behind the budget issues are issues about what we want our government to spend on, how much we want our government to cost, and who should pay for it. It would seem that of the five frames that Neuman, Just, and Crigler present, the economic frame should be the most important here. Perhaps this story could be framed even more fundamentally in terms of policy discussion: that is, a consideration of what we want our government to do and how it should do it. Policy discussion, however, seems so rare in news stories as not to be mentioned by Neuman, Just, and Crigler. As it is, even the economic frame is totally absent. In fact, in leading into the next story, Jennings dismisses the conflict between the President and Congress as economically irrelevant: "Despite the Budget crisis, it was another good day on Wall Street."

The conflict frame has overwhelmed the presentation of politics, with the politicians playing the role of combative opponents so that they can get their soundbites and pictures on the news. The political stories seem to have nothing to do with real issues, except that us ordinary folk are left powerlessly to absorb the impact. No wonder people are cynical. Even the reporters had a hard time keeping a straight face on this story. Then again, they are the ones who tell these stories, and we are the ones who watch them.

The Process Continues

As Sandra handed in her paper that Friday morning, she remembered how she had said just a few weeks before that these frames made perfect sense and were a natural way to talk about the news. She suddenly realized that she had switched her opinion entirely, that these weren't the only way to tell stories. At least for this story she wanted to hear more about the economics and policy choices of welfare, the military, and all the other areas in which the government spent money. Well, maybe which frames you chose did make a difference. She decided that she would think more about that later.

It took over a week for the teaching assistant to read and grade the papers (Thanksgiving gave everyone a break), but Sandra was pleased with the A she received. Even more, she was pleased with the steady string of marginal comments agreeing with what she said and with the final comment of the teaching assistant:

> *Your paper uses the analysis of the frames to go beyond the idea of frames. You show how the frames used in this case make us wonder about whether we are getting the full and real story. You show how the politicians themselves play to the frames in ways that distort government activity. You show that journalists in producing those frames also are cynical about them. And you show how this whole process of news production makes us all cynical about what we see of our government. Excellent work.*

On the final paper for the course, Sandra followed up on the topic of framing by examining the way futuristic talk about the Internet was framing current discussion of the media. Since she felt she now understood much more clearly what it meant to analyze something, she was much more confident when analyses were assigned in other classes. Thus this one paper was part of her continuing interaction with the class and part of her own process of growth.

Thinking About Student Writing

1. In the process of developing her essay, at various times Sandra Malowski came across different ideas, information, and methods that she would use in her final paper. She also developed her own thoughts and observations that she would later use. Go back over the story of Sandra's writing process and circle each place she ran across an idea or piece of information or developed an insight that she would use in her final paper. Where do each of these ideas, facts, observations, and methods come from? How does she use each in the final paper?

2. The first part of this chapter presents ten typical processes of writing, but notes that for different pieces of writing not all may appear, or be

in the same order, or be of the same importance. The processes may even circle back and repeat. Go over the story of Sandra Malowski's paper and note in the margin wherever you see one of the following processes at work. How important is each for Sandra's paper? How does she engage in each of the processes? How does each of the processes relate to other processes that come before and after it?

1. The process of unfolding situations
2. The process of putting your goals and the task in focus
3. The process of developing ideas
4. The process of finding and gathering resources
5. The process of thinking through your materials
6. The process of planning and organizing your statement
7. The process of producing text
8. The process of making your sources explicit
9. The process of examining and improving text
10. The process of receiving responses and moving on to the next statement

Writing for Reflection

1. Think of a paper or other piece of writing you recently wrote. Based on the various processes presented in this chapter (particularly the list of ten processes above), describe the processes that your paper was part of and the processes by which the paper was produced.

2. Interview someone working in a field in which you might be interested for your career, and ask about their writing process for a specific kind of writing they do on the job. Questions should cover not only the writing-up stage (planning, drafting, revising), but also the earlier processes of recognizing that they are in a situation calling for writing, of gathering information, of thinking through their ideas, and so on. Use the list of ten processes to help you develop interview questions. Then write up what you have found.

Getting Involved Electronically

In a few paragraphs reflect on how the availability of word processors, spell checkers, and other electronic writing tools influences your writing process. How do you use these tools? Is your writing process different when electronic tools are not available? Which electronic tools do you not use? Is that by choice or because of lack of familiarity? How might you use electronic tools differently, more fully, or more effectively?

Thriving
in the
Classroom

Two

4

Journals and Reflective Writing

AIMS OF THE CHAPTER

Reflective writing helps you make personal sense out of the rich, complex, and confusing information you are learning, ideas you are confronting, and people you are meeting. As the term implies, this writing is like a mirror, giving you an opportunity to look at your developing self. This personal connection increases your motivation, purpose, and involvement by helping you define what you want to learn and say. This chapter encourages you to explore both traditional forms of reflective writing and the new opportunities opened up by electronic communication.

KEY POINTS

1. Reflective writing is an opportunity to sort through learning and experience.

2. Journals provide space for examining your readings and thoughts in great detail, following through on your observations in whichever way strikes you as appropriate. When used as part of a course, journals help teachers respond to your ideas.

3. Electronic mail, bulletin boards, and discussion groups allow you to explore your interests and engage in informal communication with other students in the class, the instructor, and other people who share your interests on campus and throughout the world.

QUESTIONS TO THINK ABOUT

- What people, ideas, courses, readings, or other experiences have made you think new thoughts or wonder about new ideas? When and where do you think about these new experiences?

- What experiences have you had writing a journal? In what ways was the journal useful? In what ways did it seem forced or unnatural? What kinds of entries might best help you develop your feelings and thoughts about your reading and learning?

■ Have you ever used the Internet? What subjects might you like to explore in Internet discussion groups or World Wide Web information sources?

◎◌◠ A Rich and Confusing Environment

College is a new environment. You are probably surrounded by a wider variety of classmates than you experienced in high school — students of different ethnicities and nationalities; students of different economic and social backgrounds; students from more regions of the state, country, and the world; students of more interests and accomplishments; older students returning to school after varied experiences; and upperclassmen and graduate students with developed knowledge and commitments. Your professors will often be deeply involved in their areas of specialization, in ideas they have pursued over time with their colleagues, and in projects that apply their learning to improving various aspects of life. The readings you have been assigned in your courses will introduce you to new subjects and to deeper levels of understanding of subjects with which you are already familiar. The books and journals in the library and the bookstores provide opportunities to pursue ideas and learning on your own in directions not limited by the curriculum.

You also get to see special accomplishments and skills up close — the sociology professor's ability to analyze how people relate to each other, the literature professor's ability to find the right expression, the philosopher's ability to cut to the heart of an argument, the architect's ability to conceive of a graceful and useful building, the government professor's involvement in state policy making. Many of your classmates may also have abilities, skills, and knowledge you may admire — from the computer programming whiz to the wrestling champion to the classmate who is just so witty. Seeing these accomplishments may open your eyes to new goals and lead you to reassess exactly where your best talents lie.

How do you make sense of all you come in contact with and set some directions for yourself? Some questions will sort themselves out spontaneously as you become involved in a heated discussion or suddenly want to do extra reading for a course that fascinates you. Some instructors may encourage you to think about your reaction to what you are learning through discussion questions and informal assignments. They may be available for you to talk with outside of class, during office hours, or even over coffee. Informal talk with your friends and classmates also helps you sort through all the new ideas and experiences you are confronting.

Using Writing for Reflection

Writing can also be used to think through the meaning of experiences. One traditional method is to keep a journal where you consider the most puzzling, intriguing, or outrageous ideas you come across each day. E-mail discussion groups are another, newer way to try out ideas and write reflectively. Almost all colleges now have electronic mail capabilities that students can access from some terminals on campus once they establish an e-mail account. On some colleges access is extremely easy from anywhere on campus, and all students are preassigned e-mail accounts. Once you are on e-mail, you can find discussion groups on many topics. Some of these are local to your campus, and others go worldwide.

Journal Writing

The journal, even when it is assigned as part of coursework, allows you to step outside the usual channels of class communication to reflect on ideas in a comfortable way. It creates a personal space for you to pursue thoughts and connections, develop critical perspectives on your readings and lectures, make plans, and evaluate your goals with respect to projects, courses, and the overall college experience.

Teachers assign journals as part of their classes to encourage several sorts of reflection. They may want you to:

- Think about the ideas and information of the course and find what is relevant to you
- See how the teachings of the course may be applied to your experiences — such as how organizational theory explains what is going on in your part-time job or how information from your zoology class helps you identify insects in the fields beyond the edge of campus.
- Criticize the divergent viewpoints presented in the course
- Indicate what you find most interesting or most difficult in the course materials, so that in class they can speak to the needs, interests, and thinking of you and your classmates

Journals are assigned in many kinds of courses. Although the journal provides an alternative to usual classroom communications, instructors often relate journal assignments to other classroom communications, as in a reading journal, a planning journal, or a personal connections journal. In a philosophy course, for example, a journal to develop arguments about questions raised in class provides an informal opportunity to practice the kind of philosophic language that is being developed in the course and that you will have to produce on exams and in papers. Because journals provide an informal space to explore ideas and reactions, you can use them to discover and develop ideas that you may want to develop in more formal papers. Thus journals are one of the key tools of invention, as described on page 75.

❧❧ REVIEWING WRITING PROCESSES

Invention

Invention is the art of finding what you want to say or write in any circumstance. Invention is particularly necessary in college writing, where your assignments often offer a wide range of possibilities that you have to narrow to a single issue. For this you need a well-chosen paper topic.

A successful paper topic balances several competing considerations. First, it must be original and creative enough to hold your teacher's interest and set it apart from other students' papers. At the same time, it must show that you are familiar with the subject matter, and it must stick to the limits set by the assignment. It must be complex enough to show substantial thought yet not so complex that it cannot be covered in the assigned length. Finally, it must interest you. The more important the subject is to you, the more you will be committed to writing a strong paper.

Finding a good idea is not always easy, but journal writing helps. Journal writing is one of the best tools for invention, for it allows you to turn thoughts over in your mind as you work through a course. When you are given a specific assignment, you can then look back in your journal for clues about topics that interested you that might fit the assignment. You can also use the journal to test possible ideas for the assignment and see, in a low-risk setting, where they might lead.

Another way to explore a topic area is to "brainstorm," or to follow loose, unstructured chains of association until you see connections you did not see at first. For example, if you were given the assignment to write a paper on an important issue in elementary education today, you might begin listing everything that came to mind when you thought of the word *school,* things such as *teachers, blackboard, school buses, textbooks,* and *school lunch.* The last term, *school lunch,* might produce another chain of associations like the following: *high prices, free lunch programs, students who need support.* This might lead to a question that indeed raises a major issue for the future of education: Will the learning abilities of students from poor

families be hurt when child support and school support programs are cut back, and won't that impairment of learning help keep the students in poverty?

The primary purpose of a brainstorming session, whether alone or with others, is to produce a large quantity of ideas — most of which will never be used in a final paper. Many ideas that don't seem appropriate at first should still be put down because you can never know which ideas will trigger associations that might ultimately be very productive. A ridiculous-sounding notion may well be a dead end, but it might also be the starting point of a good paper topic.

❧ Three Students' Reading Journals

Here are three examples of journal entries written for an introductory philosophy course, all based on a single passage by Lao Tzu, a Chinese philosopher who lived in the sixth century B.C. In the first journal entry the student considers the meaning of the text by examining the meaning of difficult phrases and sentences. In the second the student thinks about the single philosophic concept of opposites. The last entry is more personal and open-ended. Although all three take on different tasks, in each the student develops a fuller understanding of the passage and how it relates to his or her own thinking.

Here is the passage by Lao Tzu.

The whole world recognizes the beautiful as the beautiful, yet this is only the ugly; the whole world recognizes the good as the good, yet this is only the bad.

Thus Something and Nothing produce each other;
The difficult and the easy complement each other;
The long and the short off-set each other;
The high and the low incline towards each other;
Note and sound harmonize with each other;
Before and after follow each other.

Therefore the sage keeps to the deed that consists in taking no action and practices the teaching that uses no words.

The myriad creatures rise from it yet it claims no authority;
It gives them life yet claims no possession;
It benefits them yet exacts no gratitude;
It accomplishes its task yet lays claim to no merit.
It is because it lays claim to no merit
That its merit never deserts it.

From *Tao Te Ching* by Lao Tzu, trans. D. C. Lau (New York: Penguin, 1963) 58.

Lao Tzu, founder of the Chinese religion of Taoism, was author of the *Tao Te Ching.*

老子

By permission of the Open Court Publishing Co.

LAO-TZE

Journal Entry 1 (Finding the Meaning of the Text)

This passage seems like a poem built on contradictions and paradoxes. The problem in understanding this passage seems to be to see how these contradictions and opposites can make sense. Lao Tzu begins this passage by stating that what is seen as beautiful is really ugly and that what is recognized as good is really "only the bad." While these statements seem confusing at first, his use of the phrase "the whole world recognizes . . ." before both good and beautiful suggests that the world does not recognize true beauty or true goodness. Most people, he seems to say, do not have a correct idea of either morality or beauty, so we should not trust their opinions or perceptions.

Later, the author lists a series of opposites such as "something and nothing," "difficult and easy," "long and short," and "high and low." In very poetic fashion, he states that each of these contradictory terms is somehow involved in the other: "something and nothing produce each other," "the long and the short off-set each other," and so on. These paradoxes make us think about how supposedly opposite things are actually similar. Long and short are both about length, and actually they help define each other, for without knowing what is long, how could you know what is short?

Finally, Lao Tzu writes about a "deed that consists in taking no action and practices the teaching that uses no words." This mysterious deed is something that gives life to "the myriad of creatures" yet "claims no authority"— something that "accomplishes its task" yet it "claims no merit." These final statements appear illogical because what kind of deed is not done and what teaching has no words? It seems that this kind of mysterious deed is something he is recommending to us. But it is also a puzzle as to what we should do. How can we follow his recommendation if we don't take action?

The three major parts of this passage contain three different kinds of statements that illustrate the principles of Taoism that we have been studying in class. The first part of the poem suggests that the majority of people don't perceive reality correctly, the second suggests that things we consider opposite are actually connected (like Yin and Yang), and the third suggests that we need to find a way of acting which does not try to control situations, that blends into its surroundings. All of these points go along with the philosophy of Lao Tzu and illustrate some of the important principles at the heart of his teachings.

Journal Entry 2 (Philosophical Interpretation)

The assigned reading by Lao Tzu touches on a number of the philosophical questions we have been studying this term. One of the most important subjects he treats is the nature of opposition. By including a series of opposite terms — such as something/nothing, difficult/easy, long/short, and high/low — and asking us to consider the way they are connected to each other, Lao Tzu forces us to reexamine our conception of what it means to be an "opposite." For Lao Tzu, opposites are not things that are unrelated, as they are for most of us, but things that are closely related to and cannot exist without each other.

As an example of this principle, we can look at the opposition between "cold" and "hot." We generally consider these terms to be opposites, but, in reality, they can only have meaning in reference to each other. Something that is cold is something that is not hot, and vice versa. If we were to remove either of these concepts from our society, we would also have to remove the other, since, if nobody had any idea of what it meant to be hot, they could not possibly understand what it means to be cold, since coldness is really nothing more than the absence of heat.

Maybe what Lao Tzu is trying to get across in this passage is that, if we want to experience things in life that we consider "good," we must also be willing to experience things that we consider "bad," since all of the concepts that make up this opposition depend on each other. Many people think it would be nice to live in a world without cold, darkness, ugliness, falsehood, and evil. However, what Lao Tzu says to these people is that, without these things, there could never be any warmth, light, beauty, truth, or goodness.

On the other hand, it may be that he thinks we are too concerned with either side of the opposites. Maybe it doesn't matter so much whether something is hot or cold or if it is beautiful or ugly, because each are alike, as he says. This would certainly fit with his ideas about not taking action and not using words. That is, we shouldn't try to make things one thing or another, but just take them as they are.

Journal Entry 3 (Personal Response)

I found this passage by Lao Tzu to be very confusing. All of his talk about something being nothing and long being short seemed like a lot of philosophic mumbo-jumbo. The last part of the poem, about something that "gives people life yet claims no possession" and "benefits them yet exacts no gratitude" was even more confusing, since it was difficult to understand what this "It" was. I had to read the whole passage three or four times before I started to understand it at all, and I'm still not sure that I have it right.

But, after I read it over and over again, I started to see a few of the things that he seemed to be saying. In the first half of the poem especially, I think that Lao Tzu wants us to see that words like "difficult" and "easy," or "high" and "low" aren't always opposites. In fact, they are words that can refer to the very same thing depending on who is speaking. For example, I am very good at English and not very good at math, so what is easy to me (like writing a paper) may be very difficult for someone else, and what is difficult for me (like balancing a checkbook) may be a snap for them. This difference does not mean that either one of us is right in our perceptions of what is hard or easy, just that our perceptions are different.

I can think of lots of times when I have used a word in a way that seemed clear, only to find out that the person I was talking to understood something very different. A lot of times, this kind of misunderstanding leads to arguments because one person wants to prove that their idea is the right one. I think that one of the most important things that Lao Tzu teaches us is that perceptions can be different without anyone being right or wrong.

Thinking About Student Writing

1. What purpose does each student have in writing the journal entry? How do the purposes differ? Do the purposes in any way overlap or converge?

2. In each of the three journals, which terms or phrases do each of the students find most puzzling? Which do they find most revealing? How do the three students focus attention differently?

3. What interpretation or conclusion does each student come to? Are these conclusions similar or consistent? How do they differ? In what way do the differences in conclusion arise from different purposes, different focuses of attention, and different ways of thinking about the passage from Lao Tzu?

In each journal entry, the personal reflection was framed by the reading assignment and the journal writing assignment. Within that assigned frame, students pursued their own ways of thinking about the ideas. As they saw what they wrote, they could recognize issues that concerned and puzzled them, which they might want to follow up on, and how and whether their interest in philosophy was developing.

The teacher, reading the journals later, responded by using student examples in class to create more engaging discussions, by moving the class discussion toward issues and concerns expressed by students, by suggesting readings the students might find relevant, and by returning personal comments to the journals. The journal changed the general dynamic of the class.

The journal also provides a place for you to test out ideas that you might use in later, more formal assignments. If the instructor reads and comments on your journal, you can use the feedback to focus and develop your ideas further. You can even use the journal to ask the instructor to clarify the assignment or respond to your ideas.

☙❧ Guidelines for Journals

In assigning journals, teachers usually discuss their expectations and may provide examples from previous classes. Beyond the formal or informal guidelines your teachers establish, consider the following general suggestions for using journals:

1. *Write as though talking to yourself or a close friend.*   The more you find the level of language that is closest to the way you think personally, the more you will be able to make the connection between what you are learning and those ideas and experiences that are closest to you.

2. *Dare to be original — Dare to be stupid — Dare to get involved.*   Don't censor what you are thinking ahead of time. A direction that at first looks and feels either outrageous or silly may turn into something quite focused, respectable, and strong as you work through your ideas.

3. *Don't be afraid to argue.*   If your ideas begin with a negative reaction to what you read, express that negative thought. The criticism may become more focused, fully developed, and forceful as you work through what you think. You may find that your first negative reaction is only an initial resistance that you overcome as you think through the reading, or that it is leading to an important idea in itself. In any case, since this is a personal journal, a candid expression of dislike will not immediately require you to get involved in a major public debate. Moreover, in the academic world argument and disagreement are not necessarily insults or rudeness; they can be ways of cooperating in making ideas better and advancing knowledge.

4. *Make connections to other ideas, personal experiences, other courses, and readings.*   Specific examples and more general ideas can help illuminate each other. As you see how one idea or experience relates to another, you start to expand your understanding of both things. Through comparisons you can start to see more details in both and distinctions between the two. You can find general patterns or conceptual links. You may start seeing how even more ideas and experiences may be connected to create a broader vision of the subject.

5. *Try new ways of saying things.*   Find ways to discuss what you are reading, experiencing, or thinking that differ from your previous ways of writing. You will then see events in different perspectives and make more connections among ideas. A useful approach is to put material in different frames, as in describing a historical event in legal terms. Or you could describe the feelings of a character using a sentimental, emotional vocabulary that the character uses, but which is totally alien to you. There are many other interesting ways of saying things. You can make lists of political strategies described in different campaigns in different parts of the textbook, or draw diagrams showing how two species of plants might have similar leaf structure. Varied kinds of representations may help tap more deeply into your way of thinking and may provide novel ways for you to expand your thoughts.

6. *Keep your pen moving.*   Since a journal is not a formal public presentation, you don't need to worry if everything makes sense or is stated well. Keep on writing, even if you feel you have little to say. As your pen moves, one word may lead to another, one thought may touch off a deeper or more interesting one. Don't let temporary breaks or distractions break your mental link with the ideas unfolding on the journal page. Trust the process of writing.

7. *Follow through on your thoughts and keep extending them.*   It is easy once you have an interesting idea to step back, admire it, and say that's enough for today. But an idea identified in a few sentences or a paragraph may be the opening to something much bigger and broader, so stopping after your first statement will not take you as far as you may be able to go. Find ways to continue with the thought. Perhaps you might explain each part in greater detail, find an instance where the idea would apply, or locate a good example of it. You could compare it to some alternate point of view. You can ask where the idea specifically links up with the things you have been reading. If you find yourself stuck on how to expand your idea, make up an appropriate question and then try to answer it.

8. *Read back in the journal, reflecting on what you have thought and how you are using the journal.*   This reflection will lead you to explore your thoughts in greater depth, see patterns, locate areas of interest you want to explore, remember your best ideas, and use your journal even more effectively. You may then want to make a new entry commenting on what you found.

9. *Make writing the journal a regular habit.*   If you set a time every day for writing journals, you will get better at it. Thoughts will come. You will also come to pay attention to the stray relevant thoughts that occur in the course of the day, as you say to yourself, "I have to remember that for when I write my journal tonight."

You may, of course, keep a journal even when none is assigned. Since it is time-consuming to keep up with a journal every day in every course, you might want to keep a single journal, writing about whichever course or experience each day is most on your mind. Or you may choose to keep journals for those one or two courses in which you are most involved. By articulating your ideas and being able to look them over on paper, you will be able to take them farther. Moreover, you will have more developed things to say in class, and you may want to speak to the teacher after class about some thought you are developing in your journals. Teachers generally respond positively to any student interested enough in their course to keep a journal.

Another approach is to target a single course in which you are having difficulty getting involved. By keeping a journal, you may start to find a way to become more interested. You may figure out just why you don't find much in the course or have trouble with it. Then you can use this knowledge to address and, perhaps, resolve the problem.

ꙮꙮ N E W S   F R O M   T H E   F I E L D

Richard Rodriguez's Reading Journal

In his autobiography *Hunger of Memory*, Richard Rodriguez describes his early attempts at reading and writing about the great classics of literature. Though he did not know it at the time, young Rodriguez was using many of the strategies of the reading journal in his early childhood education. Even though his early approaches to reading later seemed to him a bit naive, his reading notebooks gave him the chance to express and develop his thoughts about his reading. As he started to sense that there was more to reading than he was able to express, looking back on his early journals helped focus his dissatisfaction and drive him on to find more mature ways of understanding. After all, only by recognizing that there was something more to his reading than he was able to say could he challenge himself to deeper views.

In the fourth grade, I embarked upon a grandiose reading program. "Give me the names of important books," I would say to startled teachers. They soon found out that I had in mind "adult books." I ignored their suggestion of anything I suspected was written for children. (Not until I was in college, as a result, did I read *Huckleberry Finn* or *Alice's Adventures in Wonderland*.) Instead, I read *The Scarlet Letter* and Franklin's *Autobiography*. And whatever I read I read for extra credit. Each time I had finished a book, I reported the achievement to a teacher and basked in the praise my effort earned. Despite my best efforts, however, there seemed to be more and more books I needed to read. At the library I would literally tremble as I came upon whole shelves of books I hadn't read. So I read and I read: *Great Expectations;* all the short stories of Kipling; *The Babe Ruth Story;* the entire first volume of *The Encyclopedia Britannica* (A-ANSTEY); the *Iliad;*

Moby Dick; Gone with the Wind; The Good Earth; Ramona; Forever Amber; The Lives of the Saints; Crime and Punishment; The Pearl. . . . Librarians who initially frowned when I checked out the maximum ten books at a time started saving books they thought I might like. Teachers would say to the rest of the class, "I only wish the rest of you took reading as seriously as Richard does."

What did I see in my books? I had the idea that they were crucial for my academic success, though I couldn't have said exactly how or why. In the sixth grade I simply concluded that what gave a book its value was some major idea or theme it contained. If that core essence could be mined and memorized, I would become learned like my teachers. I decided to record in a notebook the themes of the books that I read. After reading *Robinson Crusoe,* I wrote that its theme was "the value of learning to live by oneself." When I completed *Wuthering Heights,* I noted the danger of "letting emotions get out of control." Regarding these brief moralistic appraisals usually left me disheartened. I couldn't believe that they were really the source of reading's value. But for many more years, they constituted the only means I had of describing to myself the educational value of books. (61–62)

From Richard Rodriguez. *The Hunger of Memory: The Education of Richard Rodriguez* (New York, Bantam, 1982) 62.

ssignments

JOURNALS FOR YOUR SELF, JOURNALS FOR YOUR COURSES

1. For two weeks keep a daily journal about the interesting, admirable, or odd things you come across in college. You may comment on people, ideas that occur to you, ideas and information from assigned books, comments from teachers or classmates, or anything else that attracts your attention.

2. Select one of your courses in which you do a substantial amount of reading. For two weeks keep a journal in which you respond to ideas and information you come across in that reading. Try to connect the reading material with ideas, concerns, or experiences you have had outside the course.

3. The following passages all reflect on the role of reading and learning in people's lives. Use them to prompt your own thoughts about your own experience. Write a journal entry on one of the following passages about learning and literacy.

A. From Mike Rose, *Lives on the Boundary* (New York: Free Press, 1989). Mike Rose, a noted teacher of writing, describes his own uninspiring experience as a student in an unchallenging situation.

> Students will float to the mark you set. I and the others in the vocational classes were bobbing in pretty shallow water. . . . There were a few teachers who worked hard at education; young Brother Slattery, for example, combined a stern voice with weekly quizzes to try to pass along to us a skeletal outline of world history. But mostly the teachers had no idea of how to engage the imagination of us kids who were scuttling along at the bottom of the pond.
>
> And the teachers would have needed some inventiveness, for none of us was groomed for the classroom. It wasn't just that I didn't know things — didn't know how to simplify algebraic fractions, couldn't identify different kinds of clauses, bungled Spanish translations — but that I had developed various faulty and inadequate ways of doing algebra and making sense of Spanish. Worse yet, the years of defensive tuning out in elementary school had given me a way to escape quickly while seeming at least half alert. During my time in Voc. Ed. [Vocational Education], I developed further into a mediocre student and a somnambulant problem solver, and that affected the subjects I did have the wherewithal to handle: I detested Shakespeare; I got bored with history. My attention flitted here and there. I fooled around in my class and read my books indifferently — the intellectual equivalent of playing with your food. I did what I had to do to get by, and I did it with half a mind. (26–27)

B. From *The Autobiography of Malcolm X* (New York: Penguin, 1968). Malcolm X describes how he got his real education through reading when he was in prison for armed robbery.

> My alma mater was books, a good library. Every time I catch a plane, I have with me a book that I want to read — and that's a lot of books these days. If I weren't out here every day battling the white man, I could spend the rest of my life reading, just satisfying my curiosity — because you can hardly mention anything I'm not curious about. I don't think anybody ever got more out of going to prison than I did. In fact, prison enabled me to study far more intensively than I would have if my life had gone differently and I had attended some college. I imagine that one of the biggest troubles with colleges is that there are too many distractions, too much panty-raiding, fraternities, and boola-boola and all of that. Where else but in prison could I have attacked my ignorance by being able to study intensely sometimes as much as fifteen hours a day? (275)

C. From Alan Bloom, *The Closing of the American Mind* (New York: Simon & Schuster, 1987). Alan Bloom complains that students today are harmed by not being exposed to the great thinkers. As a result they are left to get their ideas from popular entertainment.

> Lack of education simply results in students' seeking for enlightenment wherever it is readily available, without being able to distinguish between the sublime and trash, insight and propaganda. For the most part students turn to the movies, ready prey to interested moralisms such as the depictions of Gandhi or Thomas Moore — largely designed to further passing political movements and appeal to simplistic needs for greatness — or insinuating flattery of their secret aspirations and vices, giving them a sense of significance. *Kramer vs Kramer* [a 1978 movie starring Dustin Hoffman and Meryl Streep] may be up-to-date about divorces and sex roles, but anyone who does not have *Anna Karenina* or *The Red and the Black* [classic nineteenth-century novels, by Leo Tolstoy and Stendhal, respectively] as part of his viewing equipment cannot sense what might be lacking, or the difference between an honest presentation and an excuse in consciousness-raising, trashy sentimentality, and elevated sentiment.

D. From Jean-François Lyotard, *The Postmodern Condition* (Minneapolis: University of Minnesota Press, 1984). The French philosopher Jean-François Lyotard discusses how information and knowledge have become part of the economic system of production.

> It is widely accepted that knowledge has become the principal force of production over the last few decades; this has already had a noticeable effect on the composition of the work force of the most highly developed countries and constitutes the major bottleneck for the developing countries. In the postindustrial and postmodern age, science will maintain and no doubt strengthen its preeminence in the arsenal of productive capacities of the nation-states. Indeed, this situation is one of the reasons leading to the conclusion that the gap between developed and developing countries will grow even wider in the future.
>
> But this aspect of the problem should not be allowed to overshadow the other, which is complementary to it. Knowledge in the form of an informational commodity indispensable to productive power is already, and will continue to be, a major — perhaps the major — stake in the worldwide competition for power. It is conceivable that the nation-states will one day fight for control of information, just as they once battled in the past for control over territory, and afterwards for control of access to and exploitation of raw materials and cheap labor. A new field is opened for industrial and commercial strategies on the one hand, and political and military strategies on the other. (4–5)

E. From Zora Neale Hurston, *Dust Tracks on a Road* (1942) (New York: Harper and Row, 1984). The novelist Zora Neale Hurston describes some of the reading that moved her deeply when she was a child.

In that box [of books] were *Gulliver's Travels,* Grimm's Fairy Tales, *Dick Worthington,* Greek and Roman Myths, and best of all, Norse Tales. Why did the Norse tales strike so deeply into my soul? I do not know, but they did. I seemed to remember seeing Thor swing his mighty short-handled hammer as he spread across the sky in rumbling thunder, lightning flashing from the tread of his steeds and the wheels of his chariot. The great god Odin, who went down to the well of knowledge to drink, and was told that the price of a drink from the fountain was an eye. Odin drank deeply, then plucked out one eye without a murmur and handed it to the grizzly keeper, and walked away. That held majesty for me.

Of the Greeks, Hercules moved me most. I followed him eagerly on his tasks. The story of the choice of Hercules as a boy when he met Pleasure and Duty, and put his hand in that of Duty and followed her steep way to the blue hills of fame and glory, which she pointed out at the end, moved me profoundly. I resolved to be like him. The tricks and turns of the other Gods and Goddesses left me cold. There were other thin books about this

Writer Zora Neale Hurston's (1891–1960) best-known works are her novel *Their Eyes Were Watching God* and her auto-biography *Dust Tracks on a Road.*

and that sweet and gentle little girl who gave up her heart to Christ and good works. Almost always they died from it, preaching as they passed. I was utterly indifferent to their deaths. In the first place I could not conceive of death, and in the next place they never had any funerals that amounted to a hill of beans, so I didn't care how soon they rolled up their big, soulful, blue eyes and kicked the bucket. They had no meat on their bones.

. . . .

I came to start reading the Bible through my mother. She gave me a licking one afternoon for repeating something I had overheard a neighbor telling her. She locked me in her room after the whipping, and the Bible was the only thing in there for me to read. I happened to open to the place where David was doing some mighty smiting, and I got interested. David went here and he went there, and no matter where he went, he smote 'em hip and thigh. Then he sung songs to his harp awhile, and went out and smote some more. Not one time did David stop and preach about sins and things. All David wanted to know from God was who to kill and when. He took care of the other details himself. Never a quiet moment. I liked him a lot. So I read a great deal more in the Bible, hunting for some active people like David.

. . . .

In searching for more Davids, I came upon Leviticus. There were exciting things in there to a child eager to know the facts of life. I told Carrie Roberts about it, and we spent long afternoons reading what Moses told the Hebrews not to do in Leviticus. In that way I found out a number of things the old folks would not have told me. Not knowing what we were actually reading, we got a lot of praise from our elders for our devotion to the Bible.

Having finished that and scanned the Doctor Book, which my mother thought she had hidden securely from my eyes, I read all the things which children write on privy-house walls. Therefore, I lost my taste for pornographic literature. I think the people who love it got cheated in the matter of privy houses when they were children.

In a way this early reading gave me great anguish through all my childhood and adolescence. My soul was with the gods and my body in the village. People just would not act like gods. Stew beef, fried fat-back, and morning grits were no ambrosia from Valhalla. Raking back yards and carrying out chamber-pots were not the tasks of Thor. (53–56)

⨏⨒ Electronic Discussion Groups

Computer networks have brought new possibilities of personal communication. Individuals and people sharing a special interest can now communicate locally and internationally. For teachers designing courses, these networks allow greater access to more materials, give students more chances for interaction, and allow students to develop individualized interests and knowledge. At the present, electronic communication has been used in education to supplement traditional channels of communication, but over time more and more discussions, lectures, readings, and projects are likely to be mediated through electronic means. These trends are already well under way.

A basic kind of electronic communication is electronic mail (e-mail) — simply a message sent from one computer terminal to another over some network or telephone line. The message can flow from one office to the next, from a computer laboratory to a professor's office, from your home computer via modem to a central university computer (where other classmates can log on), or from your computer to an international network of people interested in similar subjects. It is a kind of electronic phone message but with certain advantages. You don't have to wait until it is convenient for the other person to be at the other end of the line — you can send the message whenever you want, and the other person can read and respond whenever he or she wants. You can also send the message to several people or a whole group on an electronic list simultaneously. Further, in many systems you can send long documents as well as short messages, so that, for example, in the middle of writing your paper, you can e-mail a question to your teacher and attach a rough draft of the relevant section; the teacher, when he or she next checks e-mail, can then get back to you with a quick response to help you with revision.

Within the context of courses, e-mail can facilitate communication between teacher and student and among students. Increasingly teachers provide students with their e-mail addresses and sometimes hand out e-mail directories for the entire class. On the most basic level, this access lets you ask teachers questions about the assignments or ideas you have. Similarly, e-mail allows you to contact classmates between classes to ask questions, coordinate projects, set up meetings, share notes, and even collaborate in writing assigned group reports.

Since details of local computer systems vary and are developing rapidly, this chapter offers no specific directions. Moreover, because interfaces are getting simpler and more user-friendly, soon most systems will probably be almost self-explanatory. Generally, however, once you log on, a simple command will show which messages are waiting for you to read and another simple command will allow you to reply or write a new message. Once you are in a message-writing mode, you are presented with a memo format, where you fill in the e-mail address you want the message sent to, the addresses of anyone who should receive a copy, and a topic headline. Then, in the appropriate space, you type in your message. Depending on the system, you may be limited in the length of the message and on the format you must follow. Moreover, the simplicity and means of editing your message will depend on the system you are working with, although these are getting easier to use every day.

E-mail can be sent out to individuals at their individual addresses or to groups whose addresses are gathered in group addresses known as *lists. Listserves* are the central computers through which all the mail to a list is routed. On most mailing systems you can also make your own group-mailing list by creating what is known as a *group alias;* then whenever you send mail to the group alias it will go to all the individuals who are part of it. Through slightly different procedures messages also can be posted to *electronic bulletin boards* and *newsgroups,* which anyone can then access and read at a later time.

Local Area Networks and Class Discussions

Electronic communication offers new ways to carry on class discussions as well, and teachers are increasingly using them in courses. Local area networks (LANs) allow communication among a limited number of terminals, and electronic classrooms are increasingly hooked up in LANs. Through LANs teachers can supervise individual work from a central location or can make an individual student's work available on all students' terminals or on a central display screen for general discussion. These procedures are particularly useful in writing classes.

Networks also allow messages to be displayed on all terminals, making it possible for all students sitting at their separate terminals to talk with each other. The teacher may begin an electronic discussion by presenting a question to consider, posing a problem to be solved by the class, or posting on the network a text to be discussed by the class. Students then post their comments, responding to questions or to the comments of other students as the discussion unfolds, just as in an ordinary discussion.

Such electronic discussion has proven to be extremely involving for students. All students can respond simultaneously without worrying about waiting until being called on or interrupting each other, and all can develop extended answers that are thought through, without the pressure of holding the floor in a classroom. Moreover, because all students can examine each other's comments at length, look back on them, and write in response to any comment instead of just the most recent things said, comments can be more directed from one student to another. In this manner students can develop their own thinking and responses in a less intimidating setting, and at the same time gain large amounts of feedback and become part of an involved discussion. At the end of class students can obtain a transcript of the day's session in either electronic or paper form. These archival transcripts may be useful as starting points for more formal essays on the subjects discussed.

Because such electronic discussions frequently create their own dynamics, with little need for direct and constant teacher intervention, teachers can take a less central role, and students in responding to each other are not under constant pressure of evaluation and communicating with the teacher. Teachers sometimes decrease the pressure further by allowing the students to use pseudonyms so that no one knows who is the source of any comment.

To create opportunities for further communication in group projects, teachers can set up specific structures for interaction using special software. For example, small electronic discussion groups can be set up for work teams. In these teams each student is expected to comment on the drafts of the other students' papers, and the other students are then to revise in light of students' comments. Software programs such as *Storyspace, Commonspace, Commentary,* and *Engineer's Notebook* allow students to attach messages to each other's messages or to comment on a shared text.

✐✐ Electronic Links

Messages may be distributed through various kinds of networks. A LAN links up all the computers and terminals within a single classroom, building, or business or college. These local networks may then be hooked into a large international network known as the *Internet,* which links up universities, businesses, governments, and private users around the world. In recent years it has grown explosively and no doubt will continue to change rapidly.

Electronic mail (or e-mail), one of the main uses of the Internet, allows you to keep in contact with friends and people of similar interests both on campus and throughout the world. Electronic discussion groups are an especially good way to explore your interests, articulate your own thoughts, come in contact with other people's thoughts on these subjects, and get others' responses to your own thoughts. These discussion groups, which are organized in listserve, newsgroup, and bulletin board formats, cover a wide range of topics, from environmental concerns and political action to science fiction fan clubs and guitar-playing technique. The World Wide Web, which we will discuss as an informational source in Chapters 7 and 11, is also becoming a site for personal expression and interaction, especially as individuals create home-pages, which present an identity for others to visit and offer links to other pages that the individual finds interesting.

Whereas the Internet provides many opportunities for out-of-class exploration, some teachers may encourage you to log on to specific subject-related bulletin boards, discussion groups, and listserves. Discussion groups allow anyone who logs on to initiate comments or questions or to follow up on previous comments, as long as they remain relevant to the topic and format defined for that board or network. Often there will be specific *Netiquettes* (or network etiquettes) defined for participation (see page 92).

Brief Guide to Netiquette

Although most of the traffic on the Internet is unregulated and unmonitored, members of the electronic community have developed a set of informal rules, or network etiquette, collectively referred to as "netiquette," to govern private and public correspondence on the Internet. Most netiquette conventions are simply the rules of polite conversation moved into the electronic community; however, there are a number of rules that are unique to the e-mail networks, and first-time users often violate the rules of netiquette innocently when they begin posting to newsgroups or discussion lists. A naive electronic mistake will usually be tolerated by more experienced users; however, flagrant and repeated violations of netiquette, when reported to local systems administrators, can jeopardize a computer user's Internet privileges. Below are some of the most common netiquette conventions.

1. Always remember that the people you are responding to are human beings and that electronic communications usually can't convey your precise intentions. Be sensitive to the fact that what to you may seem like a reasonable, dispassionate objection may be taken as a personal attack, while, on the other hand, posted messages (known as *posts*) that you consider hostile and sarcastic are probably not intended to be so. Also, avoid writing in ALL CAPS except for special emphasis; this is generally seen as the Internet version of shouting.

2. Keep posts and messages short and to the point, and avoid posting unnecessarily. Most readers of the newsgroup have a limited amount of time to devote to electronic networking, and many home users must pay a fee for every message they receive. Also avoid having extended private conversations on public bulletin boards, posting messages that do not fit with the focus of the newsgroup, and quoting large blocks of a previous post in a response.

3. Never forward private correspondence to a newsgroup or to another individual without permission of the author; this is considered extremely bad netiquette. At the same time, remember that it is easy for someone else to forward your e-mail if he or she wants to. Anything you write to anyone could potentially be read by hundreds of thousands of people within minutes of your posting it. So it is a good idea not to say anything on e-mail — especially in a public forum — that you would not want generally attributed to you.

4. Always sign your posts, and never try to remove your name or address from your header. Don't post to newsgroups anonymously or use anonymous mail to threaten or harass others. Anonymous postings and letters are considered extremely rude, and could very possibly cause you to lose your e-mail privileges.

5. Do not use newsgroups to post unauthorized commercial announce-ments. A number of USENET groups are specifically designed to ad-vertise certain items for sale. Use these when appropriate, but do not use other groups or mailing lists to advertise products or services for sale. Occasionally, the Internet has been used to forward illegal chain letters or advance pyramid schemes. Such actions are almost always dealt with severely by newsgroup moderators and systems adminis-trators.

 ## The Reflective and Reflected Self

As you find ways to state and develop your thoughts in relation to what you are learning in college, your sense of who you are in college, why you are there, and what you are gaining from your various studies will grow. Re-flecting on your situation, learning, and interests will focus your concerns, consolidate your knowledge, and direct your energies. Moreover, you can look back on what you say to gain a conscious awareness of where you are going.

Even further, you get the stimulus of responses, challenges, and ques-tions — all of which give you more to think about and respond to. Since oth-ers' challenges and questions are responses to what you have shared, their comments are as relevant to you as they can be. In seeing how others respond to your thinking, you come to understand how your thoughts are reflected through other people's perceptions and minds. In seeing how you are re-flected through the people around you, you can gain an even deeper insight into where you are and how you are coming into being in that place.

Getting Involved Electronically

After exploring the local and Internet resources available to you, identify several bulletin boards, newsgroups, or listserves that speak to your in-terests. Log on to two or three of them and follow them for several days. Find out if they have a FAQs (Frequently Asked Questions) List, and read through it if they have one. After you get a sense of the discussions, post a comment on one of them.

5

Notes and Summaries: Writing to Remember

AIMS OF THE CHAPTER

This chapter shows how writing and other acts of communication are essential parts of retaining and recalling information. Writing helps make facts meaningful and connected. Moreover, to be useful, memories need to be recalled and communicated at moments when they are needed. So the ability to produce statements of information at the appropriate time is a crucial part of the memory process.

KEY POINTS

1. Many tasks in college depend on remembering information and ideas. Restating information and ideas actively through writing can help you remember what you are learning.

2. Memory is helped by grouping pieces of information, connecting information with ideas, finding patterns in the knowledge, applying knowledge actively in situations, and finding personal connections with the information. Writing can aid in each of these processes.

3. Rewriting notes in various formats, creating diagrams and charts, using computers to take and rearrange notes, and writing summaries are different ways of representing what you are learning.

QUESTIONS TO THINK ABOUT

- When have you had to remember a lot of information? What was easy and what was difficult about the experience? What techniques helped you remember? Which were most useful? Which least?

- What subjects in or out of school do you remember most about? Which subjects or kinds of material have you had the hardest time remembering?

■ Which books have you written about for school or other situations? How much do you remember about these works? How does that compare with what you remember about books you have read at around the same time, but not written about?

Your main task in many courses is to become familiar with a body of information. Success in such courses consists of your remembering and displaying the information at appropriate times, usually in written examinations. In this manner you may have been asked to learn the major historical events in nineteenth-century America, the standard spellings of English words, the various species of animals along with their characteristics and life cycles, or the opinions advanced by various philosophers.

Writing enters into memory tasks in two ways: in learning the material and in demonstrating that you know and understand it. To explore the first part, how writing helps learning, we need to see how writing helps one remember important details and overall meaning. To explore the second part, the demonstration of knowledge, we need to look into how writing can connect information, allowing you to display to the instructor both detailed factual knowledge and understanding of relationships. This chapter focuses on learning and remembering; the next chapter focuses on displaying remembered knowledge.

Memory and display are closely linked. If you can express information fully and in your own words, your knowledge of it is firmer and more long-lasting. In expressing the material, you become attuned to details and to distinctions, which in turn help you express the material in a richer and more engaged way. That is, learning to draw the picture and learning the details of what you are drawing are so interlinked as to be simultaneous. This process becomes all the more intense and successful if you are personally engaged in the picture, which you find both interesting and important.

The skills of being able to represent your knowledge in writing are at the heart of success in college. In some courses almost all your writing will be to reproduce information presented in lectures, textbooks, and other readings. The greater writing challenges of analysis, synthesis, problem solution, and argument, presented in the later chapters of this book, also require mastery of focused and efficient representation of facts and ideas from your reading. Success in doing these more complex forms of writing about knowledge depends on your ability to first represent that knowledge when and where you need it. You can't analyze the structure of political power in the ancient Mayan state without being able to describe the facts of Mayan life and theories of political power. You can't propose a convincing solution to an environmental problem unless you can present all the relevant data and clearly identify what causes what. More complex writing tasks build on more fundamental tasks.

❧◌ **Methods for Remembering**

Psychologists still do not know exactly how memory works. In fact, memory seems to be many different kinds of things that work in different ways. Remembering an amusing story at an appropriate time in a conversation is not quite like your fingers remembering how much to turn up the volume dial on your radio, nor remembering where you left your keys, nor remembering your early childhood games. In college, however, you are concerned with a particular kind of memory — being able to reproduce information that you heard in lecture or read in your textbook under exam conditions and to recall relevant ideas and information as you are thinking through papers. Although psychologists do not fully understand how this "school memory"

Nineteenth-century phrenologists believed that each part of the brain housed specific kinds of thoughts.

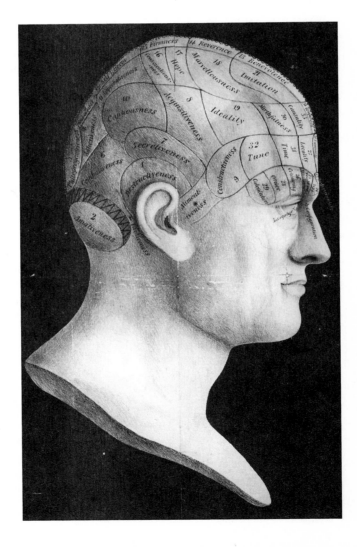

works, the active restatement of information in writing is definitely one of the things that improves retention. Each of the following proven methods of improving memory involves restatement of information and can involve writing as part of the restatement process.

1. *Using mnemonics.*   Disjointed lists of information are hard to learn. Most people have only a limited capacity to remember items from a list that has no organization. This is why most of us can only remember a very few phone numbers — the few that are most important to us. Mnemonics (memory devices), such as the rhyme for the length of the months, words whose first initials spell out some concept (such as FACE and Every Good Boy Does Fine for the spaces and lines of the treble clef in music) or phone numbers that spell out words (such as 1-800-Buy-This) are frequently used to turn a disorganized list into a single coherent item.

2. *Chunking.*   The grouping of separate items into larger units, known as chunking, allows you to put several related items in a single place in your memory. Thus your phone area code, although three digits, is usually remembered as a single number. Outlines and organized lists, paragraph clustering of information on a related topic, and other writing devices that pull information together in groups can help you chunk information and so remember it.

3. *Making meaningful patterns and connections among facts.*   Organizing material within chunks in meaningful ways and then connecting chunks in larger meaningful patterns helps you remember more. Writing allows you to connect information in larger meaningful patterns. Combining written information and visual images is particularly useful.

4. *Developing generalizations.*   As you organize, chunk, pattern, and connect information, you will be reflecting on what these various parts add up to. You will be putting the ideas and information into categories and formulating general statements that bring out the similarities among various pieces of information. The more you are able to identify and articulate these categories and generalizations, the more you will be able to create a sharply defined picture and to place and locate information within that picture.

5. *Learning by doing.*   Your knowledge becomes more certain the more you use and apply that knowledge actively. Thus if you use economics principles to make decisions for a small business, you are more likely to remember them than if you are simply studying them from a book. Similarly, hands-on work with a computer helps you make sense of and remember the instructions in the computer manual.

6. *Repeating.*   Repetition works for both intellectual knowledge and mechanical tasks. If you must remember some facts and phrases precisely, such as names of species or foreign language vocabulary, saying and writing the items repeatedly does help. However, if the meaning is more important than the exact words, it will help to repeat the meaning in different words. Thus the more you write about a poem or a series of historical events or chemical processes, the better you are likely to remember them. This writing may be informal and personal as you think through a subject in journals or notes, or it may be more formal, as in summaries, descriptions, or essays. No matter what the format, the more you review the information in your mind, think about it, and write about it, the better you will know it. This simple and obvious point is often overlooked, but you will find that the material you wind up knowing best is likely to be precisely that material you have written about.

7. *Identifying personal interest and motivation.*   When you are interested in some material, you attend both to its details and to the meaning it conveys. Writing about the information will increase this involvement by giving you more opportunities to locate the personal value and relevance of the material.

8. *Learning in the environment where you will use the information.*   Learning the material in the way you are likely to need, use, or reproduce it will make the information easier to recall. For example, learning the parts of an engine as you are repairing those parts will help you associate the names with the activity. However, they will still be hard to remember when you are sitting with a blank page in an exam room. Therefore, whenever you have to remember something for a paper-and-pencil exam situation, it is best to practice remembering it in a practice exam situation.

All these ways of improving memory suggest that we know best what we actively use, especially if we make sense of the information as we use it and establish personal connections to it.

Writing for Reflection

Describe a course where you currently have to learn a large amount of factual information. What kinds of information do you have to learn? Up to now what methods have you used to remember this information? What do you feel has been most successful, and what least? Are there any new methods you would like to try?

REMEMBERING

1. *Using mnemonics.* According to the 25th Amendment, if the President of the United States should die or become incapacitated, seventeen elected or appointed public officials would, in turn, succeed to the presidency. Imagine that you will need to re-create this chart on a test, and create a mnemonic device (or perhaps several) based on one key letter or initial in each item on the list.

   Vice President
   Speaker of the House
   President Pro Tempore of the Senate
   Secretary of State
   Secretary of the Treasury
   Secretary of Defense
   Attorney General
   Secretary of the Interior
   Secretary of Agriculture
   Secretary of Commerce
   Secretary of Labor
   Secretary of Health and Human Services
   Secretary of Housing and Urban Development
   Secretary of Transportation
   Secretary of Energy
   Secretary of Education
   Secretary of Veterans Affairs

2. *Chunking.* The following twenty-four common phobias are listed in James D. Laird and Nicholas S. Thompson's *Psychology* (Houghton Mifflin, 1992). The phobias are listed in alphabetical order; however, they would be much easier to remember if they were grouped into related categories (e.g., involving natural phenomenon, etc.). Prepare the list for easy memorization by creating four to six general categories, containing roughly equal numbers, into which the phobias can be processed in a chunked format:

   Acrophobia — fear of heights
   Agoraphobia — fear of open spaces
   Ailurophobia — fear of cats
   Algophobia — fear of pain
   Arachnophobia — fear of spiders
   Astrapophobia — fear of storms, thunder, and lightning

Aviophobia — fear of airplanes
Brontophobia — fear of thunder
Claustrophobia — fear of closed spaces
Dementophobia — fear of insanity
Genitophobia — fear of gentiles
Hematophobia — fear of blood
Microphobia — fear of germs
Monophobia — fear of being alone
Mysophobia — fear of contamination or germs
Nyctophobia — fear of the dark
Pathophobia — fear of disease
Phobophobia — fear of phobia
Pyrophobia — fear of fire
Syphilophobia — fear of syphilis
Topophobia — fear of performing
Xenophobia — fear of strangers
Zoophobia — fear of animals or some particular animal

3. *Connecting.* Annotate the accompanying map, Figure 5.1, with the following information to help yourself remember facts about the territorial expansion of the United States:

1803: President Thomas Jefferson purchases the Louisiana Territory from France for $15,000,000, effectively doubling the size of the country.

1810, 1813: The United States gradually occupies West Florida.

1818: An agreement with Britain fixes the border with Canada at the 49th parallel from Lake of the Woods, Minnesota, westward.

1819: President James Monroe purchases Florida from Spain for $5,000,000.

1842: A dispute with Canadian lumbermen leads to the Webster-Ashburton treaty which fixes the border of Maine.

1845: President James K. Polk approves admitting the Republic of Texas to the United States despite conflicting Mexican claims to the territory.

1846: America annexes the Oregon Territory (Washington, Oregon, and Idaho) in an agreement with Great Britain.

1848: Following three years of war, the Government of Mexico cedes the land that would later become California, Arizona, New Mexico, Colorado, and Utah.

1853: James Gadsden negotiates the purchase from Mexico for $10,000,000 of a strip of land along the border of Arizona and New Mexico to make a Texas-to-California railway possible.

1867: In a move widely regarded as "Seward's Folly," U. S. Secretary of State William Seward agrees to purchase Alaska from Russia for $7,200,000, or about two cents an acre.

1898: The United States Government agrees to annex the Republic of Hawaii.

4. *Connecting and generalizing.* Study the statistics in the table on page 102 about characteristics of students entering colleges in the United States from 1970 to 1994. As you study the statistics, list your observations about how the data connect and the generalizations you can form about the data. Then, after you put the table and your notes out of sight, write about two hundred words summarizing the information on the table and the interpretations you have made of that information.

| FIGURE 5.1 | Map of the United States of America |

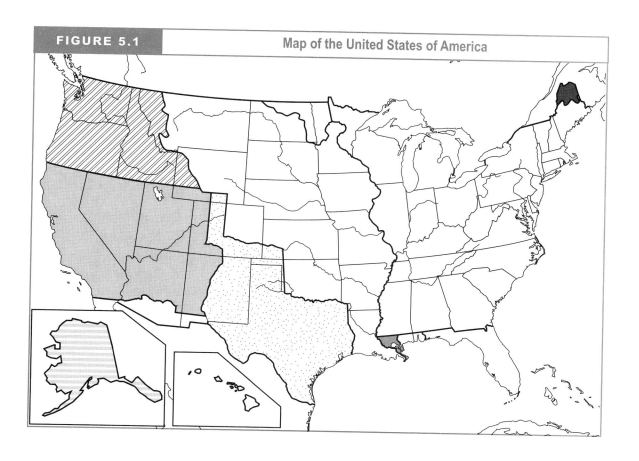

No. 294. College Freshmen—Summary Characteristics: 1970 to 1994

[In percent: As of fall for first-time full-time freshman. Based on sample survey and subject to sampling error; see source]

CHARACTERISTIC	1970	1980	1985	1989	1990	1991	1992	1993	1994
Sex: Male	55	49	48	46	46	47	46	45	46
Female	45	51	52	54	54	53	54	55	54
Applied to three or more colleges	[1]15	26	29	37	36	34	33	37	36
Average grade in high school:									
A– to A+	16	21	21	23	23	24	26	27	28
B– to B+	58	60	59	59	58	57	57	57	56
C– to C+	27	19	20	17	19	19	17	16	15
D	1	1	1	–	–	–	–	–	–
Political orientation:									
Liberal	34	20	21	22	23	24	24	25	23
Middle of the road	45	60	57	54	55	54	53	50	53
Conservative	17	17	19	21	20	19	19	21	21
Probable field of study:									
Arts and humanities	16	9	8	9	9	8	8	8	8
Biological sciences	4	4	4	4	4	4	5	6	7
Business	16	24	27	25	21	18	16	16	16
Education	11	7	7	9	10	9	10	10	10
Engineering	9	12	11	10	8	10	9	9	8
Physical science	2	3	2	2	2	2	2	3	2
Social science	14	7	8	10	10	8	9	9	10
Professional	(NA)	15	13	13	15	18	20	20	19
Technical	4	6	5	3	4	4	3	3	3
Data processing/computer programming	(NA)	2	2	1	1	1	1	1	1
Other[2]	(NA)	(NA)	16	15	16	17	17	17	17
Communications	(NA)	2	2	3	2	2	2	2	2
Computer science	(NA)	1	2	2	2	2	1	2	2
Recipient of financial aid:									
Pell grant	(NA)	33	19	22	23	23	23	24	23
Supplemental educational opportunity grant	(NA)	8	5	6	7	7	6	6	6
State scholarship or grant	(NA)	16	14	15	16	13	14	14	16
College grant	(NA)	13	19	20	22	22	24	24	26
Federal guaranteed student loan	(NA)	21	23	23	23	22	23	28	29
Perkins loan[3]	(NA)	9	6	2	8	7	8	8	9
College loan	(NA)	4	4	8	6	5	6	6	8
College work-study grant	(NA)	15	10	10	10	11	12	12	13
Attitudes—agree or strongly agree:									
Activities of married women are best confined to home and family	48	27	22	26	25	26	26	24	25
Capital punishment should be abolished	56	34	27	21	22	21	21	22	20
Legalize marijuana	38	39	22	17	19	21	23	28	32
There is too much concern for the rights of criminals	52	66	(NA)	69	(NA)	65	67	68	73
Abortion should be legalized	(NA)	54	55	65	65	63	64	62	60
Aspires to an advanced degree	49	49	51	60	61	60	55	65	66

– Represents or rounds to zero. NA Not available. [1]1969 data. [2]Includes other fields, not shown separately. [3]National Direct Student Loan prior to 1990.

Source: U.S. Bureau of the Census, *Statistical Abstract of the United States: 1995* (115th edition). Washington, D.C., 1995. Page 187, table 294.

5. *Repeating.* Read the following Sonnet No. 73 by William Shakespeare and memorize it by repeating the lines until they are familiar. You may also be able to use chunking and other patterns. See how long it takes you before you are able to repeat the poem verbatim. Then wait a week and see if you can still recall all of the words.

That time of year thou mayst in me behold
When yellow leaves, or none, or few, do hang
Upon those boughs which shake against the cold,
Bare ruined choirs, where late the sweet birds sang.

In me thou see'st the twilight of such day
As after sunset fadeth in the west,
Which by and by black night doth take away,
Death's second self that seals up all the rest.

In me thou see'st the glowing of such fire,
That on the ashes of his youth doth lie,
As the death-bed, whereon it must expire
Consumed with that which it was nourished by.

This thou perceiv'st, which makes thy love more strong
To love that well, which thou must leave ere long.

Some Ways to Represent Knowledge to Yourself

By this point, you have already developed several ways to use writing to study: You probably use underlining, highlighting, marginal comments, reading notes, and lecture notes. In all these activities you take a pen in hand, make a decision, and make a mark. However, these activities may require no more than selecting what you think important. The following ways of using writing will help you organize material using a more active understanding.

Rewriting Notes in Various Formats

One simple way to make deeper sense out of your notes is to rewrite them in hierarchically ordered lists. That is, you list less important information underneath more important ideas and categories. Here are some formats typically used.

Unable to find a Hi-Liter, Wayne Merlman
used a black Magic Marker to cross out all
the stuff he didn't want to read again.

- Traditional outlining uses levels of headings and indentation to show which ideas and facts are most important and which are subordinate.

OVERALL TOPIC

I. First main idea
   A. Subordinate idea
      1. Details
      2. Details
   B. Subordinate idea

II. Second main idea

- A hierarchical tree diagram, Figure 5.3A, divides topics into parts that expand downwards on the page.
- Network diagrams, Figure 5.3B, cluster information around key concepts that are then linked up.

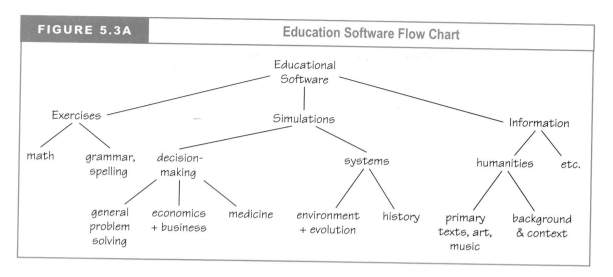

FIGURE 5.3A   Education Software Flow Chart

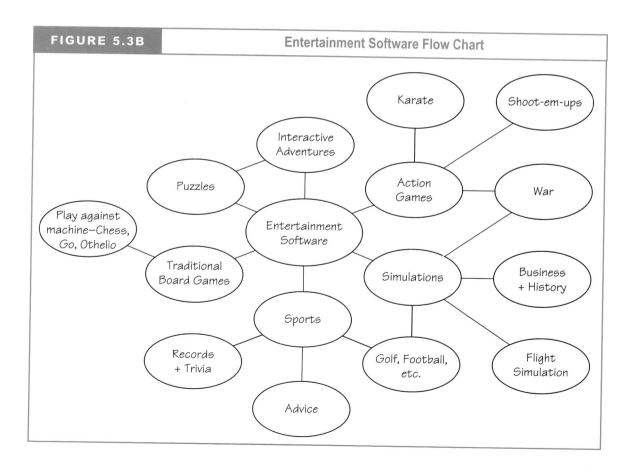

FIGURE 5.3B   Entertainment Software Flow Chart

FIGURE 5.3C	Separation of Powers and Checks and Balances		

Branches of Government

		Legislative	Executive	Judiciary
Separation of Powers and Checks and Balances	Legislative functions	Makes laws	Can veto laws	Reviews laws for constitutionality
	Executive powers	Can override vetos	Enforces laws	Issues injunctions Can review executive action
	Judicial decision making	Impeach Creates or eliminates courts	Grants pardons Nominates judges	Interprets laws

Adapted from Ken Janda, Jeff Berry, and Jerry Goldman, *The Challenge of Democracy*, 4/e. Copyright © 1995 by Houghton Mifflin Company.

- Charts and matrices, Figure 5.3C, arrange information in categories defined by intersecting columns and lines.

Keeping your notes on a computer also gives you many options for reordering and organizing. If you take notes on any word processor, you can easily rearrange them to create logical categories or form an outline. Other programs allow you to set up tree structures or idea networks and move parts around. Hypertext programs like Hypercard and Storyspace give you great flexibility in organizing notes in different ways.

Personal Summary Statements

Simply writing a paragraph identifying the overall meaning and most important information you learned in a lecture or after reading your assignments will help you make sense of your material. By staying in the lecture room for a few minutes after class to write some summary statements or by not getting up for a study break until you write a few sentences of overview, you can ensure that you are constantly reflecting on what the information means and how it fits together. You can set aside part of your notebook for these study journals, which you can then use to help orient yourself to more detailed notes and textbook annotations when you go back to study.

⟨⟨◎ ◎⟩⟩   R E V I E W I N G   W R I T I N G   P R O C E S S E S

Writing Summaries for Yourself

1. *Read for the general sense* of the overall passage.
2. *Identify the gist* or main idea for each section, ranging from several paragraphs to a subheaded unit in a textbook. Use this statement to write a paragraph topic sentence or a heading for an outline format.
3. *Select major points* or details that elaborate this gist. In the remaining sentences of the paragraph or in the subordinate parts of the outline, show how these details relate to the main point.
4. *Restate each point* in your own terms for your summary, adding more detailed information from the text.
5. If the textbook has a beginning of the chapter preview or end-of-chapter summary, use these to help guide your attention, but locate where in the text each point is made.
6. *Identify the source* you are summarizing so that when you are using your notes later to write, you can give credit to your sources (see page 112) and avoid plagiarism (see pages 112–114).

You can also write study journals along with reading journals, as discussed in the previous chapter, perhaps setting aside left-hand pages for response, or simply alternating types of entry but marking clearly which is which. Increasingly, professors in many courses are assigning summary and response journals (see pages 81–83) to engage students more actively. Here are some examples from a History of Western Civilization course:

Student Sample

The following journal entry by Jane Eames is in response to a passage in the beginning of Plato's *Apology*. The first paragraph of the journal entry is a brief summary of the passage, and the second is a personal response.

> Summary:
>   In the assigned passage of *The Apology,* Socrates is trying to explain to the judges why some of the people of Athens, led by Meletus, dislike him enough to bring him to trial. Socrates begins by explaining that he never considered himself wise or intelligent, so he began to seek out people who had a reputation for wisdom. He found a learned politician and, after talking to him for some time, discovered that the man was not really wise, but that he only thought himself wise. Socrates knew that he himself was not wise, but he felt that he

was wiser than the politician because he was at least
willing to admit that he knew nothing. Socrates repeated this procedure with the great poets and artisans
of Athens and discovered that none of them were really
wise and that the only true wisdom in life is to know
that you know nothing.

Personal Response:
   I don't think that Socrates is being very sincere in
this speech. He is pretending that he is foolish and
unwise, and he makes a big deal out of saying that he
knows nothing, but I really get the idea that he thinks
he knows a great deal. The way he was going around
telling people that they don't know anything reminds me
of a guy I knew in high school who thought he was a
great debater. Every time anyone said anything, this
guy would jump in and argue the point until everyone
around him got mad and left. This guy wasn't very popular, and he never seemed to realize that people weren't
impressed by his debating ability because he was always
using it against them. It sounds like Socrates was a
royal pain in the neck to the people of Athens, and,
while I don't agree that he should have been put to
death for what he did, I can certainly see why people
didn't like him very much.

Thinking About Student Writing

1. According to the summary, what is the key issue Socrates is concerned with in this passage? What is Socrates' point?

2. What aspect of the passage does the student Jane Eames respond to?
   What point does the student make about this passage? How does the
   student develop her point? Do you find her response warranted?

3. Based on your reading of the summary, what other possible responses might students have to Socrates' argument?

1. Using either the current catalogue of your college or a departmental handout, create a concept network or flowchart that illustrates the requirements for normal progress toward graduation during each of the years that you will be in school.

2. Obtain a copy of two health insurance policies — one of which should be the student insurance plan at your college — and read them both carefully. Create a map or diagram that illustrates important comparisons between the two plans. Include such factors as amount of coverage, deductibles, out-of-pocket expenses, and situations covered or not covered.

3. Write a summary and response for the first chapter of this book.

4. From a textbook for another course, choose a selection of several pages that you will have to know well for an upcoming quiz or exam. Write a summary of the passage, and then write a response.

5. From your personal library, choose a book that has an important personal, philosophical, or ethical meaning for you. From this book select a three- to five-page passage. Write a summary and response, identifying the important meaning of the passage and then explaining its personal value to you.

6. The following passage is taken from Plato's *Crito* and contains the attempt of one of Socrates' disciples to convince him to break out of jail and flee Athens rather than accept his death sentence. Read the passage carefully and write a journal entry following the two-part summary response pattern.

SOCRATES: Do the laws speak truly, or do they not?

CRITO: I think that they do.

SOCRATES: Then the laws will say: "Consider, Socrates, if we are speaking truly that in your present attempt you are going to do us an injury, for, having brought you into the world, and nurtured and educated you, and given you and every other citizen a share in every good which we had to give, we further proclaim to any Athenian by the liberty which we allow him, that if he does not like us when he has become of age and has seen the ways of the city, and made our acquaintance, he may go where he pleases and take his goods with him. None of our laws will forbid him or interfere with him. Anyone who does not like us and the city, and who wants to emigrate to a colony or to any other city, may go where he likes, retaining his property. But he who has experience of the manner in which we order justice and administer the state, and still remains, has entered into an

implied contract that he will do as we command him. And he who disobeys us is, as we maintain, thrice wrong; first, because in disobeying us he is disobeying his parents; secondly, because we are the authors of his education; thirdly, because he has made an agreement with us that he will duly obey our commandments; and he neither obeys them nor convinces us that our commands are unjust; and we do not rudely impose them, but give him the alternative of obeying or convincing us; that is what we offer, and he does neither." These are the sort of accusations to which, as we were saying, you, Socrates, will be exposed if you accomplish your intentions; you above all other Athenians.

Suppose now I ask, why I rather than anybody else? They will justly retort upon me that I above all other men have acknowledged the agreement. "There is clear proof," they will say, "Socrates, that we and the city were not displeasing to you. Of all Athenians you have been the most constant resident of the city, which, as you never leave, you may be supposed to love. . . . Moreover, you might in the course of the trial, if you had liked, have fixed the penalty at banishment; the state which refuses to let you go now would have let you go then. But you pretended that you preferred death to exile, and that you were not unwilling to die. And now you have forgotten these fine sentiments, and pay no respect to us, the laws, of whom you are the destroyer; and are doing what only a miserable slave would do, running away and turning your back on the compacts and agreements which you made as a citizen. And, first of all, answer this very question: Are we right in saying that you agreed to be governed according to us in deed, and not in word only? Is that true or not?" How shall we answer, Crito? Must we not assent?

From Walter J. Black, trans., "Crito," in *Five Great Dialogues of Plato* (New York: Walter J. Black, 1942) 75–77.

∾ Overview Summaries

At appropriate times in a course, such as at the end of a major topic or before periodic exams, an overview and summary of what you have learned can help you pull a coherent picture together. After skimming your textbook and notes, try to come up with a few main statements about the material. Then think how to organize those main ideas in some sequence or pattern. Use this sequence of statements to provide topic sentences for each of the paragraphs, which you then can elaborate with some of the more specific details from your coursework. In this way you will develop a personally meaningful framework for thinking about the course material. Be sure to use connecting phrases at the beginning of each paragraph to show how the ideas connect and relate to the overall themes of the course. As an introductory or concluding paragraph, it is useful to come up with an overview statement.

The following is a sample of a unit summary by Mike Caruso, a student in an Introduction to Economics course:

> The current unit in economics is on Supply, Demand, and the Price System. The unit discusses the way that, in a free market, the laws of supply and demand ensure that the price of economic goods will always move toward a fair market equilibrium.
>
> The principal term for this unit is <u>market</u>, which is defined by the textbook (<u>Economics</u>, 2nd ed., by William Boyes and Michael Melvin) as "a place or service that enables buyers and sellers to exchange goods and services (p. 52)." Markets can be small-scale, like the local farmer's market, or international in scope, like the world stock markets — but they all operate on several basic economic principles including the laws of supply and demand.
>
> <u>Demand</u> is an abstract term that describes the amount of a good or a service that people are willing to purchase at every possible price, whereas the <u>quantity demanded</u> refers to the demand for a product at a specific price. Similarly, the <u>supply</u> of a product refers to the amount of a good or a service that producers are willing and able to offer at every possible price, whereas the <u>quantity supplied</u> refers to the amount of that product that producers will offer at a given price.
>
> Both supply and demand functions can be plotted on a graph, with different prices producing differences in both the consumer's willingness to buy, and the producer's willingness to sell, a given economic product. The laws of economics dictate that, as prices increase, producers' desire to supply that product increases, while consumers' desire to purchase it decreases. The fair market price for any good or service, then, is at the equilibrium point where the producers are willing to supply at that price the same amount that consumers demand. When the price of an item goes above this equilibrium, the result is a surplus; when the price goes below the equilibrium, the result is a shortage. Although markets are not always, at any given time, in perfect equilibrium, surpluses and shortages work to

> ensure that, in the long term, items are priced at
> their fair market level.
>
> According to Professor Morton, these rules will al-
> ways work as long as a market is free. However, as gov-
> ernments and societies intervene in the free market,
> there arise two types of controls that interfere with
> market functions. Price floors, such as government sub-
> sidies on agricultural products, establish a minimum
> price for certain goods, thus creating a surplus. Price
> ceilings, such as rent-controlled apartments in high-
> rent areas, establish a maximum price which suppliers
> are not allowed to exceed. In both cases, additional
> government action is necessary to ensure that the econ-
> omy functions smoothly despite the additional controls.

Since these summaries are for your use alone, you may be somewhat schematic about them, using lists and outlines and whatever else may help. The important task is to bring out the connections, logic, and overview. Being explicit helps develop thinking and memory. The effort to write an overview in full form is worthwhile because you then make a full set of connections and coherences.

At exam time such summaries provide an overview of the course, topic by topic. Think of these summaries as a minitextbook for a few years from now — what you will want to remember from this course or for a friend who does not have access to the course materials. Indeed, if you are part of a study group, which we will discuss below, such topic or book summaries are useful to both yourself and your group. Comparing summaries is a good way to develop one's perceptions.

REVIEWING WRITING PROCESSES

Revealing Sources and Avoiding Plagiarism

Plagiarism is the crime of passing off as your own another person's written work — their unique ideas as well as their exact words. The term comes from the Latin word *plagiarius,* which means to kidnap. This false representation is of specific concern in different contexts. In commercial publishing, where people make money from unique written texts, plagiarism is equivalent to stealing, and is punishable in law by both criminal and commercial penalties. Here it is likely to become an issue primarily concerning financially successful creations, such as popular songs and movie scripts or best-selling books. In academic and professional careers, where one's credentials depend on what one has written, plagiarism amounts to lying about one's own accomplishments and stealing another person's. When plagiarism is uncovered in such cases, it means loss of professional credibility and often loss of one's job.

In student life, where original thinking and work are constantly encouraged and student work is always being evaluated, passing off another person's work as your own is a form of cheating. If you are caught plagiarizing, you may be punished by failing grades or even expulsion from college.

The answer is not to avoid other people's words and ideas. You learn from other people's words and ideas. As students you constantly depend on textbooks and other readings to inform you about the ideas and facts other people have developed so you can use them. If you hear a good idea or a way of phrasing things that appeals to you, those ideas and phrases are likely to stick in your mind and mix in with your own ideas and your own ways of saying things. Your professors also expect you to be able to repeat and use the ideas and information from a course. Much of learning to write, as well, is based on imitating models and building a large repertoire of things to say and ways of saying them.

In fact, when you write in college you are very much in the middle of a world of *intertextuality* — that is, each piece of writing (or text) is connected to many other surrounding texts (see page 231). Whenever your write, you are surrounded by the words of others. You are producing just one statement as part of a whole communication system, where each statement responds to the statements around it. Particularly when you are summarizing a text, answering a question based on information from a textbook, reporting library research, or discussing someone else's writing, you are working very closely with the words, ideas, and information of others. You *have* to use their words and ideas and information in your writing.

So how do you avoid plagiarism? You must always identify the source of your information, ideas, and phrasing when you are working directly from someone else's words.

For library research papers, this means providing bibliographic references (see page 240) for special ideas and information, although if certain ideas and information are well known and appear in several sources, you can assume they are common knowledge and do not belong to anyone in particular, so you do not have to attribute them to one particular source. If you also use the exact words from any of your sources, you need to put those words in quotation marks or block quotes (see page 240). The accurate citation of material from sources also helps establish that you have done solid library research and are basing your work on good sources. In addition, your own contribution stands out clearly if all the source-based material is clearly marked.

If you are writing a paper discussing someone else's ideas or writing, you must always identify whose work you are discussing, where that work appeared, and what ideas and information were presented in the source. If you repeat any words from the source, you must put those words in quotation marks. This accurate identification sets it apart from your own commentary.

If you are summarizing someone else's writing, you must always mention the author and text and the exact pages you are summarizing. You may do this by mentioning the source of the summary (". . . as Robert Kennesaw points out on pages 53–58 of *The Truth of Life . . .*"), or an end tag ("summarized from Robert Kennesaw, *The Truth of Life,* pages 53–58"). You need to do this even if the summaries are just for your own notes, because when you return to the notes you need to be able to remind yourself where they are from. Moreover, if your summary takes special words or phrases from the original, you should note those also by quotation marks. These quotation marks also help identify characteristic ways the original author had of expressing ideas. The biggest cause of inadvertent student plagiarism, particularly in research papers, comes from relying on notes from other sources without noting the source or exact quotations; later, when students write the papers, they forget the sources they used and mistake their notes for their own writing.

Even if you use only assigned readings and the textbook to answer questions, it still helps to identify the source you are relying on, especially if you have done several different readings in the term. The authors might have different views or cover different aspects of the questions. Demonstrating to the teacher that you understand the differences among the works will also show how carefully you have followed the work of the course. If, however, you have been only using a single textbook, and everyone understands that all information for the course comes from that textbook, then you may not have to repeat this fact.

Some sources do not have to be cited, however. This includes ideas, general knowledge, and phrasing that you are not directly discussing or relying on for a particular piece of writing but that still influence your writing. These materials have worked their way into your mind and into your way of expressing yourself. They have become so mixed in with other things you have read, learned, and thought that they no longer directly reflect any one other writer. It is not plagiarism to draw on all you know to make an original statement. If, for example, you have been reading many authors to help you think about justice, you do not need to mention them all in every paper you write on current social problems. You should only mention those that help you make your point clearly.

Don't be afraid to use what you have learned. Just be careful to give credit to those writers who you are directly relying on.

✪ Questions and Answers

Often on exams and essays you are given questions that ask you to bring together information in a new way. In that case making up in advance and answering for yourself the kinds of questions you might expect is a powerful study technique. Writing the questions makes you think through the material at least as much as writing the answers.

You can write questions by applying the information and ideas of the course to new problems of social or personal importance. Questions may also reflect the interests and concerns the teacher has expressed in lectures and discussions. You may look at previous exams to develop models for your questions, paying attention to such things as the level of generality the teacher asks about, the kinds of concepts asked about, the kinds of examples used and problems posed, and the typical phrasing of the questions. Try to frame the kinds of questions your instructor might ask.

Questions are also very useful for study groups, especially if they are in anticipation of the kinds of questions teachers are going to give. Some instructors even give out a list of questions or issues that may turn up on exams to help individual students and study groups focus their efforts.

Here are some examples of one student's questions and answers for a business class. The student prepared these questions as a way of studying a textbook chapter on theories of employee motivation in a corporate environment.

Questions on <u>Business</u> by William Pride, Robert Hughes, and Jack Kapoor (Houghton Mifflin, 1993), pp. 231–57.

1. What is employee motivation, and how can managers influence motivation?

   Motivation is defined as "the individual, internal process that energizes, directs, and sustains behavior." Motivated employees are more satisfied with their jobs, more loyal to their supervisors, and more productive for their companies. Employers cannot produce a high level of motivation in employees, since it is by definition an internal process. Ultimately, employees must motivate themselves. However, good managers can increase an employee's "morale," or satisfaction with their job and their working environment, and by doing so encourage their employees to become more motivated.

2. What is the Hawthorne Effect, and why is it important to businesses?

   The Hawthorne Effect is a phenomenon first documented by Elton Mayo at Western Electric's Hawthorne Plant in Chicago. Mayo was attempting to study the effects of lighting on employee productivity. He established an experimental group of workers and increased their lighting, which, predictably, led to an increase in productivity. However, when Mayo decreased the lighting of a second group, he found that their productivity also increased. The conclusion he reached was that it was not the lighting that determined productivity, but the fact that the workers were participating in an experiment that made them feel important. The Hawthorne Effect is an important consideration in business because it shows that human factors are just as important to worker productivity as mechanical factors.

3. What is Maslow's Hierarchy of Needs, and how does it relate to employee motivation?

Maslow's Hierarchy of Needs is an attempt by psychologist Abraham Maslow to arrange the various needs and desires of most human beings into five basic levels: physiological needs (food, water, sleep), safety needs (the need for physical and emotional security), social needs (need for love, affection, and a sense of belonging), esteem needs (need for respect, recognition, and praise), and self-realization needs (need to grow and develop in unique and personal ways). According to Maslow, people work to satisfy the physiological needs first and then, once those needs are satisfied, they move up to higher-level needs. The most important need at any one time is the most basic (lowest-level) need that has not been satisfied; however, once a low-level need has been satisfied, it ceases to become a viable motivator. Maslow's hierarchy is important to employers who want to know how to motivate their employees even after basic physiological and safety needs have been met.

ᕙ Study Groups

Study groups of three to six classmates give you the opportunity to compare notes about what you are learning. By meeting regularly throughout the term, you can talk about what you are learning. You gain the advantage of each other's insights, and as one or another of you run into difficulties and pressures, you can provide mutual support.

Study groups work best when each person is assigned to prepare a summary, a discussion of a topic, or a question for each meeting. When you are aware that others are relying on you, you think more carefully and deeply. Just by contributing to the group you will learn more than from working on your own, no matter what else you learn from the members themselves. Moreover, by comparing ideas you can identify different perspectives, clear up misunderstandings, and discuss further the meaning of valid differences. Different members of your group, because of their different interests, knowledges, and skills, can help you see more about your subject and the variety of perspectives that may be taken.

Electronic communication can help make group studying easier because it allows you to share study notes and ask each other questions easily. It is not difficult to send messages to all members of the group simultaneously, and you may even be able to set up an alias (which allows you to send mail to the whole group through a single address). In this way you can get the benefit of working with people, gaining their support, and feeling what it means to contribute actively even if you are at home or cannot arrange actual meeting times. There is often much to be gained in the spontaneity and immediacy of face-to-face meetings, especially if you are having a hard time "getting into" the material. The presence of other people concerned with learning the same material can help each of you focus on the material and engage with it.

 xercises

WRITING AND REMEMBERING

1. Write a unit summary for one of your classes. Include relevant information from both the textbook and the course lectures, integrated in a way to show that you have thought about the material and begun to make important connections.

2. Research a career or profession that you hope to enter and prepare a brief summary of the current state of that career. Include such facts as amount of education required, availability of employment, starting salary, and opportunities for advancement.

3. Think of a class you are currently taking that requires a large amount of recall. Imagine that you have been hired by the other students in the class to teach a tutorial seminar. Design a memorization strategy that takes into account the unique nature of the material. Feel free to use any of the strategies listed in this chapter, in any combination, and any others that you might think of.

4. Write a series of questions and answers for the following section from a textbook on broadcasting in America. The passage describes recent changes in technology that have affected the broadcasting industry.

Home Media Center

Improvements in television receivers have paralleled viewers' increasing ability to control their entire home electronic media environment. Home video recorders and players now allow viewers to purchase and copy programs of their own choosing — and to watch them at their leisure, instead of having to accept common signals sent to large, undifferentiated, widely dispersed audiences (see Figure 5.4).

VCRs: Giving Viewers Control

The home video recorder dates back to at least 1972, when Japan's Sony Corporation introduced the first *Videocassette*

recorder (VCR), the U-Matic, for educational and business applications. Three years later Sony marketed its Betamax machine for the home market at an initial price of $1,300. Futurists predicted a

---

FIGURE 5.4   **Home Media Center**

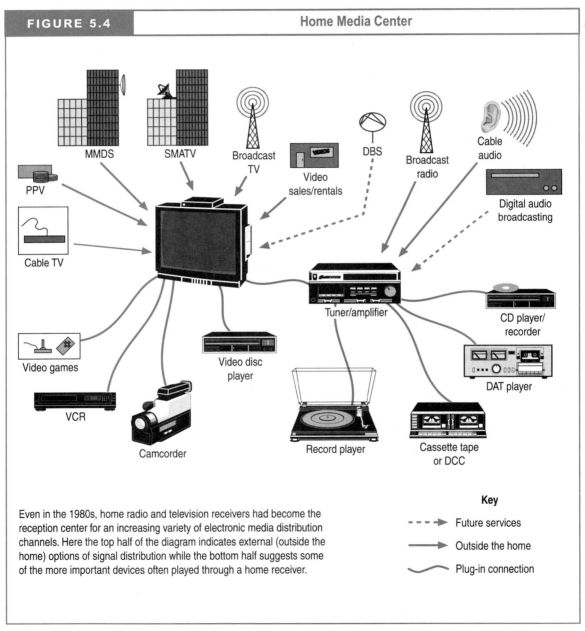

MMDS · SMATV · Broadcast TV · Video sales/rentals · DBS · Broadcast radio · Cable audio · PPV · Cable TV · Digital audio broadcasting · Video games · Video disc player · Tuner/amplifier · CD player/recorder · DAT player · VCR · Camcorder · Record player · Cassette tape or DCC

Even in the 1980s, home radio and television receivers had become the reception center for an increasing variety of electronic media distribution channels. Here the top half of the diagram indicates external (outside the home) options of signal distribution while the bottom half suggests some of the more important devices often played through a home receiver.

Key

- - - ▶ Future services

──────▶ Outside the home

∼∼∼∼ Plug-in connection

Source: From Sydney Head and Christopher Sterling, *Broadcasting in America, 7/e.* Copyright © 1994 by Houghton Mifflin Company. Used by permission.

new video revolution, now that consumers could choose not only *when* they would view something but also *what* they would view at that time — broadcast or cable programs, prerecorded cassettes, or their own home-recorded sources. . . .

Sony's monopoly (which had angered other Japanese manufacturers) ended in 1977 when Matsushita introduced its technically incompatible VHS (Video Home System). By offering longer recording times, VHS gradually monopolized consumer VCR markets. Various "bells and whistles" stimulated sales, bringing prices down from an average of more than $1,000 in the late 1970s to about a third of that a decade later.

By the mid-1980s several trends had combined to create the long-promised home video revolution. Sales of VCRs after 1975 closely paralleled the 1959–1966 "take-off" years of color television receiver sales (see Figure 5.5). By 1992 more than three quarters of all American homes had a VCR — and about 15 percent had at least two.

As VCR penetration increased, Hollywood recognized a new market for retailing older motion pictures. Soon thousands of films could be bought (or more often rented) for home showing, thus further encouraging VCR sales. VCR users could easily duplicate tapes, leading to widespread piracy. Film distributors changed their marketing strategies to forestall illicit copying: outlets rented films for just a dollar or two a night, which was cheaper than copying. Such inexpensive rentals encouraged still more VCR buying. By the late 1980s, the purchase price of leading motion pictures on cassette had dropped from $80 to $30 or less, thus encouraging even more purchases — and still greater VCR use. When the blockbuster film *E.T.* finally reached the home-sale market, it sold a record 14 million copies at $29.95 each.

VCRs encourage *time shifting,* the recording of broadcast or cable programs (some cable networks encourage VCR use in their promotional materials) — not to keep but to view at a later time. . . . VCRs have an important psychological effect: viewers can control what they see and when. Furthermore, the machines make it easy to cut out commercials during recording *(zapping)* or playback *(zipping)* — a selling point for VCRs, but hardly popular with broadcasters and advertisers.

Cable systems see VCRs as competitors, for the same reason that TV stations view cable as competitive: the newer medium diverts viewers from the old. In fact, HBO and other pay-cable services enjoyed little audience growth after the mid-1980s, largely because of competition from VCR film rentals. As noted earlier, the addition of multiple PPV channels has been one important cable response to the VCR threat. On the other hand, cable has not had much to fear from videodiscs.

FIGURE 5.5 — VCR Growth Indicators

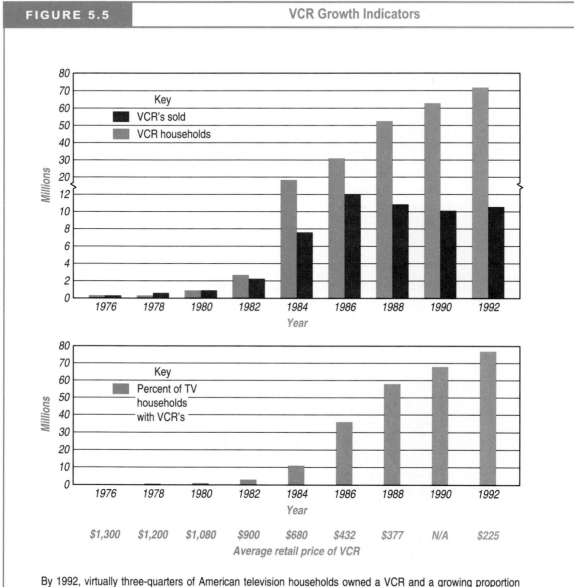

By 1992, virtually three-quarters of American television households owned a VCR and a growing proportion had more than one. As prices dropped in the 1980's, sales shot up. That the VCR industry is "mature" rather than growing, and that sales are now largely replacement or second-unit rather than first-purchase sales is indicated in the flat sales figures since 1986.

Source: Data from Electronic Industries Association and Television Bureau of Advertising.

Videodiscs — Round One

Magnavox introduced the first consumer videodisc player in 1978. Although it could not record, it cost only half as much as a VCR and offered a superior picture in playback. Then RCA's incompatible *non*laser "Selectavision" came on the market in 1981. Mass marketing brought down VCR prices faster than expected, wiping out videodisc cost advantage. Coupled with the inability to record and confusion over different standards, price competition from VCRs proved fatal to consumer potential of videodiscs, although they continued to play a role in training for education and business. In 1984 RCA pulled out of the home videodisc market, taking a loss of some $500 million. The videodisc appeared to be yet another consumer product washout.

Compact Discs

The first new audio product since tape recorders, compact disc (CD) players appeared in 1983. . . . CDs use recording methods similar to video laser discs: a laser beam plays back digital musical signals, achieving nearly perfect sound reproduction with no surface noise or distortion. CD technology was expensive at first (players cost about $800 and discs at least $20 each), but mass production pushed prices down (to about $150 for players and under $10 for many discs) such that, by the late 1980s, the CD could be said to "have had the most successful product introduction in consumer electronics history" (EIA, 1988: 31). By 1992 about 35 percent of homes owned a CD player . . . , and the LP record, mainstay of music recording for four decades, had virtually disappeared from store shelves.

Videodiscs — Round Two

CD technology came to the rescue of the moribund videodisc industry. Videodisc players capable of playing either audio or video appeared, and videodisc programs — mainly motion pictures — became more readily available. Most popular by the early 1990s were multifunction players able to handle standard 5-inch audio CDs as well as 8- and 12-inch laser videodiscs. Their ability to play digital stereo sound has prompted strong sales of classical and popular music video recordings. Still, this videodisc "round two" has been limited, as only about one percent of households owned a laserdisc video player by 1992. . . .

Getting Involved Electronically

Locate computer programs that might help you study for any course you are currently taking, such as vocabulary and grammar practice programs if you are taking a language course or a multimedia database if you are taking a history course. Try out whatever programs are available in your college computer lab or through any other source. In a few paragraphs describe the programs and how useful you think they will be in helping you study. If you have not found any useful programs, describe what you think might be an ideal program to help you in a subject.

6

Exam Writing: Displaying Knowledge

AIMS OF THE CHAPTER

This chapter develops the concept of writing to display knowledge. When you write on an exam, your aim is to show the evaluator that you are familiar with the material. You will be graded on how explicitly you present the ideas and details and on how well you connect them.

KEY POINTS

1. Although learning may be for yourself, you display that learning so teachers can evaluate what you know.

2. For purposes of evaluation, knowledge is displayed within tasks set by teachers and in the format that they request.

3. Essay exam questions give more opportunity to display one's understanding of a subject than do short-answer questions.

4. Some questions require you to rethink the material and reorganize it. For thematic questions and open-ended summary tasks, you find larger patterns in the separate topics, issues, and materials studied over the term. To respond to these questions, you step back from the details and think about them.

QUESTIONS TO THINK ABOUT

- Have you ever wondered why you are explaining things to teachers that they already know?

- Have teachers ever graded you down for not writing something on an exam even though you knew the material thoroughly?

■ Have teachers ever graded you down for not answering the question or
not giving the answer in the right form, even though you thought you
showed that you knew all the facts and ideas you were expected to
know?

Many assignments in college ask you to write on original subjects — to
report on fresh materials from your experience or research, to present your
own ideas, or to carry out analyses and arguments. In these assignments you
have the chance to be evaluated for your special contribution. However, in
many courses your task is simply to learn a well-defined body of information
and ideas and to demonstrate your familiarity with that material. In taking
exams for these courses, you simply display through writing what you have
learned. Your task is not necessarily to add to the instructor's understanding,
for the instructor probably has all the knowledge already. You are writing
solely to show what you know.

Although learning for your own purposes and long-term knowledge is
the goal of any course, your immediate reward is in the grades that evaluate
your efforts. Good grades, of course, bring rewards in the job market or in
admission to a professional school, and thus can be seen as an extrinsic or external reward. However, grades also have an intrinsic value because they signal how well you are doing. They indicate that you have been accomplishing
the kind of learning and work your instructors consider valuable. Insofar as
you value what they value, you may feel personally very good about a good
grade. (The comparative value of extrinsic and intrinsic rewards is discussed
on pages 172-173.)

To get high grades, you display your knowledge in the fashion determined by the instructor. During the opening class sessions and perhaps on a
syllabus sheet, teachers often explicitly identify the requirements, the form in
which you will have to show what you have learned, and the criteria by
which these displays will be evaluated. It is worth paying close attention to
these details, especially because they may not be repeated later. The specific
requirements of the course identify specific goals for your learning, which
can then help you set your personal goals for the term (see the discussion of
goal-setting on page 125).

Goal-Setting Research

Teachers, motivators, and moralists have long believed that setting goals contributes to success in any enterprise. However, it is only within the last thirty years that the precise relationship between goal setting and increased productivity has been studied by psychologists, sociologists, and organizational behaviorists. The modern scientific study of goal setting began in 1966, when Edwin Locke, a psychologist at the University of Maryland, published a study in the *Journal of Applied Psychology* (5: 60–66) entitled "The Relationship of Intentions to Level of Performance."

In this ground-breaking study, Locke divided student volunteers into three randomly determined groups and assigned individuals within each group a specific task. Participants were given an adjective (e.g., *hot*) and told to list things that could be described by that adjective for one minute. The only difference between the three groups was that each group was given a different "standard of success" to beat. Students in the first group were told that a successful test required them to list at least five items. Students in the second group were told that they should list at least ten items. Students in the third group were given the almost unattainable goal of fifteen items as their standard for successful completion of the experiment.

The experiment showed a high degree of correlation between expectations and performance. Each group's average accomplishment was just below the goal set for it: after fifteen trials, those in the first group averaged slightly fewer than four items per test; those in the second group averaged nearly nine items; and those in the third group averaged slightly more than fourteen items. From these data, Locke concluded (1) that higher goals produce higher results — even when a task is so difficult that it can be completed successfully only 10 percent of the time; and (2) that specific, known goals are much more motivating than general instructions to "do your best" or "list as many as you can."

Since Locke's study, dozens of other researchers have duplicated his results in a number of different contexts. The theory of goal setting that has emerged from these studies identifies at least three reasons for the motivating power of specific, difficult goals:

1. Specific goals direct people's effort in specific directions. When people are given vague goals such as "do your best" or "be productive," they expend their energies in different directions. However, when presented with specific goals, people tend to focus their attention in a single direction.

2. Goals regulate energy expenditure. Most people tend to work hard in proportion to their perception of how much they feel they should work. This is not to say that people will always work as hard as they

are expected to, but that even underachievers will achieve more if they are working toward a more difficult goal.

3. Goals lead to more persistence. When people have specific goals to work toward, they usually try harder to meet those goals than they would otherwise.

The goal-setting research of Locke and others has dramatically changed the way that business managers look at production, but it also has important implications for students. Success in school, as in any other enterprise, requires specific, challenging goals, perhaps so challenging as to appear almost unattainable. Classroom instructors generally attempt to set these goals for students. Students respond to expectations and take an active part in working toward goals.

✐ Short-Answer Examinations

Often you will be asked to display your memory of a course's material through a short-answer examination. This type of exam is common in subjects such as psychology or biology where you are expected to absorb much information. In these multiple-choice, sometimes machine-graded tests, all you need to do is select and note your choice. The format gives you few options for how to express your knowledge, and the questions usually provide little context to jog your memory. You just move from one question to the next, and at each question your mind must focus on some new aspect of the subject. Although sometimes a series of short-answer questions may be structured around a single problem or topic, usually the topics jump around — making it harder to recall the information.

When you take a course in which your work is primarily to be evaluated by short-answer questions, the first challenge is to find a way to involve yourself with the material; if you think of the course material as separate facts to be memorized, you may have a hard time remembering a disjointed array of statements. In such courses, then, it is all the more important to construct your own framework of meaning throughout the term. When you are in a test situation, if the fact does not come back immediately, you can use the framework to reconstruct the relevant area of knowledge and so increase your chances of recall. Even if you can't remember, for example, all the characteristics of REM (rapid eye movement) sleep in a psychology exam, if you have put the details together into an overall sense of what REM sleep is like, you may be able to reconstruct what you need to know. The association of rapid eye movements with dreaming may lead you to remember that muscle twitches, varying heart rate and blood pressure, and various forms of bodily stimulation can occur in relation to the nervous stimulation of the dreams, and that people absorbed in dreams are hard to awaken.

The second challenge of such courses is that short-answer questions invite only preset answers. With short fill-in questions, you must find either the exact words that the instructor is looking for or something close to them. Although this rigidity makes such tests efficient to grade, it gives you little opportunity either to explore your own interests in the material or to engage the instructor in your thinking about the coursework. So it is all the more important for you to find your own ways to increase your involvement in the course outside the limited classroom channels of communication, such as through personal journals or study groups.

One way to do this is to take closely related courses at the same time so that they feed back on each other. You may also discuss the subject with the instructor or the teaching assistant through office hours, discussion sections, or e-mail. When you study for short-answer tests or quizzes, it is helpful to read the material with the discussion, activities, issues, and problems of the class in mind rather than as a way to cram for a quiz. If you are engaged in the larger educational processes of the class and pay reasonable attention to your reading, more details are likely to stick with you.

Fortunately, short-answer exams and quizzes often are only part of a course's evaluation. They are often mixed with essay questions or complex problems, which give you opportunity for becoming engaged, displaying your understanding, and interacting with the instructor.

Writing for Reflection

Describe a course you are taking that will test you through short-answer questions. Describe the materials you are working with, the quizzes and exams you will take, and the specific kinds of questions you may be asked. Then develop a plan for studying for this course.

Summary Questions

To allow you to display more of your understanding on homework and exams, teachers may ask you to summarize material. Answers may range from a sentence to several paragraphs in length. Such questions may not require reorganizing or rethinking the material from lectures or textbooks, but only repeating that information in a certain format. You identify what aspect of the material is appropriate to the question and find a compact way to reexpress it. To make a coherent statement rather than a disjointed list of facts, you need to develop an overall understanding of the material.

The following passage from a textbook on business communications is followed by a summary study question.

What makes one person more likely than someone else to engage in arguments? What happens when other people who are arguing about issues refocus their attention on each other? Although we briefly touched on the subject of group conflict [previously], here we show you how to evaluate your own tendencies in this area and their implications for communication in your career. The tendency to view argumentation positively is called argumentativeness. More specifically, Dominique Infante contends that "argumentativeness includes the ability to recognize controversial issues in communication situations, to present and defend positions on the issues, and to attack the positions which other people take."

Generally speaking, argumentativeness in the workplace is a positive and constructive strategy. Arguing for causes, positions, and ideas within organizations is often viewed favorably because people who are effective arguers achieve their goals more often. Research has shown that subordinates prefer superiors who are high in argumentativeness because they feel their bosses will be more successful with their superiors and the entire unit or department will benefit from effective argumentation skills. The review of critical thinking skills is designed to improve your ability to argue constructively.

The tendency to attack other people instead of arguments is termed verbal aggressiveness. Dominique Infante and Charles Wigely provided the following definition: "Verbal aggressiveness . . . denotes attacking the self-concept of another person instead of, or in addition to, the person's position on a topic of communication." When comparing argumentativeness with verbal aggressiveness, you discover that the difference between these two traits is the focus of the attack. Argumentative people concentrate on positions, issues, reasoning, and evidence. Verbally aggressive people concentrate on attacking others personally.

The difference is very important in how others view the arguer/aggressor and in how the trait affects career relationships, productivity in groups, and ability to achieve organizational goals. According to Infante, people can possess both traits, although interestingly, people with a high degree of argumentativeness are less likely to use verbally aggressive standards.

Study Question: What is the difference between argumentativeness and verbal aggressiveness? What are the implications of each for organizational communication?

Source: From Dan O'Hair and Gustav Friedrich, *Strategic Communication* (Boston: Houghton Mifflin, 1992) 349–50. Copyright © 1992 by Houghton Mifflin Company. Used by permission.

Like most study questions, this one strings several related questions together and asks you to comment on both a selected fact and a possible implication.

To answer the question, you pare down the passage to its essential parts. The wording of the question encourages you to do this by directing you toward those concepts in the passage that the authors consider most vital: (1) a definition of "argumentativeness"; (2) a definition of "verbal aggressiveness"; and (3) an explanation of how each functions in a workplace environment. Using these three points as a basic organizational framework, one student wrote the following summary:

> Argumentativeness is the ability to argue and attack ideas, positions, and evidence. Verbal aggressiveness, on the other hand, is the tendency to attack and insult individual people instead of, or along with, their ideas. Argumentativeness is usually a positive trait in the workplace, since people feel comfortable working for someone who communicates and argues effectively. Verbal aggressiveness, on the other hand, leads to personal attacks, poor communication, and bad feelings.

From O'Hair and Friedrich, 349–50.

Thinking About Student Writing

1. Which specific points did the summary keep from the original? Which ones did it delete? Why?

2. What overall points tie the summary together? How does this focus compare with the focus of the original?

3. How well does the summary respond to the study question?

Writing Summaries for Others

Preparing a formal summary for others to read requires more careful work than preparing a summary for your own use, as was discussed in Chapter 5 on "Writing to Remember." In addition to the guidelines on summary writing presented in the previous chapter (see page 107), you can also consider the following steps in writing a summary for a class:

1. *Follow directions.* Note the instructor's specific directions and requirements.
2. *Understand.* Before beginning work, make sure you understand what the passage says in all its details. Look up any unknown words, and

work through the meaning of any phrase or sentence that remains unclear.

3. *Select.* Choose the material you think important enough to appear in the summary. You may do this by underlining or otherwise identifying important words and phrases, crossing out or eliminating less important passages, or writing sentences or notes that capture the central idea of each paragraph or unit.

4. *Organize.* Sort the material you have selected, following the general pattern of the original. Combine material from several sentences in the original in a single sentence of the summary to show how the pieces connect.

5. *Provide an overview.* State the main point in the first sentence.

6. *Use transitions.* Use connecting words and phrases to tie the parts together and to show the relationship among the many ideas.

7. *Review.* Read over the final version to make sure the various parts are connected and that the whole summary provides a coherent picture.

8. *Identify the source.* Tell your reader the exact source of the original passage that you are summarizing through a title or a tag line (see example at end of summary, page 129).

⟨◎⟩◎ USEFUL CONCEPTS FROM RHETORIC

Sentence Combining

One of the best ways to increase the amount of information as well as to show the relationship among various pieces of information is to combine several different ideas into one sentence. Instead of presenting only one assertion, description, or fact, a single sentence can tie several facts, details, and ideas into a coherent statement.

Although the following techniques may be very familiar, they can be reconsidered as strategic tools to increase the communicative power of your summaries:

1. *Coordination.*   Coordination uses conjunctions such as *and, but,* and *or* to link different ideas together in an equal relationship: one event happens *and* then another. You may coordinate whole clauses or smaller sentence parts. The following material on social control from an introductory sociology course reads like a list of short assertions:

> Social control may be exerted through schools. Families also serve to define appropriate behavior for youths. Community organizations such as churches and athletic clubs also attempt to influence the youngster to behave according to certain standards. This social control can be achieved through rewards and positive experiences. Social control also can be expressed through demands. The leaders of the organizations may feel they have the

best interest of the young at heart. Youth may experience these demands as a social pressure to conform.

This summary can be made more efficient and meaningful through coordination, as in the following revision:

> Schools, families, *and* community organizations may all exert social control on youths. They may try to influence youth by rewards *and* positive experiences, *or* they may demand certain standards of behavior. The leaders of the organizations may feel they have the best interest of the young at heart, *but* youths may experience these demands as a social pressure to conform.

2. *Subordination.*   Subordination puts clauses into an unequal relationship, making one statement the main one and the other supporting: one event happens *because* of another or *before* another or *if* another. Subordination uses conjunctions such as *before, after, since, because, while, when, as, although, so, so that, in order that,* or *if.* The following paragraph suffers because it does not use subordination:

> Some youths respond well to social pressure to succeed in school. Many others fail to meet the academic expectations that their families and educators place on them. Young people don't always measure up to the demands placed on them by various social groups. This often causes them to feel guilty and inadequate.

With effective use of subordination, we can cut the number of sentences in half and strengthen the relationships among the statements:

> *Whereas* some youths respond well to social pressures to succeed in school, many others fail to meet the academic expectations that their families and educators place on them. *When* young people don't measure up to the demands placed on them by various social groups, they often feel guilty and inadequate.

3. *Apposition.*   An appositive renames or restates a noun or pronoun, as in "Miguel Cervantes, the author of *Don Quixote.*" Very often, a sentence that does nothing more than define or describe something can be turned into an appositive in another sentence. Consider another excerpt on social control:

> The goal of most educators is to meet each student's individual needs. This goal cannot ever be fully realized in a competitive classroom. One of society's main goals is to train students for a competitive business environment by fostering competition in schools. Because of this social goal, teachers often cannot create the kinds of grade-free, cooperative environment that many sociologists feel would meet the needs of many students.

By using appositives, we can combine the sentences to read:

The goal of most educators, to meet each student's individual needs, can never be fully realized in a competitive classroom. One of the main goals of society — to train students for a competitive business environment through school competition — prevents teachers from creating grade-free, cooperative environments that many sociologists feel would meet the needs of many students.

4. *Embedding.*   Sentences frequently present only a single key point. That key point can often be expressed in a phrase that can be embedded into another sentence. In this way the important information from a number of sentences can be combined smoothly and coherently into a single sentence. Consider the following four sentences:

Teachers are first and foremost employees of a society. Society always has social control mechanisms that it wants teachers to enforce. Teachers must act as agents of society in regards to these social control mechanisms. If they don't, they risk losing their jobs.

We can combine the important information in all four sentences into one solid statement:

Teachers, employed by society, must act as agents for that society's social control mechanisms or risk losing their jobs.

5. *Superordination.* Superordination is the technique of combining similar or related words by using one inclusive term. By using superordination, you can eliminate confusion and combine several lists into one sentence. The following paragraph has several lists that could be usefully combined under single terms:

Pressure to succeed in a competitive academic environment comes not only from teachers, principles, school administrators, and guidance counsellors. Students also face pressures from their mothers and fathers and from their brothers and sisters. In addition to these factors, there are also groups of students in school, church, and community groups who put pressure on each other to succeed.

Each of the lists can be reduced to a single term, making sentence combination simple:

Pressure to succeed in a competitive academic environment comes, not only from *educators*, but also from *family* and *peer groups*.

6. *Economical prose.*   When one is combining sentences, every word should have a purpose. In particular, the main subject, verb, and objects of each sentence should contain the most important words. The sentence subject should be a specific noun; the main verb should be an active, concrete verb. With this strong subject and strong verb, the main clause will let you know exactly what is going on. The rest of the sentence should avoid empty phrases and wordy expressions. One solid, informational sentence is always better than three inflated ones. Consider the following inflated conclusion to the summary of social control mechanisms:

> It can be seen that the employment of various social control mechanisms by those who have been entrusted with students' education contributes to a feeling of failure and inadequacy among students who don't perform well in a competitive environment. However, as much as students would like to blame their teachers for making school miserable, it must be ultimately perceived that social forces, rather than individual teachers, are to blame for creating an environment in which competitive attributes are rewarded and failure is heavily punished.

By eliminating unnecessary words and combining the major ideas, we can rewrite this summary as a single, direct, easy-to-understand sentence.

> Teachers who use socially mandated control mechanisms often make their students feel like failures, but society creates this competitive environment.

Sentences, by their very nature, must contain related ideas. The trick to combining sentences, then, is to create relationships among ideas that would otherwise require separate sentences. By coordinating, subordinating, embedding, and combining phrases and clauses, you evaluate the importance of various ideas and determine how they relate to one another. In this case, as in so many others, good writing does more than reflect good thinking: Good writing encourages good thinking.

✆ EXERCISE: SENTENCE COMBINING

1. Rewrite the following passage using the sentence-combining techniques described on pages 130-133. Bring out the relationship of various facts while eliminating unnecessary phrasing.

> In 1993, the Nobel Prize for Literature went to Toni Morrison. Toni Morrison is an African-American writer. She is also a woman. She has written six novels. Most of her novels deal with African-American women. All of these novels have been praised by readers and critics alike. The most famous of her novels is *Beloved*. *Beloved* was awarded the Pulitzer Prize in 1988. *Beloved* is the story of a woman who kills her two-year-old child in order to save her from slavery. It is a tragic story. It is also a profound story. It dramatizes the suffering of slavery. It also illustrates the anguish of women who tried to raise their children as slaves.

Toni Morrison (b.
1931), Nobel Prize–
winning novelist.

This book is already considered a classic of contemporary literature. It secures Toni Morrison's place beside the greatest writers
of our time.

2. Take several paragraphs you have written recently for this or another
   course and rewrite them using the sentence-combining techniques
   described on pages 130-133. Bring out the relationship of various
   ideas and statements while eliminating unnecessary phrasing.

❧❧ Questions Requiring Reorganization

Some questions require more than a direct summary of the sources: They also
ask you to select and reorganize material around certain issues or problems.

Students sometimes mistake these as standard summary questions, but they are actually asking for more of a response. They ask you to think about the material.

To succeed at questions that ask for more than a summary, you connect what you know with the question asked. The teacher needs to see how you use the material you have been learning to think about issues posed in the questions. The more sense you have made of that material in your studying, the more flexible you can be in responding to the questions.

If you do not focus on the question and make a clear connection between the question and your answer, your instructor may make a very harsh judgment. One of the most common complaints of instructors is that students don't respond to questions asked on exams and assignments; they often comment that this lack of responsiveness indicates that students don't know how to read or think. This very common criticism shows how much weight instructors put on being able to speak directly to the question.

No matter how long the question statement is, usually the question is focused in a direct sentence or two. Sometimes it is preceded by an introduction of a few sentences to a page reminding you of certain issues or presenting a particular situation, problem, or argument to consider. This introductory statement is then usually followed by specific instructions, such as what issues you need to cover and how long your response should be. Sometimes the instructor might offer some suggestions on how you might proceed with your answer. The crucial part in all this material is the core question. You might even underline it to help you keep attention focused on it.

After identifying the core question, you analyze exactly what it asks for. Frequently the core question (for both exams and essays) consists of three parts: the general subject, the specific focus, and the task. The *subject* is the general topic area; it is usually indicated by a familiar word or phrase that has been emphasized in the course. The *focus* is the specific aspect of the subject on which you need to elaborate; it is often contained in qualifying phrases around the subject. The *task* defines exactly what you need to do in an answer; it is often signaled by a key question word (see pages 137–139). For example, in the following questions from a biology exam, even if you do not know the specific details the question asks for, a careful reading of the questions can give you a good idea of what sort of answer is needed.

1. Identify the chemical processes by which the liver produces bile.
2. Explain how the liver aids the digestive process.
3. Explain how the liver interacts with the rest of the digestive system.
4. Evaluate the fragility of the liver in relation to the other organ systems that contribute to the digestive process.

The subject of all these questions is the liver. You would likely find all the material to answer the questions in the chapter or section on the liver. However, each question also has a different focus. The first question focuses on the production of bile, and even more specifically on the chemical processes by which this occurs. The second and third both focus on the liver's activity within the digestive system, but the second asks only for what the liver contributes to the system, whereas the third asks you to consider the total interaction. The fourth focuses on the fragility of the organ within the context of the secondary subject of the fragility of other organ systems. Questions with a comparative or relational task usually have two or more subjects that need to be considered together.

These four questions also have specificity of task. The first asks for a specific identification of the chemical processes. This would require naming the chemicals and processes, placing them in sequence, and showing how one leads to another; including specific chemical equations and transformations would further strengthen the answer. The second and third "explain how" questions call for more general answers on the impact of the liver on the digestive processes. For the second you would need to describe the digestive process at the point where bile is placed within it and how that fluid carries the digestive process along. For the third, you would describe how the digestive process signals and regulates the liver so it can make its contribution. The fourth question turns you in the entirely different direction of what can go wrong and how easily — including malfunctions, imbalances, overloads, and diseases — and then asks you to compare the susceptibility of the liver to other organs of the digestive process.

Obviously, although all these seem at first glance to be on the same subject, each requires a distinctly different answer. If you just repeat everything you remember from the liver chapter, you are likely to answer none of the questions accurately.

A careful reading of the question will help you start recalling the information you need to develop your answer. Then identifying what kinds of things you need for an appropriate answer should start bringing the relevant details to mind. If the specific details you need still haven't already occurred to you, you can begin a more systematic search of your memory, knowing exactly what kind of details you are looking for.

USEFUL CONCEPTS FROM RHETORIC

Key Question Words

The following list of key question words defines and gives examples of the different tasks you may be asked to carry out on an essay examination.

Agree, Disagree, Comment on, Criticize, Evaluate

Give your opinion about a book, quotation, statement, or concept and then present the reasons for your opinion. If the question says agree or disagree, you express either a positive or a negative opinion. If the question says comment on, criticize, or evaluate, your answer can include both positive and negative points.

> "Our society has a zero-sum economy in which every economic gain by one person necessitates an equal loss by someone else. Agree or disagree."

Analyze

Break down a topic into all its parts. Be sure to include all the parts and to tell what makes each part different from the others.

> "Analyze the role of religion in the English Succession Crisis of 1681."

Compare

Show how two subjects are both alike and different. Be sure to discuss each subject and give both likenesses and differences.

> "Compare the prescribed treatment of women in two early legal systems: the Code of Hammurabi and the Law of Moses."

Contrast

Show only the differences between two subjects. Be sure to talk about each one.

> "Contrast the reproductive systems of birds with the reproductive systems of reptiles."

Define

Give the exact meaning of a word, phrase, or concept. Show how what you are defining is different from everything else of its type. Cite examples.

> "Define the concept of 'dialectical materialism' as it was used by Marx and Engels."

Explain Why

Give the main reasons why an event happened or happens.

> "Explain why a star becomes a white dwarf after its energy has been expended."

Describe, Discuss

Tell what happened, what a subject looks like, or what a subject is.

> "Describe the process of photosynthesis and discuss its role in the ecosystem."

Illustrate

Give one or more examples to support a general statement.

> "Illustrate the relationship between financial reward and worker productivity by citing examples from major studies in the area."

Interpret

Explain the meaning of the facts that are given. The question may ask you to use a specific method of interpretation. Be sure to go beyond just repeating facts.

> "Interpret the results of Abraham Lincoln's election in 1860 in light of Anthony Esler's theory of generational change."

Justify, Prove

Give reasons to show why a statement is true.

> "Using what we have learned about the revolutions in France, Spain, and Russia, justify Thomas Hobbes's famous statement that life in the absence of a strong civil government is 'solitary, poor, nasty, brutish, and short.'"

List, State

Itemize important points. Be sure to list all the items asked for in the question. Do not give examples unless they are requested.

> "List Freud's five stages of psychosexual development and briefly describe each one."

Outline, Review, Summarize

Give all the main points of a quotation, book, or theory. You do not have to include minor points.

> "Review the major Civil Rights campaigns by the Southern Christian Leadership Conference between 1957 and 1961."

Relate

Show how one object has an effect on another. Be sure to identify the connection between them.

> "Relate the rise of computer literacy to the steady decline of blue-collar jobs in the American economy."

Trace, List the Steps or Stages

List a series of important events, leading up to a final item or point. Be sure not to leave any item out or include more than the question asks for. This type of question may refer to historical events, recall a process, or ask for detailed directions.

> "Trace the important political, military, and religious developments that culminated in the 'fall' of the Western Roman Empire in the fifth century A.D."

Responding to Essay Exam Questions: A Review

1. *Read the question.* Identify the topic, focus, and task.
2. *Think about the question.* What does the question call for? What kind of answer would adequately address the task? What kind of answer might display a deeper understanding?
3. *Think about the course and course materials.* Ask yourself: How does the question relate overall to the course materials and goals of the course? What materials from the course would be relevant to the answer? What ideas that the teacher emphasized might be relevant? What specific details from the course might provide useful examples or evidence?
4. *Decide on your general answer to the question.* Figure out in blunt and direct terms the major point you want to make in answering the question. Think of this as the 25-words-or-less version. Make sure this speaks directly to the question and provides a clear-cut answer. Are you answering yes or no? What are the specific causes you are identifying? How many stages are you including in the process you are asked to describe?
5. *Outline your answer informally.* A few notes on the direction of the answer and the key points you want to make should be enough to focus your answer and keep you on track.
6. *Write an opening.* Make sure your opening statement responds directly to the question, giving your general answer and identifying the specific ways in which the remainder of the question will flesh out the answer. You may want to use parts of your 25-words-or-less version. The opening sentence is important both because it sets your answer in the right direction and because it announces to whoever is grading the question that you are addressing exactly what the question asks you to address.
7. *Write the body of the answer.* Include all the material the question requires. Do not ignore any parts of the question as asked. Make sure that all parts of your answer do indeed relate to and follow through on the question and that you explain that connection.
8. *Write a conclusion that ties the points you make back to the focus and task raised in the question.* This is your last chance to make sure that your answer is not just a loose connection of statements on the general subject of the question, but is rather a precise response to the specific issues the teacher was asking about. It is also your last chance to show the teacher how well you have addressed the question and understood the material.

To anticipate the kinds of questions the instructor is likely to ask on an exam, pay attention throughout the term to the questions asked in class and in homework assignments. You may even wish to keep a list of such questions and use them to help organize your work, either by yourself or as part of a group. In study groups you can also use the instructor's questions as models to make up more questions to ask each other (see pages 116-117). If the teacher is likely to ask a variety of questions that go beyond rote summary, you cannot follow a preset organization of the textbook or lectures; in these cases, you find ways to reorganize the material around different issues, ideas, or problems. What are the underlying kinds of thinking your teacher wants you to do with the material? Then organize your studying around those issues and tasks.

ssignments

ASKING AND ANSWERING QUESTIONS

1. Read the following excerpts from the Supreme Court decision in a recent controversial case concerning freedom of religion. Then briefly answer (in a paragraph or so) each of the questions that follow. In class discuss how the different questions require different sorts of answers.

   The case concerns the right to sacrifice animals in religious services. In 1987, the city of Hialeah, Florida, passed a series of ordinances designed to prevent members of the Santeria religion — a Cuban-based fusion of traditional African religion and Roman Catholicism — from practicing animal sacrifices. The city asserted that such sacrifices violated the moral values of the community. The church members petitioned the federal courts to overturn the ordinances, arguing that the animal sacrifice was vital to the practice of their religion. The right to practice their religion with its animal sacrifice was protected, they claimed, under the First Amendment to the U.S. Constitution (the free speech amendment), and particularly by the clause that guarantees the "free exercise" of religion.

   In 1993, the Supreme Court ruled unanimously that the city's ordinances were in violation of the free exercise of religion clause of the First Amendment. The decision, authored by Associate Justice Anthony Kennedy, has become an important reference point in cases where individual freedoms are pitted against community standards. Here are several excerpts from that opinion:

   Church of the Lukumi Babalu Aye, Inc., and Ernesto Pichardo v. *City of Hialeah.* Decided June 11, 1993.

   Our review confirms that the laws in question were enacted by officials who did not understand, failed to perceive, or chose to ignore the fact that their official actions violated the Nation's essential commitment to religious freedom. The challenged laws had an impermissible object; and in all events the principle of general applicability was violated because the secular ends asserted in defense of the laws were pursued only with respect to conduct motivated by religious beliefs. . . .

The Free Exercise Clause of the First Amendment, which has been applied to the States through the Fourteenth Amendment . . . provides that "Congress shall make no law respecting an establishment of religion, or prohibiting the free exercise thereof. . . ." The city does not argue that Santeria is not a "religion" within the meaning of the First Amendment. Nor could it. Although the practice of animal sacrifice may seem abhorrent to some, "religious beliefs need not be acceptable, logical, consistent, or comprehensible to others in order to merit First Amendment protection." (Thomas v. Review Board of Indiana Employment Security Division . . . 1981). . . . Neither the city nor the courts below, moreover, have questioned the sincerity of petitioners' professed desire to conduct animal sacrifices for religious reasons. We must consider petitioners' First Amendment claim.

In addressing the constitutional protection for free exercise of religion, our cases establish the general proposition that a law that is neutral and of general applicability need not be justified by a compelling governmental interest even if the law has the incidental effect of burdening a particular religious practice. . . . Neutrality and general applicability are interrelated and, as becomes apparent in this case, failure to satisfy one requirement is a likely indication that the other has not been satisfied. A law failing to satisfy these requirements must be justified by a compelling governmental interest. These ordinances fail to satisfy [these] requirements. We begin by discussing neutrality. . . .

Ordinance 87-40 incorporates the Florida animal cruelty statute, Fla Stat 828.12 (1987). Its prohibition is broad on its face, punishing "whoever . . . unnecessarily . . . kills any animal." The city claims that this ordinance is the epitome of a neutral prohibition. . . . The problem, however, is the interpretation given to the ordinance by respondent and the Florida attorney general. Killings for religious reasons are deemed unnecessary, whereas most other killings fall outside the prohibition. The city . . . deems hunting, slaughter of animals for food, eradication of insects and pests, and euthanasia as necessary. . . . There is no indication in the record that the respondent has concluded that hunting or fishing for sport is unnecessary. Indeed, one of the few reported Florida cases decided under 828.12 concludes that the use of live rabbits to train greyhounds is not unnecessary. . . . Respondent's application of the ordinance's test of necessity devalues religious reasons for killing by judging them to be of lesser import than nonreligious reasons. Thus, religious practice is being singled out for discriminatory treatment. . . .

In sum, the neutrality inquiry leads to one conclusion: The ordinances had as their object the suppression of religion. The pattern we have recited discloses animosity to Santeria adherents and their religious practices; the ordinances by their own terms target this religious exercise; the texts of the ordinances were gerrymandered [written to have unequal effect] with care to proscribe religious killings of animals but to exclude almost all secular [nonreligious] killings; and the ordinances suppress much more religious conduct than is necessary in order to achieve the legitimate ends asserted in their defense. These ordinances are not neutral, and the court below committed clear error in failing to reach this conclusion. . . .

The Free Exercise Clause commits government itself to religious tolerance, and upon even slight suspicion that proposals for state intervention stem from animosity to religion or distrust of its practices, all officials must pause to remember their own high duty to the Constitution and to the rights it secures. Those in office must be resolute in resisting importunate [overly persistent] demands and must ensure that the sole reasons for imposing the burden of law and regulation are secular. Legislators may not devise mechanisms, overt or disguised, designed to persecute or oppress a religion or its practices. The laws here in question were enacted contrary to these constitutional principles, and they are void.

Questions

a. Describe the issues in the case *Lukumi* v. *Hialeah.*

b. Define the term *neutrality* as used by Justice Kennedy in this decision.

c. Analyze the reasoning behind the Supreme Court's decision that the Florida law in question is unconstitutional.

d. In this decision, Justice Kennedy reasons that religious freedom should take precedence over community values unless there is a compelling state interest to restrict religious activity. Do you agree or disagree?

e. Explain the significance of the Supreme Court's decision in terms of individual freedoms versus community standards.

f. Compare the ethical issues involved with killing animals for secular reasons (food, sport, pest control) with the same issues involved in killing animals as part of a religious ordinance.

2. Consider the following excerpt from the Supreme Court decision in *Brown* v. *Board of Education* (1954), the decision that outlawed segregated schools throughout America. The unanimous (9 to 0) decision was written by Chief Justice Earl Warren. The *Brown* v. *Board* decision

overturned the earlier decision, *Plessy* v. *Ferguson* (1869), in which the Court ruled that "separate but equal" schools did not violate the Fourteenth Amendment to the Constitution.

Read the passage carefully and think of five questions about it that require answers going beyond mere summary. Write the questions down and then answer them using the strategies reviewed on pages 139–140.

Brown v. *Board of Education of Topeka.* Decided May 1954.

The plaintiffs contend that segregated public schools are not "equal," and cannot be made "equal," and that hence they are deprived of the equal protection of the laws. Because of the obvious importance of the question presented, the Court took jurisdiction. Argument was heard in the 1952 Term, and reargument was heard this Term on certain questions propounded by the Court. . . .

In approaching this problem, we cannot turn the clock back to 1868 when the [Fourteenth] Amendment was adopted, or even to 1896 when *Plessy* v. *Ferguson* was written. We must consider public education in the light of its full development and its present place in American life throughout the Nation. Only in this way can it be determined if segregation in public schools deprives these plaintiffs of the equal protection of the laws.

Today, education is perhaps the most important function of the state and local governments. Compulsory school attendance laws and the great expenditures for education both demonstrate our recognition of the importance of education to our democratic society. It is required in the performance of our most basic public responsibilities, even service in the armed forces. It is the very foundation of good citizenship. Today it is a principal instrument in awakening the child to cultural values, in preparing him for later professional training, and in helping him to adjust normally to his environment. In these days, it is doubtful that any child may be reasonably expected to succeed in life if he is denied the opportunity of an education. Such an opportunity, where the state has undertaken to provide it, is a right which must be made available to all on equal terms.

We come then to the question presented: Does segregation of children in public schools solely on the basis of race, even though the physical facilities and other "tangible" factors may be equal, deprive the children of the minority group of equal opportunities? We believe that it does. . . .

We conclude that in the field of public education the doctrine of "separate but equal" has no place. Separate educational

facilities are inherently unequal. Therefore, we hold that the plaintiffs and others similarly situated for whom the actions have been brought are, by reason of the segregation complained of, deprived of the equal protection of the laws guaranteed by the Fourteenth Amendment.

3. For a chapter in a textbook you are currently studying in another course, ask five questions, each using a different key question word (see pages 136–138), and then answer as you might on an exam.

4. Bring in questions from recent assignments, quizzes, or exams in other courses and discuss with the class how you might go about answering each.

REVIEWING WRITING PROCESSES

Proofreading

Before you turn in any assignment to an instructor, even a quickly written answer to a quiz question or a homework summary of the night's reading, proofread it to eliminate misspellings, mechanical errors, and typing mistakes. Careless mistakes can detract from even the best writing, and teachers will often subtract points for mistakes that you could have corrected easily with a little extra effort. Here are some proof-reading suggestions:

1. *Allow yourself plenty of time to correct errors and, if appropriate, to reprint your document.* If you proofread right before the paper is due, or you are writing in class, you will have to make corrections with a pen or pencil. Although it is generally better to pencil in a correction than to ignore an error altogether, it is always much better to reprint the page (if you are using a computer) or to make the correction on a type-writer. Instructors expect papers prepared before class to look neat and professional, but all teachers prefer neatly inserted corrections to no corrections. Here are some useful symbols for making handwrit-ten corrections:

∧	insert	I left out ∧ word. this
∿	transpose	My hands slipped when (was I) typing.
≡	use a capital	State names like ohio should be capitalized.
/	use lower case	Subject names like Mathemat-ics and History don't need cap-itals.
◠	close up space	I le◠ft a space.
¶	start a new paragraph	. . . the last sentence. ¶ I begin a new paragraph.

2. *If the situation allows, read your paper out loud.* When you read silently, your mind often compensates for missing words, extra words, wrong words, or misplaced punctuation. When you read your paper out loud, you catch things that you would miss otherwise.

3. *Ask someone else to read your paper over for mistakes.* Sometimes you can be too close to your writing to recognize all of the errors. It is always a good idea to have a friend, family member, or roommate read over your paper to find mistakes that you might have missed. Of course, don't try this in an exam.

4. *Don't assume that, just because a document has been checked on a computer, it does not contain errors.* Computer spell-checkers and grammar checkers are useful tools for catching some kinds of errors, but they do not catch everything. If you are using a computer checker, you should still look carefully for wrong words, similar words with different spellings, missing words, extra words, and mechanical problems that the computer is not programmed to identify.

Questions for At-Home Essays

For at-home essays you have more time to think about the question assigned, to organize your thoughts, to write carefully, to expand on your discussion, and to revise. You also have access to notes and books, and even additional sources you might want to bring in from related books or the library. This means that you need to take advantage of the increased time and access to material to produce a well-thought-out, clearly presented, detailed response.

In these assignments, not only are you likely to have better conditions for writing, but your instructor will likely have better conditions for reading, and so will have time to notice subtlety of thought, organization, and supporting details. This is in contrast to exam essays, which are typically read rapidly to get the grades in on time. There the grader looks for clearly displayed and direct points in response to the question. Any indirection or complication may lead the grader to miss the relevance of the answer as he or she goes on to the next paper in the stack. This pattern of reading is only reinforced by graders' knowledge of the rushed conditions under which students write in exams. They suspect that anything that does not go directly to the target must be off the mark. On the other hand, in grading at-home essays, instructors generally have more time and are also aware that students may have spent substantial time and work on the project. For these reasons, they are likely to read more carefully, trying to construct the student's line of reasoning and seeing how far the student can take the idea. Thus you get more leeway to give something other than the most obvious answer.

Since at-home knowledge-display assignments generally move toward the kinds of essay assignments described in the following chapters, they are not discussed here. Instead we will discuss two types of questions that are close to the summary but require substantial thinking: the large overview question and the open-ended summary question. These kinds of questions ask you to find big patterns in the material you are studying — showing that you are making sense of both the meaning of each part and the connections among the parts.

The *large overview question* points you to some underlying theme and asks you to pull the material together around that theme. The following are examples of the kinds of large thematic questions that might help you tie together the different work you have done over the term in various kinds of classes:

1. *History.* How did the concept of a popular revolution change and develop in the years between the French Revolution in 1789 and the Russian Revolution of 1917?
2. *Political Science.* In what ways does the tension between individual rights and social cohesion shape current approaches to public policy?
3. *Philosophy.* In what ways have philosophers attempted to deal with the apparent contradiction between a God who is perfectly good and a world that is experienced as evil?
4. *Literature.* How might the shift in twentieth-century poetry away from rhymed, metered verses toward free verse and experimental forms point to underlying changes in the philosophies, values, or attitudes of poets?
5. *Anthropology.* What are some of the primary differences in the way that preindustrial and postindustrial societies perceive nature?

These questions usually give a strong hint about the kind of pattern the instructor is looking for, as well as some criteria for determining whether your answer will address the teacher's expectations.

The *open-ended summary question* is less directive, giving you an opportunity to tell what you know in the way you want to tell it. This is more difficult because it is up to you to identify a significant *pattern* around which to organize the material and then to connect substantial amounts of material to that pattern.

In answering such complex questions, you need to step back from the details you have been learning to develop overviews of the subject. Thought representation devices such as concept networks, matrixes, or diagrams are most useful (see pages 104–107). If you are working on an at-home essay, you can try some freewriting or a journal. With the big question in mind, it is also helpful to review your notes, the table of contents of your textbooks, or the course syllabus to remind yourself of the material that might be relevant to the question. The more constructive preliminary work you put into figuring out the underlying patterns, the more focused and powerful your final answer is likely to be.

Once you have identified the underlying pattern in the material you want to describe, you then find the most direct and easily understandable way you can of expressing that pattern precisely. You may see a set of connections, but if you cannot express those connections clearly, the instructor will not know what it is you are seeing, and may assume you only have some loose and poorly conceived associations rather than a strong pattern you are trying to demonstrate. In finding a way to describe the pattern clearly and forcefully, you are likely to refine your idea further. As you heighten the outlines of the pattern for others, you will also do it for yourself.

The statement of the pattern can then form the core of your opening paragraph and become the basis for the outline of details to follow. You plan the outline to elaborate the pattern in a section-by-section manner, showing each part in greater detail but always connecting it to the larger pattern.

✐ Beyond Classroom Learning

In this and the previous chapter we have been considering a process whereby you can become more involved in the ideas and information that are presented to you in books and lectures. Rather than superficially memorizing a few words and phrases by rote just long enough to reproduce them on an exam, you can make the material part of your thinking by learning to talk and write about it in various ways. These facts and concepts become part of statements you yourself make and patterns of knowledge you yourself have seen and articulated. You have made your learning part of yourself, part of the understanding of the world you have with you at all times, because it is knowledge you have not only overheard, but knowledge you have remade by stating it in your way, reflecting how you have placed that knowledge in your mind. Moreover, by restating that knowledge in ways that can be recognized as valid and thoughtful by others, even the distant people who may grade your examination, you have confirmed the validity and strength of your perception of the subject. You have found a way of putting your knowledge on the line, and putting yourself behind that knowledge.

Nonetheless, there are limitations to the kind of involvement created by the knowledge building discussed in the last two chapters. We have been discussing knowledge contained within the four walls of the classroom, accepted on the authority of the textbook and instructor; it is not necessarily integrated with your previous beliefs and experiences, nor necessarily directed toward the ways you might want to use it once you are no longer a student. You have developed yourself by participating in this specialized classroom communication activity of receiving, remembering, rearticulating, and displaying knowledge, but it is only a classroom self that has been developed.

Some instructors may create opportunities to help you think about how your learning relates to what you have seen or heard or done previously in school or out, or to the opinions common in your community. Teachers may even give you some opportunity to critically evaluate what you are learning and to determine how much you agree with the propositions presented or how much you appreciate the literature or art you are studying. Obviously there is more room for such personal judgment in courses like philosophy, literature, and art appreciation than in physics, mathematics, or biology. Instructors may also help you look beyond the classroom to see how your learning relates to problems and issues current in society or research. Through discussion, case studies, and real-world problems, instructors can help you start to make a link between what you study in the classroom and professional tasks and problems you will confront later in your career.

These kinds of connections expand and make more complex the communication system of the classroom, and they are the subjects of other chapters in the book. Some courses are totally engaged in these extensions, whereas others make only small gestures in those directions. In those cases, you need to make those connections on your own, even if all the classes you take are narrowly bound to the small communication circuit of knowledge reception and display, because it is those connections beyond the classroom that will deepen your commitment, understanding, and involvement in the subject matter, making it more than just a matter of classroom learning.

Assignments

GOALS AND SUMMARY WRITING

1. Make a list of academic goals for the remainder of the current term. Make the goals specific and challenging. Instead of saying "work harder on psychology course," commit yourself to "prepare reading notes on reading assignments before class and go over lecture after each class to identify main themes and points." Be detailed about what things you wish to accomplish and what you need to do to accomplish them. Write the goals down and post them in a conspicuous place where you will see them every day.

2. Reread all the course information provided by your instructors this term and make a list of the goals they have set for their classes. Compare these goals with the goals that you have set for yourself.

3. Read the following paragraph and combine as many sentences together as you can while still preserving the meaning and continuity of the passage.

   Alfred Binet developed a test for intelligence. He was a French psychologist. He developed the test in 1904. It is a famous test. It is still used by psychologists today. It is called the Stanford-Binet test. It asks questions about common knowledge. It measures a person's mental age. Psychologists divide this mental age by the person's chronological age. They then multiply the number by 100. This number is called the IQ. IQ stands for "intelligence quotient." There are many problems with measuring intelligence this way. It is difficult to define "intelligence." It is difficult to define "common knowledge." These factors affect the value of IQ tests. They cannot be considered completely reliable. They may predict achievement in some areas and not others. Their predictions may be culturally biased. Mental age is itself a culturally defined concept. It is not clear exactly what the tests measure. There may be

kinds of intelligence that do not correlate with the test. They may give an inaccurate idea of intelligence. Intelligence may not be a separable personal attribute. Intelligence may be a set of responses to situations. Intelligence may be developed through experience. Intelligence may not be just how you work alone. Intelligence may have to do with what you can do with others. IQ scores make intelligence appear like an inborn fixed horsepower.

4. Design a final exam for a course you are taking this quarter. Decide how much of the exam should consist of objective questions (multiple-choice, true-false, etc.), how much should consist of short-answer or short essay questions, and how much should consist of longer overview or summary essays. Write all of the questions in the way that you think your instructor would write them and then take your own final as a practice for the real thing.

5. Imagine that you have been commissioned to write a formal summary of a movie for publication in a newspaper. You have been allocated 250 words and will be expected to provide a thorough, professional synopsis of important plot, character, and thematic elements. Select a movie that you have seen recently and summarize it as completely as possible in the assigned length.

6. Select a course that you have taken recently or are currently taking and write down three important themes that have recurred throughout this course. Write a general overview question about each of these recurring themes, and then answer one of the three.

Getting Involved Electronically

1. Find out if any courses on campus use electronic exams. If so, find out about their formats and how they are used in the courses. Write a few paragraphs describing what you have found.

2. Investigate the spell-checker, grammar checker, and other proofreading tools available on the word processor you use or available at your college computer lab. Try out these tools that are designed to improve the final appearance of your writing. Write a few paragraphs describing how these programs work and how useful they are.

Using
Concepts
to View
the World

P A R T

Three

7

Illustrative Writing: Connecting Concepts and Real Examples

AIMS OF THE CHAPTER

Academic knowledge has meaning and value beyond the classroom. To help you understand the meaning and power of what you are learning for the many kinds of events that happen, your teachers may ask you to connect your learning with events that occur outside the walls of the university. This chapter aims to help you see that academic study has powerful connections to many parts of life.

KEY POINTS

1. Each discipline, or area of academic study, provides a way of looking at, understanding, and acting in the world. It provides a way of getting involved in and improving some important human activity.

2. Instructors are likely to believe deeply in the value of their subjects and will try to express that value by showing how learning relates to the world outside the classroom.

3. In discussions and assignments you may be asked to make specific connections between course materials and contemporary events presented through newspaper and magazine articles or in videos and films produced for nonacademic audiences.

4. In writing about contemporary events, you need to make detailed and frequent connections between the academic concepts or information and the specific details of the events.

QUESTIONS TO THINK ABOUT

■ Why do teachers and researchers study the specialized and unusual things you are being taught?

■ Just what do your teachers get enthusiastic about and why?

- Have you ever felt either in school or on your own that you have learned something really important and useful? When?

- How can what you learn in your coursework give you a better understanding of the world?

Most professors deeply believe that their subjects are important and useful ways of looking at the world and life. For example, psychologists really are curious about how their own and other people's minds operate and why people think and behave as they do. To them knowledge of psychology can be immediately and profoundly helpful. It can help people use their minds more effectively, overcome personal difficulties, find more satisfying ways of living, and understand how people interact. Moreover, if you ask psychologists how they view the world around them, their descriptions will be saturated with concepts and perspectives they have developed as part of their professional experience. Although they may be cautious about overgeneralizing from current psychological knowledge or making judgments about aspects of personality and behavior that they don't yet fully understand, they approach daily life as psychologists.

Similarly, economists look at the world through the lens of their economic knowledge. They look at people, businesses, and governments in terms of finances and exchange. As professionals and as private citizens they are likely to offer others economic analyses and advice about how to conduct economic affairs.

Almost all teachers believe that the study of their subject can lead to more satisfying lives. Teachers of literature, art, music, history, and philosophy see their subjects as their passions and their way of being in the world. Teachers in the sciences see beauty in their subjects. In the knowledge of their fields, they find powerful ways of understanding the world, creating new technologies, and addressing problems, whether in medicine, the future of the planet's ecology, or the sources of energy. Professors of applied fields believe that much human happiness depends on creating wiser and more competent public administrators, lawyers, businesspeople, teachers, engineers, and counselors.

⌔ Snapshots of the World

Because of their commitment, instructors want students also to understand the beauty and strength of their subjects. They want students to see how specialized knowledge can reveal and change the world beyond the classroom.

Sometimes this desire may only be an undercurrent of the class, perhaps increasing the teacher's personal intensity. In passing, the teacher may com-

ment on how what you are studying explains some familiar daily phenomenon. The biology teacher may remark that a chemical process first noticed in
the nervous system of flatworms may hold the key to improving human
memory, or a literature teacher may point out that the development of symbols of nationhood in Renaissance poetry helps us understand how we think
about nations today. Such comments may have little direct effect on what is
expected of you; you will still be expected to understand the major systems
of flatworms and to interpret sixteenth-century poems. Nonetheless, these
insights into the implications of the knowledge will increase your personal
sense of connection, motivation, and commitment.

In some courses, teachers go further and bring the world outside of the
classroom directly into the communications of the classroom, in ways that
become a central part of the course.

Representations of the World

Teachers can bring the world into the classroom through articles from current magazines and newspapers, through films and videos of contemporary
events and communities, or through Internet access. These representations of
current situations and issues help you think about the meaning and implications of what you are studying. In an economics course on international
trade, the teacher may use debates in a news magazine over free trade agreements to trigger a discussion of current economic developments. In an urban
anthropology class a documentary film concerning the life in the *favillas*
(shantytowns) of Buenos Aires might reveal how the social forces discussed
in texts affect real lives. An art history class examining the relationship of art
to the rise of museums might consider recent controversies over public funding for the exhibition of avant-garde art. You can probably think of many
other examples from your own courses.

The Internet also is providing a large amount of information about different aspects of the world, especially through the *World Wide Web*. The Web
allows easy access in convenient format to information, magazines, data, or
whatever people wish to make available, from the latest facts about health
foods or a political movement to the full text of classic books of literature and
religion. You can even get a visual tour of famous art galleries around the
world or sound recordings of political speeches. Many kinds of material are
now being posted onto World Wide Web servers, and in the next few years
the Web will provide nearly instant access to enormous stores of information
linked together. The links are created in *hyper-text* format, meaning that
cross-references from one document to another are directly linked electronically. If a document about some research in Missouri mentions a research
group doing similar work in Bolivia, you can retrieve information about the
Bolivian group and their work by clicking your *mouse* (a device that points to
items on the screen) on a marked word or button.

These current articles, films, and electronic documents will probably not

have been created for classroom use in the way textbooks are; they are directed to the world outside the classroom. You might be tempted to treat them in the same way you do when you see them in the morning paper, on television in the evening, or while surfing the net in your spare time. However, in the class you need to see such "real-world" documents in relation to the concepts and methods of the course or in comparison to other cases you have studied. The teacher may first draw these connections, and in class discussion and papers you may be asked to follow up, expanding on the connections the instructor has made or bringing in new examples from the news or other media. Here are the basic steps:

- Identify what aspect of the course materials this event or situation is related to. Is this case meant to be a comparison with a historical case? Or is it an illustration of an analytic concept you have been working with?

- Given the specific relevance of the materials for the work of the course, identify which details or aspects of the materials are most important.

- Given the connection between course and materials, analyze, evaluate, or otherwise think about the contemporary materials in a way appropriate to the course. Construct an account of the case or situation that is relevant to the course.

In other words, you identify (1) how the case fits the course; (2) what details to focus on; and (3) how the approach of the course suggests thinking about it. For example, if you have been studying group loyalties in a sociology course and your teacher assigns a magazine article based on undercover interviews with a local youth gang, you know that the teacher is asking you to consider how group loyalties hold the gang together. With the issue of group loyalties in mind, you then find in the article all the signs and factors related to group loyalty that you have considered throughout the course, such as similarity in dress and appearance, claims of kinship with other members of the gangs, fears expressed about the world outside the group, locales and times for gathering, rituals, and so on. Finally, you might consider which ideas about group loyalty this case fits best. In class discussions, instructors may draw you through this process in a step-by-step way.

FINDING REAL-LIFE EXAMPLES

1. Choose a course that presents material that might apply to contemporary events or situations. Examine your local newspaper for several days and clip several articles that seem to exemplify or otherwise relate to concepts, events, processes, or other things you are studying in that course. Write three questions that relate your clippings to the course materials. Then bring your clippings and questions to this writing class along with textbook passages and discuss the different ways in which school learning applies to the world.

2. Access the World Wide Web through one of the terminals in the college library or campus computer center. After exploring the Web for awhile, locate some pages that are interesting and relevant to a course you are currently taking. If you can, print out images of several of these pages to bring to class. If not, take notes on the information on the page and the links to other pages. Keep a record of the URL addresses of the most interesting pages so that you can revisit them.

3. Read several of the sidebars in this book entitled "Useful Concepts from Rhetoric." From newspapers, magazines, or other printed materials, bring into class three real-life situations in which any of these concepts might apply. Be ready to discuss how the concepts apply to the examples.

Writing Papers About Real-Life Situations

Although some class discussions of outside contemporary materials may be passing events in a course to highlight certain concepts, instructors may use those discussions as the basis for more extended assignments or papers. In certain courses, applying learning to current issues and case studies may also be the specific purpose of the course, as in courses on contemporary social problems. When you write a paper on a real-world case or a current event, the following steps can help you develop ideas:

■ *Consider what the question asks you to do with the material.* Particularly, see if it indicates what elements of the course ought to be related to the case or current event, and in what way. Does the question specify the methods you might use to collect information? Does the question define what attitude you should take to the material or what task you must accomplish? Are you to take the material as a case to be solved, an illustration of ideas you are learning, or as an exception? Are you asked to consider how the participants in the case view events and how those views match up with the concepts you are studying? Are you to provide a critique of or evaluate current policies adopted for the situation? Does the question specify certain formats you might use to present your answer? In short, what does the assignment ask you to do?

■ *Identify which materials, methods, and models from the course are most relevant for the assignment.* For your working notes, make a list of those concepts, theories, or facts from the course that might be most useful to understand the case or events you are examining. If necessary, review your notes and readings. Review discipline-specific methods of collecting information that might be useful for the assignment. Also search your course readings and lecture notes for any examples that might give you a model for what your final paper might look like. Try to identify the typical ways of discussing example cases in this subject area.

■ *Develop a general approach to the question.* Identify what you wish to accomplish, what you need to cover, and what kinds of discussion you will have to present. Then write a brief one- or two-sentence direct answer to the question as you best understand the issues. In the course of working on the paper, you may wish to refine, develop, or even change this main idea or thesis statement. Nevertheless, identifying a tentative main idea in the beginning helps focus your thought, direct your activity, and provide a framework for developing the essay.

■ *Go through the case materials again, keeping in mind the question that you are developing.* Identify the specific details, facts, and statements that are most relevant to the issues on which you are focusing. These can be recorded by highlighting, annotating, or making a set of working notes.

■ *Connect the specifics of the case with the relevant materials from the course.* You may first do this by keeping a set of journals or notes that start to sketch out your ideas. As seems appropriate, go back to the course notes and readings to pull out details, quotations, definitions, charts, or other items that will help elaborate the ideas more fully in relation to the case. At the end of this process, bring together your ideas in a single page with the details of the case so you can see how course materials and case fit together.

■ *Plan an organized answer.* The answer should address the task and bring in a detailed examination of materials from both class and case. In every section of the planned essay (or every heading in the outline), bring the class and case materials together. You do not want just two separate sections, one about the course materials and one about the case: you want the two brought together at every point. Write sentences that explicitly connect the two.

■ *In the final paper, show the interaction between case and course.* The relation between the two should help bring out the meaning of both. The paper should be presented to make that interaction evident:

1. The *introduction* of the essay should directly address the task and identify how course materials and case materials inform each other. Explicitly state the relationship between the two sets of materials in a thesis sentence, a clear statement of the main point.

2. *Each paragraph in the essay's body* should support the main point, discussing some aspect of how the case sheds light on the ideas of the course or how the course ideas shed light on the case. As mentioned above, make explicit connections between the case and the course, especially in the introductory sentences of the paragraphs. These connections should also add up in a coherent way and be presented in a comprehensible order, with one idea leading to the next.

3. The *conclusion* should again directly address the primary task set by the question, showing how the case fits into course issues, or how course issues would help understand, resolve, or provide a more sophisticated way of handling the case. Based on the analysis and discussion of the paper, the conclusion should provide some specific evaluations, recommendations, insights, or other advances on thinking.

ꙮ   R E V I E W I N G   W R I T I N G   P R O C E S S E S

Revision and Drafting

Professional writers rarely submit *first drafts* (their first attempt at a piece of writing) for publication or presentation. Many writers see first drafts merely as broad outlines of what they eventually intend to say. Good writing usually means *revision:* looking again at your writing to see how you can make it better. Students tend to see revision much differently than professional writers. Some students only look over a paper to correct obvious mistakes or typographical errors. Such correction is really only *proofreading* (see page 145). Others look over their papers to try to make their meaning more precise or their prose more economical. This sharpening of the phrasing is what is called *editing* (see pages 184–186). The most successful students, however, realize that revising means looking over everything: the statement of the main idea, the logic and reasoning, the major supporting ideas, the organization, and the examples and details, as well as the grammar, word choice, and spelling.

Contemporary writing research shows that, whereas inexperienced writers tend to divide the writing process into a "thinking" stage and a "writing" stage, experienced writers see their writing as a part of their thinking process. The English novelist E. M. Forster once said, "How can I know what I think until I see what I say?" From Forster's perspective, writing becomes a way to create, refine, and modify ideas, rather than just a way to express thoughts that have already been sufficiently formed. Through each draft you bring your thoughts more into being, as you look at the shape your ideas are taking and bring out that shape more fully.

Most students have had the experience of writing a paper and discov-

Calvin and Hobbes   by Bill Watterson

ering that, by the time they reach their conclusion, they are expressing ideas that had not occurred to them when they began. When this happens, inexperienced writers often think they have done something wrong. Experienced writers, on the other hand, recognize that their writing has helped them create new ideas. They then go back to the beginning to incorporate these insights into their writing, eliminating the stray statements they needed at first to warm up. After writing another draft, a writer may discover even more new ideas that need to be included.

Writing on a computer or a word processor makes revising a paper much easier. But even students who use word processors must make a conscious effort to rework and rethink their ideas during every stage of writing. This requires foresight and planning, since papers hastily prepared the night before they are due will almost always be unrevised first drafts. Where possible, you should try to complete your first draft several days before the paper is due, giving yourself time to come back several times to revise your prose and work through the main ideas. When you do this, you may find that your final paper might not look anything like your original version.

Sample Student Essay

The following student essay was written for an introductory Psychology course. After reading a chapter entitled "The Individual and the Social Group" from the textbook, students were asked to find and discuss a news story that exemplified one of the concepts presented in the chapter. The student James Dilling found a story in a political magazine describing the decline of a New England fishing community that seemed to fit precisely with the concept of "tragedy of the commons." The essay presents both the main points of the concept and the primary facts of the case, and then clearly discusses how the case fits the concept.

A Common Tragedy in Gloucester
by James Dilling

We often assume that rational individuals will create rational public policies; however, this assumption does not always hold true. Individuals acting intelligently, rationally, and defensibly in their own best interests can often contribute to the decline of the communities to which they belong. Deborah Cramer's article "The One That Got Away" on pages 40-41 of the July/August 1994 issue of *Mother Jones Magazine* tells the story of Gloucester, Massachusetts, a small fishing village that has learned this lesson the hard way. The Gloucester case illustrates the psychological principle known as the "tragedy of the commons." This principle states that in cases of communal property or resources, the best interests of rational individuals are often at odds with the best interests of the communities to which they belong.

The idea of the tragedy of the commons was first identified by a psychologist named Garret Hardin in 1968. Hardin used the image of the village commons — large areas in the middle of a town where everyone had the right to graze their cattle — as a metaphor for all of the commonly held resources in our society today. Consider the case of a town where ten townspeople each kept two cows on the commons. Everyone prospered by this arrangement. If, however, one of the ten put a

The town common in Sterling, Massachusetts.

third cow on the commons, then that one person would
have an increased yield by 33 percent, and the difference to the rest would have been unnoticeable. However,
as Laird and Thompson point out in *Psychology,* what
makes sense for one person proves disastrous for a community:

> The problem is that what one villager found reason-
> able, other villagers did too. Soon each villager
> had three, then four cows on the commons. They added
> more and more cows until the commons was no longer a
> pasture, until there was too little grass to support
> even one cow. . . . The cumulative effect of individu-
> ally rational behavior was the destruction of the
> commons. (556)

Fishermen's desire to increase their individual catch depleted the fish population, leading to a decline in the industry.

While Hardin deals primarily with a theoretical commons in a fictional town, Deborah Cramer presents an all-too-real example of this tragedy. Once a thriving fishing village, Gloucester has experienced a sharp decline in business as the fish population off its coast has steadily declined. For years, boats would travel out to sea and come home full of fish, and, even though the fish population is now at a "record low" (40), industry advocates are reluctant to accept conservation standards that would limit the number of fish caught now in order to rebuild the population of fish for future generations. Even important and moderate regulations — such as regulating the time that a fishing boat can spend at sea and increasing the size of the holes in the nets to protect smaller fish who have yet to spawn — have been shouted down by angry fishers who are "yelling and hollering that the council is trying to put them out of business" (41).

The angry reactions of the townspeople can best be understood when viewed as an example of Hardin's psychology of the commons. Each individual fishing operation is concerned, first and foremost, with its own best interests. For these individual operations, this means that, to act rationally and in their own best interest, they should try to catch as many fish as they possibly can — even though such a strategy will eventually destroy the common fishery. For any one operation to stop its fishing unilaterally would be irrational, since others would still find it profitable to overfish the same area and the only losers would be those who stopped. Unless everyone decreases fishing operations together, nobody stands to gain by decreasing them alone. To put it in Hardin's terms, what would be rational and far-sighted for the collective level becomes irrational and self-defeating for the individual.

This all-too-common tragedy serves as an eloquent rebuttal to the popular theory of laissez faire economics, or the belief that government industries regulate their resources best when the government takes a strict hands-off approach. Without some government regulation, the common fishing grounds of Gloucester and other New England ports are doomed to certain extinction. Individuals cannot rationally decrease their fishing efforts, but the industry as a whole must do so in order to survive. In order to preserve the resource for the future, local, state, and national government regulators must step in and place reasonable controls on all members of the fishing industry equally. While such regulations may be unpopular, they are made necessary by the peculiar psychology of the commons that Hardin identified in his research in 1968.

Works Cited

Cramer, Deborah. "The One That Got Away." <u>Mother Jones Magazine</u> Jul.-Aug. 1994:40-41.
Laird, James, and Nicholas Thompson. <u>Psychology</u>. Boston: Houghton Mifflin, 1991.

Thinking About Student Writing

1. What points does James Dilling present to explain the concept of the tragedy of the commons? What sources does he use to present the concept? Where in the essay does he use these sources, and in what form does he present the material from them?

2. What facts does Dilling present about the case of Gloucester fishermen? What source does he use for this information, and in what form does he present information from that source?

3. What connection does Dilling make between the concept and the Gloucester case? On the basis of that connection, what further point does Dilling make about politics and government policy?

4. How does Dilling organize the parts of his essay to bring different points together into a whole?

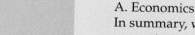

Assignments

WRITING ABOUT REAL-LIFE SITUATIONS

1. Select one of the following readings from an academic discipline and then locate a recent news item that relates to it. Study the news item and write a brief (500- to 750-word) essay explaining the story in light of the reading.

A. Economics
In summary, when trade has opened up, and when each country concentrates on its area of comparative advantage, everyone is better off. Workers in each region can obtain a larger quantity of comparative advantage and trade their own production for

goods in which they have a relative disadvantage. When borders are opened to international trade, the national income of each and every trading country rises.

From Paul A. Samuelson and William D. Nordhaus, *Economics* (New York: McGraw-Hill, 1989) 904.

B. Sociology

The media provide instant coverage of social events and social changes, ranging from news and opinions to fads and fashions. They offer role models, viewpoints, and glimpses of lifestyles that people might otherwise never have access to. Through the media, children can learn about courtroom lawyers, cowboys, police detectives, or even such improbable characters as Batman, E.T., and Rambo. (The fact that many of these images are not very realistic does not necessarily lessen their influence.) Through media advertising, too, the young learn about their future roles as consumers in the marketplace, and about the high value the society places on youth, success, beauty, and materialism. Changing social norms and values are quickly reflected in the media and may be readily adopted by people who might not otherwise be exposed to them. The rapid spread of the new trends in youth culture, for example, depends heavily on such media as popular records, television, FM radio, youth-oriented magazines, and movies.

From Ian Robertson, *Sociology* (New York: Worth, 1987) 130.

C. Psychology

A subtle process that contributes to prejudice is the *just-world phenomenon* — another special case of the balance principle, that good goes with good. Many people behave as if they believed in a just world, in which bad things don't happen to good people. Of course, the world isn't just; and earthquakes, hurricanes, famine, and disease all strike at random. However, to the extent that people follow the just-world principle, they tend to think that the victims of tragedy somehow deserve their fate. Certainly we all know better; but as with other cases in which balance processes occur, if we are not paying attention we may tend to exhibit the just-world phenomenon.

From James Laird and Nicholas Thompson, *Psychology* (Boston: Houghton Mifflin, 1992) 509.

D. Anthropology

Law and order in stratified societies depends on an infinitely variable mixture of physical compulsion through police-military force and thought control. . . . In general, the more marked the social inequalities and the more intense the labor exploitation, the heavier must be the contribution of both forms of control. The regimes relying most heavily on brutal doses of police-military intervention are not necessarily those that display the greatest amount of visible social inequity. Rather, the most brutal systems of police-military control seem to be associated with periods of major transformations, during which the governing classes are insecure and prone to overreact. Periods of dynastic upheaval and of prerevolutionary and postrevolutionary turmoil are especially conducive to brutality.

From Marvin Harris, *Culture, People, Nature: An Introduction to General Anthropology* (New York: HarperCollins, 1988) 389.

2. Find an article in a newspaper, magazine, news broadcast, or other source of current information that describes how a professional or a researcher used his or her knowledge to resolve a conflict or solve a problem. In a few paragraphs, describe the events or findings presented in the article, and then write several more paragraphs discussing the value of the kind of knowledge and research described in the article.

3. In a newspaper, magazine, television program, or other source of current information, locate a story that reveals the relevance of any material you have studied in any course this term. Write an essay of five hundred words describing the relationship between the story and the concepts or information from your class. Give your instructor copies of course or media materials he or she might need to understand or evaluate your essay.

Getting Involved Electronically

Search the World Wide Web to find materials relevant to any topic you are studying in one of your courses. Write a few paragraphs describing your findings.

8

Autobiographical Writing: Connecting Concepts and Experience

AIMS OF THE CHAPTER

The richest source of knowledge you bring to the class is yourself. This chapter describes how you can connect your own experiences and memories with what you learn in class, especially when your instructor gives you the opportunity to do so. Making this connection will increase your presence as a contributor to the class interaction.

KEY POINTS

1. Writing about your own experiences in relation to the subject matter of the course helps you understand the meaning and relevance of academic concepts.

2. While writing about your experience puts you on the line, and while you always have a right to have your privacy respected, thinking about personal experience in relation to academic concepts deepens your understanding of the material and heightens the reality of your learning. Hearing and reading the relevant experiences of other members of the class also extends your understanding.

3. An essay of illustration describes something that you have witnessed or experienced as an example of some category, concept, pattern, process, phenomenon, or other general idea that you have studied in the course.

4. An essay comparing everyday common-sense views of your experience with more specialized disciplinary ways of looking at those events deepens your appreciation of course material.

QUESTIONS TO THINK ABOUT

■ When have teachers asked you to write or talk about your own experience? When have you found such writing most useful?

- Have you ever felt uncomfortable sharing personal information with a teacher or a class? What boundaries would you set up to define what you would or would not care to share?

- What material have you learned that has helped you understand some part of your experience? What experiences have you had that have helped you understand the material you have studied?

Each of you as you enter the classroom brings broad swaths of the world with you. Depending on the subject, each of you may have had experiences that relate to the ideas and information presented in class. Whether the issue is the political process, human behavior and psychology, symbols in culture, the mass media, or literature and the arts, each of you has seen and been through much that relates directly to class studies. If you are discussing the influence of the media on children, you have watched many hours of television and have seen its effect on yourself, your peers, and your relatives. If you are discussing changes in American economy, you have witnessed the changing presence of corporations and business, the changing marketing of products, and changing employment opportunities. If you are discussing the plot structure of narratives, you have movie, video, and novel plots in your memory. If you are discussing the effects of stress on behavior, your personal and college life may provide many incidents to think about.

By asking students to speak and write about their experiences, instructors help students examine the personal relevance of what they are learning. Other classmates' experiences and analyses of those experiences further enrich this understanding.

Personal Issues and Privacy

However, as lively and motivating as personal experience is to consider in the classroom, it is not always easy to work with. Discussing your experience

Calvin and Hobbes   by Bill Watterson

reveals something of who you are and what you think about life. These complications are great advantages for making the subject real and personally important, but they can make discussions more challenging or threatening. As you examine your life and experience in new ways, you may come to question long-held assumptions and beliefs. Moreover, in some cases, the pressure to draw on your own experience may ask you to reveal more of yourself than you want to share. What seems like a lively discussion to one person can seem like an invasion of privacy to another.

Those things you have witnessed and experienced are part of yourself. Your sense of identity has in part developed through what you have learned to deal with and how you have learned to deal with it. In describing what you have observed and lived you expose both your experience and the way you look at things.

Most teachers who ask for personal experiences are aware of these issues of privacy, even though they may have different thoughts and expectations about the assignment. Whatever a teacher's approach may be, you should always have the right not to discuss some matter or view that you feel is private, that you feel is inappropriate for the classroom, or that you feel uncomfortable about sharing with any particular group. You also have the right to raise the question of privacy with the instructor. Most teachers are quite reasonable if you approach them about these reservations. Similarly, if your instructor shares student writing with the rest of the class, you should let the teacher know when you feel a piece of writing is too private for other class members to read.

It is useful to keep in mind that teachers asking for personal experiences are not usually asking for deep dark secrets, but just ordinary everyday things students see about them, such as how clothes-buying decisions are affected by the media. Often instructors and classmates are surprised when a student responds to a question about experience with an intimately personal story. In those cases, no one forces the student to share such a story, but the student trusts the class and feels the need to tell it. However, this kind of response should always be voluntary.

✺ Sharing in the Classroom

These cautions aside, once students start to bring more of themselves into the classroom, the teacher can respond more to them and to the material they present. For example, I have had truly wonderful discussions with students of all backgrounds about social mobility as they examine their family histories to see the kinds of opportunities and obstacles provided by society in different countries, regions, and time periods, and how their parents, grandparents, and other relatives coped with the hand life dealt them. Moreover, these students were then able to reflect on how their own choices about college and major fit into their ideas about how society is organized and how they can make their own best and most satisfying way in it. Because of their different backgrounds and experiences, students have different patterns of perception. A student who grew up in a rural country with few choices except to follow in his parents' footsteps can see the many opportunities of a modern urban economy but may not grasp the many ways that parents try to protect economic and social position for their children in a society where family class position can easily fall in a single generation. On the other hand, a student from an affluent background may see her family's rise in individualistic terms that emphasize the persistence, hard work, or just good luck of particular ancestors but that same student may have a hard time seeing how opportunities depend on the structure of society and the economy. As students start to see how they view the social-economic terrain, they come to understand each other and the complexity of the subject.

Participation in a discussion of personal experiences requires directness, honesty, and an openness to people's experiences. While granting authority to each individual to speak for his or her own experience, these discussions also create a picture that is bigger than any one person's story. When you leave a classroom, you can always reject the collective terms developed there, and inside the classroom you can hold an alternate position and argue for it. But it is important to entertain the possibility that the experience of the class as a whole adds up to more than the experiences or thoughts of any one person.

Different classes have different languages in which students learn to express experiences. If a sociology class is discussing family history, the discussion will use sociological terms and concepts. If that same material is discussed as part of an economics course, the discussion will use economic terms and concepts. Nonetheless, the particular histories that students tell will focus and change the discussion in light of the experiences the students bring.

In some cases personal experience papers are directed just to the teacher, who will then respond to them in detail. In that case the thinking you develop will enter into wider class discussion only indirectly through your classroom comments, which are likely to draw on the specifics of the essays. Your papers are also likely to influence how the teacher directs the class. If your papers are to be read by your classmates, they become a way of representing your experience to others who have not seen what you have seen or had the perspective you have had. The papers then become part of a larger body of material for the whole class to think about.

Assignment   USING READING TO THINK ABOUT YOUR LIFE

Write a journal entry about one of the following autobiographical passages. Compare the quotation to your own experiences and describe any insight into your life that the passage gives you.

1. In New Mexico the land is made of many colors. When I was a boy I rode out over the red and yellow and purple earth to the west of Jemz Pueblo. My horse was a small red roan, fast and easy-riding. I rode among the dunes, along the bases of mesas and cliffs, into canyons and arroyos. I came to know that country,

not in the way a traveler knows the landmarks he sees in the distance, but more truly and intimately, in every season, from a thousand points of view. I know the living motion of a horse and the sound of hooves. I know what it is, on a hot day in August or September, to ride into a bank of cold, fresh rain.

From N. Scott Momaday, *The Way to Rainy Mountain* (Albuquerque: University of New Mexico Press, 1969) p. 67.

2. We children lived and breathed our history — our Pittsburgh history, so crucial to our country's story and so typical of it as well — without knowing or believing any of it. For how can anyone know or believe stories she dreamed in her sleep, information for which and to which she feels herself to be in no way responsible? A child is asleep. Her private life unwinds inside her skin and skull; only as she sheds childhood, first one decade and then another, can she locate the actual, historical stream, see the setting of her dreaming private life — the nation, the city, the neighborhood, the house where the family lives — as an actual project under way, a project living people willed, and made well

N. Scott Momaday (b. 1934), a Native American of the Kiowa tribe, won the Pulitzer Prize for his novel *House Made of Dawn*.

or failed, and are still making, herself among them. I breathed the air of history all unaware, and walked oblivious through its littered layers.

From Annie Dillard, *An American Childhood* (New York: Harper & Row, 1987), p. 74.

3. In the world of the southern black community I grew up in, "back talk" and "talking back" meant speaking as an equal to an authority figure. It meant daring to disagree and sometimes it meant just having an opinion. In the "old school," children were meant to be seen and not heard. My great-grandparents, grandparents, and parents were all from the old school. To make yourself heard if you were a child was to invite punishment, the back-hand lick, the slap across the face that would catch you unaware, or the feel of switches stinging your arms and legs.

   To speak then when one was not spoken to was a courageous act — an act of risk and daring. And yet it was hard not to speak in warm rooms where heated discussions began at the crack of dawn, women's voices filling the air, giving orders, making threats, fussing. Black men may have excelled in the art of poetic preaching in the male-dominated church, but in the church of the home, where everyday rules of how to live and how to act were established, it was the black women who preached. There, black women spoke in a language so rich, so poetic, that it felt to me like being shut off from life, smothered to death if one were not allowed to participate.

From bell hooks, *Talking Back* (Boston: South End Press, 1988).

4. The professor spoke like an Englishman, although he was an American. He played the part of Continental sophisticate — mentioning Josephine Baker, American jazz, and the like. He graded our compositions anonymously. One day he was reading my composition as an example of an A theme, praising the flow, the length of sentences, and so on. About midway he had a question and asked whose paper it was. I raised my black hand and like magic the quality of the paper went from A to F. He ripped it to shreds from that point on. I received a C for the course. From Sumner's standpoint, blacks could sing, dance, and play jazz, but what could they possibly know about English composition.

From James P. Comer, M.D. *Maggie's American Dream* (Penguin Books, 1989), p. 157.

5. I was to grow up an ugly child. Or one who thought himself ugly. *(Feo.)* One night when I was eleven or twelve years old, I locked myself in the bathroom and carefully regarded my reflection in the mirror over the sink. Without any pleasure I studied my skin. I turned on the faucet. (In my mind I heard the swirling

voices of aunts, and even my mother's voice, whispering, whispering incessantly about lemon juice solutions and dark, *feo* children.) With a bar of soap, I fashioned a thick ball of lather. I began soaping my arms. I took my father's straight razor out of the medicine cabinet. Slowly, with steady deliberateness, I put the blade against my flesh, pressed it as close as I could without cutting, and moved it up and down across my skin to see if I could get out, somehow lessen, the dark. All I succeeded in doing, however, was in shaving my arms bare of their hair. For as I noted with disappointment, the dark would not come out. It remained. Trapped. Deep in the cells of my skin.

From Richard Rodriguez, *Hunger of Memory* (New York: Bantam Books, 1982) pp. 124–25

NEWS FROM THE FIELD

Intrinsic Motivation and Doing Something for Its Own Sake

While receiving a reward for accomplishing the goals that others set for you can motivate hard work and can make you a more productive student, as Edwin Locke has shown (see pages 175–176), externally set goals and rewards, such as grades, at some point reach a limit. Some psychological and organizational researchers point out that the highest, longest-lasting, and most productive motivation comes when an activity is rewarding in itself. In his 1993 book *Punished by Rewards: The Trouble with Gold Stars, Incentive Plans, A's, Praise, and Other Bribes,* Alfie Kohn examines the limitations of systems that motivate by offering rewards. Kohn considers a "reward" to be anything that a parent, educator, manager, or employer uses to acknowledge and encourage specific positive behaviors. Rewards can come in the form of verbal praise, high grades, money, or tangible prizes, but they all have the same basic effects.

Kohn points out that *rewards and externally set goals ignore your reasons for wanting to do things.* Rewards and incentives focus on the results of a behavior instead of its causes, and therefore they treat surface symptoms only. When students do badly in class or when employees perform poorly on the job, they do so for some reason. Setting goals and offering rewards may improve short-term results, but will do nothing to get to the real problems behind the behavior; once the reward is no longer offered, the problems will almost always resurface. Thus to really improve your ability to learn in the long run, you need to explore your underlying reasons for wanting to learn as well as the underlying reasons that might be inhibiting your learning.

External goals and rewards discourage risk taking. When people work toward a goal for a reward, they tend to work only for the reward and to ignore anything that will not directly qualify them to receive it. Kohn points out that this often decreases people's overall productivity by narrowing their focus to those things that will ensure the reward. For example, a student who is working only for an A in a class will learn everything that it takes to pass tests and write papers but will be unlikely to learn or retain other things that do not directly relate to evaluations. Rewards decrease our field of vision and emphasize short-term accomplishment over long-term growth.

Finally, *externally set goals and rewards decrease intrinsic motivation.* Intrinsic motivation is the personal satisfaction that comes from the activity itself, as well as from the satisfaction of doing it well. Enjoying playing soccer or working on the computer and the feeling that you are doing it well are far more likely to lead you to spend more time with greater attention at those activities than if you are paid an hourly rate to be on the field or in front of a computer.

A study by a psychologist at the University of Rochester in the early 1970s supports the assertion that rewards actually decrease interest in a task. In the study, two groups of college students were asked to work on a spatial relations puzzle. One group was promised money for their participation and another group was not. After a set amount of time, the students were told that the first phase of the study was over and that they should sit alone in a room and wait for the next phase. The researchers observed that the students who had not been paid were far more likely to continue working on the puzzle than those who had received a monetary reward. The students who had been paid had come to be motivated primarily by the money, but the students who received no reward developed an intrinsic interest in the puzzle that motivated them to want to solve it.

For Kohn, and for many other researchers and motivators, the ideal school or work environment is the one in which tasks become their own rewards. External motivation can only increase productivity temporarily and superficially, but internal motivation can increase satisfaction, cooperation, and output permanently. Students study best when they love the subjects they study, and workers work best when they love their jobs. Although your instructors may try to build your motivation by sharing their enthusiasm for the subject or helping you develop your own goals, only you can really identify what it is you find important and rewarding.

✑✑ Two Kinds of Personal Experience Paper

Although instructors may find many formats and ways of asking you to bring your experience to the classroom, these assignments are generally variants of two basic processes: presentation and discussion. You may be asked to present some relevant experience in a way that *illustrates* what you have learned from the course, or you may be asked to *discuss* experience in ways that have been developed in the course.

⚲〜 Experience as Illustration

An essay of illustration describes something that you have witnessed or experienced as an example of some category, concept, pattern, process, phenomenon, or other general idea studied in the course. The general idea is central to the paper, and the experience is selected for how well it fits the idea. Then the experience is described to make that connection obvious.

In assigning such exercises the teacher usually wants you to see that what is talked about in class also exists in the world, that you can associate specific events with those classroom ideas, and that you can use the classroom concepts to identify details, aspects, or parts in the actual experience. If, for example, in psychology you have been studying how people deal with inconsistent or contradictory thoughts (called *cognitive dissonance*), in discussing a personal illustration you do more than tell a story about your thought processes and just call it cognitive dissonance; you *show* how the discomfort and attitude change you went through fit with the typical ways people react to cognitive dissonance *as described in the textbook.*

Developing a Personal Illustration

The following suggestions are guides to the process of developing an essay that uses personal experience to illustrate a concept from an academic discipline:

- Identify the concept, pattern, phenomenon, or idea that the teacher is asking you to illustrate. Review the relevant course materials to make sure you understand the concept. If the teacher offers you a choice of concepts to work with, select the one that you suspect has the most direct and interesting connections with experiences you might write about.

- Locate an area of experience that seems to be relevant to the concerns of the course and the specific concept to be discussed. Then list various specific experiences that you might discuss, and mentally walk through them. If the topic is related to work, for example, you could review the various jobs you have had by listing them and then jotting down possible examples for your paper. If the topic concerns marketing, you could think of the products you use regularly and the marketing campaigns associated with them. To remind yourself about the marketing of common products, you might want to leaf through a magazine or walk through a shopping mall.

- Think about which example will give the richest presentation in both detail and concept. A bare-bones example that fits the precise specifics of the concept will usually produce an adequate answer. More elaborated presentations will probably be seen as more advanced work and be rewarded accordingly. You can also think about the kinds of examples the teacher has presented in lecture and discussion.

- Once you have selected an incident or situation to retell, then brainstorm details from memory. To refresh your memory, you might look at photographs, memorabilia, or other things you associate with the event, or perhaps speak with a friend or relative who is familiar with the event. The textbook or lecture definition or discussion can be used as a framework through which to recall further details. See how the concept and its parts remind you of new aspects of the incident, make the incident look different, or give you a new angle on the events.

■ As the details build, you create a mental picture of the event, object, or experience. As you build up the picture, you need to keep adding details, using charts, networks, diagrams, or whatever kind of representation is helpful.

■ Write out a first sketch of the experience. As you read it over, underline those aspects that most directly relate to the central idea. Think about how you could elaborate those aspects with even more details and specifically identify their relevance.

Writing an Essay of Personal Illustration

The essay should open with an overview, summary, or definition of the central concept, pattern, or phenomenon to be illustrated, along with some indication of the specific experience that will be described.

The main body should recount the experience while also emphasizing the connection to the general concept. *Each sentence* should make a clear connection with the concept or pattern you are illustrating, even if only with a word or phrase that comes from the conceptual definition. Each detail should be told to bring out its connection to the general pattern or idea. Expand most on those parts that are most related to the main theme. Summary or overview sentences at the beginning or end of each paragraph should expand on the relation to the concept.

If any aspects of the illustration do not fit well with the main idea or even seem to point in a contradictory direction, you should point that out, not try to hide the difficulty by not mentioning the contradicting details or slipping past them rapidly and without comment.

Writing this kind of essay involves always doing two things at once. Even as you keep the readers' attention on the idea behind the description, you also always make sure they get a clear picture of the events or experiences being described. Nonetheless, even as you get involved in painting your picture, you try not to lose sight of the concept being illustrated.

In your conclusion you can expand upon what the illustration shows about the concept or pattern, whether it shows how the concept changes in the real world, how further details fit in, or how forcefully reality illustrates the abstractions taught in the classroom.

Sample Student Essay

In the following essay Ai-Lin Young discusses the way she has experienced racism. She builds her discussion around the concept of racism described in the paragraph by writer James Comer earlier in this chapter. First she clearly explains the concept of racism Comer uses. Then she applies that concept to illustrations from her own life. Before reading this essay, reread the paragraph by Comer on pages 171–172.

```
No I Don't Speak Chinese, I'm an American
Ai-Lin Young


     In a short description of a classroom experience,
James Comer presents racist stereotypes as appearing to
have two sides, positive and negative, but ultimately
both sides are harmfully racist. In this incident the
professor first demonstrates that he holds seemingly
positive stereotypes of black culture. The professor
admires jazz and the famous American black singer
Josephine Baker. But then he shows that he holds nega-
tive stereotypes when he changes his opinion about
Comer's writing once he realizes who wrote it. The
racism is not just in the negative stereotype, it is
also in the positive one. Both are harmful in that they
define what is expected of a person, that there are cer-
tain things they are supposed to know and do on the ba-
sis of their race, just as they define what a person is
supposed not to be able to know and do. What neither
the positive nor the negative stereotype allows is the
person to define his or her self based on who he or she
is. My experience of people's reaction to my race shows
```

People growing up in the United States share in the experiences the country has to offer.

how this works, even though they may express no obvious
negative feelings.

As an Asian-American woman at a primarily white
school, I often find myself occupying a strange and
strained position. So far I have not encountered obvious kinds of negative racism directed towards me personally; no one has called me a "chink" or a "jap" or a
"gook." In fact, more often than not, the people I meet
are curious about my cultural heritage. They will ask
me what my name means when I first meet them, and then
they will ask me if I speak Chinese. Perhaps then they
might even compliment me on my straight, long black
hair.

All of this attention is supposed to be good, isn't
it? Then why am I so often left with a bad taste in my
mouth, as though accepting these compliments and responding to these enquiries is something my stomach
can't quite handle? When other students ask me if I
speak Chinese (after they have established to their
satisfaction that that is what I am) I often wonder,
and sometimes ask, if they speak the language of their
parents and grandparents who immigrated to this nation?
When I ask it, this question usually comes as a surprise, as though no one has ever suggested before that
they might speak anything but English or be anything
but "Americans."

But I'm an "American" too. As a young girl, I
watched the same T.V. shows, listened to the same music, went through the same school system, and read the
same books and magazines as everybody else in my generation. Even though my mother is a first generation immi-
grant from Hong Kong, she never really spoke to me in
Chinese—perhaps because she was always trying to perfect her English. My stepfather, a fourth generation
Chinese American, had to go to school to pick up the
stilted Cantonese he uses when discussing money matters. So I wonder, when white students look at me, why
is it they imagine I don't really speak the same language as they do? Why is it they imagine I have some
secret knowledge of authentic Chinese culture, when I
have been only a visitor to Chinatown and have never
even seen China?

The difference between what I know and what they
know is not as large as they imagine, but how can I
convince them of this when even my teachers will ask me
to share my secret knowledge in the classroom? When we

read Maxine Hong Kingston's *Woman Warrior* in an English class, my instructor turned to me and asked if the book really described "the way it really was" to be Chinese. I had no idea how to answer. My mother had never talked to me of ghosts, and I had never felt unvalued or unappreciated as a female child in our home. I really didn't know enough about "the way it really was" to answer the question. Though I know that this instructor wasn't trying to be overtly prejudiced, he did put me on the spot unfairly because he made unwarranted assumptions about me based on my name and the color of my skin. Ultimately, isn't that what "racism" really is? Isn't that what James Comer experienced?

Though I have never been overtly insulted or dismissed or marked down on the basis of race as James Comer has, I have had many experiences of a more subtle kind of prejudice. Whenever a friend or a classmate assumes that I speak a different language or have a different background than they do, they are suggesting that I am not as "American" as they are. Whenever a teacher acts as though I am the resident expert on an Asian subject, I feel like I don't quite belong to the class as much as other students do. They assume who I am rather than letting me tell them. Though I know that, for the most part, these are liberal, open-minded individuals who do not consider themselves racist or prejudiced in the slightest degree, their occasional inability to look beyond my foreign-sounding name and my darker-than-average skin shows that even our most tolerant citizens have a long way to go in recognizing that racism is still a pervasive problem in our society.

Thinking About Student Writing

1. What is the issue that Ai-Lin Young finds in James Comer's description? How does this issue relate to her life?

2. In what way do others treat the author as Chinese? What do they assume she knows and has experienced? To what aspects of her are they responding in making these assumptions?

3. Why does Ai-Lin Young consider herself an American? On what aspects of herself is that identification made? How is her knowledge and experience similar to that of her classmates? To what extent do her teachers and classmates recognize that similarity? What is the effect of their assumptions about her experience?

4. How does the author define racism? In what way does that definition fit her experience? What has been the effect of that racism? Do you agree with her definition of racism and her characterization of the meaning of her experience?

5. In what sentences does the author focus on the concept of racism? In what sentences does she focus on her experience? In what sentences are the two brought together? How is the linkage made in those sentences?

6. In what way has Ai-Lin Young's experience helped you understand some aspects of racism more clearly?

7. If you were the author, how might you have felt about writing this essay about yourself and then having your classmates read it?

 **ssignments**

ESSAYS OF PERSONAL ILLUSTRATION

1. Using the quotation from James Comer or one of the other quotations on pages 169 to 172, write a 500-word essay using your own experience to illustrate a concept presented in the quotation you choose.

2. Identify a personal experience that illustrates the concepts presented in one of the following passages. Write an essay of personal illustration of 500 to 800 words about your experience in relation to those concepts.

A. Falling in Love

Of all the misconceptions about love the most powerful and pervasive is the belief that "falling in love" is love or at least one of the manifestations of love. It is a potent misconception because falling in love is subjectively experienced in a very powerful fashion as an experience of love. When a person falls in love what he or she certainly feels is "I love him" or "I love her." But two problems are immediately apparent. The first is that the experience of falling in love is specifically a sex-linked erotic experience. We do not fall in love with our children even though we may love them very deeply. We do not fall in love with our friends of the same sex — unless we are homosexually oriented — even though we may care for them greatly. We fall in love only when we are consciously or unconsciously sexually motivated. The second problem is that the experience of falling in love is invariably temporary. No matter whom we fall in love

with, we sooner or later fall out of love if the relationship continues long enough. This is not to say that we invariably cease lov-
ing the person with whom we fell in love. But it is to say that the
feeling of ecstatic lovingness that characterizes the experiences of
falling in love always passes. The honeymoon always ends. The
bloom of romance always fades.

From M. Scott Peck, *The Road Less Traveled* (New York: Touchstone, 1978), pp. 84–85.

B. Social Identity

The socialized part of the self is commonly called *identity*. Every
society may be viewed as holding a repertoire of identities — little boy, little girl, father, mother, policeman, professor, thief, archbishop, general, and so forth. By a kind of invisible lottery, these
identities are assigned to different individuals. Some of them are
assigned from birth, such as little boy or little girl. Others are assigned later in life, such as clever little boy or pretty little girl (or,
conversely, stupid little boy or ugly little girl). Other identities are
put up, as it were, for subscription, and individuals may obtain
them by deliberate effort, such as policeman or archbishop. But
whether an identity is assigned or achieved, in each case it is ap-
propriated by the individual through a process of interaction
with others. Only if an identity is confirmed by others is it possible for that identity to be real to the individual holding it. In
other words, identity is the product of an interplay of identification and self-identification.

From Peter L. Berger and Brigitte Berger, *Sociology, A Biographical Approach* (New York: Basic
Books, 1972) 66.

C. Opportunity Costs

A choice is simply a comparison of alternatives: to attend college
or not to attend college, to change jobs or not to change jobs, to
purchase a new car or to keep the old one. An individual compares the benefits that one option is expected to bring and selects
the one with the greatest *anticipated* benefits. Of course, when one
option is chosen, the benefits of the alternatives are foregone. You
choose not to attend college and you forego the benefits of attending college; you buy a new car and forego the benefits of
having the money to use in other ways. *Economists refer to the foregone opportunities or foregone benefits of the next best alternative as*
opportunity costs — the highest-value alternative that must be
foregone when a choice is made.

From William Boyes and Michael Melvin, *Economics*, 2nd ed. (Boston: Houghton Mifflin,
1994) 33–34.

D. A Legal Definition of Nuisance

A nuisance exists when an owner's use of his or her property un-
reasonably infringes on other persons' use and enjoyment of their
property rights. Nuisances are classified as public, private, or
both. A public nuisance exists when a given use of land poses a
generalized threat to the public. It is redressed by criminal prose-
cution and injunctive relief. Examples of public nuisances include
houses of prostitution, actions affecting the public health (such as
water and air pollution), crack houses, and dance halls. A private
nuisance is a tort [that is, a private injury or wrong] that requires
proof of an injury that is distinct from that suffered by the general public. (It differs from trespass because the offensive activity
does not occur on the victim's property.) A party injured by a private nuisance can obtain both damages and injunctive relief.

From Harold Grilliot and Frank Schubert, *Introduction to Law and the Legal System,* 5th ed.
(Boston: Houghton Mifflin, 1992) 385–87.

From Illustration to Discussion

Once you bring your own experience into class, it is available to think about
in the context of your courses. The instructor will ask you to think in new
ways about events and experiences. In the past you probably used common
sense to think about experience, but now you are being asked to think in
ways that relate to disciplines. These specialized ways of thinking enable you
to see events in ways that extend beyond everyday approaches. You may
find that common-sense thinking serves some important purposes, and disciplinary thinking serves others.

Comparing Everyday and Disciplinary Thinking

As we take part in daily events and observe the behavior of others, we make
sense of what we see through various commonsense methods — attributing
motives to people, recognizing typical causes for events, believing certain actions will have certain consequences. Those same events, whether they are
political, economic, interpersonal, or international, are also the subject of various fields or disciplines. However, these specialized disciplines have developed special ways of seeing these same events. They highlight certain facts,
consider some issues worth doing research on, and use special concepts and
theories to organize their perceptions and facts. Thus a disciplinary account
of an event may be very different from a common-sense one.

Consider the explanations people give for their actions. For example, we
are having lunch with a friend. If the friend tells us that he went to Boston

last weekend and explains that he wanted to visit a high school friend now at a different college, we might take the reason at face value and ask how the friend was and whether they had a good time. If we think that reason is not the full story, we may ask probing questions to get at the real reason — such as a need to escape the pressures of the college or a budding romance with someone in Boston. But these reasons still assume self-conscious intentions, desires, and motivations.

On the other hand, social scientists may approach the reasons from other perspectives. One might look at what is called "accounting behavior" and therefore consider what kind of account the person was creating for his actions and what the situation was that established the need to create an account. That is, what kind of story was the friend telling, and why was he telling it at that moment? Perhaps he was simply being polite in response to a question, or perhaps he gave a simple, easily accepted standard story because he wanted to maintain the appearance among his friends of being a conventional young man who did things for ordinary reasons.

Another social scientist might look at how lunchroom conversations are part of a process of building friendships. Still another, interested in how people take turns in conversations, might examine when people interrupt each other. And yet another researcher, interested in power, would look at who has the final word. Each of these approaches offers new insights into the situation, and each is worth considering.

In college courses teachers are interested in teaching certain specialized approaches to events. They may ask you not only to describe events in specialized ways (as in the previous assignment) but to compare how the events look from the specialized perspective and from the everyday common-sense perspective.

This is not to say that disciplinary perspectives are necessarily opposed to common sense — as though common sense were deluded and specialized knowledge could see clearly. Sometimes it may be like this, as when we discover a poem has a powerful effect not because of its disturbing subject but because of its disrupted rhythms and its clashing images. But at other times disciplines can build a more elaborate and precise view on the basis of a familiar common-sense point of view, as when the idea that people will vote for their own interests becomes the basis for complex quantitative studies of voting patterns. The connection between disciplinary knowledge and common sense may also run the other way, as disciplinary concepts enter into everyday thinking; for example, much of our everyday thinking about people is now filled with such professional psychological concepts as anxiety, repressed thoughts, or phobias. You may find that as you become convinced of the value of the disciplinary perspectives you are studying, you may incorporate some of those perspectives in your everyday approach to life. On the other hand, sometimes you may have very good reasons to hold two different kinds of views — a commonsense way of relating to friends and a more disciplined way of understanding what role the relationships play in your life.

It is not always easy to see an event in two separate ways. If you have already been involved in the course, your point of view probably already incorporates some disciplinary perspectives, so you already are seeing through special lenses. In that case, to recover a commonsense point of view, you go backwards to recall how you viewed events before studying this subject. As you recall your earlier understanding, you may also become aware of how different it is from your newer view.

Developing a Comparison of Everyday and Disciplinary Thinking

The following suggestions can help you develop an essay comparing everyday and disciplinary perspectives on an event.

- *Identify a relevant event.* Identify an event that is relevant to the course and concepts but about which you and others have a fairly developed commonsense view.

- *Develop a neutral account of the event.* Having identified such an event, you need to get some view of it independent of the disciplinary considerations presented in the course. Unlike in the previous assignment, here you begin by keeping some distance from both commonsense and disciplinary thinking. You describe the event in as neutral and concrete terms as possible, without explanations, causes and effects, motivations, evaluations, or other comments. In discussing actions, you do not attribute reasons or feelings to those people you are describing or take any pattern or general category for granted. You simply report what people said and did — that is, what happened.

- *Recover commonsense explanations.* Once the facts are down, you then recover what commonsense explanations people might give them. People give explanations for various reasons: so they know how to act in the situation, or so they can explain the events, categorize them for memory, and not be puzzled or troubled by them anymore. One way to recover the commonsense point of view is simply to recall your state of mind when you saw the event as it happened, especially if it was important and your feelings and perceptions stayed with you. Even better would be an instance where you retold the story a number of times, such as an often-repeated family story about your childhood or the reactions of your high-school class to a shocking incident. In this way you can recover how you and others characterized the events. A written document presenting your views at the time, such as a letter, would be especially helpful.

    You may also remember what other people said at the time or the explanations they gave after the event. Another approach is to speak with someone who has observed or participated in the event but has not studied the subject for which you are writing the paper. Finally, you may take some published but nonprofessional account, as in a local newspaper, to represent a commonsense view.

- *Develop a disciplinary perspective on the events.* As in the previous assignment of illustrative description, identify those concepts you have studied that are most relevant to the event. Then describe each detail in relation to those concepts. If disciplinary terms suggest further details, try to recall them, or at least point out their absence from commonsense memory or standard news reports. Think about what additional information you would have gathered had you been a discipline-trained researcher present at the event. You may gather your thoughts and descriptions together in a sketch, outline, or informal series of freewritten paragraphs.

■ *Compare the disciplinary and commonsense views.* As you start to develop the two accounts, set them side by side in some chart or matrix so you can see what kinds of details and patterns the disciplinary account clarifies versus what kinds of details and patterns common sense points to. As you start to draw conclusions, write a few sentences that encapsulate the difference between the two perspectives. When your thoughts and notes are developed, you are ready to draft the paper.

Writing an Essay Comparing Everyday and Disciplinary Thinking

In this paper, the final form can reflect to some extent the organization of the work that brought you to your conclusions. The paper can begin with a neutral, concrete account of the events or phenomena to be discussed, and then a statement indicating that you are comparing two ways of looking at these events.

The next section can elaborate on how participants, or you in your commonsense mode, saw the events, and perhaps how that perception was related to how you and others acted. Then you might explain the disciplinary perspective that relates to the event. You might even recount the event as seen from that perspective.

Having established the two points of view, you can then discuss what the disciplinary perspective highlights or explains in contrast to the commonsense view, and vice versa. Your aim is to show what is gained and lost from either view. You may also wish to discuss how the two perspectives make visible different aspects of the event, based on the different goals of participants and disciplinary researchers. The conclusion can talk about the nature or value of either view or of both.

Another approach is to narrate how your understanding of the event changed as you moved from a commonsense perspective to a disciplinary one, and then evaluate the implications of that change. That is the strategy taken in the following sample essay.

❧❧ REVIEWING WRITING PROCESSES

Editing

Even after several drafts of a paper have been written, editing is still important. In editing, try to step back from the paper and read it as someone encountering it for the first time. After spending a long time struggling with ideas, it is easy to assume that the reader shares your knowledge of the topic. But things that seem obvious to you may not make sense at all to the reader. Often you need to add clear transitions between major ideas and define unfamiliar terms and concepts so that the reader will not be lost.

Editing is also done to improve style — including word choice and sentence construction (see the discussion of sentence combining on pages 130–135). The following guidelines help in making appropriate stylistic decisions. They are suggestions only; final decisions should be based on what is appropriate for the assignment.

- **Look for ways to replace passive-voice constructions with active-voice ones.**

  Unedited: *It is believed* currently that the Bering Strait *was crossed* by people from the Asian continent who became the first inhabitants of America.

  Edited: Anthropologists currently *believe* that people from the Asian continent *crossed* the Bering Strait and *became* the first inhabitants of America.

- **Avoid slang, jargon, or unnecessarily big words.**

  Unedited: The laudatory reception of the novel in the journalistic media that appealed to the working-class audiences impressively demonstrated the pseudo-Romantic revolutionary impulses of a trammeled industrial proletariat.

  Edited: The favorable reviews of the novel in the popular newspapers showed that many English workers were frustrated with the conditions in their own country.

- **Express ideas concisely; never use five words where two will do.**

  Unedited: It is a well-respected, commonly held belief that violent actions seen on TV can precipitate imitations of that violence among those who constitute the TV audience.

  Edited: Many people believe that violence on television causes people to behave violently.

- **Vary your sentence length; combine strings of short sentences into longer ones.**

  Unedited: In A.D. 350, Rome extended into parts of Europe, Asia, and Africa. The Romans provided a stable political environment for many people.

  Edited: In A.D. 350, Rome provided a stable political environment for people in parts of Europe, Asia, and Africa.

- **Avoid multiple prepositional phrases.**

  Unedited: A crucial part *of* psychology is the study *of* the tendencies *in* human beings *for* kinds *of* inclinations that lead to anti-social behavior.

  Edited: Psychology studies human tendencies to engage in anti-social behavior.

- **Express parallel ideas with parallel grammatical constructions.**

  Unedited: Some sociologists prefer a functionalist view of society, whereas a conflict perspective is advocated by others.
  Edited: Some sociologists prefer a functionalist view of society, whereas others prefer a conflict perspective.

- **Limit the use of "there is" and "there are."**

  Unedited: There are a number of problems with Marx's view of worker revolution.
  Edited: Marx's view of worker revolution has many problems.

- **Use strong verbs instead of nouns formed from verbs.**

  Unedited: Electrification led to the *transformation* of domestic *lighting* to electricity and the *abandonment* of gas as a light source, leaving gas *utilization* for heating.
  Edited: When people *started to light* their homes with electricity, they *began to use* gas more for heating.

Sample Student Essay

In the following essay Jenn Rosario discusses how the rhetorical way of thinking about writing she gained from the opening chapters of this book helped clear up confusions she had about writing. Those confusions came from a common everyday idea that there is a one best way to write. Rhetoric gave her a way to make sense of the many different things people had told her about the "best" way to write.

```
High School English Teachers
and "the Right Way" to Write
Jenn Rosario


    In school over the years, I have written essays in a
fair number of classes and have usually gotten good
grades. I am not saying I have written as much as I
ideally should have or am an ideal writer, but I seem
to have satisfied my teachers. But in satisfying the
teachers' demands I have gotten confused as to what
they want. Each asks for something different and criti-
cizes different things. They each acted as though they
each knew exactly what good writing was, but the prob-
lem was that they didn't agree. Good writing was a dif-
ferent thing for each of them. To deal with the
different demands of each class, I developed a common-
```

sense rule: "Don't try to make sense of it. Just find out what they want and give it to them."

I am not alone in thinking this was good common sense. Every time we had an assignment due, my friends would make jokes about what this or that teacher wanted, and we would trade tips about how to do well. There was even a folklore that got passed down from one class to the next about what you needed to do to make each teacher happy. Our collective common sense was that writing made no sense. We might like writing something, we might feel we had learned something by the writing, but we should never get too secure that we knew how to write. Inevitably, the next teacher we had would tell us that we got it all wrong.

Let me tell you some examples. When I was a junior in high school, my English teacher, Mrs. Spaulding, opened my eyes to a new way of writing. She taught me to explore my thoughts and feelings and use writing as a tool to understand myself in a new and interesting way. She encouraged a very personal writing style and taught me that my own experiences really were worth writing about. We wrote personal journals, and when we wrote about literature we put ourselves in the characters' positions to feel what they must have felt. I did well on all of the papers, got an A in the class, and left that year so confident of my writing ability that I couldn't wait to take senior English the next year.

However, my senior English teacher, Mr. Dauite, immediately stifled my enthusiasm. Our first assignment was to analyze the pressures that led a character in a novel to act as she did. I wrote that paper the way Mrs. Spaulding had taught me, but I did everything the wrong way. He criticized my use of personal experiences as "irrelevant and subjective." He told me that my narrative style was "rambling and loosely organized" and that I "needed to come to a point quickly and defend that point throughout the entire paper." At the end of the paper, he wrote a big, fat "C−." After a couple of papers, though, I did find out what he was asking for and I got back to getting my A's. And I learned something about how to analyze ideas without putting myself in the middle of it. But if someone asked me what good writing was, I could only tell them I was confused.

In fact I went through the term with two opposite ideas running through my head:

1. Mrs. Spaulding had taught me the wrong way to write and that, even though she made me feel good about myself, she had done me a disservice by failing to teach me the correct principles;

2. Mr. Dauite was old-fashioned and unreasonable and wasn't aware of the modern writing techniques that Mrs. Spaulding knew.

Since I couldn't decide between these two ideas, I just decided, along with my friends, that writing made no sense.

   The problem was that all of us, Mrs. Spaulding, Mr. Dauite, my friends, and myself all were going on the assumption that there is one "correct" way to write and that the duty of good writing teachers is to teach that method — and nothing else — to their students. I wasn't quite sure which of my teachers had been derelict, but, working from this assumption, I was sure that one of them had to be guilty of teaching flawed material to un-suspecting students.

   Since I have learned how to adopt a rhetorical per-spective on writing, however, I have a new view of what went on, a way that makes sense out of what went on in the different classes. No one was at fault; no one did anything wrong. In each of the classes the teachers taught me and my friends important things about writ-ing, and we improved our writing abilities. Our only mistake was to look for a single "right way" to write. Rhetoric teaches that there are many ways to write, de-pending on where you are and what you are doing. Chap-ter One of the textbook for this course sums up the rhetorical point of view:

> Successful communication varies from person to per-son and situation to situation. There is no simple, single "good rhetoric," no one way to write. You must always think about the specifics of the situa-tion; what you want to accomplish, with whom, and through what available means. (6)

   From this perspective, Mrs. Spaulding and Mr. Dauite were two different audiences with two different sets of rhetorical expectations. Mrs. Spaulding's purpose in the class was to teach writing as a method of self-exploration and discovery. She told us on a number of occasions that we could use writing to communicate with ourselves and make sense out of our own experiences. Mr. Dauite, on the other hand, believed that the primary purpose of writing was to construct well-reasoned arguments that communicated our ideas effectively to others. He continually stressed the importance of good communication and effective presentation of one's position.

Each teacher taught me something valuable. Both types of writing they taught have their place, and both have contributed to my development as a writer. But an even more important lesson is the one that I learned by putting the two experiences together: that there is no "correct" way to write a paper. Since there is no one way to write a paper, my responsibility, as a student, is to evaluate each rhetorical situation I approach and determine what kind of writing fits the activities going on. The way of writing I choose is just part of taking part in the kind of learning that the classroom offers, and there are many kinds of learning. I have already begun to notice that teachers often give hints about what they want, and even though these hints may not be too specific and may change from teacher to teacher, they do give me a good place to start thinking about what kind of writing is called for in each case. But even more than those little hints, I am noticing that teachers usually make it very clear what kinds of things they want students to learn and what they will be evaluating the students on. What I have to do is think about what kind of writing best shows the kind of learning the teachers are looking for.

Of course, I would still like it much better if there actually were set guidelines that I could simply follow all the time. Life would be simpler. But since life is complicated, and learning is complicated, and school is complicated, it really helps to know that I should stop looking for that one way to write "correct" papers and start looking for what works in each situation. That is my new common sense.

Work Cited

Bazerman, Charles. <u>Involved: Writing for College, Writing for Your Self.</u> Boston: Houghton Mifflin Company, 1997.

Thinking About Student Writing

1. What was Jenn Rosario's common-sense view of writing? What experiences seemed to confirm it? How did that common-sense view lead her to react to assignments in different classes? To what extent was that view useful? In what way did it have less fortunate consequences?

2. How does the author present her experiences to show clearly that a common-sense explanation was not adequate?

3. What is her new view? How does this new view lead her to reevaluate her previous experiences? What aspect of her previous view does she call a mistake? What aspects of her previous experience and views does she still find useful? What kind of guidance does her new view give her in facing new writing assignments and situations? In what way has her new view become a new kind of common sense?

4. Where does Jenn Rosario first present her new view? How does she elaborate on that view and show its value? How does the presentation of the new view allow her to re-present her experience from a new perspective?

5. How does Jenn Rosario's use of her personal experience help her develop and present her ideas clearly and forcefully?

6. If you were the author, how might you have felt about writing this essay about yourself and then allowing your classmates to read it?

Assignments

COMPARING EVERYDAY AND
DISCIPLINARY THINKING

1. Choose one concept that you have learned from this book or this course that has given you a new way to think about some aspect of writing. Write a paper about your own experience in writing, comparing your new way of thinking about that writing with your previous way.

2. Identify one powerful concept or topic you have learned in one of your courses this year that has changed the way you look at something. Write an essay of 800 to 1,000 words comparing how you see events using this disciplinary approach with how you used to think of the events using everyday common sense.

3. Using one of the selections from question 2 on pages 179–181, write an essay of 500 words comparing how the concept presented in the

selection differs from more everyday ways of looking at the subject. Use your own experience to illustrate the different ways of looking at events.

4. Select a controversial political or social issue in your community. Write an essay of 800 to 1,000 words describing how certain concepts or ways of thinking used in one of your college courses might help people resolve their differences, understand their difficulties, or come to a reasonable solution.

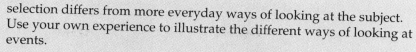

Getting Involved Electronically

Locate on the World Wide Web personal home pages set up by individuals, and pick one that interests you. Examine both how the person represents himself or herself and his or her interests and what kind of links are made to other Web resources. Pay particular attention to links people might make to academic or other professional information on the Web: that is, to what extent people tie their personal statements to knowledge and issues explored in a serious academic or professional way. Write up your impressions of how one individual represents himself or herself on the Web.

Analytical Writing: Looking Closely

AIMS OF THE CHAPTER

Academic disciplines introduce new ways of looking at things. These new ways are often analytical: you look at parts of phenomena and determine how the parts work together. Analysis is one of the central intellectual skills in academic life. This chapter discusses how analysis works and how you can write more analytically. By increasing your analytic skills you will be able to develop your individual point of view into effective contributions to academic and professional inquiry.

KEY POINTS

1. Analysis means to cut a whole into various parts or categories to understand what it is or how it works.

2. Analysis is often tied to specific disciplinary methods. Underlying every analysis usually is a theory.

3. Analysis helps you observe and understand many things about disciplinary, professional, and public problems.

4. Specific procedures can help you analyze phenomena and write up analyses.

QUESTIONS TO THINK ABOUT

■ Which things do you understand that sometimes other people don't? How does your insight depend on understanding how these things work or fit together? What do you see that allows you to analyze those things? On the other hand, when have you been totally confused about how something works or why things happen as they do? Understanding what parts of that situation or object might help you understand the whole?

- How often do your instructors use the words *analysis* or *analytical*? In what situations do they use terms related to analysis, and what are the tasks or thoughts they are referring to?

- How do you determine what the parts of an object or situation are? Where can you get the terms of your analysis from?

- How can looking at the parts of an object or situation help you resolve some problem you are facing?

ᘓᘓ Analytical Insight

Disciplinary knowledge shows the parts and processes of things we usually treat as a whole in daily life. By offering explanations of how things are put together and how they work, the various disciplines give you a way of looking at events and objects in greater detail. Such detailed understanding allows you to diagnose what goes right and wrong and to intervene in focused, effective ways. This pulling apart of objects and events and looking inside to see their components is known as analysis.

In many courses instructors want you to become skilled in the methods of analysis that are appropriate to the field. Rather than just tell you that the formula for a situation is thus and such, or that a condition is caused by these factors, they ask you to look at the situation, pull it apart, and tell *them* what is going on.

Sometimes analysis is obviously combined with other activities, as when in a political science class you analyze the structure of a legislative body in order to understand who can influence legislation in what ways. In a mechanical engineering course you might analyze an engine so that you can design a more efficient one or solve problems with the current one. Sometimes analysis is the primary activity, as when a neurobiologist analyzes the process by which a sensory impulse sets off brain activities, or when an art historian analyzes the style of a particular painter.

ᘓᘓ Some Key Features of Analysis

The procedures, methods, and uses of analysis vary widely in the disciplines, and even within a single discipline there are many types of analysis, which need to be presented and discussed in a range of ways. Nonetheless, several key elements are part of almost all analytical processes.

Analysis is initiated by some need or desire to know the components, dynamics, structure, or workings of some phenomenon in greater detail than is at first evident. Thus the central activity is seeing more deeply, more closely, in greater detail, something that looks at first glance to be a whole, or a unit. To understand a computer program, you need to know its parts; to understand how to build a bridge, you need to know the components that give it strength; to settle a philosophic argument, you need to know the issues that contribute to the larger problem. Analysis is crucial to most disciplines because they frequently want to understand why things happen as they do, so they open up the hood and look inside to see the parts.

Analysis looks for those things that are not obvious on the surface, that seem to be hidden to casual inspection. Analysis uncovers the unseen. Where there is nothing hidden, nothing smaller than meets the eye or common-sense judgment, there is little to analyze. Thus to find interesting or significant things you look in certain kinds of places in certain kinds of ways. Much of the art of analyzing is finding the right subject to analyze — interesting enough to tell you what you want, but not too complicated to make sense of. For this reason biologists often work with simpler animals that have less developed systems than humans; for example, because the flatworm *Aplysia* has one very large nerve cell, it is ideal for understanding nerve cell operation. Sometimes it may seem obvious what to analyze; for example, in studying why a company is profitable, it may seem obvious to begin with the balance sheet. However, the crucial place to look may be far from obvious; the real answer may lie in the patterns of motivation among the workers, or in the association of a name brand with a cultural hero.

Each object or phenomenon may be viewed through many different forms of analysis. Some of these will be more appropriate and revealing for your purposes than others. Psychiatric analysis will not tell you much about a stone, but various kinds of geologic and chemical analyses will. Depending on what you need or want to know, you pick the right mode of analysis for the stone — radioactive dating, spectroscopic analysis, assays for specific minerals, comparison of composition and structure to surrounding geologic formations, and so on. Sometimes the appropriateness of a particular analytic method is clear, as when you are given a method for analyzing problems of force and motion in physics or are asked to analyze the grammatical structure of a sentence. At other times the choice of method is based on a hunch, as when you *think* that a particular poem's effect depends on metaphors. If you then notice that several metaphors are repeated in the poem, you are more sure that you have a useful approach.

Each mode of analysis identifies specific procedures that make particular elements visible or accessible. Chemical analyses require precise laboratory procedures for preparing a sample, adding reagents, and measuring results. If you have decided to explore the economic situation of the voters in the district, you need to get appropriate economic data and carry out certain statistical procedures. Having decided that you want to look at the conflict of characters in a play, you identify the opposing concerns of the characters and the specific moments of conflict that occur on stage.

Some methods of analysis are so well defined that all the steps are predetermined, whereas others require more creativity. With certain well-known chemical procedures, the results will follow unproblematically if all the steps are followed. However, when you are given substances whose structure we only partly understand, you have to bring to bear all you know about the subject to make sense of the clues. Then you may need to create further analytical procedures to develop new conclusions. In analyzing poems, political situations, or human psychology — where each situation is different and complex — you almost always have to move beyond familiar, defined procedures.

Each level of analysis involves working with identifiable aspects or parts, isolating those parts from each other, and seeing the specifics of each of the parts. If you are working with the mineral components of a geologic sample, you identify what the various components are and the amount of each in the sample. In working with the metaphors of a poem, you identify the different strains of metaphor in the poem, then how frequently, in what places, and with what effect each kind of metaphor is used. In working with the socioeconomic background of voters, you identify what categories you place the voters in and how many belong in each.

An analysis may require several levels or aspects of examination. Having seen a problem or issue at one level, you may decide to look more deeply to find what you need. Thus, after looking at the current socioeconomic status of voters, you may decide that no clear pattern of voting emerges. However, when you look deeper into the voters' past and economic situation and their attitude toward the future, you find that people who believe they can become middle class tend to vote for middle-class interests. You may also want to explore some related aspects, such as the voters' religious background and ethnic affiliation, to see how they affect attitudes toward economic advancement and thus political loyalties.

Frequently the analysis takes something apart and then puts the parts back together to show how they make up the whole. After having found the components and percentages of some chemicals, you may need to consider what happens when they are brought together. You may find that several variables influence a voter; but to understand how any one voter votes, you will have to look at how socioeconomic status, perception of mobility, religion, ethnicity, education, and many other variables come together in a single voting choice.

Usually a theory underlies the analysis. Each analysis creates a certain picture of how something works or how it is composed. Many different kinds of pictures can be drawn for one object. The analysis of geologic formations, for example, is based on beliefs that are not immediately evident and have not necessarily been believed for all time, such as that the earth is billions of years old and has been formed in a process of cooling down, that there is an interior movement in a fluid center, and that there is surface movement of large plates. If you believe in Freudian psychology, which connects early experience, repressed emotions, and current symbolic expressions like dreams and jokes, you will analyze dreams differently than if you believe that dreams are the overflow of cognitive processes or messages from beyond the earth.

When there is a current debate or division over which of several theories is strongest, several types of analyses may go on simultaneously. One group of political scientists may study the symbols of political culture, others may examine group affiliations and interests, and still others may study only economics. Each group believes that its theory explains all political processes. When favored theories change, the kind of analysis generally practiced also changes. In literary and other cultural studies in the middle of the century, people believed that texts operated within themselves, so most analyses were confined to what appeared on the page or in the picture. Today many strong theories have emerged making connections among power, politics, social organization, and the objects of culture, so that now analyses often reach into the social, political, and economic context of each text or picture.

Analysis in the Classroom

Because analysis is so crucial to academic disciplines and professional activity, in most fields much emphasis is placed on analysis. In almost all fields you will be doing substantial analyses by the time you take upper-division courses. The analysis may be carried out in classroom activity, as in discussions or lab work. Frequently, however, you will analyze something with a group or by yourself and then present your analysis in written form. The analysis may be connected with data you have gathered or with data already presented, as in a case study (see Chapter 14).

Depending on the style of the discipline and the teaching strategy of the teacher, the analytical methods may be more or less clearly explained. On one extreme, teachers list specific procedures that must be followed and then supervise you, as in statistical analysis within economics. Others use informal discussion using a variety of analytical approaches, as in a literature class where the teacher talks about short stories in a variety of ways but never explicitly says what those are. Open discussion, directed by a few teacher questions, may give you practice in these methods, but they still are never laid out as an explicit method or formulaic set of procedures. In the middle are situations where the lecture or discussion examines a case in detail and provides a model, or where the instructor, in discussing the implications of a theory, uses that theory to analyze a case in class discussion. Sometimes the instructor sets up a problem and asks students to develop their own method of analysis.

Group work frequently requires developing some appropriate method of analysis of the project so that you will develop common ways of seeing the issues and coordinating your perception, observation, ideas, and work. Also, the group needs to break the project into parts for different people to work on at different times. The more deeply you analyze the task and issues at hand, the more deeply you will share a way of seeing what you are doing, and the more effectively you will work together.

ssignments

ANALYZING ANALYSES

1. Describe some of the common types of analyses in a discipline you are studying or a profession in which you are interested. Are the analyses given specific names? What do they find out? For what purpose? What might happen if the analysis is incorrect? In what ways might the analysis go wrong? What kinds of data or phenomena are analyzed? What are the methods of analysis? Are specific terms used to identify the parts revealed in the analyses? At what point do people entering that profession or discipline start learning how to do these analyses? How are they taught?

2. Describe analytical tasks you have been asked to do in classrooms. What was the class? What kind of analysis was it? What kinds of data or phenomena did you analyze? What were you trying to find out? How did you carry out the analysis? How precisely did the instructor define what you were to do, and what did you have to improvise on your own? What special terminology did you use? What did you learn?

3. Compare the kinds of analysis you have done in literature classes with the kinds you have done in social science classes and in science and math classes.

4. Examine the following three passages of analysis: one from the biological sciences, one from the physical sciences, and one from the humanities. Then choose one to describe and analyze in a short essay that answers the following questions: What is being analyzed? What is the writer trying to show or find out by the analysis? What are the categories or parts used in the analysis? What specific data are associated with each category or part? What does the separation of the parts indicate about what is being analyzed? Does the writer try to show connections among the parts, and, if so, what are they?

A. Biology: Samuel Scudder

It was more than fifteen years ago that I entered the laboratory of Professor Agassiz, and told him I had enrolled my name in the Scientific School as a student of natural history. He asked me a few questions about my object in coming, my antecedents generally, the mode in which I afterwards proposed to use the knowledge I might acquire, and, finally, whether I wished to study any special branch. To the latter I replied that, while I wished to be well grounded in all departments of zoology, I purposed to devote myself specially to insects.

"When do you wish to begin?" he asked.

"Now," I replied.

Louis Agassiz
(1807–1873), noted
for his study of fossil
fish, was the leading
American naturalist
of his day.

This seemed to please him, and with an energetic "Very well!"
he reached from a shelf a huge jar of specimens in yellow alcohol.
"Take this fish," he said, "and look at it; we call it a haemulon; by
and by I will ask what you have seen."

With that he left me, but in a moment returned with explicit
instructions as to the care of the object entrusted to me.

"No man is fit to be a naturalist," said he, "who does not know
how to take care of specimens."

I was to keep the fish before me in a tin tray, and occasionally
moisten the surface with alcohol from the jar, always taking care
to replace the stopper tightly. Those were not the days of ground-

glass stoppers and elegantly shaped exhibition jars; all the old students will recall the huge necklace glass bottles with their leaky, wax-besmeared corks, half eaten by insects, and begrimed with cellar dust. Entomology was a cleaner science than ichthyology, but the example of the Professor, who had unhesitatingly plunged to the bottom of the jar to produce the fish, was infectious; and though this alcohol had a "very ancient and fishlike smell," I really dared not show any aversion within these sacred precincts, and treated the alcohol as though it were pure water. Still I was conscious of a passing feeling of disappointment, for gazing at a fish did not commend itself to an ardent entomologist. My friends at home, too, were annoyed when they discovered that no amount of eau-de-Cologne would drown the perfume which haunted me like a shadow.

In ten minutes I had seen all that could be seen in that fish, and started in search of the Professor — who had, however, left the Museum; and when I returned, after lingering over some of the odd animals stored in the upper apartment, my specimen was dry all over. I dashed the fluid over the fish as if to resuscitate the beast from a fainting fit, and looked with anxiety for a return of the normal sloppy appearance. This little excitement over, nothing was to be done but to return to a steadfast gaze at my mute companion. Half an hour passed — an hour — another hour; the fish began to look loathsome. I turned it over and around; looked it in the face — ghastly; from behind, beneath, above, sideways, at a three-quarters view — just as ghastly. I was in despair; at an early hour I concluded that lunch was necessary; so, with infinite relief, the fish was carefully replaced in the jar, and for an hour I was free.

On my return, I learned that Professor Agassiz had been at the Museum, but had gone, and would not return for several hours. My fellow-students were too busy to be disturbed by continued conversation. Slowly I drew forth that hideous fish, and with a feeling of desperation again looked at it. I might not use a magnifying-glass; instruments of all kinds were interdicted. My two hands, my two eyes, and the fish: it seemed a most limited field. I pushed my finger down its throat to feel how sharp the teeth were. I began to count the scales in the different rows, until I was convinced that was nonsense. At last a happy thought struck me — I would draw the fish; and now with surprise I began to discover new features in the creature. Just then the Professor returned.

"That is right," said he; "a pencil is one of the best of eyes. I am glad to notice, too, that you keep your specimen wet, and your bottle corked."

With these encouraging words, he added:

"Well, what is it like?"

He listened attentively to my brief rehearsal of the structure of parts whose names were still unknown to me: the fringed gill-arches and movable operculum; the pores of the head, fleshy lips and lidless eyes; the lateral line, the spinous fins and forked tail; the compressed and arched body. When I finished, he waited as if expecting more, and then, with an air of disappointment:

"You have not looked very carefully; why," he continued more earnestly, "you haven't even seen one of the most conspicuous features of the animal, which is plainly before your eyes as the fish itself; look again, look again!" and he left me to my misery.

I was piqued; I was mortified. Still more of that wretched fish! But now I set myself to my task with a will, and discovered one new thing after another, until I saw how just the Professor's criticism had been. The afternoon passed quickly; and when, towards its close, the Professor inquired:

"Do you see it yet?"

"No," I replied, "I am certain I do not, but I see how little I saw before."

"That is next best," said he, earnestly, "but I won't hear you now; put away your fish and go home; perhaps you will be ready with a better answer in the morning. I will examine you before you look at the fish."

This was disconcerting. Not only must I think of my fish all night, studying, without the object before me, what this unknown but most visible feature might be; but also, without reviewing my discoveries, I must give an exact account of them the next day. I had a bad memory; so I walked home by Charles River in a distracted state, with my two perplexities.

The cordial greeting from the Professor the next morning was reassuring; here was a man who seemed to be quite as anxious as I that I should see for myself what he saw.

"Do you perhaps mean," I asked, "that the fish has symmetrical sides with paired organs?"

His thoroughly pleased "Of course! Of course!" repaid the wakeful hours of the previous night. After he had discoursed most happily and enthusiastically — as he always did — upon the importance of this point, I ventured to ask what I should do next.

"Oh, look at your fish!" he said, and left me again to my own devices. In a little more than an hour he returned, heard my new catalogue.

"That is good, that is good!" he repeated; "but that is not all; go on"; and so for three long days he placed that fish before my eyes, forbidding me to look at anything else, or to use any artificial aid. "Look, look, look," was his repeated injunction.

This was the best entomological lesson I ever had — a lesson whose influence has extended to the details of every subsequent study; a legacy the Professor had left to me, as he has left it to so many others, of inestimable value, which we could not buy, with which we cannot part.

A year afterward, some of us were amusing ourselves with chalking outlandish beasts on the Museum blackboard. We drew prancing starfishes; frogs in mortal combat; hydra-headed worms; stately crawfishes, standing on their tails, bearing aloft umbrellas; and grotesque fishes with gaping mouths and staring eyes. The Professor came in shortly after, and was as amused as any at our experiments. He looked at the fishes.

"Haemulons, every one of them," he said; "Mr. _____ drew them."

True; and to this day, if I attempt a fish, I can draw nothing but haemulons.

The fourth day, a second fish of the same group was placed beside the first, and I was bidden to point out the resemblances and differences between the two; another and another followed, until the entire family lay before me, and a whole legion of jars covered the table and surrounding shelves; the odor had become a pleasant perfume; and even now, the sight of an old, six-inch, worm-eaten cork brings fragrant memories.

The whole group of haemulons was thus brought in review; and, whether engaged upon the dissection of the internal organs, the preparation and examination of the bony framework, or the description of the various parts, Agassiz's training method of observing facts and their orderly arrangement was ever accompanied by the urgent exhortation not to be content with them.

"Facts are stupid things," he would say, "until brought into connection with some general law."

At the end of eight months, it was almost with reluctance that I left these friends and turned to insects; but what I had gained by this outside experience has been of greater value than years of later investigation in my favorite groups.

Source: Samuel Scudder, "Take this Fish and Look at It."

B. Chemistry: C. Carl Sagan

Let us approach a much more modest question: not whether we can know the universe or the Milky Way Galaxy or a star or a world. Can we know, ultimately and in detail, a grain of salt? Consider one microgram of table salt, a speck just barely large enough for someone with keen eyesight to make out without a microscope. In that grain of salt there are about 10^{16} sodium and chlorine atoms. This is a 1 followed by 16 zeros, 10 million billion atoms. If we wish to know a grain of salt, we must know at least the three-dimensional positions of each of these atoms. (In fact, there is much more to be known — for example, the nature of the forces between the atoms — but we are making only a modest calculation.) Now, is this number more or less than the number of things which the brain can know?

How much *can* the brain know? There are perhaps 10^{11} neurons in the brain, the circuit elements and switches that are responsible in their electrical and chemical activity for the functioning of our minds. A typical brain neuron has perhaps a thousand little wires, called dendrites, which connect it with its fellows. If, as seems likely, every bit of information in the brain corresponds to one of these connections, the total number of things knowable by the brain is no more than 10^{14}, one hundred trillion. But this number is only one percent of the number of atoms in our speck of salt.

So in this sense the universe is intractable, astonishingly immune to any human attempt at full knowledge. We cannot on this level understand a grain of salt, much less the universe.

But let us look a little more deeply at our microgram of salt. Salt happens to be a crystal in which, except for defects in the structure of the crystal lattice, the position of every sodium and chlorine atom is predetermined. If we could shrink ourselves into this crystalline world, we would see rank upon rank of atoms in an ordered array, a regularly alternating structure — sodium, chlorine, sodium, chlorine, specifying the sheet of atoms we are standing on and all the sheets above us and below us. An absolutely pure crystal of salt could have the position of every atom specified by something like 10 bits of information.* This would not strain the information-carrying capacity of the brain.

If the universe had natural laws that governed its behavior to the same degree of regularity that determines a crystal of salt, then, of course, the universe would be knowable. Even if there were many such laws, each of considerable complexity, human beings might have the capability to understand them all. Even if such knowledge exceeded the information-carrying capacity of the brain, we might store the additional information outside our bodies — in books, for example, or in computer memories — and still, in some sense, know the universe.

*Chlorine is a deadly poison gas employed on European battlefields in World War I. Sodium is a corrosive metal which burns upon contact with water. Together they make a placid and unpoisonous material, table salt. Why each of these substances has the properties it does is a subject called chemistry, which requires more than 10 bits of information to understand.

Source: Carl Sagan, *Broca's Brain*, New York: Random House, 1979, pp. 17–19.

C. English: Robert Scholes

The field of English is organized by two primary gestures of differentiation, dividing and redividing the field by binary opposition. First of all, we divide the field into two categories: literature and non-literature. This is, of course, an invidious distinction, for we mark those texts labeled literature as good or important and dismiss those non-literary texts as beneath our notice. This division is traversed and supported by another, which is just as important, though somewhat less visible. We distinguish between the production and the consumption of texts, and, as might be expected in a society like ours, we privilege consumption over production, just as the larger culture privileges the consuming class over the producing class (as noted, for example, by Paula Johnson in "Writing Programs and the English Department").

One further distinction and our basic structure will be complete. This is the least obvious, the most problematic, and, therefore, perhaps the most important. We distinguish between what is "real" and what is "academic" to our own disadvantage. At some level we accept the myth of the ivory tower and secretly despise our own activities as trivial unless we can link them to a "reality" outside academic life. Thus we may consume "literature," which comes from outside our classrooms, but we cannot produce literature in classes, nor can we teach its production. Instead, we teach something called "creative writing"— the production of pseudo-literary texts.

The proper consumption of literature we call "interpretation," and the teaching of this skill, like the displaying of it in academic papers, articles, and books, is our greatest glory. The production of literature is regarded as beyond us, to the point where even those writers who are hired by academies to teach creative writing are felt to dwindle into academics themselves, and we suspect that their work may only be creative writing, too. How often are the works of the faculty of the Iowa Writers Workshop studied in the classrooms of the Iowa English department?

The consumption of non-literature can be taught. It is called "reading," and most college and university English departments are content to hope that it has been dealt with in secondary school — a hope that seems less and less well founded as we go on. But actual non-literature is perceived as grounded in the realities of existence, where it is produced in response to personal or socio-economic imperatives and therefore justifies itself functionally. By its very usefulness, its non-literariness, it eludes our grasp. It can be read but not interpreted, because it supposedly lacks those secret-hidden-deeper meanings so dear to our pedagogic hearts. Nor can it be produced when cut off from the exi-

---

FIGURE 9.1

PRODUCTION	TEXTS	CONSUMPTION
	literature	interpretation
creative writing	pseudo-literature	
	non-literature	reading
composition	pseudo-non-literature	

Source: Robert Scholes, *Textual Power,* New Haven: Yale University Press, 1985, pp. 5–7.

gencies of its real situations. What *can* be produced within the academy is an unreal version of it, "pseudo-non-literature," which is indeed produced in an appalling volume. We call the production of this stuff "composition."

✑✑ Analysis and Your Authority

The more a class provides opportunities for analysis, the more authority you gain as a participant in the discipline. The teacher then is no longer the single authority in the classroom, because you will have your own analytical results to add. As you gain skill in disciplinary practices, your responses include disciplinary perception within your personal vision. You go beyond being able to identify examples of concepts out in the world to seeing how they are composed and work. You are then in a position to argue for the validity of one set of findings over another. You will be responsible for presenting your analyses as conceptually precise, theoretically sound, methodologically appropriate and careful, and insightfully creative (see Chapter 15).

At this point the instructor serves as a coach, helping you see and articulate stronger perceptions about those phenomena you study. Although you still to some extent write to demonstrate skill and accomplishment, your main goal is to produce statements of relevance. Your relationships with your classmates also change as you become colleagues sharing disciplined perceptions of events. You are in a position to share insights with each other, help each other see new things, and argue with each other over findings and interpretations.

These changing relationships change the way you write. You now present serious interpretations of events to show and persuade others of something they might not yet have seen themselves. Your statements contribute to the learning of the entire class. You have the opportunity both to gain increased respect and to influence others by presenting persuasive and insightful accounts of the objects studied. But this also puts you more on a spot, as you have to present things more as you see it. This changing relationship also pertains to the kinds of writing discussed in the remaining chapters of this book: investigating, synthesizing, problem solving, and arguing — also all activities carried out by full professionals in your field.

Skillful Practice Is More Than a Set of Rules

Your instructor in each subject will provide guidance in setting up analytical tasks and helping you accomplish them. Since the tasks, instructions, and procedures will vary from discipline to discipline and from problem to problem, you should attend closely to explicit instructions as well as to indirect hints. Some special skills may not be fully and clearly articulated in instructions and must be figured out by just watching the instructor.

As mentioned before, the analytical procedures appropriate for a particular situation may be quite strictly defined by disciplinary standards or may hardly be defined at all. Various levels and kinds of guidance fall in between. There are many reasons for this variation, including the way problems are formulated in the field, the availability of tools, the reigning theories, the kind of arguments, and the range of concerns in the field, and as you learn more it is worth inquiring into the reasons why your field follows its particular analytical practices.

If you are given a wider freedom in selecting, developing, or finding novel ways of carrying out your analysis, you need to become even more aware of the choices you are making. It may be useful to discuss with your instructor the consequences of proceeding one way or another. These more open-ended analytical situations give you greater creativity and allow you to use more of what you know. In even the most highly developed and rule-governed field, there is always some open area for novelty and advance, and those who use this opportunity to become leaders in the field.

Computer Tools and Analysis

Computer tools aid analysis in many fields. These tools include spreadsheets for organizing data and graphing programs for displaying data in many formats. Statistical packages allow you to find correlations among numerical data and control for the effect of different variables. Other computer tools help in finding patterns in texts, analyzing the motions of pole vaulters, or noticing at a glance the heat absorption of different parts of the earth as monitored by satellite.

These remarkable tools allow you to deal with massive amounts of data in coherent and intelligible ways, as well as in alternative configurations. They allow you to see patterns and correlations that would be inconceivable without modern computing. Nonetheless, it is up to you to make sense of the data and to understand what the tool is doing. If you don't understand, you can be faced with mountains of data and calculations that make no sense. By simply loading numbers or visual images in a computer, pushing some buttons, and then looking for any result that might come out at the other end, you are guessing about what is going on and in danger of oversimplifying the issues. You may be looking at entirely the wrong things, just because the computer makes certain calculations easy. For this reason it is always important to understand what kind of calculations the machine is doing and how to interpret the results.

WRITING FOR REFLECTION

1. Reflect on or describe an incident when you had to analyze a problem in a class, on the job, or in your family.

2. Describe an area where you are able to analyze problems or events easily. You may be able to analyze the recipe of a dish you eat or what happens in a football play, what makes a successful party, or what has caused your car to break down. In describing the kind of analysis you regularly do, tell what kind of information you gather, what issues you look for, and what categories you use to make sense of the information. Describe how your analysis goes beyond gathering data to helping you see new things.

REVIEWING WRITING PROCESSES

Planning to Write

Like most ventures in life, successful writing requires advance planning. Some of the most important work that writers do occurs before they write a single word. Many of the chapters of this book, such as this chapter, offer specific advice to help you plan the particular kind of writing described in that chapter. There are, however, some general principles that apply to most writing situations.

Before you begin a paper, check that you have selected an appropriate topic, thought of the main points you want to make, worked through the arguments that will support these points, and decided on an organizational framework that will present these ideas effectively to your audience. Sometimes appropriate structures are suggested in the assignment, but more often you will analyze your main assertions and decide for yourself how to arrange and present them.

Imagine, for example, that your instructor has assigned a paper comparing or contrasting the use of color in two different paintings. You might decide to treat the first painting in the first half of the paper and the second painting in the second half. This would allow you to construct strong arguments about both paintings and examine internal comparisons within each work. Or you might want to compare one element in the first painting with a similar element in the second and then to return to a second element in the first. This would allow you to go back and forth between the paintings in a "Ping-Pong" fashion and compare different features more directly than the first kind of paper.

There are many possible ways to organize your information for any given paper, and no one way is inherently better than any other. However, when you consider the material you wish to present and the objectives you wish to achieve, certain patterns will seem more advantageous than others. For this reason it is important to spend time considering how you want to present your material.

The time that you spend formulating a plan will pay off in several important ways. First, it will give you a strong sense of purpose and confidence. When you start a paper with a strong sense of your overall structure in mind, you will always know what you have to do next and how long it will probably take to get there. Second, planned writing takes much less time than haphazard writing, since you will not have to spend time groping for ideas or following dead ends. Finally, and most importantly, a good organizational framework allows you to present your ideas in a more organized, logical fashion to your audience. Since most college teachers place a great deal of value on organization, good planning is an essential part of successful writing.

❧ Writing and Analyzing

When you carry out analytical tasks in a class, there is almost always some element of simply practicing a skill and demonstrating to your teacher what you can do. When this is your goal, you explain as much of your procedure and thinking as you can so that your instructor can see how you carried out the task and can suggest ways to find out more or analyze the facts more precisely.

Sometimes you may have a more personal stake in presenting your analysis. You may be convinced that your analysis of bilingual education has some important implications for policy, or that your analysis of a short story reveals important truths about emotions. In this case you still need to present your reasoning and procedures clearly to persuade readers of your view, but you do not need to exhibit as much of your backstage thinking for coaching and guidance. The analytical procedure becomes a way of generating evidence and findings rather than an end in itself.

The processes of analyzing and writing up your analysis are closely linked. When you are first thinking about what to analyze or how to go about it, you are also aware that you will be producing an analytical statement at the end of the process. You are thinking about all the things you need to do so that you will have appropriate material and ideas to write about. The more clearly you know what you want to put in your final statement, the more you will know what you need to do to carry out the analysis — everything from what kinds of procedures you will follow and what details you will want to record, to how much you need to think through the theoretical implications of your method and findings or how broadly you need to investigate alternative methods or objections people may raise.

By the time you write your first draft, you are likely to have many formulations written that you can use — perhaps early journal entries about what you will do, descriptions of the object you are studying, notes from your data collection, ideas you have come up with by talking with others, or outlines and sketches. When you start to draw these pieces together, you may find that you need to rethink the connection of the parts or perhaps do some more digging into further details or follow-up issues. So there is constant interaction between taking your object of study apart and putting your ideas and information together in writing. Analysis and writing go hand in hand.

The following section presents general guidelines for producing an analysis in all courses. Afterwards, samples from analytical essays in a variety of courses are presented.

✆✇ General Procedures for Analysis

These guidelines are presented in very general terms to allow you to adapt them to any situation that requires analysis. As you work with these guidelines in different situations, you will develop a more concrete sense of how analysis works.

1. Understand your aim.
2. Think about the object or kind of object you need to analyze to accomplish that task.
3. Identify, define, and if possible isolate the object of analysis.

4. Identify an appropriate method of analysis.
5. Examine the object carefully in light of the task and method, trying to understand it and gathering relevant data.
6. Establish the specific categories suggested by your problem and method.
7. See how the categories apply to your object.
8. Isolate and record relevant details according to the categories or process.
9. Examine the reorganized data carefully to answer your underlying question, whether it is to understand how the object is constructed, to explain how the event unfolds, or to identify what went wrong.
10. Formulate your analytical conclusions.
11. Develop further implications and conclusions.
12. Sketch out an outline.
13. Write the first draft.
14. Revise to highlight the most important issues for the task and make clear the reasoning that ties the sections together.

❧❧ USEFUL CONCEPTS FROM RHETORIC

Genre

Genre means a type, as in a type of writing, a type of movie, or a type of song. We all recognize many types of things. In listening to the radio, from the first few bars of a song you can recognize if it is a soft-rock love song or a heavy-metal headbanger. You can guess what much of the song will sound like, and you know the kinds of words that will be in the lyrics, the kinds of chords the music will use, and the kinds of special ornaments and improvisations the soloists will add to the basic music. You would be surprised to hear heavy-metal lyrics to a soft-rock sound. Even more, you know the kinds of feelings and experience you will get from listening to the music, and you can make a quick decision about whether you want to listen.

Text genres are the same way. By recognizing the kind of text you are reading, you can make good guesses about the kind of language and details that will be used, the kind of tasks that will be accomplished, and the kind of organization the text will use. You also know something about how the writer is relating to you and what kind of responses the text will try to evoke. You can then focus your mind, mood, and expectations so as to understand, interpret, think about, and appreciate what you are reading. For example, as you read through the morning newspaper, even though all the articles appear in the same publication, you rapidly shift your frame of mind as you quickly notice whether you are reading a news story, a news analysis, an editorial, a human interest story, an entertainment story, a sports story, a love-lorn column, a classified automobile advertisement, or any one of the dozen other genres that appear every day.

Similarly, as a writer, by identifying the genre you are working in, you can focus on the tasks, language, details, organization, and other features that you will use. You can get a strong sense of the kind of thinking you need to do and the kind of text you are trying to produce. If you are writing a letter to your friend from high school days, you immediately set out on a different kind of work and in a different mood than if you are writing an analysis of a short story for your literature class.

This textbook in its different chapters describes many of the typical genres students work in: journals, summaries, personal experience papers, analyses, library research reports, and so on. Nonetheless, even within these types disciplines establish particular varieties. You can immediately recognize if you are reading a psychological analysis of a social problem or an engineering analysis of an electrical problem, and not only because they are using different words.

To improve your ability to work in the specific forms of writing in your major, you should examine the various genres used in that field, both at the student and the professional level, to figure out what makes them distinctive. What kinds of tasks do they accomplish? What kinds of language do they use? How are they organized? What kinds of details, illustrations, or evidence do they present? What kinds of reasoning do they display? The more rapidly and precisely you can identify the kinds of things you are reading and writing, the better you can focus your work and the more intelligently you can communicate within the forms appropriate to your field. Ultimately, too, you can decide whether any of the standard forms are too restricting in some way or don't accomplish what you feel needs accomplishing. Then you can try to change or combine genres to go in new directions while still meeting the needs and expectations of people who will be reading what you write.

☙ Writing an Analytical Essay

The form for reporting analyses varies from discipline to discipline and situation to situation. The following general guidelines, however, may help you identify what you need to include.

1. Early in the essay, identify the problem or task you are addressing, the specific object, event, or other phenomenon you are analyzing, and the method of analysis you have used.
2. Also early in the essay, discuss why it is important to study the object or event and what you hope to learn from it.
3. Before you begin the full analysis, provide specific details about the method you use, from the way you gathered and recorded your data to the specific procedures for defining categories and assigning elements

to those categories. Make sure you identify all the key steps and describe all the special considerations that were necessary in carrying out the analysis. All analytical categories you will use need to be identified, defined, and discussed. Discuss as well the reasons for the choice of method.

4. Report the problems in carrying out the analysis and difficulties that turned up in the course of work. This is especially important for classroom situations, where instructors need to monitor how you are carrying out the procedures.

5. Report your findings and results, using the analytical categories you defined earlier.

6. Discuss the meaning of your findings and draw conclusions that address the original task or problem.

Sample Analyses from Different Disciplines

The following four opening paragraphs from analytical essays in different disciplines give a sense of the many ways analysis is used in different fields. In reading through them, notice the fundamental problem each analysis is addressing, the categories used to show the parts of the issue or phenomenon, and the way the categories are used to develop a view of the issue or phenomenon.

The fifth sample is a complete analytical essay. The two primary analytical concepts established in the opening paragraph (freedom of religion and separation of church and state) are elaborated by examining constitutional phrasing and supreme court decisions, and then are used to reveal the tension involved in any school prayer controversy.

Literature: An Analysis of Gender in a Pop Song
Claire Richards

The sixties, we have always been told, were a time of radical change and revolution, and nothing contributed to these new radical values more than the music of people like Bob Dylan and the Beatles. However, for all of the radical theories of these pop icons about social justice, their attitudes towards women remained remarkably backward. The songs of the sixties are full of lyrics that justify the objectification and devaluation of women and women's roles. This devaluation of the feminine ranges in tone from the fun-loving celebration of female passivity in "I Wanna Hold Your Hand" by the Beatles to the equation of femininity with Satanic darkness in Led Zeppelin's "Dazed and Confused." Somewhere between these two extremes, Bob Dylan's influential pop anthem "Like a Rolling Stone" maintains an attitude of

contempt for women by continually associating traditional women's roles with dishonesty and deception.

Chemistry: An Analysis of What Happens When Metal Corrodes
Andrew Mancey

Most people know that many metals, when exposed to
moisture, air, or other environmental factors, will
corrode. Corrosion can come in the form of rust on iron
or steel, black tarnish on silver, or the green patina
that often covers things made of brass or copper. Less
well known, perhaps, are the chemical reactions that
cause these easily observable effects. All three forms
of corrosion result from the chemical processes of oxi-
dation and reduction that take elements from the atmosphere and combine them with elements in the metals in
order to produce new chemical compositions.

Business: An Analysis of a Marketing Research Report
Ken Fuscolini

Recently, the Wasatch Feed Factory, a large farm-supply
concern, hired a market research firm to contact 500 of
its past customers for a customer satisfaction survey.
The data collected by this survey indicate that, while
very few consumers were dissatisfied with Wasatch's service, not very many felt any customer loyalty to the firm
either. In the following analysis, we will examine statistical responses in three key areas — product satisfaction, price, and service — in an attempt to suggest ways
that Wasatch might successfully retain more customers.

Earth Sciences: An Analysis of an Earthquake
Patrice Ferrin

Every year there are nearly a million earthquakes in
the world. The overwhelming majority of these are too
small to be detected without sophisticated equipment;
however, large earthquakes have been among the most
devastating natural disasters in the world's history,
releasing energy many times in excess of that released
by the most powerful nuclear weapon. While the details
of nuclear fission have occupied scientists for years,
the physical mechanics of an earthquake are actually
quite simple: 1) the heat coming from the earth's interior puts tremendous pressure on rocks in the earth's

crust; 2) this stress causes the earth's crust to break
and slip; and 3) shock waves from this slippage travel
along the earth's surface at high speeds.

Political Science: An Analysis of Prayer in School: Constitutional Rights in Conflict
Andre D'Onville

When the United States Supreme Court first ruled that
students could not offer prayers in public schools, religious students and their parents began protesting the
infringement of their rights. In recent years, restor-
ing this "right" to pray in schools has become one of
the main items on the agenda of the religious right. On
the other side of the political spectrum, liberal
groups such as the ACLU have concentrated on preventing
any prayers in public or educational settings. They argue that the most important right in question is not
the right of religious students to pray, but the right
of all students not to have religious ideals forced
upon them. The issue of school prayer has required the
government to negotiate some kind of compromise between
two legitimate but conflicting Constitutional principles: the separation of Church and State and the right
to freedom of religion.

Both of the rights in question can be found in the
First Amendment to the Constitution, which states, in
part, that "Congress shall make no law respecting an
establishment of religion or prohibiting the free exercise thereof." This single sentence contains two distinct and important individual clauses. The first, or
the "establishment clause," mandates that the state not
be permitted to advocate or mandate any specific religious beliefs; the second, the "free exercise clause,"
requires that the government respect the right of each
individual to worship — or not to worship — according to
the dictates of their own consciences.

School prayer proponents base their arguments on the
latter of these two clauses. The well-known conservative talk-show host Rush Limbaugh, for example, argues
that the free-exercise clause of the First Amendment
precludes any prohibition on voluntary prayer in
school, or anywhere else for that matter (282). This is
so, Limbaugh maintains, because praying is part of the
way that many people exercise religion, and, as long as
they are not trying to force these beliefs on anyone
else, they should be able to exercise their religion

anywhere. To some extent, the Supreme Court agrees with this interpretation: in the 1991 *Lamb's Chapel* v. *Center Moriches School District* decision, the Court ruled that religious groups must be free to use school facilities for religious purposes — including prayer — on the same terms that other clubs and community groups use them. Thus, if a school allows a group of students to come together voluntarily during non-school hours and play chess or discuss politics, it must also allow them to meet in the same way to read the Bible or say prayers.

However, when schools do anything to endorse or encourage prayers, they run the risk of violating the establishment clause of the First Amendment, which forms the Constitutional basis for the Separation of Church and State. Originally, this clause was meant to prevent the federal government or any state from establishing, supporting, or requiring attendance at a state Church. As America has grown more culturally and religiously diverse, however, the Supreme Court has consistently ruled that the establishment clause prevents any state encouragement of or support for any beliefs that favor one religion or belief system over another.

In 1962, the Court ruled in *Engle* v. *Vitale* that official prayers at public schools violated the First Amendment's Establishment Clause by requiring non-Christian and non-religious students to participate in a religious activity of specific faiths. In 1985, the Court ruled in *Wallace* v. *Jaffree* that even voluntary "moments of silence" violate the free exercise clause since they tacitly encourage prayers and could alienate or embarrass students who prefer not to pray. This does not mean that students cannot pray silently while they are in school. Spontaneous individual prayers have always been protected by the Constitution — wherever they occur. However, teachers and school officials cannot subsidize, support, offer, or encourage prayers of any kind during school hours. To do so, the Supreme Court has ruled, would violate the Constitution's prohibition against the establishment of religion.

The establishment clause and the free exercise clause represent two distinct and often conflicting attitudes about the relationship between religion and government. By including both of these clauses in the Constitution, its framers required future generations to walk a thin line between respecting all religions and supporting none. The debate over school prayer requires us to look at both parts of the First Amendment and attempt to negotiate a position that protects the

```
broadest spectrum of individual interests. Such negoti-
ations are never easy, and they rarely result in total
victory for either position, but they are an essential
part of the process of democratic rule that our Consti-
tution outlines.
```

Thinking About Student Writing

1. In each of the five opening paragraphs, what is the problem being addressed? What is the phenomenon being examined? What categories are used to break up the phenomenon? How do the categories help address the problem?

2. In the political science essay on school prayer, what are the two rights analyzed as being in conflict? What is the basis or origin of each of these rights? How have these rights evolved in the history of the United States? How do various people argue that those rights apply to school prayer?

3. What Supreme Court cases concerning school prayer are discussed in the essay by Andre D'Onville? How do these cases relate to the earlier analysis of conflicting rights?

4. What conclusions does Andre D'Onville draw from his analysis? Do you agree with him? To what extent and in what way has his analysis made clear to you the issues at stake in the school prayer controversy? Do you see other relevant issues raised by this controversy that are not included in his analysis? How might you analyze this controversy?

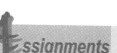

Assignments

ANALYSIS

1. Analyze the general education requirements in your college catalogue. Look at the required courses and formulate some general philosophy that seems to explain the college's choices.

2. Analyze the different notions of romance in two popular songs. Determine each song's attitude about romantic love and show how these attitudes come through in the texts and the music.

3. Look up news articles about a recent presidential or congressional election and analyze the voting patterns or trends that determined the final result.

4. Write a brief, 500-word essay analyzing the effect of television violence on youth culture.

5. Write a journal entry analyzing the way that one class you have taken this quarter has changed the way you think about an issue you have studied.

6. Examine the tables on pages 217–218 concerning employment and wages in the United States. Then develop some analytic questions to use on the data, choose the relevant data, and arrange it according to the categories appropriate to your analytical questions. After analyzing the selected data, write a 500-word essay describing your analysis and what you found. For example, you may be interested in understanding whether the kinds of work that pay best are in the fastest growing segments of the job market. Or you may be interested in comparing the wages of male and female workers in various industries.

Getting Involved Electronically

1. Describe a computer tool that you have found useful or that is used for an area in which you are interested. What does the tool do, and what doesn't it do? What can it tell you, and what does it not tell you? What problems will it solve, and what won't it? For example, if you are examining a writing style analyzer, you might notice that it provides a word count, a sentence length analyzer, and a spell-checker. How do these measures support your writing? How might they mislead you? What do you have to know to use the information the style analyzer provides? What do you need to know about writing that programs don't help you with? What other criteria do you use to analyze and evaluate your writing that are not supported by automated analyzers?

2. For any subject you are now studying or are interested in studying soon, identify some of the computerized tools used in that field. For example, you might look at statistical and graphing programs in the social sciences or economic simulation packages that examine the effect of different economic factors on a situation. In languages you may look at grammar parsing programs. Describe what programs you find, what they do, and how they are used in your subject of interest.

FIGURE 9.2	Employment in the Fastest Growing and Fastest Declining Occupations: 1992 to 2005

OCCUPATION	EMPLOYMENT (1,000)				PERCENT CHANGE 1992-2005		
	1992	2005¹			Low	Moderate	High
		Low	Moderate	High			
Total, all occupations²	121,099	139,007	147,482	154,430	14.8	21.8	27.5
FASTEST GROWING							
Home health aides	347	794	827	835	128.7	138.1	140.6
Human services workers	189	429	445	451	127.6	135.9	139.2
Personal and home care aides	127	283	293	296	122.0	129.8	132.0
Computer engineers and scientists	211	409	447	484	93.9	111.9	129.2
Systems analysts	455	891	956	1,001	95.7	110.1	120.0
Physical and corrective therapy assistants and aides	61	113	118	119	84.6	92.7	95.1
Physical therapists	90	163	170	173	80.2	88.0	91.4
Paralegals	95	166	176	180	75.8	86.1	89.8
Occupational therapy assistants and aides	12	20	21	21	70.5	78.1	80.1
Electronic pagination systems workers	18	29	32	33	65.1	77.9	84.0
Teachers, special education	358	594	625	648	65.9	74.4	81.0
Medical assistants	181	296	308	313	63.5	70.5	73.0
Detectives, except public	59	94	100	104	60.1	70.2	76.8
Correction officers	282	452	479	503	60.0	69.9	78.1
Child care workers	684	1,100	1,135	1,183	60.6	65.8	72.8
Travel agents	115	167	191	196	45.2	65.7	69.9
Radiologic technologists and technicians	162	252	264	267	55.4	62.7	64.6
Nursery (farm) workers	72	110	116	123	53.1	62.0	71.3
Medical records technicians	76	118	123	125	54.4	61.5	63.6
Operations research analysts	45	67	72	75	50.1	61.4	68.0
Occupational therapists	40	61	64	65	52.9	59.6	62.5
Subway and streetcar operators	22	33	35	37	48.1	57.2	64.9
Legal secretaries	280	415	439	447	48.3	57.1	59.9
Teachers, preschool and kindergarten	434	646	669	682	48.9	54.3	57.2
Manicurists	35	54	55	56	51.2	54.1	58.3
EEG technologists	6	9	10	10	46.6	53.8	55.4
Producers, directors, actors, and entertainers	129	190	198	205	47.0	53.5	58.7
Speech-language pathologists and audiologists	73	105	110	113	44.6	51.3	55.7
Flight attendants	93	121	140	144	30.3	51.0	55.5
Guards	803	1,138	1,211	1,255	41.7	50.8	56.2
Nuclear medicine technologists	12	17	18	18	43.1	50.1	51.6
Insurance adjusters, examiners, and investigators	147	205	220	220	39.3	49.1	49.5
Respiratory therapists	74	104	109	110	41.4	48.3	49.9
Psychologists	143	204	212	222	42.1	48.0	54.7
FASTEST DECLINING							
Frame wirers, central office	11	2	3	3	-77.4	-75.3	-74.7
Signal or track switch maintainers	3	1	1	1	-76.6	-74.6	-72.9
Peripheral EDP equipment operators	30	11	12	12	-62.6	-60.2	-59.0
Directory assistance operators	27	12	13	14	-54.9	-50.6	-49.4
Central office operators	48	22	24	24	-54.7	-50.3	-49.1
Station installers and repairers, telephone	40	18	20	20	-54.7	-50.3	-49.1
Portable machine cutters	11	5	6	6	-48.3	-40.1	-39.4
Computer operators, except peripheral equipment	266	151	161	168	-43.2	-39.3	-36.6
Shoe sewing machine operators and tenders	16	9	10	10	-46.3	-38.4	-35.8
Central office and PBX installers and repairers	70	41	45	46	-41.3	-35.6	-34.1
Child care workers, private household	350	220	227	242	-37.1	-35.1	-31.0
Job printers	15	9	10	10	-39.4	-35.0	-33.2
Roustabouts	33	20	22	32	-38.4	-33.2	-2.0
Separating and still machine operators and tenders	21	13	14	15	-37.0	-32.8	-29.8
Cleaners and servants, private household	483	316	326	347	-34.6	-32.5	-28.2
Coil winders, tapers, and finishers	20	12	14	16	-41.2	-32.4	-22.1
Billing, posting, and calculating machine operators	93	62	66	68	-33.6	-29.5	-27.0
Sewing machine operators, garment	556	338	393	396	-39.1	-29.2	-28.7
Compositors and typesetters, precision	11	7	8	8	-30.7	-26.5	-23.3
Data entry keyers, composing	16	11	12	12	-31.7	-26.4	-23.8
Motion picture projectionists	9	7	7	7	-29.3	-25.8	-24.0
Telephone and cable TV line installers and repairers	165	117	125	134	-29.4	-24.4	-18.7
Cutting and slicing machine setters³	94	68	73	76	-28.1	-22.6	-19.5
Watchmakers	9	7	7	8	-26.5	-11.6	-18.4
Tire building machine operators	14	10	11	12	-29.4	-22.3	-19.0
Packaging and filling machine operators and tenders	319	232	248	257	-27.1	-22.3	-19.4
Head sawyers and sawing machine operators and tenders⁴	59	44	46	53	-25.7	-22.3	-10.3
Switchboard operators	239	177	188	194	-25.9	-21.3	-18.8
Farmers	1,088	831	857	914	-23.7	-21.2	-16.0
Machine forming operators and tenders, metal and plastic	155	113	123	133	-27.8	-20.8	-14.3
Cement and gluing machine operators and tenders	35	26	28	30	-25.7	-20.2	-12.7

[1]Based on low, moderate, or high trend assumptions. [2]Included other occupations, not shown separately. [3]Includes operators and tenders. [4]includes setters and set-up operators.
Source: U.S. Bureau of Labor Statistics, *Monthly Labor Review*, November 1993.

FIGURE 9.2	Full Time Wage and Salary Workers—Number and Earnings: 1983 to 1994

CHARACTERISTIC	NUMBER OF WORKERS (1,000)				MEDIAN WEEKLY EARNINGS (Dollars)			
	1983	1985	1990	1994[1]	1983	1985	1990	1994[1]
All workers[2]	**70,976**	**77,002**	**85,082**	**87,379**	**313**	**343**	**415**	**467**
Male	42,309	45,589	49,015	49,992	378	406	485	522
16 to 24 years old	6,702	6,956	6,313	6,040	223	240	283	294
25 years old and over	35,607	38,632	42,702	43,952	406	442	514	576
Female	28,667	31,414	36,068	37,386	252	277	348	399
16 to 24 years old	5,345	5,621	5,001	4,403	197	210	254	276
25 years old and over	23,322	25,793	31,066	32,983	267	296	370	421
White	61,739	66,481	72,637	73,500	319	355	427	484
Male	37,378	40,030	42,563	42,816	387	417	497	547
Female	24,361	26,452	30,075	30,685	254	281	355	408
Black	7,373	8,393	9,642	10,199	261	277	329	371
Male	3,883	4,367	4,909	5,099	293	304	360	400
Female	3,490	4,026	4,733	5,100	231	252	308	346
Hispanic origin[3]	(NA)	(NA)	6,993	8,274	(NA)	(NA)	307	324
Male	(NA)	(NA)	4,410	5,295	(NA)	(NA)	322	343
Female	(NA)	(NA)	2,583	2,979	(NA)	(NA)	280	305
Family relationship:								
Husbands	28,720	30,260	31,326	(NA)	410	455	532	(NA)
Wives	14,884	16,270	18,666	(NA)	257	285	363	(NA)
Women who maintain families	3,948	4,333	5,007	(NA)	256	278	339	(NA)
Men who maintain families	1,331	1,313	1,786	(NA)	377	396	444	(NA)
Other persons in families:								
Men	5,518	6,173	6,434	(NA)	219	238	296	(NA)
Women	4,032	4,309	4,475	(NA)	201	213	271	(NA)
All other men[4]	6,740	7,841	9,468	(NA)	350	380	442	(NA)
All other women[4]	5,803	6,503	7,920	(NA)	274	305	376	(NA)
Occupation, male:								
Managerial and professional	10,312	11,078	12,263	13,021	516	583	731	803
Exec., admin., managerial	5,344	5,835	6,401	6,785	530	593	742	797
Professional specialty	4,967	5,243	5,863	6,236	506	571	720	809
Technical, sales, and administrative support	8,125	8,803	9,596	9,764	385	420	496	548
Tech. and related support	1,428	1,563	1,747	1,638	424	472	570	622
Sales	3,853	4,227	4,666	4,836	389	431	505	575
Admin. support, including clerical	2,844	3,013	3,183	3,289	362	391	440	482
Service	3,723	3,947	4,476	4,784	255	272	320	350
Private household	11	13	12	14	(B)	(B)	(B)	(B)
Protective	1,314	1,327	1,523	1,674	355	391	477	538
Other service	2,398	2,607	2,942	3,096	217	230	273	293
Precision production[5]	9,180	10,026	10,169	9,824	387	408	488	515
Mechanics and repairers	3,418	3,752	3,669	3,593	377	400	477	519
Construction trades	2,966	3,308	3,603	3,407	375	394	480	492
Other	2,796	2,966	2,897	2,824	408	433	510	553
Operators, fabricators and laborers	9,833	10,585	11,257	11,333	308	325	378	406
Machine operators, assemblers, and inspectors	4,138	4,403	4,510	4,469	319	341	391	415
Transportation and material moving	3,199	3,459	3,721	3,854	335	369	418	469
Handlers, equipment cleaners, helpers, and laborers	2,496	2,724	3,027	3,010	251	261	308	319
Farming, forestry, and fishing	1,137	1,150	1,253	1,266	200	216	263	290
Occupation, female:								
Managerial and professional	7,139	8,302	10,595	12,187	357	399	511	592
Exec., admin., managerial	2,772	3,492	4,764	5,548	339	383	485	541
Professional specialty	4,367	4,810	5,831	6,639	367	408	534	623
Technical, sales, and administrative support	13,517	14,622	16,202	15,954	247	269	322	376
Tech. and related support	1,146	1,200	1,470	1,536	299	331	417	466
Sales	2,460	2,929	3,531	3,633	204	226	292	324
Admin. support, including clerical	9,911	10,494	11,202	10,785	248	270	332	374
Service	3,598	3,963	4,531	4,702	173	185	230	257
Private household	267	330	298	311	116	130	171	177
Protective	139	156	216	277	250	278	405	430
Other service	3,139	3,477	4,017	4,115	176	188	231	256
Precision production[5]	784	906	893	970	256	268	316	370
Mechanics and repairers	120	144	139	160	337	392	459	520
Construction trades	45	53	50	52	(B)	265	394	408
Other	619	709	704	758	244	253	300	342
Operators, fabricators and laborers	3,486	3,482	3,675	3,412	204	216	262	293
Machine operators, assemblers, and inspectors	2,853	2,778	2,840	2,563	202	216	260	292
Transportation and material moving	159	189	227	242	253	252	314	361
Handlers, equipment cleaners, helpers, and laborers	474	514	608	608	211	209	250	279
Farming, forestry, and fishing	143	138	171	161	169	185	216	234

B Data not shown where base is less than 50,000. NA Not available. [1]See footnote 2, table 626. [2]Includes other races, not shown separately. [3]Persons of Hispanic origin may be of any race. [4]The majority of these persons are living alone or with nonrelatives. Also included are persons in families where the husband, wife or other person maintaining the family is in the Armed Forces, and persons in unrelated subfamilies. [5]Includes craft and repair.
Source: U.S. Bureau of the Census, *Statistical Abstract of the United States: 1995* (115th edition.) Washington, D.C., 1995. Pages 415, 433; tables 651, 677.

Investigating

Four

10

The Investigative Process

AIMS OF THE CHAPTER

This brief chapter introduces assignments involving library research, field-work, and laboratory experiments. It explains the basic process of gathering information to think about and analyze before coming to a conclusion and making a written statement. These kinds of research assignments are then examined in more detail in Chapters 11 and 12.

KEY POINTS

1. In doing research you find new subjects and events to bring back into class discussion.

2. Research can be done in the library, in the field, and in the laboratory. Each kind of research provides a different kind of information and is carried out according to different procedures.

3. Research projects are driven by underlying questions or problems. The basic issue needs to be focused into an investigative question that will be explored by examining a specific research site. Research design brings together specific concepts, questions, and methods. Results are presented in a format appropriate to the subject.

QUESTIONS TO THINK ABOUT

- When have you found out something on your own that went beyond what was taught in class? How did you find it out? Were you able to present your finding to the teacher or class? In what form did you present it?

- What research have you heard about that you admire? What do you know about how that research was carried out, by whom, and with what specific findings? What do you find interesting or important about that research?

- What research have you heard of that strikes you as silly or useless? Why do you think so? What might the researchers have been thinking that made the research seem worth doing?

- What kind of research is most common for the fields you are studying? Why is this research useful for each of those disciplines or professions? Where do researchers usually go to carry out this research? What methods do these researchers usually use?

- With whom do researchers in your field usually share their research findings — with other researchers, professionals serving clients, the public, or students? What means do these researchers use to present their findings?

Sometimes coursework sends you out of the classroom to look at something. You may observe ecosystems or work on a political campaign. You may interview survivors of a recent disaster or search old newspapers in the library. You may test an electric generator or run a psychological experiment concerning people's visual perception. In each of these cases you investigate the world to understand some aspect of it better, and then you write up the results of that investigation so that you can bring it into the conversation with your instructor, classmates, and academic discipline.

You may also go outside the classroom to help solve real problems — engineering design problems, community social problems, the problem of educating students in the primary and secondary schools, the problem of helping clean up the environment, or the problem of getting a candidate elected. Then you may bring back your solutions to be discussed and examined in class. Presentations of problems and their solution are discussed in Chapter 14. In this and the next two chapters we focus on the processes of investigating, describing, and understanding.

The Three Sites of Investigation: Library, Field, and Laboratory

Three primary ways to find out more about the world outside the classroom are through library work, fieldwork, and laboratory work. These three sources provide the material for most investigations at all levels of the professions and disciplines.

In library work you examine the records of past events and the thoughts and analyses done by others: that is, you draw on how others have represented events and ideas. By using all that is in the library, the classroom discussion can potentially include all that has been discussed by humans. A modern library is truly a wonderful thing, making available the entire history of recorded thought and information.

The Library

In the library, it is easy to get lost in piles of words and books or in avalanches of electronic data available on CD-ROM and on-line databases. But these records are not just bits of printed paper and electronic bits; they are the recorded observations and thoughts of observers, scholars, researchers, and thinkers throughout history, as well as the statistics and facts collected by governments and other organizations, the collected public representations of news in magazines and newspapers, and the collected debates over politics. Even the smallest college library has a wide selection of such materials, and the larger university libraries are amazing collections of all that we have learned and known, along with those things we no longer believe. Moreover, with microfilm, CD-ROM, and on-line databases, even small libraries have access to extensive collections. Finally, through interlibrary loan you have access to the resources of major research libraries no matter how small your library is. The library may look like just another building with a lot of books, but a great portion of the world is represented there, as gathered and drawn by the people most involved in making, observing, and thinking about that world.

The Field

In fieldwork you gather data about real events as they unfold using the methods and stance of your discipline. You go out into the messy world —

Libraries offer access to the thoughts, knowledge, and records of people in many countries by many authors.

the "field"— to see what is going on for yourself. But you don't go out naive and unarmed; you bring with you a disciplined way of observing. Concepts give names to and identify what you are seeing and problems to solve. Tools for observation — whether instruments like Geiger counters, psychological texts, or ways of looking and note taking as carried out by anthropological ethnographers — help you notice, characterize, and record what you are seeing. Disciplines also provide methods of analysis to help you observe more closely, and what you see may send you back to look for more details to support patterns that emerge in your analysis.

The total effect of these disciplinary tools is to help you see more than an unprepared observer would see. Then you gather and record that information in ways that will be useful and persuasive for the academic discussion that occurs when you return to the university. Your fieldwork then can enter as another voice in the disciplinary discussion: "This is what I have seen and recorded and interpreted and this is how it adds to, challenges, or contradicts what other people have seen or thought."

The Laboratory

In laboratory work you observe special events created to display certain phenomena so that you can resolve specific questions. In a sense you bring back a piece of the messy world to examine under less confusing conditions. The laboratory conditions try to remove disturbing factors that might influence the phenomena you are investigating. You design them to highlight just a few factors you are able to control so that you can get clean and focused information about this representative piece of the world. You then use that information to see how well it can describe events once they are thrown back out in the confusion of the world. If the pattern you notice in the relative calm in the laboratory is so firm or robust to also hold true out in the less controlled world, then you have found a significant pattern.

Investigative Work in Courses

In asking you to take these excursions beyond the walls of the classroom, teachers may have several motives:

- To teach you disciplinary methods of gathering information about the world. Through your own experience you find out how a chemist discovers the characteristics of materials or how a sociologist diagnoses problems in a dysfunctional family.

- To help you confront material that interests you using the investigatory and intellectual tools of the subject. You learn to approach significant issues as a disciplined professional would.

- To bring real and immediate cases back into the classroom to enrich the discussion of the course. Your research into the history of big business sports could add much to the discussion of an economics class; your fieldwork with a film production crew could help illustrate the practical meaning of concepts learned in film production classes.

Issues in Investigation

To gain information that will tell you something useful and important, you first think about what you want to find out and why. In all three methods of investigation, you have several preliminary issues to resolve before you rush out with your note pad. These provide an underlying approach to investigative problems, which then can be elaborated through methods appropriate to each investigative technique and each disciplinary domain.

The Basic Problem or Question

This is the fundamental issue you hope to understand or address by your research. Direct and bold underlying questions, such as "Why do people join gangs?" or "How can computers facilitate classroom instruction?" underline the importance of your work and keep the details of your investigation in perspective. Although your investigation is not likely to answer these questions fully, your results may help you understand them.

The Focusing or Specifying Question

This takes your fundamental question and focuses it on a more specific problem. For example, the basic question, Why do people join gangs? can be specified in a variety of ways: What economic or emotional factors influence gang membership? What demographic factors characterize gang members? What influences a good student to join a gang? Does the presence of several gangs in a neighborhood influence whether youth will join gangs? At what age do youth start to affiliate with gangs, and what is the path by which they get involved?

Similarly, the question on computers in the classroom can be specified in many ways: How have electronic bulletin boards or e-mail groups been used in college classrooms? What happens when several classes are linked together in electronic discussion? What learning occurs when students use computer simulations of economic processes? How does word processing facilitate writing in college classrooms? Are any students turned off by computer use in classrooms? Does the use of electronic media interfere with or facilitate the relationship between student and teacher? How do multimedia presentations affect different kinds of learning? What happens to motivation in language learning when all student activities are computer mediated?

These more focused questions will begin to suggest useful information that would help you understand the issue. They are small enough to make some headway on while still being important enough to tell you something significant.

The Investigative Site

This is a specific incident, place, system, or phenomenon that provides an opportunity to investigate the specifying question. Ideally this is a site that puts the issues in sharp relief, more than other sites. It should also be a site to which you have access. To investigate the process by which a young person is drawn into a gang, for example, you may know people who were formerly or are currently in gangs and would be willing to talk about the experience. Even better, if they have siblings who did not join the gang, you could get several perspectives on what happened to the one person and compare that experience with those of the other children, some who resisted the draw of the gang.

If you are interested in studying computers in the classroom, there may be some course that is introducing new technology. Perhaps the basic economics course, for which you are enrolled, is introducing a market simulation program to give students practical experience in how markets operate under various conditions. This would provide a wonderful opportunity not only for you to experience the new technology but also to interview the professor. You could also observe what happens in the class and interview students.

The choice of a site, of course, must be determined by what is available — what is in your college library, what laboratory facilities you have available, and what field sites you can conveniently get into. But once you have a good grasp of your fundamental and specifying questions, you may notice many possibilities for research sites and how you could use them.

The Investigative Design: Concepts, Questions, Method

To decide exactly what to look for in your research site and how to gather your data, you develop a research design. First, after thinking about the possibilities of the site, you think about which concepts are likely to help you describe, define, and understand the situation. These investigative concepts must be relevant to the kind of information that you can gain from your site. For example, if you have only demographic data about gang memberships, concepts referring to class, economics, race, and family size might be most relevant; concepts relating to psychological feelings would be less relevant. On the other hand, if the research site allows for personal interviews that may reveal something about feelings, then psychological concepts may be most useful.

Often the theory and research you are learning about in class will provide a relevant range of concepts. So if you are working on the process of gang membership for a sociology course, you may want to draw on the concept of *reference group* — the group of people who provide the individual's measure of self-value. If you are studying the same material for a psychology course, you might want to use concepts of *anxiety* and *threat*.

The design then narrows your research question down to a concrete question about the site. This investigative question should apply the investigative concepts to the specific site to tell you exactly which data you are looking for. So if you are interested in the role of emotions, particularly anxiety, on gang membership, you might want to ask, "Exactly what threats did new gang members feel before they joined the gang, and how did joining the gang affect those feelings?" If, instead, you are interested in the role of reference groups in encouraging people to affiliate with gangs, you might ask, "What did individual youths do to seek approval from the gang members? How did the gang members respond to these efforts for approval?"

Each set of problems and concepts calls for its own appropriate methods of investigation and procedures for interpreting the data. The gang study about the effect of reference group behavior might proceed largely by interview. You would frame questions around issues of how members learned to fit in with the gang and what they got out of it. But since you are dealing with an obviously important and sensitive subject, you might want to have largely positive and open-ended questions, letting the interviewees choose what to tell you. Because the matter is so personal, you would not want to use too many technical terms and concepts. You might use them to plan the questions and later analyze the responses, but in the actual interviews you need to find friendly and common-sense ways to encourage people to tell you their story.

On the other hand, in studying computer simulations in the economics class, depending on your investigative question, you might want to get test scores of students who used the simulations and those who didn't. You might want detailed descriptions of what happened in classes that did and did not use the simulations, or you might want students to fill out attitudinal surveys telling whether they liked using computers in that class.

All these decisions are part of the design. Each field has developed its own typical research designs — specific criteria and procedures for finding out about the world that are aimed at making the data most useful for the kinds of problems they investigate and the kinds of ideas they have developed. In upper-division courses of your major, perhaps in courses on research methodology, you will learn the more specific methods of investigation developed in your field.

The Investigative Report

The report on your findings will address the following questions:

- *What is the interest or importance of what you found out?* This question generally is answered in the introduction.

- *How did you find out, gather, or observe the information?* In field and laboratory work this is often described explicitly in a "methods" section (see pages 225-226). In library research, the sources of your information are usually presented through citations, either in footnotes or in a bibliography (see pages 242-247).

- *What did you find?* In scientific work this is usually presented in a "results" section (see pages 267-269). In humanities writing your findings generally make up the main body of the essay.

- *What are the meaning and implications of what you found?* In scientific writing, meanings and implications are usually presented in separate "discussion" and "conclusions" sections. In humanities writing, the meaning and implications may be intermixed with the main presentation of the findings; the final paragraphs, however, usually focus on developing meanings and conclusions of the research.

The first and last questions (about importance and about meaning) connect your research with the issues and concepts of the course or discipline. They prompt you to think about what you have found in terms of the discussion that has been going on all term and to present your work in relation to that discussion. If you pursue those two questions energetically, your report will clearly relate your research methods and findings to the issues of the course.

Getting Involved Electronically

Locate an on-line journal or abstract service for some research field that interests you. After examining articles or abstracts, briefly describe some kinds of research being done in the field and the kinds of methods used.

11 Investigating the Archive: Library Research Writing

AIMS OF THE CHAPTER

The college library and other archives (such as those now being made available on the Internet) provide enormous amounts of information for you to think about and analyze. This chapter presents the archival research paper as a process of thought and discovery.

KEY POINTS

1. When you are developing a library research paper, your thoughts are interacting with your findings. As you discover more about your subject, you are able to focus on the questions you want to answer, the topic you will investigate, and the claims you want to make.

2. Modern libraries provide access to many sorts of materials in book, audio, visual, microform, and electronic format, both on site and off site. Specific index and abstract tools help identify available materials.

3. As you find materials, you evaluate their meaning and reliability, as well as think through their implications for your research project.

4. Your final paper takes best advantage of your research by referring to your sources in a detailed and thoughtful way. You then document your sources in a standard format.

QUESTIONS TO THINK ABOUT

- Have you ever felt lost or confused in your college library? How did you get your bearings? Did you find what you needed, or did you leave unsatisfied? What strategies might you have used to make your inquiry easier or more successful?

- When you were given some choice of topic on library research, why did you choose the topic you did? What consequences did that choice have for the success, usefulness, and interest of the paper that resulted and the value of that assignment for you?

- Have you ever found something in the library on the Internet that surprised you, made you see something new or in a new way, or otherwise made you think?

Library research is probably most familiar to you from previous schooling. From early grades you may have been asked to look up some information in an encyclopedia or in magazine articles and describe what you have found. By now you realize, however, that not all questions you have are answered directly by one source in precisely the answer you would like. For the kinds of questions and issues you are examining in the university, a prepackaged encyclopedia article will hardly do. You have to gather and think through a variety of sources and come to your own conclusions.

In the library research you now do, you will find that viewpoints may conflict. Moreover, since people may have been interested in questions that differ from yours, you may have to extend their findings and ideas to fit your interests. Perhaps you may even treat the sources you find in the library not as direct sources of information but as themselves the thing to investigate. That is, newspaper reports from the Civil War may tell you as much about the newspaper industry and about the attitudes and interests of the newspapers and readers as about the facts of the various battles. Articles on the latest breakthroughs in biochemistry may tell you more about what the big issues and popular approaches are than about what is definitely known.

◎◎ An Interactive Discovery Process

As you develop a library research paper, your thoughts interact with what you are finding. Although you may start with a general idea of what you are looking for and why, you can't know exactly what you will find. As you find out what material is available and the facts presented in the material, you should get new ideas and rethink some of your earlier ones. New ideas may in turn send you out looking for additional sources.

The library assignments presented in this chapter require a relatively short research process. Such smaller assignments often specify the task and a narrow range of topics to investigate. They may even specify the sources you should examine (such as the newspapers of the period or the state legislative record). Even when you are directed to general catalogues and indexes of materials, it will be clear what sources you should search — for example, all articles mentioning your historical event, all work by a particular author, or all zoning variances during a certain period.

As you become involved in more elaborate projects in other courses, a

Modern libraries mix traditional print holdings with electronic resources.

single research project can involve you for a term or even several years. As projects lengthen and deepen, your conception of the project is likely to change radically as you start to uncover material and as your changing ideas suggest new material to look for. The bigger and more open-ended the assignment, the more complicated is the problem of knowing where to look for materials. You need to get beyond the obvious sources to look at background, parallel cases, relevant theory, sidelong connections, or other kinds of materials that do not have your subject labeled across the top. Instead you will have to dig into these sources to find the relevant facts and reconnect them in ways that other people haven't. In addition, when projects are big, you may need to consult many different kinds of sources. Part of such assignments is in fact your ingenuity and persistence in discovering relevant sources and seeing new connections among the different kinds of material.

This discovery process is *recursive*: that is, it keeps looping back on itself. Thus it is necessary to alternate between focusing your ideas, setting out after material, thinking about analyzing what you have found, and then refocusing your ideas and setting out again. In this way you gradually build a picture of your subject or issue. As you start to fill in the picture, you may wish to go after more precise details or check out a related area. For example, in examining the controversy over affirmative action programs, you may discover that they began as a court-ordered remedy to break patterns of hiring discrimination. You then may wish to go back to examine those early court cases or how government policy changed to forestall further court action.

In this discovery process, be careful about coming to fixed conclusions too early. Be prepared for surprises, such as contradictory information that might force you to a higher level of thinking or a crucial case that sheds new light on the subject.

✑✐ USEFUL CONCEPTS FROM RHETORIC

Intertextuality

Every essay you write, every statement you make, echoes the words of earlier statements by yourself and others. The term *intertextuality* refers to the fact that we always draw on the words of people who came before us. Sometimes we may explicitly discuss what others have said and what we think about them, as in reading journals (see Chapter 4) or more formal essays of interpretation and commentary. In essays of argument (see Chapter 15), we may explicitly use the statements of some people to support our views and oppose the words of others. In library research papers (as discussed in this chapter), what we have to say is built on the information and ideas we find in the writings of others. We explicitly refer to our sources (see pages 240–242) and document them (see pages 242–247) to show exactly what we are drawing on from the archives of the library. These references call attention to the connection between our current statement and other texts that have preceded it. They make clear what the immediate prior conversation was and how we have added to it. If we fail to acknowledge that history of discussion and simply pass it all off as our own creation, we are guilty of plagiarism (see pages 112–114).

Even if we do not explicitly quote or otherwise refer to the words of others, we still rely on them. If we use words that are characteristic of or associated with an individual or a group, we bring those people to mind. If, for example, I encouraged you to try the Internet by saying "Just say yes," I would be reminding you intertextually of the "Just say no" antidrug campaign. I might also remind you of all the uses — straight, comic, and ironic — that people have made of that phrase since then. These phrases often expressed complex attitudes toward commands issued by authorities about activities that are judged to be good or bad for us. So if I, as author of this textbook and thus an authority figure, urged, "Just say yes to the Internet," you could rightfully see layers of irony in the statement.

In a more general sense, intertextuality reveals how much our language is part of our social heritage. If I am in a cooking class and talk to the other students using the language of cooking we have learned, my classmates recognize what I am talking about, which pan or spice or cooking procedure I am referring to; moreover, my classmates recognize me as someone sharing with them an activity where such words are important.

The fact that we rely on words that we first read or heard from others, however, does not mean we do not develop our own things to say. We take those words and put them together for our own purposes. We express our own attitudes with them, and we combine them to create new statements and carry out new actions that fit our new situation. As Mikhail Bakhtin, a theorist who helped develop the concept of intertextuality, noted, words we borrow from others become our own once we make them alive again with our own intentions.

Directing Your Research

In the previous chapter we mentioned some general issues concerning research and research writing (see pages 224-227). Because of the nature of library research, these issues may be handled with more flexibility than in other forms of research that require more rigorous prior planning. However, they still need to be addressed in the course of the research.

For example, you may leave your subject unsettled and open for the first one or two visits to the library as you explore possibilities. It can be a great deal of fun seeing the many ways people have approached a subject or getting a sense of a historical time and place by reading old magazines and newspapers. After your preliminary explorations, however, you need to focus and organize your search to answer your research question. Then you must address the orienting issues in ways appropriate for library research.

The Basic Problem or Question

From the very beginning of your research, you should have some sense of why you are engaged in it. You try to state to yourself in notes or in a journal the interest that is driving you — perhaps a curiosity about what was going on in a period of history, a desire to learn about the life of an author in order to understand the novels you like, a concern for a social problem, a confusion as to why a government agency or a large organization does not accomplish what it should, and so on. If you never articulate a personally significant motivation for the research beyond simply completing the assignment, you are not likely to pursue the research with much energy or come up with interesting ideas and findings.

The Focusing or Specifying Question and the Investigative Site

In your early investigations in the library, perhaps by examining overview works like encyclopedias or general books and articles on your area of interest, you look for a more specific way to follow through on your research. You look both for questions that narrow your task and for specific sources of information that can provide a single instance, case, or area that you can examine in some detail and care.

For example, to find out about the period of history that fascinates you — perhaps the period of industrial growth in the United States after the Civil War — you may have looked at a few chapters in a general American history book. There you found references to the crucial role of inventors and inventions such as the railroad, telegraph, telephone, and electric light in changing the economy. This might lead you to a question such as "How did inventions influence the post–Civil War economy?" and lead you specifically to investigate the development of the telephone.

The Investigative Design: Concepts, Questions, Method

Library research usually involves deciding what kind of material to search out, what kind of notes to take, and what kind of analysis to do on the material collected. Library method means specifying the available sources and determining what they can tell you. In the example of the growth of the telephone in the post–Civil War period, you may want to look at books about the development of the communications industries and biographies of some of the chief inventors such as Alexander Graham Bell, Elisha Grey, and Thomas Edison. However, to gain firsthand information through primary sources, you may wish to search out articles in *Scientific American* and other journals of technology and industry.

As you examine the material, you develop specific questions that will help you see how to interpret, evaluate, and use what you find to answer your larger research questions. In reading about Alexander Graham Bell, for example, you may want to ask how private research connected with industrial financiers and how the early uses of the telephone affected economic growth. As you look at articles in *Scientific American,* you might look for how the reports of technical advances were presented as being economically beneficial.

Similarly, you develop concepts that will help draw your information and ideas together. These concepts may arise fairly directly from the sources or from somewhere else. In the telephone research, concepts of investment in technology, financial opportunities, and expansion of industry may come directly from the ways in which your sources talk about the period, but you may also wish to use some modern economic concepts about systems, networks, and the communications revolution to help explain what was going on.

The Investigative Report

The results of library research may be written up without a formal report structure. Historical research may be written as a narrative of events that focuses on the details that relate to your research questions, or as a causal essay that identifies the causes or consequences of an event. Other library research may follow other patterns, simply incorporating the research material as detailed evidence within the discussion. Whatever organization you give to the presentation of your research, early in the text you need to focus the issues you are pursuing and the claims you are making, and throughout the report you need to cite your sources.

Using the Library in the Electronic Age

The library is likely to hold many materials that are potentially relevant and important for your interests, but the problem is to identify and find those materials and then keep track of them. Not so long ago, libraries had mostly books, journals, and some old newspapers. By using the card catalogue and a few periodical indexes, you could find what you needed and then pull the materials from the shelves. Microfilm, microfiche, videos, and other storage devices then allowed more kinds of materials (such as newspapers and magazines, government records, patent records, private papers, and rare books) to be stored in greater numbers, so you had to look in more catalogues and in more places in the libraries to locate relevant materials. In particular, each microfilm or microfiche collection may have had a specialized finder or index that you needed to use to locate what was available in the collection.

Then card catalogues started to be placed on line; these card catalogues were also linked so that through your college catalogue you could examine all the library catalogues in the state. Materials from other libraries could be requested by interlibrary loan.

As disciplinary research became specialized, specialized indexes and abstract services appeared, so you had to know which index to use. Recently many of these indexes have been placed on line, others have been made available on CD-ROM, and still others exist only in hard copy. These electronic indexes allow you to search quickly through many titles to find your materials. Often the search tools attached to these indexes allow you to combine descriptors. So, for instance, you can locate all articles on a certain subject published in 1993 and written in German. Or you can search for all articles that combine two different subjects, such as *telephone* and *consumers*.

Most recently, the Internet has made electronic retrieval of archives available throughout the world, using such electronic tools as *Gopher, Fetch, Archie,* and *World Wide Web.* More and more materials are being made available on the Internet every day, and the tools for accessing them are becoming more and more convenient. Nonetheless, because the situation is in transition, finding information on the Internet still is very much a matter of random luck or personal information that someone passes on to you. On the other hand, once you start exploring the Internet, you will find many materials at your fingertips. By the time you read this, finding your way around the Internet may have become simpler; central indexing sites are currently being developed, and there are search tools (one is called *Yahoo*) that will search widely for subject names you identify. The best way to start exploring is to have someone demonstrate to you the tools available at your computer site, and then just see what you can find.

World Wide Web in particular is organized to let one information site lead you to another. It is organized on hyper-text principles, where each location is linked to other locations by hot-buttons. Once you have found something at all related to your interests, you are likely to be led to a whole range of relevant materials. In particular, many subject index pages are being

The World Wide Web makes available resources from libraries, universities, governments, newspapers, political groups, and other organizations and individuals from around the world.

developed by individuals and groups; these pages will lead you to what the authors of that page think are the most useful or interesting World Wide Web sites on that subject as well as to other related index pages. If you find the right index page for your subject, you may be led to mountains of material. However, since Web sites are changing so rapidly and the addresses often change, there is little purpose in providing you with current sites and addresses that may no longer be the same when you need them. Your college's library or computer lab or classmates may provide you with some good starting places.

Ultimately libraries are working to integrate the indexing of materials and simplify access; however, with so many new opportunities and resources developing, it may be a long time before research access is again a simple thing. Because libraries are becoming so rich and complex and because each library is different, the advice offered in this chapter and in the sidebars can only serve as a starting point for becoming acquainted with your college library. You can gain an orientation to your library through scheduled library tours, through handouts and pamphlets available in your library, through on-line help on the library computer system, through workshops, and even through taking a course on using the library. A course introducing you to the full resources of the library may be one of the most valuable courses you take. Finally, you should regularly make use of your reference librarians, who know how to get to what you need most directly and rapidly.

It is worth learning to find your way through all the access tools and materials of your library, because every additional piece of relevant material you find gives you more resources to accomplish your task. Finding the right materials buried in the library can make an ordinary project into a remarkable one. You may find something you truly had no idea of before you began searching.

Some Commonly Used Indexes

This list may give you some idea of the range of indexes available and may help you find those indexes most relevant to your subject. Each of these indexes provides information, usually at the front of each volume, on how it is organized and how it may be best used. Many of these are now available on CD-ROM or On line.

Indexes to General Circulation Periodicals

     General Science Index
     Humanities Index
     Public Affairs Information Service
     Reader's Guide to Periodical Literature
     Social Sciences Index

Indexes to Newspapers

> *New York Times Index*
> *The Times Index* (London)
> *Wall Street Journal Index*
> *Washington Post Index*

Index to Government Publications

> *American Statistics Index*
> *Monthly Catalog of U.S. Government Publications*

Indexes to Specialized Journals

> *Accountants' Index*
> *Anthropological Index*
> *Art Index*
> *Bibliography and Index of Geology*
> *Biological Abstracts*
> *Business Periodicals Index*
> *Chemical Abstracts*
> *Criminology Index*
> *Education Index*
> *Film Literature Index*
> *Hospital Literature Index*
> *Index Medicus*
> *International Bibliography of Economics*
> *International Bibliography of Historical Sciences*
> *International Bibliography of Political Science*
> *International Bibliography of Sociology*
> *Lexus*
> *MLA International Bibliography*
> *Music Article Index*
> *Philosopher's Index*
> *Physics Abstracts*
> *Popular Music Periodical Index*
> *Psychological Abstracts*
> *Resources in Education*
> *Science Citation Index*
> *Social Sciences Citation Index*
> *Sociological Abstracts*
> *Women's Studies Abstracts*

GETTING ORIENTED TO YOUR LIBRARY

Go to your college library and collect all the handouts that describe the on-line catalogue, available indexes and abstract services, databases, and special collections and archives. Read the materials and then locate each of the services mentioned, both by logging on to the computer catalogue and by walking through the library.

Evaluating What You Find

Although the library contains many remarkable resources, all these resources are not to be taken at face value as unquestioned truth. Each text represents a statement made by real people at a certain moment in history; each text has the limitations not only of what the writers knew and were interested in, but also of the situation for which it was written. That is, each bit of information in the library comes from a person like you, who sees and does certain things and does not see or do other things. One book may have been written as part of a political campaign, another as part of an evolving debate over anthropological theories. One book may have been written to be a best seller, playing upon popular fascination with the film industry, whereas another may have been written to defend the actions of a public personality who has been sent to prison. One newspaper article may have been written while a battle was in progress and accurate detailed information was not yet available, and another may have been written years after to examine the consequences of that battle for current military policy. Every text, even those you come to rely on directly for your facts, has a story behind it. To know how you can best interpret and use each piece of material, you need to start understanding the story. Two sets of distinctions, sometimes used by historians and literary scholars, may help you start to understand how you can interpret and use various sources.

Primary and Secondary Sources

Primary sources are sources written at the time of the events and represent the information, ideas, interests, and orientations of the people who were directly involved — whether it is a historical event such as a presidential election, an academic debate such as over the validity of a new experiment, or an artistic production such as a novel or musical performance. So, for example, a primary source for an academic debate would be an article written by one of the debaters themselves, and a primary source for a novel would be the novel itself and perhaps some letters written by the author to his sister.

Secondary sources are written after the events, looking back on the events and retelling and commenting on those events. So a secondary source for the presidential election might be a book recounting the changing political alignment of voters over the period. A secondary source on the academic debate might be a later article sorting out and evaluating what new ideas and findings resulted from the debate, and a secondary source on the artistic event might be a literary analysis or biographical account of the composer's life and works.

Reliable Information Sources and Individual Statement Sources

Although every text is some person's representation, reflecting individual ideas and perceptions or desires to influence others, some texts tell you more than just what the author thought or was trying to do. After evaluation, you can come to rely on some tests as useful or accurate characterizations of the facts of the situation.

There is no simple way to judge between these two. In each case you have to evaluate the quality of the source, how it compares with other accounts, the interests and knowledgeability of the author as well as the author's access to other information sources, and other factors that might influence the detail and accuracy of the account. However, over time you will come to rely on some sources for information more than others. Some newspapers attempt to be more comprehensive and less driven by immediate political stances than others. Although some government statistics may reflect a picture that government wants to give out, over time some governments and some agencies develop a greater reputation for reliability. It may even be in their own interests to present unbiased information to allow their citizens to make informed choices. Academic scholars, because they have to meet the criticism of their professional peers, often try to develop a more accurate and detailed view of subjects than people writing for the popular or political press, but again, some scholarly writers are more careful and impartial than others, just as some political and popular writers are more accurate and impartial than others.

The point is that you constantly need to make judgments about the quality of your sources and how they should be interpreted. Moreover, even if you determine that a source is factually unreliable, that does not mean it is useless. It still may reflect that at a certain time certain people held certain views, used certain arguments, and even attempted to distort debates through lies and obfuscations. Every text is itself a historical fact. Even forgeries are facts, though not the facts they claim to be.

Referring to Your Sources

In the course of writing your essay based on library research, you will want to mention the materials you have found. You can bring these source materials into your essay in several ways.

1. *Quotation.* In quotation you use the exact words of your source. When you do this, you need quotation marks or block quotation format, as in this example:

   ```
        Karl Marx, in one of his many discussions of
   the alienation of labor, comments:

                  The more the worker expends himself in
                  work, the more powerful becomes the
                  world of objects which he creates in
                  face of himself, and the poorer he him-
                  self becomes in his inner life, the less
                  he belongs to himself. . . . The alien-
                  ation of the worker in his product means
                  not only that his labour becomes an ob-
                  ject, takes on its own existence, but
                  that it exists outside him, indepen-
                  dently, and alien to him, and that it
                  stands opposed to him as an autonomous
                  power. The life which he has given to
                  the object sets itself against him as an
                  alien and hostile force. (170)

   This passage ties the concept of alienation to the
   notion of objects and objectification, so that alien-
   ation consists of the separation of the worker from
   the objects the worker makes.
   ```

   Notice how three periods (. . .), with a fourth to indicate a sentence end, are used to indicate deleted material.

   Quotation gives direct evidence of what your source said, evidence that allows you to analyze the statement or take advantage of the particular eloquence or precision of the phrasing. However, because it hands over the voice of your essay to someone else, it does not directly indicate what *you* are saying.

2. *Paraphrase.* In paraphrase you rephrase the ideas and information from the source in your own words, as in the following example:

```
        Karl Marx claimed that every time a worker
produced something, the worker created more objects
that existed outside of himself, until he became sur-
rounded by a world of objects that was no longer a
part of himself. The worker thus became alienated
from his world, having nothing left inside, but only
possessing objects which no longer had personal mean-
ing. The worker's spirit is drained in the process of
producing objects for the market. These objects then
become his enemy because they keep him from himself.
So not only does his labor become meaningless as he
produces goods which are of no value to him, but the
world he produces no longer has meaning. He is caught
in an alien world and thus suffers alienation. (Marx
170)
```

Paraphrase allows you to keep the detail of the original while still maintaining control of the direction of the paper. With paraphrase you can keep the writing going in the direction you want and interpret the passage. However, paraphrase loses the power of the original and often requires much lengthy explanation of ideas.

3. *Summary.* When you refer to someone else's ideas by summary as part of your own essay, you usually pick out specific points to summarize rather than give a summary of the other person's whole argument, as in the following example:

```
        For Karl Marx the concept of alienation de-
fined the relation between the worker and his produc-
tion. The production of goods separates the worker
from his labor, turning that labor into an object no
longer attached to the spirit of the worker (Marx
170). Unlike Adam Smith, who celebrated the produc-
tive capacity of humans, Marx saw mass production of
commodities as a degradation of the human spirit.
```

Summary allows you to pick out the most relevant points from your sources and work them into your discussion.

4. *Mention only.* You can make a brief and rapid reference by simply mentioning the name of an idea, invention, discovery, creation, or other source:

```
        Karl Marx's concept of alienation (Marx 170)
presents a problem to all those who wish to create
socialist states in an industrial world, because all
```

```
states now depend on mass production for their pros-
perity.
```

One drawback of this approach is that your readers may not be familiar with the concepts or material you quickly mention. Even if they are,
they may not know what aspect or part you find relevant to your discussion. The quick mention won't let you know what Marx's concept of alien-
ation is, nor will it tell you what aspects of that concept are at odds with
mass production. So unless you are sure your readers will know exactly
what you mean by a brief mention, it is best to spell out more fully in a
summary, paraphrase, or quotation what you wish to refer to.

Whichever way you bring the sources into your essay, you need to introduce and then discuss these materials so the readers will know why you
are presenting this material, how you are using it, and what they should get
from it. Finally, whatever format you use, you need to give credit for all materials you use. This can be done through footnotes or through parenthetical
references to the sources linked to a Works Cited bibliography (see pages
242–247). Thus the writer on Marx cited Marx in parentheses with a page
number and then gave the following information at the end of the essay:

```
                     Work Cited

Marx, Karl. Selected Writings in Sociology and Social
        Philosophy.  Trans. T. B. Bottomore.  New
        York: McGraw-Hill, 1956.
```

◎◎ Giving Credit in Modern Language Association (MLA) Style

Each discipline or subject area has its own style of giving credit to sources.
Although footnotes are still used in some subjects, most disciplines now prefer that credit be given through a Reference or Works Cited list at the end of
the essay or report. Consequently, this book will describe this latter method.
Here the Modern Language Association (MLA) Style, widely used in the humanities, will be presented. On page 246 the American Psychological Association style, widely used in the social sciences, will also be presented. There
are many other style manuals for different fields. Your teachers in various
subjects will give you directions about the style you are to follow for their
course.

In-Text Parenthetical References

According to the MLA style, right after you use material from a source,
whether by quotation, summary, paraphrase, or mention only, you place the

author's name in parentheses. If you refer to specific material from a specific page, you also include page numbers. In the following sample paragraph, notice that when there are two sources by the same author, additional information is provided in the parentheses (in the sample below, Cowan has two titles, so a brief title is given). If two authors have the same last name, you should also use an initial. These references are then linked to more complete references in the Works Cited list that follows, as in the following sample:

> Feminism and the history of technology have met in the examination of the impact of household technologies (Rothschild; Cowan, "Industrial"). Ruth Schwartz Cowan, especially, has examined how these technologies, while claiming to alleviate the burden on women, have increased the obligations under which women live (Cowan, *More Work*). Other scholars have examined phrases like "laborsaving devices" (Bose, Bereano, and Malloy 53) and keywords like "efficiency" (Altman 98) to demonstrate how these have been used to manipulate perceptions of technology. Using such critiques, one can develop a feminist perspective on technical communication (Gurak and Bayer).

Works Cited

Altman, Karen E. "Modern Discourse on American Home Technologies." Communication and the Culture of Technology. Ed. Martin J. Medhurst, Alberto Ganzalez, and Tarla Rai Peterson. Pullman: Washington State UP, 1991. 95–111.

Bose, Christine, Philip Bereano, and Mary Malloy. "Household Technology and the Social Construction of Housework." Technology and Culture 25 (1984): 53–82.

Cowan, Ruth Schwartz. "The Industrial Revolution in the Home: Household Technology and Social Change in the 20th Century." Technology and Culture 17.1 (1976): 1–23.

Cowan, Ruth Schwartz. More Work for Mother: The Ironies of Household Technology from the Open Hearth to the Microwave. New York: Basic Books, 1983.

Gurak, Laura, and Nancy Bayer. "Making Gender Visible: Extending Feminist Critiques of Technology to Technical Communication." Technical Communication Quarterly 3 (1994): 257–70.

Rothschild, Joan. Teaching Technology from a Feminist Perspective. New York: Pergamon, 1988.

The Works Cited list should be placed at the end of the essay or report. Each work mentioned in the essay or report must be listed here, in alphabetical order, by the author's last name. The following rules specify the basics of the format.

Basic MLA Bibliography Punctuation

For a Book

- First line flush with left margin; second and following lines indented.
- Author's last name first, followed by comma and first name.
- Book title underlined or italicized.
- Colon between place of publication and publisher.
- Periods between major parts and at end.

For an Article in an Anthology

- Article title in quotation marks; book title underlined or italicized.
- Editor after book title, name in normal order.
- Inclusive pagination of article at end; second page number abbreviated.

For an Article in a Periodical

- Article title in quotation marks; periodical title underlined.
- Volume number after periodical title.
- Date of issue in parentheses, followed by a colon.
- Inclusive pagination of article at end.
- If the article appears on nonconsecutive pages, give first page followed by +.
- For popular journals and newspapers, the volume number can be eliminated if the exact date is given; for academic journals that have continuous pagination throughout the volume or year, the exact issue and date can be eliminated as long as the volume and year are presented.

```
Author.   "Title of Article."   Everytown Daily News 23
          January 1997: A8.
Author.   "Title of Article."   Entertainment Week 15
          January 1997: 37-43.
Author.   "Title of Article."   Journal of Scholarship 58
          (1997): 368-86.
```

For Material in Electronic Media

- For material also available in print, such as a magazine or newspaper, first list the print information, and then identify the electronic source, including the medium (such as Diskette, CD-ROM, or On line):

```
Author.   "Title of Article."   Everytown Daily News 23
          January 1997: A8.   Everytown Daily News Ondisc.
          CD-ROM.   March 1997.
```

- For material with no print version, provide the following information, as available, in the following order:

        Author.   "Title."   Date of material.   <u>Title of Data-
                base</u>.   Publication medium.   Vendor.   Electronic
                publication date.

- For material from electronic journals or conferences, provide the following information, as available, in the following order:

        Author.   "Title of Article."   <u>Name of Journal or Con-
                ference</u>.   Volume or issue number (date of pub-
                lication): number of pages or paragraphs.   On
                line.   Name of Computer Network.   Date of ac-
                cess.

Modifications and Special Situations

Author
If no author is given, begin directly with the title. Also:

> If two authors: `Collins, Roberta, and James Delugga.`
> If three authors: `Collins, Roberta, James Delluga, and Felicia`
`Rivera.`
> If four or more authors: `Collins, Roberta, et al.`

Edition
If other than the first edition, list the edition after the main title:

        Author.   Title.   Rev ed.   City: Publisher, date.

Translator or Editor
List this after the edition information:

        Author.   Title.   2nd ed.   Trans. Ken Kracouer.   Ed. Ed-
                ward Mianus.   City: Publisher, date.

Book Review
If an article in a periodical is a book review, directly after the title place "Rev. of" followed by title of book and author. If the article has no title, simply use "Rev. of."

        Siegel, Renata.   "I Liked It."   Rev. of <u>A Good Book</u>, by
                Sandra Melawi.   <u>Monthly Journal</u> Sept. 1996:
                32-33.

The sample paper on pages 248–252 follows the MLA format.

For greater detail, consult
    Gibaldi, Joseph, and Walter Achtert. *The MLA Handbook for Writers of Research Papers.* 4th ed. New York: Modern Language Association, 1995.

✑ Giving Credit in American Psychological Association (APA) Style

The American Psychological Association (APA) style for giving credit differs in some details from that adopted by the Modern Language Association. The following are general guidelines of the APA style widely used in the social sciences.

In-Text Parenthetical References

References placed in parentheses in the body of the text should include author and date of publication, and may include specific page references if you are citing a specific fact or quotation. These references should then match works that appear in a Reference list at the end. The following example of APA bibliographic style should be compared to the MLA style presentation of the same material on page 243.

> Feminism and the history of technology have met in the examination of the impact of household technologies (Rothschild, 1988; Cowan, 1976). Ruth Schwartz Cowan, especially, has examined how these technologies, while claiming to alleviate the burden on women, have increased the obligations under which women live (Cowan, 1983). Other scholars have examined phrases like "laborsaving devices" (Bose, Bereano, & Malloy, 1984, p. 53) and keywords like "efficiency" (Altman, 1991, p. 98) to demonstrate how these have been used to manipulate perceptions of technology. Using such critiques, one can develop a feminist perspective on technical communication (Gurak & Bayer, 1994).

References

Altman, K. E. (1991). Modern discourse on American home technologies. In M. J. Medhurst, A. Ganzalez, & T. R. Peterson (Eds.), Communication and the culture of technology (pp. 95–111). Pullman: Washington State University Press.

Bose, C., Bereano, P., & Malloy, M. (1984). Household technology and the social construction of housework. Technology and Culture, 25, 53–82.

Cowan, R. S. (1976). The industrial revolution in the home: Household technology and social change in the 20th century. Technology and Culture, 17, 1–23.

Cowan, R. S. (1983). <u>More work for mother: The ironies of household technology from the open hearth to the microwave</u>. New York: Basic Books.

Gurak, L., & Bayer, N. (1994). Making gender visible: Extending feminist critiques of technology to technical communication." <u>Technical Communication Quarterly</u>, <u>3</u>, 257–270.

Rothschild, J. (1988). <u>Teaching technology from a feminist perspective</u>. New York: Pergamon Press.

Basic APA Bibliography Punctuation

For a Book

- First line flush with left margin; second and following lines indented.
- Author's last name first, followed by comma and initials.
- Two or more authors separated by & (not *and*); last name first for all names.
- Date of publication in parentheses, following author's name.
- Book title underlined or italicized, only the first word capitalized except for proper nouns.
- Colon between place of publication and publisher.
- Periods between major parts and at end.

For an Article in an Anthology

- No quotation marks for article title, only first word capitalized.
- Book editors preceded by "In"; names in normal order, using abbreviations for first names; followed by "(Eds.)."
- Book title after editors, underlined or italicized, only first word capitalized.
- Article page numbers appear in parentheses after the book title.

For an Article in a Periodical

- Year in parentheses after author's name.
- No quotation marks for article title, only first word capitalized.
- Periodical title underlined, all major words capitalized, followed by volume number and inclusive pages, all separated by commas.
- Volume number underlined or italicized.

For greater detail, consult
American Psychological Association. *Publication Manual.* 4th ed. Washington, DC: American Psychological Association, 1994.

❧ Sample Student Paper

The following student paper, using MLA bibliographic style, provides a historical perspective that helps clarify the issues in a public controversy. The assignment was to identify an issue or story currently covered in newspapers and other news media, to look into the history and other background of the story through library research, and then to write a short paper showing how the background explains the current story.

The student, Karen Jurgstrom, was writing for a political science assignment to investigate the historical background of a current political issue. She chose to examine the history of affirmative action programs, which were coming under attack in the spring of 1995 with a number of proposals to retract or dismantle existing programs and guidelines. She wondered how affirmative actions came about and why they had originally gained support when so many people now were calling them unfair.

Karen Jurgstrom
The History of Affirmative Action

For many civil rights activists and legal scholars, affirmative action programs achieve "equal protection under the law," but to others they seem anything but equal. In an article for The Christian Century, Glenn Hewitt expresses his fear that even the best-intentioned affirmative action programs can cause white males to become "victimized by justice" (146). Many other white males, lacking Hewitt's sensitivity to race and gender issues, feel they are being punished for historical crimes that they did not commit. Such feelings have led to political movements to outlaw affirmative action programs. However, as our nation continues the crucial dialogue about equality of opportunity in all aspects of work and society, we need to understand that the hiring programs in question did not begin as, and were never intended to be, a punishment against the privileged. Nor were they intended to create an advantage for one group over another. Affirmative action programs in the United States attempted to provide equal opportunity for all people by counteracting the effects of long-term historical inequities. Affirmative action programs were meant to break through the deep social causes that kept certain groups at an enduring disadvantage.

Affirmative action has its roots in the Civil Rights Act of 1964. Before this landmark legislation,

state and federal organizations had attempted to limit
discrimination in specific areas, such as voting rights,
but there had never been a comprehensive national anti-
discrimination law. The Civil Rights Act of 1964, which
has been described as "the most comprehensive legislative attempt ever to erase racial discrimination in the
United States," outlawed discrimination on the grounds
of race, color, religion, or national origin (Janda
588). Following the 1964 Civil Rights Act, individuals
and businesses could no longer refuse to hire, serve,
or sell to African-Americans. In the years between 1964
and 1969, a number of other important pieces of civil
rights legislation were passed, including the Elementary and Secondary Education Act of 1965, the Voting
Rights Act of 1965, and the Fair Housing Act of 1968
(Janda 590).

The immediate effect of these laws was that individuals and corporations could no longer refuse to
hire, serve, sell to, educate, or rent apartments to
African-American citizens. However, from the very beginning, civil rights activists knew that equality was
more complicated than just declaring an end to centuries of discrimination and assuming that everyone
would suddenly be equal. President Lyndon Johnson, who

Affirmative Action
attempts to overcome
the effect of generations
of discrimination. Here
is a 1968 protest march
in Memphis, Tennessee.

signed the Civil Rights Act into law, argued that true
equality of opportunity required overcoming the effect
of past inequality:

> You do not take a person who for years has
> been hobbled by chains, liberate him,
> bring him up to the starting line of a
> race, and then say, "You are free to com-
> pete with all the others," and still
> justly believe that you have been com-
> pletely fair. Thus, it is not enough just
> to open the gates of opportunity; all our
> citizens must have the opportunity to walk
> through those gates. (Urofsky 17)

In this passage, Johnson gives the main reason for affirmative action programs: equality is a complicated
thing, and society cannot remedy a history of inequality simply by eliminating the barriers to success that
have stood for centuries.

The Supreme Court acknowledged this fact in its
1971 Griggs v. Duke Power Co. decision. The plaintiffs
in this case were thirteen African-Americans who had
been denied employment or promotion at a North Carolina
power company on the basis of their education or their
performance on objective competence tests. The company
argued that, as long as they could prove that their
testing procedures were racially neutral, then they
were justified under Title VII of hiring and promoting
whites over blacks. However, in a unanimous decision,
the Court ruled that the Civil Rights Act of 1964 for-
bade the use of job criteria that had the effect of
discriminating against members of a specific ethnic
group — even if the company manifests no direct intention to do so.

The key issue at stake in the Griggs decision
was Title VII of the Civil Rights Act, which outlawed
discrimination on the basis of race. Both sides believed that they were interpreting Title VII correctly:
the company argued that, if they were to promote a
black candidate over a white candidate who had scored
better on a test, they would be guilty of discriminating against the white candidate. The plaintiffs,
though, argued successfully that discrimination against

a group, by devising criteria that are inherently discriminatory, was as illegal as discrimination against
an individual. Herman Belz, the author of a book-length
history of affirmative action, cites the Court's response to this argument as the beginning of modern affirmative action:

> Griggs shifted civil rights policy to a
> group-rights, equality-of-result rationale
> that made the social consequences of em-
> ployment practices, rather than their pur-
> poses, intent, or motivation, the decisive
> consideration in determining their lawful-
> ness. The decision supplied a theoretical
> basis for preferential treatment as well
> as a practical incentive for extending
> race conscious preference. (51)

From the Griggs decision and later directives
by both Congress and the Supreme Court, there has
emerged a large network of educational and hiring programs that, collectively, go by the name of "affirmative
action." The debate over these programs has become a
divisive element in American politics, and many conservative politicians have come to power on the promise to
end "reverse discrimination" and "preferential treatment of minorities." Contrary to many people's opinions, however, affirmative action programs were not
designed to exact retribution for centuries of persecu-
tion and oppression, nor were they meant to create inequality. Rather, these programs recognize that past
oppressions have resulted in very real, very present
inequalities in educational training and income level,
and these inequalities cannot be corrected without some
reference to the historical situations that produced
them.

Works Cited

Belz, Herman. Equality Transformed: A Quarter-Century
     of Affirmative Action. New Brunswick: Transac-
     tion, 1991.
Hewitt, Glenn. "Victimized by Justice." Christian
     Century 23 September 1987. Rpt. in The Refer-
     ence Shelf; Affirmative Action. Ed. Daniel
     Altschiller. New York: H.W. Wilson, 1991.
     144–47.

Janda, Kenneth, et al. The Challenge of Democracy.
        Boston: Houghton Mifflin, 1992.
Urofsky, Melvin I. A Conflict of Rights: The Supreme
        Court and Affirmative Action. New York: Scrib-
        ners, 1991.

Thinking About Student Writing

1. What is the issue that Karen Jurgstrom addresses in her research essay? In what way is this currently a political issue? How does Karen Jurgstrom present the views of people with different political positions on this issue? To what extent and in what way does she present her own view on the issue?

2. What is the main point that Karen Jurgstrom found about the history of affirmative action? What specific evidence leads her to this conclusion? What are the key historical moments she examines? Why do you think she chose each of those moments?

3. What documents did she rely on to find out about the history of affirmative action and that she used as sources of evidence? Why do you think she chose those documents? What other documents might she have used?

4. Whose points of view are expressed in each of the moments she examined and the documents she used? Why are those points of view significant? Do you think she might have come to different conclusions and become aware of different points of view if she had examined different moments and documents? What other specific kinds of events and documents might have affected her conclusions? In what way?

5. How does this historical account help us understand the current political issues?

Assignments

LIBRARY RESEARCH

1. Choose a current news story of interest to you. Through library research, obtain background information and a history about the event and write an essay of about 1,000 words explaining the meaning of the current story in light of the background.

2. Using local newspapers and other sources, write the story of a recent crucial election or public controversy in your town. Identify the people who played a major role and discuss what they stood for, who backed them, and how the debate or struggle unfolded. In light of what you find, describe and interpret the meaning of the events and their outcome in a research essay of 1,000 words.

3. Using materials in your college archive, write a narrative of some event in the history of your college.

4. Choose an old movie, a television show you have enjoyed in reruns, or musical performers of a previous period. Using newspaper and magazine reviews as well as books and articles about the entertainment industry of the relevant period, write an essay describing how the movie, show, or group were perceived and evaluated when they originally appeared.

5. Write a brief essay describing the events and cultural climate during the month of your birth. Use contemporary newspaper, magazine, and video sources as well as later historical accounts.

Getting Involved Electronically

Examine the various electronic bibliographic resources available in your library that are relevant to subject areas in which you are interested. List and briefly describe the most useful catalogues, databases, indexes, abstract services, or other resources you have found.

12

New Investigations: Fieldwork and Laboratories

AIMS OF THE CHAPTER

Field and laboratory research, although requiring special investigative techniques, are similar to other college writing in presenting information in relation to concepts and conclusions. This chapter explains the logic and general practice of field and laboratory research and how reports of such work ought to be written. As you advance in your major, you will do such specialized research projects in the discipline of your choice.

KEY POINTS

1. Because unfolding events are complex, in fieldwork, you carefully plan what information to gather, how to gather it, and how to record it. You make these choices on the basis of the question you are trying to answer and on how you think your research site will shed light on that question.

2. When you analyze the data and write the research report, you explain the meaning of the events that may have been too complex to understand while they were going on.

3. Experiments are special events created by researchers so that they can see how certain phenomena or processes work out in simplified circumstances that display the phenomena most clearly.

4. Reports on experiments place the story of what happened (the results) within the story of how the researcher created the circumstances for the events (the experimental design and procedure). These stories are then framed by the stories of the researchers trying to understand phenomena and of what we currently understand about those phenomena (introduction, review of literature, and discussion and conclusions).

QUESTIONS TO THINK ABOUT

- Where and how might you observe in action the concepts and phenomena you are studying in class?

- What kinds of field observations and experiments do researchers in the subjects you study tend to make? What observational techniques do they use?

- How do field studies and experiments help develop knowledge in subjects you study?

- What field and laboratory courses are you likely to take as part of your major or professional training?

In library research you rely on what has already been recorded. But if you are interested in how people talk to each other in everyday conversation, where are you going to find that record? If you want to know what people in your community feel about plans to sell off city lands to private developers, where are you going to find that information? You have to go out into the field to gather the information yourself, in the form that is most useful for your inquiry.

When you go out into the world, you find it is a messy and confusing place. Many things happen simultaneously, potentially influenced by many factors. So in doing fieldwork you need to develop a precise sense of what you are looking for, how you will get the information you need, and what you will not pay attention to, interesting though those complications and distractions may be.

The choices you must make in fieldwork are always questionable. You can't gather all the information you always want; events go by too fast, and you can't place recording devices at every location. You could always have gathered other sorts of information. The events you are trying to understand may have been significantly influenced by something that you just cannot or did not collect data about.

For certain kinds of problems, one way to overcome the confusion of the world is to create a cleaned-up and simplified situation in which you examine events that you select and design. In the laboratory you can simplify and focus events to try to reveal precisely what you want to learn about them. In this setting the challenge is to control the circumstances in which the phenomena are displayed so as to reveal aspects that would remain hidden under more usual circumstances.

Getting the Story in the Field

As already mentioned, in fieldwork your task is to record a small corner of the world. If you tried to record everything, you would be pretty busy and would use more videotape and more computer memory than anyone has. The world passes by too quickly and too fully to make any kind of complete record.

Even just a small corner of the world has too much. Imagine trying to keep an absolute record of everything that happens in your class in just five minutes — what gets said and whispered, what gets recorded in the notebooks, every change of expression on everyone's face, every squirming in the seat, every increase and decrease in heart rate and brain wave function, and perhaps every thought that races through every mind. You have to make your choices, to decide what is worth recording and what can be recorded reasonably efficiently and accurately.

The Importance of the Fundamental Question or Problem

Even if you could record everything, the question remains why you would want to. A complete record on its own won't make any more sense than the original experience; it won't answer any questions or give you guidance. You have to start looking for particular things based on the problem you are trying to solve, the question you are trying to answer, or the phenomenon you are trying to understand. The problem or question or phenomenon will help you define what you need to record and how. It will tell you when to start taking notes or set the cameras rolling, and what to focus on.

In planning to do fieldwork, therefore, from the very beginning you need to have the basic problem or question of your research firmly in mind. In li-

Students measure water quality as part of environmental field research.

brary work you may be able to dive into materials with only a general sense of your interests and then stitch together some kind of picture out of prerecorded material as you move through the project. Furthermore, you can always get back to the library to find the missing pieces once you have figured out what's interesting. In fieldwork, however, if you don't know why you are out there and what you are looking for, you will be overwhelmed and undirected. If you ever do figure out what you are interested in, you would already have missed most of the relevant data.

Finding a Site for Fieldwork

The site you choose for fieldwork, especially during your undergraduate years, often depends on what is available and convenient. You usually don't have the time, money, or opportunity to travel far and into unusual settings to answer your questions. Much of your fieldwork will have to be done on or near campus or in a nearby community.

At the same time, choosing a research site that has no relation to your question only because it is there can be disastrous. Although the site can probably provide endless data, those data may tell you nothing about your questions. The student center snack bar presents many people in motion and might provide wonderful opportunities for studying irony in the speech of young adults or responses to random meetings, but if you are interested in childrearing techniques or the operations of legislative bodies, you might have to wait a long time before you come up with any useful observations.

You may need to be ingenious, therefore, in thinking about the sites available to you and what any particular site can tell you about the questions you are investigating. Although the snack bar may be the last place you would think to examine the way people are recruited into political movements, you may notice that a group of activist students regularly gather at one table, which then provides a place for curious students to hang out and learn in an informal way about events, plans, and issues. Now you do have a place to study the processes of political recruitment.

Concepts, Method, and Planning

Because you need to know exactly what you are looking for and how you are going to gather and record the information, fieldwork needs to be very well planned. Of course, this planning will vary according to the discipline in which you are working, your questions, the kind of investigation you are carrying out, your own resources, and the particulars of the site. In courses where you will be assigned fieldwork, your instructor is likely to give you specific advice about how to choose your research site and plan your work. The instructor may also devote substantial class discussion and office conference time to helping you think through your plan.

If you will be gathering statistical data or using questionnaires, you need to be especially careful in your planning, because statistics and questionnaires are hard to adapt in response to what you observe in the field. They both narrow your focus of attention so that you only pick up a narrow range of information; moreover, to maintain the validity of the data and method, you need to follow through on the statistical categories and questions you have established at the beginning.

If you are entering a discipline that regularly uses field methods, you will probably take specialized methods and statistics courses as part of your major, where these issues will be examined in much greater detail.

Record Keeping

Methods of recording data will vary, from the highly stylized methods of baseball scorekeeping or recording of dance choreography, to extensive note taking and journal keeping, in which one simply describes what one sees according to the categories of observation. Each discipline and kind of work has its own style of record keeping, but you may also have to adapt or develop your own to fit the needs of your project. The more care you put into record keeping, the better your work is likely to be, because when the events and observations are over, your records will be all you are left with to analyze and present. You probably won't be able to go back to fill in what you missed.

Analyzing Fieldwork

While you are collecting data in the field, you will be quite busy. Concerned with observing and recording, you may have little time to think about the meaning of what you find. This is different from library research, during which you regularly look up from the books to think about what you are finding. Even the selection of the next place to look in the library requires adding up the meaning of your research to that point. In fieldwork, however, your data collection is organized by your previous plan, and you may not have much opportunity to assess what you have collected until the plan is completed.

When your information is in, you need to look it all over, think about it, and try different methods of appropriate analysis. The techniques of looking over the data and analyzing it will vary from discipline to discipline, topic to topic, and study to study.

Reporting Fieldwork

Fieldwork can be presented in a great variety of ways, from a direct narrative describing your journey to your field site and what you saw there to a technical statistical report. In the classes where you write field reports and in related courses you will probably read and discuss published field studies, and you can then use these as models. Your textbook may cite studies you may want to look up. Journals and books in the discipline are also likely to hold many models. If you continue studying in a discipline that uses fieldwork, in addition to reading many field studies that can serve as models for your own work, you are likely to become familiar with how certain problems are discussed and with certain reporting styles. For example, in recent decades there has been a particularly vigorous debate over the research and writing of ethnographic reports in anthropology.

No matter what style the report is written in, it should include several kinds of information. That information is contained in both professional sociologist Gary Alan Fine's textbook account of some of his field research into Little League, written in a more narrative form (see pages 260–262), and in student Leonore Racker's study of study habits at her college's library, written in more of a technical report form (see pages 263–265). As you examine both examples, you should look at how they answer each of these questions.

What is it? What are you studying, generally and specifically?   The report should first of all identify what you are studying. You need to make clear both the larger issues or phenomena you are interested in as well as the specific site and investigative questions. Thus in the sample student paper below, Leonore Racker establishes the larger issue of how students consider study breaks and the specific site of her college library where she carried out the research.

So what? Why is the study worth paying attention to?   You need to establish that your subject is of interest and importance and that the results will help us understand significant issues or solve particular problems. No matter how fascinated you are with what you have been studying, others are always likely to ask "So what?" It is best to address the "so what?" question right up front, because readers will focus their attention only on what they consider valuable.

What did you do? What method have you chosen to carry out this research, and how, in detail, did you carry it out?   In order to interpret what you found, the readers need to see how you found it. If readers know you gathered your information about classroom learning by sitting in a class for a term and observing what went on, they will get a different picture of your information than if they knew you interviewed teachers and students extensively, or than if they knew that you gathered samples of work and tests. Information about your method also lets the readers evaluate how well the kind of data you have gathered can support the kinds of conclusions you draw.

What did you find? What information were you able to gather from the scene, and what picture does it give?   This reporting of what you found is of course the heart of your report. This is the news you carry from the field. The findings should be reported in detail, backed up by specific data that are appropriate to the subject, including statistics, survey answers, quotations from interviews, diagrams of what you observed, or photographs or other recordings. At the same time, you must not confuse the readers with irrelevant details, just because you collected them. You must be selective in providing only the most relevant information and presenting it in the clearest, most organized way possible.

What does it mean? How do you analyze and interpret the findings?   In analyzing the events you observed and on which you collected data, you are fulfilling the promises of the issues you raised in the opening parts of your presentation. Your analysis, while explaining what you found and while being true to the details, should also speak to the "so what?" question by letting the readers know why your discovery is valuable.

Report of a Professional Field Study

In the following, sociologist Gary Alan Fine writes about his fieldwork with Little League baseball. Although he has written about this work at greater length and in more formal ways in books and articles, this informal retelling still maintains all the characteristics of a field research report. Notice particularly how directly he deals with the "so what?" question right from the beginning. Notice also how carefully he explains all his research and method decisions. This explanation helps us understand what he was looking for and what he found. In this way, his findings, when he gets to them, are more meaningful.

Learning with the Boys

Gary Alan Fine

A sociologist who explores leisure and popular culture must withstand skeptical glances. It seems like too much fun. How can useful knowledge come from social scenes that seem so "trivial"? It is a fair question, especially as there is a sense that many academics, with their large chunks of discretionary time, avoid tasks that aren't enjoyable. As I tell my classes, "It's a dirty job, but someone's got to do it." Still, there are many important insights that can come from this research.

For three seasons I studied Little League baseball teams in suburban communities in New England and the Midwest. My decision to observe these teams didn't stem from the fact that I had played Little League when I was a kid or that I had a son of that age or even that I was fascinated by the world of sport. Actually, I had been observing how small groups of Harvard University undergraduates behaved in a social psychology laboratory. One can learn much from such artificial situations, but some topics cannot be studied in a lab. What are groups "really like" when members are free to do as they choose? What do members talk about, and how do they judge each other in a "real world"?

My desire to observe natural groups, coupled with interests in leisure and in the learning experiences of preadolescent boys, led me to consider studying boys who played Little League baseball. Here were natural groups that had as their goals both task success and personal friendships. The boys wanted to win games and to have fun doing it. I did not intend to *describe* Little League baseball as an end in itself. Although that might be interesting as journalism, it is questionable sociology. Our goal must be to generalize from the particular scene we study.

Baseball teams can be studied in many ways. One could simply examine the standing of the team, the batting averages of the players, and the other statistics that are collected by baseball record-keepers. This is archival (secondary) research. Another possibility is to distribute questionnaires to team members. Survey research, such as this, might tell us about whether players on better teams are happier than those on less successful teams (they are), but it couldn't tell us much about the meaning or emotions of the experience of winning and losing. Finally, if one could arrange it, one might manipulate the teams, such as by selecting which players play on which team, to test hypotheses, as in experimental research. The research techniques that I selected, however, were in-depth interviewing and participant observation (sometimes labeled ethnography). In the interviews, my research assistants and I spent over an hour with each child asking open-ended questions to which we hoped that the boys would respond at length. We wanted to see the world as the players saw it, rather than shoving words in their mouths. The key to participant observation is to spend as much time with one's subjects as one can, noting their behavior and their explanations for that behavior.

Preadolescent boys live in a rough-and-tumble culture. Remember when you were that age. Male college students reading

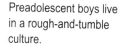

Preadolescent boys live in a rough-and-tumble culture.

this may wince at their own antics. Girls were probably not a part of this world, except perhaps during fifth and sixth grade. A paradox that I addressed was how could boys, who were personally nice and polite, behave in ways that most adults would find disreputable. This is the problem of "Good Children and Dirty Play" (girls sometimes behave in this way, too). I listened to boys talking about the pranks or vandalism that they or their pals engaged in. Some boys used racist language and delighted in aggressive sexual and sexist talk. For instance, most preadolescent boys delight in discussing the anatomy and alleged sexual activity of the girls they know. Such talk stems from the needs of preadolescents to differentiate themselves from other groups — to strengthen their community, a community that takes its boundaries from the messages that are transmitted from adult society. Preadolescents learn from adults that gender, race, and age are critical grouping variables. From this it is easy to recognize how preadolescents attempt to define their own group as specially virtuous and make negative comparisons to other groups. With regard to sexual and aggressive talk and behavior, preadolescents attempt to act in ways that they consider "mature." Maturity for children means that they will behave in ways that are dramatically different from how they had previously acted. They rely on those social traditions that they have just learned and those that are considered hidden or secret. Sexual talk is an example of this hidden, secret information.

Only through spending time with these preadolescents, being *with the boys,* can the knowledge of their sometimes hidden world be glimpsed. Preadolescents have learned, correctly, that adults are shocked at their private talk and may not even want to know about it. Listening to kids and spending time with them in a nonjudgmental way opens the door to a secret, rich, and colorful world.

Leisure activities, despite their lightness, are a window through which we can peer into the dynamics of group life. Here people behave as they choose. It is a dirty job, but some of us really should do it.

From Gary Alan Fine, "Learning with the Boys," in *Sociology,* ed. Beth B. Hess, Elizabeth W. Markson, and Peter J. Stein, 4th ed. (New York: Macmillan, 1993): p. 37.

Sample Student Field Report

Leonore Racker, as part of her writing course, was asked to write a field report on some aspect of undergraduate learning (see question 1 on page 265) to be shared with her classmates. She decided to survey what other students thought about the value of study breaks. She herself was unsure about whether she was taking too many breaks whenever she studied. Although she felt only too glad to get up to chat with friends or have a soda, she was afraid that she was enjoying herself too much. After asking students in the library a few basic questions, Leonore gained more confidence in her own study plans. If she had received special training in fieldwork, survey techniques, or statistics, the methods she chose would no doubt have been more accurate and precise; nonetheless, this survey told her and us a few things worth knowing.

Leonore Racker
Study Breaks and Student Effectiveness: A Field Report

Description of the Study
The chief purpose of this study was to determine (1) whether or not students who consider themselves successful studiers take frequent breaks while they are studying; and (2) whether or not students see study breaks as an effective part of the studying process. To collect the necessary data, I conducted a random survey of 25 students who were studying in the University of California, Santa Barbara, library between 12:00 and 2:00 on a weekday afternoon in the eighth week of the ten-week fall quarter. All grade levels were represented by the sample in the following proportions: four freshmen (16%), five sophomores (20%), seven juniors (28%), six seniors (24%), and three graduate students (12%).

I asked each student to rate him- or herself as being "not effective," "somewhat effective," "effective," or "highly effective" in his or her personal studies. For the purposes of this presentation, I have combined the students into two groups: "less effective" students are students who rated themselves in one of the first two groups, and "more effective" students are those who rated themselves in one of the last two. Of the 25 students, then, 18 (72%) considered themselves "more effective" and seven (28%) as "less effective." I should stress, though, that these labels only apply to the students' perceptions of their study habits and not the actual learning effectiveness of those habits; I did not ask any questions about academic performance or grade point average. I asked all 25 of the students a series of questions designed to determine the place of study breaks in their overall study strategies.

Summary of Data
Predictably, students who saw themselves as more effective reported spending more time studying

than students who saw themselves as less effective. Fifty-five percent of the more effective students reported studying more than 16 hours a week, compared to only 28% of the less effective students, and only 22% of the more effective students reported studying 10 hours or less during a week, while 71% of the less effective students fell into this category. Nearly all of the students, however, said that they took breaks during their study time. Only one respondent in each category reported that he or she did all of his or her studying in one sitting. The remaining students in both categories were fairly evenly divided in the number of study breaks they took, with the less effective students slightly more prone to take 1-2 or 3-4 breaks in a study session, and the more effective students more likely to take more breaks (presumably because they study for longer periods of time). The following table shows the number of study breaks reported by students in each category:

Study Breaks	0	1-2	3-4	4-5	5+
Less Effective	14%	43%	43%		
More Effective	6%	28%	33%	28%	6%

While nearly all of the students said that they took study breaks, they did not always report feeling the same way about them. Six of the seven less effective students (86%) said that they agreed with the following statement: "I probably should be more diligent when I study, but sometimes I just feel that I need a break." In contrast, not one of the more effective students agreed with this statement, and 88% of them agreed with this opposing statement: "I can only study effectively for a certain amount of time, so I need to take periodic breaks in order to always be at my best." Only one of the less effective students agreed with this statement.

Conclusions

While the study showed that almost all students take breaks when they study, students who consider themselves effective studiers are much more likely to view these breaks as a beneficial element of an overall study strategy. Furthermore, effective students are more likely to have an overall study strategy, while less effective students are more likely to study, or take a break, without working with an overall plan. Students in both categories reported that, after a certain (and widely varied) amount of time, they could no longer study effectively; however, the more effective students anticipated this and worked other activities and breaks into their study plans. It is this ability to plan and organize study time, taking into account the need for periodic breaks, that, more than anything else, set apart the students who considered themselves more effective from the ones who considered themselves less effective.

Thinking About Student Writing

1. What research question does Leonore Racker pose? Why might that be a useful or interesting question to ask?

2. Where does she carry out the field study to answer the question? What is the design of the field study? What method does Leonore Racker use to gather and record data? How well do the location and design address the question? What weaknesses do you see in the design? What strengths?

3. How does Leonore Racker present her results? Do you get a clear and precise picture of what she observed?

4. What does Leonore Racker find? What conclusions does she draw from what she finds? Do you think her conclusions are warranted on the basis of her findings?

5. What do her conclusions suggest to you about the best way to study? How well do her conclusions correspond to your study habits?

Assignments

DOING FIELDWORK

1. In order to investigate any of the issues, concepts, or processes of academic reading and writing discussed in this course or book, conduct a field study. This study might be a survey of students' study and/or writing habits, a study of students' thoughts as part of their writing process (in which you ask them to talk aloud into a tape recorder as they write), an interview study of professors concerning their goals and practices in assigning writing or their feelings about student writing that they receive, an ethnographic observation of the interac-

tion between students and a teaching assistant as they discuss an upcoming writing assignment, a description of a situation in which people are arguing over the meaning or value of something they have
read, or any other kind of study that might reveal something about
the academic literacy process on your campus. Even though you may
have no training in the method of collecting data that is most appropriate for the subject you want to investigate, do your best to think
through and plan your study to get accurate and revealing results.

2. In order to understand the variety of groups, organizations, and activities on campus or your community, visit and observe a meeting or
gathering of a group you have not previously been part of. If possible, also interview some participants in the group concerning what
they do as part of the group and the meaning of that participation for
them. Write up your results as a field observation to share with your
classmates.

3. To see whether certain groups or individuals dominate or take certain
roles in class discussions, make an audio tape recording of one day's
meeting of this or another class you are taking that has only a small
number of students. Keep notes to indicate who is talking at each
point in the class so that you can identify the speakers on the tape.
Then design a method for analyzing these data (or any shorter sequence, if appropriate). For example, measuring the total time or the
number of comments various people speak in the course of an entire
classroom might give you a way of studying gender dominance patterns, whereas close study of a short sequence where people interrupt
each other might tell you about what patterns of talk allow one to get
the last word in. Write a short report on your findings.

4. To examine processes of decision making in small groups, attend a
meeting of either a student or a faculty committee. You may use any
concepts that you find most useful from your courses in political science, psychology, sociology, anthropology, communication, or any
other appropriate subject to help you design the study and analyze
the data. Record the data in any way most appropriate for the concepts and issues you are studying. Write up your results in a short report, presenting a precise claim about the processes you observed in
action.

5. Do a field study of how people greet each other in some public place,
such as an airport, the school cafeteria, or the entrance to the student
center. Sit inconspicuously at a distance and record the gender, age,
and other visible characteristics of people who greet each other, and
then record the way they do it (a few words, a wave, a handshake,
bear hugs, romantic embraces, etc.) and then what happens after the
greeting (walking on, talking with each other, going off together, etc.).

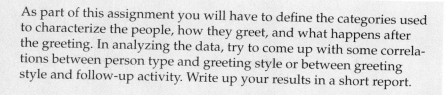

As part of this assignment you will have to define the categories used to characterize the people, how they greet, and what happens after the greeting. In analyzing the data, try to come up with some correlations between person type and greeting style or between greeting style and follow-up activity. Write up your results in a short report.

Experiments: Events Created to Be Observed

Sometimes novelists talk about putting characters together in a story and seeing what they will do. Then the novelist just claims to tell the story as the characters made the writer tell it. Of course, even if the characters seem to have their own will, they only exist in the writer's imagination and on the pages of the unfolding manuscript.

Experiments take place in real physical laboratories, and what happens is not a fiction of the experimenter's imagination. Yet there are still some similarities. The experimenter decides what to place in the laboratory, what elements to put together with what apparatus, and then how to set things in motion. The experimenter sets up a story and then watches what happens. Moreover, the experimenter watches the events from a defined point of view, gathering particular data through appropriate instruments and applying relevant concepts to make sense of events. But in the end the data that turn up on the recording instruments are beyond the control of the experimenter. Although the experimenter might have some idea or hypothesis about what might happen, he or she cannot know how the story ends, or what the results will be, until the experiment runs its course. Then the hypothesis may be confirmed or some other idea about what went on may be supported, or the experimenter may be puzzled — unable to explain the events, unable to find a meaning in the story.

Experiments are a precise mix of a controlled, staged performance to tell a particular kind of story and an uncontrolled reality that does what it wants. In this mixture we find the way in which experiments serve as revealing tools for investigation. Because reality is so messy, uncertain, and obscure in its workings, experimenters find ways to narrow down the variables, control the uncertainties, and make visible things that often can't be seen. By staging unusual events where they to some degree control and limit the circumstances, experimenters try to display events with simplicity and clarity — to see what happens in these special circumstances. The experiment then becomes a way to investigate how something operates when you don't let too many factors confuse the picture or when you push some process to an extreme that it does not get to in ordinary life.

The art of doing experimental designs sometimes requires extensive resources of time, money, and brainpower. The study of high-energy physics, for example, needs expensive particle accelerators, exotic measuring devices, and large research teams to observe operations of minute particles we have no ways of perceiving through more ordinary forms of observation. But sometimes extremely clever experiments can also be simple and inexpensive, as when a psychologist asks people to draw a penny using only their recollection, in order to see what long-term memory we hold of common objects.

Experiments are also useful for applied design research, to see what factors influence a design and how the design responds to particular conditions. Thus materials engineers will run experiments to test the strength of alloys under various stresses. Computer programmers will run experiments to see what results their programs produce with various changed inputs or altered instructions. Policy planners will run experiments to test how proposals for welfare reform work out with small groups of people before applying new rules to the whole state.

In writing up the experiment, you show both how you staged the event and what happened once you let the events take their own course. That is, you describe the experimental design and then the results. However, since

Laboratories allow you to observe, measure, and experiment with specimens of the outside world under controlled conditions.

the event was designed to develop understanding of the phenomena, you frame the story of the laboratory with an introduction defining the problem you are investigating (placing it in a history of investigations other people have carried out) and with a discussion and conclusion that interpret the meaning of the results. In this way you get the standard format for an experimental report.

1. *Introduction.*   The introduction defines the problem and reviews the literature on the subject (that is, previous published studies investigating this and related phenomena). See below for a further discussion of typical introductions.
2. *Method.*   This section describes the experiment you designed to investigate the phenomenon, how you set up the laboratory, what actions you took to set the experiment in motion, and what instruments and techniques you used to make a record of the events. The experimental design needs to be specifically relevant to the issues you claim to be investigating and the procedures need to be appropriate to fulfill the promise of the design. That is, it needs to be clear exactly why you are doing what you do, how what you are doing will advance our understanding of the phenomena you are investigating, and how you will produce results that will be reliable and appropriate.
3. *Results.*   This section presents what happened once you let the events take their course. Here accuracy and detail are of highest importance, so that readers will perceive exactly what went on and will trust your account.
4. *Discussion and Conclusion.*   This section explores the meaning and implications of the results, connecting the results to the findings of other researchers, and suggesting where investigations might go from this point. Here your reasoning is most important, both in the way you put together the data and in the way you connect these data with other people's findings and other principles of your field.

◎◎ USEFUL CONCEPTS FROM RHETORIC

The Three Moves in Research Article Introductions

Linguist John Swales, after studying many introductions and reviews of literature of research articles, has found that these article openings typically follow a three-part structure. These parts can be thought of as moves justifying the research that will be reported:

Move 1. Establishing a territory

Move 2. Establishing a niche

Move 3. Occupying the niche

In the first move the author states that there is a topic of some importance and reviews what others might have said about the topic.

In the second move the author points out that there is some limitation, weakness, flaw, or omission in that research that needs filling.

In the third move the author announces how the current piece of research fills that missing need.

The following introduction of the research article reporting the memory-of-a-penny experiment neatly reveals this pattern; the first three paragraphs carry out the moves in order.

Many things can be recognized on the basis of their visual characteristics. Moreover, laboratory studies have shown that people are quite adept at discriminating between complex pictures they have seen a short time before and those they have not, even when given hundreds (Nickerson, 1965; Shepard, 1967) or thousands (Standing, 1973; Standing, Conezio, & Haber, 1970) of pictures to remember and allowed to inspect each for only a few seconds. Both of those observations are consistent with the idea of a visual memory that readily assimilates and retains an abundance of information about the stimuli to which it is exposed.

In fact neither introspection nor the results of picture recognition studies tells us how much information regarding any particular visual pattern has been stored. When people demonstrate the ability to recognize something, they may be demonstrating only that they can place that thing in an appropriate conceptual category. And the category may be more or less broadly defined, depending on one's purpose — as when an object is recognized as an automobile, as opposed to being recognized as a Volkswagen, or as the specific Volkswagen that belongs to John Doe. Similarly, when people show that they can distinguish a picture they have seen before from one they are looking at for the first time, they show only that they have retained enough information about the "old" picture to distinguish it from the new one. Given that one typically cannot say how much information *must be* retained in order to permit such categorizations and distinctions, one cannot rule out the possibility that they may be made on the basis of a small portion of the information that the patterns contain.

The experiments reported in this paper are addressed to the question of how accurately and completely the visual details of a common object, a United States penny, are represented in people's memories. We chose to study people's knowledge of a common object rather than of laboratory stimuli because we are interested in the nature of the information that normally accrues in memory. As a stimulus, a penny has the advantage of being complex enough to be interesting but simple enough to be analyzed and manipulated. And it is an object that all of our subjects would have seen frequently.

Laboratory Courses

Because designing and carrying out experiments are such skilled perfor-mances, extensive training is often needed for original experimental investi-gations. Although some of your early laboratory experience may be designed to give you a hands-on feel for investigation, much of your laboratory work is probably highly structured. The procedures will be well defined in a labo-ratory manual, and the results are likely to be unsurprising. Such experi-ments are more to demonstrate to you how well-known phenomena work and to increase your own skill in experimental procedure. The experimental write-up is also likely to be highly structured, again through your lab man-ual, which may even provide tear-out fill-in sheets.

In grading your laboratory reports, your lab instructors will be making sure that you carry out all the tasks accurately, that you report the results pre-cisely in the prescribed manner, that you analyze the results accurately, and that you understand how concepts relate to the experimental events you have witnessed. Thus your primary task will be to report and explain accu-rately and precisely what you did, what went on, and what the results meant. Since the experiment and the format of the report are probably prescribed by your lab manual, you probably will not have to think through the design of the experiment, the organization of the report, or what to include in the re-port.

However, if you continue in a major that relies on experiments, you will be given tasks that are more open-ended and more difficult to control. These more advanced laboratory projects require more curiosity, original thought, and design on your part. At each point, your instructors will probably spell out what additional work you will need to do. For example, as the physical manipulation of the experiments becomes more difficult and the results less certain, your instructors may ask you to comment on the difficulties in car-rying out the experiment or the sources of possible error. At some point you may be asked to design your own experiment. This process (including the form of the experimental report) is likely to be guided by more skilled exper-imenters, and to be specific to the requirements of your field. You will grad-ually be led into the experimental practices of your field, often as part of research teams.

The Four Stories of the Experimental Report

What is important to know at this point is that even though an experiment re-quires much specialized skill in design and technique and even though an experimental report is a distinctive form of writing (or genre, see pages 209–210), it nonetheless is just another kind of investigative writing, present-ing findings for other people to consider. As we have discussed, the lab re-port tells four kinds of stories nested within each other:

1. The innermost story is the events in the lab, or the results.
2. The results are nested within the story of the design and the performance of the experiment that sets the stage for the results. This story of design is largely carried in the methods section.
3. The experiment itself is nested within the story of scientists trying to understand phenomena and each other's results. Much of that story is carried in the review of the literature and in the discussion part of your paper.
4. All this is buried within the largest but incomplete framing story of how nature or the phenomena under question operate. The hypotheses and conclusions try to put forward pieces of this largest story, and all the smaller stories nested within the article are part of the process of trying to figure out what should go into this overall story.

When you are first being trained in laboratory technique, the largest two stories (of nature and of scientists investigating nature) are controlled for you, since you are not really part of the front-line investigation. The scientific meaning is usually already given you in the textbook and lab manual. The experimental design is also usually provided, but the performance is up to you — and you usually need to retell some of the details of the performance. Getting results and reporting them are usually what you are held accountable for in beginning work. As you advance in experimental fields, you take on more responsibility for the outer frames of the story.

NEWS FROM THE FIELD

A Social Experiment Inside Mental Hospitals

What if the treatment of patients with psychological problems only created more problems?

The effect on mental patients of the social conditions under which they are treated is difficult to determine, because the behavior of patients can readily be attributed to their mental condition and the treatment given them can be explained as responses to the psychological problems exhibited by the patients. But some sociologists and psychologists have come to believe that the social organization of the mental hospital itself has an effect on the patients. In order to test this idea, in 1973 David Rosenhan, a research sociologist, carried out a field experiment. Rather than just carrying out a field study of the conditions in mental institutions, he created a special kind of situation in which the people who took on the role of the patients had no recognizable psychological problem. What happened then could only be explained by the social processes in the institution and not by the psychological condition of the patients.

Rosenhan and seven other adults gained entry into the psychiatric wards of twelve hospitals in five states. Three of these "pseudopatients" were psychologists, one was a psychiatrist, one was a graduate student in psychology, and two had no connection to the mental health profession. Though none of the patients had any history of mental illness, all of them were accepted into the hospitals by claiming that they had been "hearing voices" that said such things as "empty," "hollow," and "thud." The presence of the researchers was generally not known to the hospital doctors or staff, and they were instructed that they could not leave until they could prove themselves sane enough to be released.

In eleven of the twelve cases, the patient was diagnosed with schizophrenia, and in one with a manic-depressive disorder. All were admitted to the hospital immediately without undue questions or investigation. Patients used pseudonyms, but otherwise gave accurate personal and medical histories. Although most of the patients feared that they would be discovered by the staff and exposed, none ever were. All of them took copious notes on the behavior of other patients and of staff members, but none were ever interrupted or asked to stop. Whereas many of the other patients in the hospitals became suspicious of their observations and note taking, the members of the staff simply interpreted this behavior as another manifestation of mental illness.

Once in the hospital, the pseudopatients spoke and acted completely sane and displayed no further symptoms. They never complained further of hearing voices, and they underwent regular psychiatric treatment for their mental disorder. The length of stay in the hospitals ranged from 7 to 52 days, with an average stay of 19 days. None of the subjects were ever declared "sane," and all eleven of the volunteers were discharged with the label "schizophrenia in remission."

One of the most important things that this experiment found is that, once a diagnosis of mental illness was made, the staff saw nearly all of the pseudopatients' behaviors — no matter how seemingly "sane"— in light of this diagnosis. Even the normal personal histories that the participants gave to psychologists tended to be interpreted as abnormal. On one occasion, for example, a patient told a staff psychologist that he felt remote from his father as a child but that they had later become "close friends." The psychologist transformed this relatively common phenomenon into a tell-tale sign of schizophrenic reaction:

> This white 39-year-old male manifests a long history of considerable ambivalence in close relationships, which begins in early childhood. A warm relationship with his mother cools during adolescence. A distant relationship with his father is described as becoming very intense. Affective status is absent. (252)

Rosenhan's study raises serious questions about the validity of labels such as "sane" and "insane." All of the participants in the study were respected professionals whom society had labeled mentally fit. However, once a label of "insane" was attached to these supposedly sane individuals, competent medical authorities interpreted all of their actions as the actions of an insane person.

(Complete details of this study are available in D. L. Rosenhan, "On Being Sane in Insane Places," *Science* 179 (1973): 250–58.)

✑∽ A Sample Student Experiment

The following experimental report by a first-year student in a writing course provides an example of some of the basic features of an experiment, although it does not rely on any advanced techniques of experimental disciplines.

Frank Petrine
How to Get Help in the Library: A Field Experiment

Introduction
        Students, when they have assignments requiring library research, are frequently told by their teachers to seek the help of reference librarians. But no one ever tells us what to say to the librarian to get the help we need. After several attempts to gain help from reference librarians, some successful and some unsuccessful, I began to wonder what was the best way to approach a librarian for help. Last year, my high school history teacher suggested that the best way to get help was to be prepared and know what I was asking for; then the librarian could hone in on exactly what I needed. My older brother, who has just finished college, tells me, however, that the best tip is just to be persistent and not leave the librarian until you have an answer. I decided to test which of these two strategies was the more successful by carrying out an experiment at the college library.

Description of Experiment Methodology
        The purpose of the experiment was to determine the way that librarians at the Middle State University Undergraduate Library responded to requests for help in light of two variables: the persistence and the perceived knowledgeability of the person asking for help. Over the course of two months, I asked six different

volunteers to approach the information counter at the
library and ask for help in finding a book. In each
case, the book they requested did not actually exist
and could therefore not be found by the librarian. I
instructed three of the volunteers to be "extremely
persistent" with their inquiries and to insist that the
book was in the library and that they absolutely needed
to find it as soon as possible. I instructed the other
three participants to be "not persistent"—to ask for
the book only once and to leave as soon as a librarian
indicated that he or she was unable to locate it.

In addition to instructing the participants to
be "persistent" and "not persistent," I also instructed
them to display three different levels of knowledge
about the book in question. I instructed one person in
each group to pretend to know nothing but the author's
approximate last name and one or two title words from
the book. I instructed a second pair (one from each
group) to know the author's full name, the full title
of the book, and to have a general understanding of the
subject matter. I told the final pair to display a high
level of professional knowledge about the book and the
subject matter and to act as if the item were a common
one that any respectable library should be able to locate immediately. To control for possible racial, gender, or age-related biases, all of the participants
were white females between the ages of 18 and 23.

Results of the Experiment

All of the librarian responses fit into four basic response types: (1) looking in a computerized database of library holdings; (2) looking in the Books in
Print catalog or other printed listings of books that
may or may not be in the library holdings; (3) referring the participant to a senior librarian or adminis-
trator; and (4) calling one or more other libraries on
behalf of the participant. Librarians tended to follow
the steps in order, first looking in a computerized
database, then looking in a printed catalog, then referring the participant to another librarian, and finally calling another library, though, on one occasion
(subject 5) steps two and three were reversed. Twice,
the librarians responded in all four ways, and, in the
other cases, they stopped short of calling another library. The following table represents the distribution
of results with all six experimental subjects:

Participant	1	2	3	4
(1) not persistent, not knowledgeable	Yes	No	No	No
(2) not persistent, medium knowledgeable	Yes	Yes	No	No
(3) not persistent, extremely knowledgeable	Yes	Yes	No	No
(4) persistent, not knowledgeable	Yes	Yes	Yes	No
(5) persistent, medium knowledgeable	Yes	Yes	Yes	Yes
(6) persistent, extremely knowledgeable	Yes	Yes	Yes	Yes

Conclusions

While both knowledge and persistence correlated
positively with the amount of help that the participant
received, the correlation for persistence was much
higher. All three of the subjects who were instructed
to be "extremely persistent" received a high level of
service from the librarian. Of these three subjects,
only the first, who could produce neither a book title
nor an author's full name, did not receive every level
of help that the library offered. On the other hand,
none of the subjects who were "not persistent" received
more than two of the four possible services the library
offered. In libraries, as in many other human institutions, it helps to be knowledgeable, but it really pays
to be persistent.

Thinking About Student Writing

1. What research question does Frank Petrine pose? Why might that be a useful or interesting question to ask?

2. What are the two possible hypotheses he presents? What are the sources of these hypotheses? Where in the article are the hypotheses and the sources presented?

3. What is the design of his experiment to answer his research question and test his hypotheses? How well does his design address the question? What weaknesses do you see in the design? What strengths?

4. What are the results of the experiment? What conclusions does Frank Petrine draw? Do you think his conclusions are warranted on the basis of his method and results?

5. What do his conclusions suggest to you about the best way to approach librarians? Do his conclusions correspond with or contradict your common sense about the best way to get information from librarians?

Assignments

UNDERSTANDING EXPERIMENTS

1. Design an experiment to test any one piece of advice from this book or from any other teacher concerning writing. Carry out and write up the results of your experiment.

2. If you are currently taking a laboratory course, or have recently taken one, examine the format of a typical lab report required by the manual or other instructions given by the teacher. Write several paragraphs on how well the format conforms to the general structure of the experimental report described in this section and how much work of what kind was required of you versus how much of the work was already done by the laboratory instructions. Consider the report format and requirements in relation to the four levels of the experimental story as presented on pages 272–273.

3. In your college library examine a journal from an experimental field that interests you. Then write several paragraphs describing one experimental article, its format, and how it conforms to or differs from the format described in this section.

Getting Involved Electronically

Find and examine an electronic tool for researching, observing, or recording some phenomenon in a field of interest to you. Describe the tool, what it does, and how it is used by researchers.

Dealing with Complexity

PART

Five

13

Writing About Complex Worlds

AIMS OF THE CHAPTER

The more you find out about subjects, the more there is to think about. Your writing then begins to deal with this greater complexity. This chapter discusses how to write clearly while also recognizing that many facts, ideas, and viewpoints bear on one's subject.

KEY POINTS

1. In college you are often confronted by complex texts and complex issues. Material isn't simplified to provide easy answers or a single way of looking at something, especially if there is serious disagreement or if multiple factors are involved.

2. To write about complex subjects, you identify the several distinct ideas or elements that are simultaneously present.

3. One kind of complexity is an event or phenomenon that has many aspects, causes, factors, or consequences. The task here is to describe in clearest terms the multiple parts of the topic and how they fit together.

4. Another kind of complexity occurs when opinions conflict over an issue. In this case you have to understand the multiple viewpoints before you can come to your own understanding of the issue.

QUESTIONS TO THINK ABOUT

- In writing an essay, have you ever felt you had to oversimplify what you were discussing to make a clear point? How did you simplify your task? What did you leave out? What was the effect of leaving it out?

- In writing about a subject, did you ever have information that didn't fit together easily, or even conflicted? What did you do?

- What do you do when you discover credible authorities who disagree about a subject?

There are often many simple ways to talk about a subject, but they are often too simple. They leave things out, lead to poor decisions, or ignore the reality that other people with good reasons see things differently. Writing about complex subjects involves explaining them as simply and directly as you can but without hiding or distorting any of their complexity.

Textbooks at lower levels often present one single, authoritative way of looking at a subject so that students know what they have to learn. But as you advance in the subject, you find that often there are alternative points of view about many of its aspects, from the interpretation of current results to basic viewpoints. You move into areas about which there is little certainty and agreement, and into areas we all know less about. Professors often confront students with this complexity because they want them to be able to address the puzzles that still confront their disciplines.

In fact, university courses are often designed to immerse you in the complexity of problems and issues that you may have originally thought simple. Part of professors' professional task is to be as knowledgeable about their areas as possible so that they can develop accurate research and statements that will lead to more intelligent analysis and action. Their job is not to oversimplify. If they can find simple statements that explain much and do not overlook important data, then indeed they are fortunate — they have made a great discovery, a new theory that many people may find useful. However, breakthroughs to accurate and simple statements usually come only after one is immersed in the full confusion and complexity of a problem for a long time, for the solution has to draw together all those details. Even then, the new simplification may be difficult to understand. Quantum theory, although greatly simplifying our general understanding of the behavior of particles and energy, still remains complicated to understand and work with. Linguistic descriptions of grammar, although seeking accurate and powerful ways of understanding the complexity of language, nonetheless are often a challenge to understand and use.

Calvin and Hobbes

by Bill Watterson

The Simple Paper Clip Isn't So Simple

Everyday items that seem simple and self-evident often have complicated stories behind them. Every year, manufacturers produce more than 20 billion paper clips, most of which share the same basic design: a single piece of wire bent into an elongated loop with a second loop inside the first one. This paper clip design is so simple and functional that it would be difficult to imagine any other, but, in fact, the current design of the paper clip is less than a hundred years old, and reflects centuries of design evolution and improvement. In his book *The Evolution of Useful Things,* Henry Petroski, a civil engineering professor at Duke University, devotes 26 pages to tracing the history and development of the common paper clip.

Petroski writes that, for centuries after the invention of paper in first-century China, people bound multiple sheets of paper by cutting a small hole in them and tying them together with a piece of twine or thread. In the Middle Ages, people fastened paper together with straight pins, which, unlike paper clips, could be mass-produced without industrial technology. In his famous book *Wealth of Nations* (1776), Adam Smith noted that ten people working in a factory could produce 48,000 pins in a single day. While many of these pins would be used for sewing and other household

Illust. **b** *Angling.* A gaff or hook for use in landing the fish, as in salmon or trout fishing. *Scot. & Dial. Eng.* **c** A grappling iron. **d** A clasp or holder for letters, bills, clippings, etc. **e** An embracing strap, as of iron or brass, for connecting parts together ; specif., the iron strap, with loop, at either end of a whiffletree. **f** Any of various devices for confining the

Various forms of Clips for papers.

bottom of a trousers leg, used in bicycling. **g** A device to hold several, usually five, cartridges for charging the maga-

2. That which clips, or clasps; a device for clasping and holding tightly, as: **a** A grappling iron. **b** A clasp or holder for letters, bills, clippings, etc. **c** An embracing strap, as of iron or brass, for connecting parts together; specif., the iron strap, with loop, at either end of a whiffletree. **d** Any of various devices for confining the bottom of a trousers leg, used in bicycling. **e** *Scot. & Dial. Eng.*

Various forms of Clips for papers.

An instrument for lifting pots, etc., from a fire, or for carrying barrels, etc.

operations, many more would be used by banks, businesses, and offices for the purpose of binding important documents together.

With the Industrial Revolution of the nineteenth century, machines soon replaced human labor as the chief manufacturer of straight pins. And since machines were capable of bending wire as easily as cutting it, manufacturers of "bank pins" (pins marketed for use in offices) began to introduce improvements. In 1864, a patent was issued for a "paper fastener" that turned out to be "a decorative metal device whose two small teeth pierced the papers and were folded over another piece of metal placed against the back side of the sheets, thus clasping them together." Though the paper fastener did not solve the main problem of straight pins — the fact that they left holes in the papers they attached — it did solve the problem of sharp points snagging other papers in the vicinity.

In 1887, a Philadelphia inventor named Ethelbert Middleton patented a paper fastener that did not use a paper-piercing point. This early prototype of the paper clip consisted of "malleable metal stamped in curious patterns whose use involved the action of folding various wings over the corners of the papers." The invention was useful but too complicated for mass appeal, since it required complicated manipulations of "various wings" to achieve its end. However, Middleton's invention was one of many signals that, by the latter half of the nineteenth century, engineers were taking the invention and improvement of paper fasteners seriously.

The search for a better paper fastener was guided by the principles of Hooke's Law. Named for its seventeenth-century discoverer, a British physicist named Robert Hooke, Hooke's Law states that metals will behave "elastically" up to a point — they will spring back to their original shape after being bent. But if they are stretched beyond a certain point, they will lose their spring and not return to their original shape. Toward the end of the nineteenth century, inventors began to apply the principles of Hooke's Law to bent pieces of wire in an attempt to discover a design that would use the elastic property of metal to hold pieces of paper together effectively.

The actual invention of the current paper clip cannot be accurately credited to any one inventor, though several patents issued at the turn of the century give us some clues. Many accounts credit the Norwegian inventor Johan Vaaler with the invention in 1899, and Vaaler did obtain an American patent of a "paper clip or holder" in 1901. However, earlier patents were granted to Americans Matthew Schooley (1896) and Cornelius Brosnan (1900), both of whose patent applications acknowledged the existence of other bent-wire devices that they were improving upon. Brosnan's invention, marketed as the "Konaclip," came close to the contemporary design except that, instead of featuring a loop within a loop like modern paper clips, it had an outside loop with a single piece of wire running down the center, making it more difficult to grasp and hold several pieces of paper at once.

The design that has come to dominate the paper clips of the twentieth century is known as the "gem" clip, and it has never actually been patented. However, in 1899 a patent was granted to William Middlebrook of Waterbury, Connecticut, for a machine designed to manufacture them. The drawings that Middlebrook submitted to the patent office showed a perfectly proportioned gem paper clip, suggesting that the design was known and used years before Vaaler, Schooley, and Brosnan claimed to "invent" their designs. By 1908, catalogues advertised the gem clip as "the most popular clip" and "the only satisfactory device for temporary attachment of papers" (69). The gem soon replaced the Konaclip as the paper fastener of choice, and has now become synonymous with the word *paper clip* throughout the world.

The gem paper clip is a complex piece of engineering whose subtleties eluded inventors for centuries. Before the paper clip could be developed and successfully manufactured, physicists had to understand the behavior of metal, and machinists had to perfect complicated methods for bending wire without the need of human intervention. However, this complex history usually remains hidden behind the apparent simplicity of the device — and this is not unique to paper clips.

✑〜✎ Complexity Presented to You and Complexity You Find

Complexity can turn up in a variety of places in a course. Sometimes it can turn up in the professor's lectures or in a book you read: that is, a subject or issue is presented to you as complex or many-sided. However, the professor's lectures or the book will also provide some guidance by presenting the parts, pieces, or sides in an organized way, perhaps even showing a relationship among the parts. Thus the complexity is already presented to you with a coherence and a shape, the result of someone's hard thinking and work.

Consider the following passage from Charles Darwin's *The Origin of Species*. In the chapter from which this passage comes, Darwin is anticipating various objections to his theory of natural selection and attempting to answer them in advance. In this passage, he deals with the objection that the long-term, inexact process of selection would not be capable of producing a complicated, perfect organ such as the eye. He argues that the eye could have evolved in a series of stages, each useful and well formed for the creature that possessed it.

> To suppose that the eye with all its inimitable contrivances for adjusting the focus to different distances, for admitting different amounts of light, and for the correction of spherical and chromatic aberration [that is, blurring and color distortion that occur when light passes through lenses], could have been formed by natural selection seems, I freely confess, absurd in the highest degree. When

it was first said that the sun stood still and the world turned round, the common sense of mankind declared the doctrine false; but the old saying of *Vox populi, vox Dei* [that is, "The voice of the masses is the voice of God," or "Popular opinion is true"], as every philosopher knows, cannot be trusted in science. Reason tells me, that if numerous gradations from a simple and imperfect eye to one complex and perfect can be shown to exist, each grade being useful to its possessor, as is certainly the case; if further, the eye ever varies and the variations be inherited, as is likewise certainly the case; and if such variations should be useful to any animal under changing conditions of life, then the difficulty of believing that a perfect and complex eye could be formed by natural selection, though insuperable by our imagination, should not be considered as subversive of the theory.

From Charles Darwin, *The Origin of Species* (New York: Mentor, 1958): 168–69.

To understand the complexity of this passage, one must first understand the rhetorical aim of its author. In the book *The Origin of Species,* Darwin has argued that the various traits of different species evolve through a process of "natural selection" in which accidental mutations that benefit a species are gradually absorbed by the species. Darwin felt that the biological evidence in favor of his theory was overwhelming, but he also knew that it went against most people's notions of "common sense." In this passage, Darwin is setting up a lengthy presentation of biological evidence. He does not actually present the evidence in this paragraph; instead, he establishes a framework for his argument by doing three things:

1. He acknowledges that his theory goes against common expectations.
2. He asserts — through argument and example — that common opinion is not a good measure of scientific truth.
3. He states that, if he is able to demonstrate with scientific evidence that the eye has undergone mutations and improvements in the past, then he is justified in claiming that such mutations were indeed capable of producing the eye in its present complexity.

In class discussions, essays, and examinations, you will need to be able to avoid oversimplifications and to discuss the subject in a way that recognizes all the complexities suggested in the lecturer or book. But in doing this you need only follow the path already opened up by others. Once you have been given several examples of complex topics, the instructor may begin to expect more out of you. As you approach new subjects and topics, you may be expected to find the same kinds of complexities presented to you in previous cases and topics. The earlier examples will often be treated as models you should use for developing your own thoughts.

If you keep notes describing how complicated topics are treated in your readings and lectures, then you may have a better clue as to the kinds of thinking your professor would like you to develop. For example, a student reading the above passage might make the following comment in a personal journal:

> This is an amazing passage, typical of what Darwin is doing throughout the <u>The Origin of Species</u>. He gets us to see opposite things about the eye at the same time. He shows us how wonderful, coordinated, and well-designed the eye is, solving complex problems in optics; at the same time he says that the wonderful design did not have to develop in a single coordinated way, but could be the result of simpler eyes, each of which worked at its level. Each level could then have evolved for the next.
>
> In addition to making his point about how the eye evolved, he is setting us up for all the detailed evidence he has found in nature for different levels of the eye. So now we know how to make sense of the many examples that follow. Evolution becomes a way of making sense of the great complexity of nature recorded in the book. Thus evolution as a theory tries to make complex things simple and understandable.

This student, by making sense of the passage, is also making sense of the meaning of Darwin's book and theory.

ssignment

READING ABOUT COMPLEXITY

Read the following passages. Pick two that interest you and comment on their meaning in an informal journal entry. Consider how the author brings a complex situation together into a coherent description.

1. Psychology

Sigmund Freud (*Civilization and Its Discontents*, trans. James Strachey [New York: Norton, 1961]: 61) discusses how difficult it is for humans to live without aggressiveness.

> It is clearly not easy for men to give up the satisfaction of this inclination to aggression. They do not feel comfortable without it. The advantage which a comparatively small cultural group offers of allowing this instinct an outlet in the form of hostility against intruders is not to be despised. It is always possible to bind together a considerable number of people in love, so long as there are other people left over to receive the manifestations of their

aggressiveness. I once discussed the phenomenon that it is precisely communities with adjoining territories, and related to each other in other ways as well, who are engaged in constant feuds and in ridiculing each other — like the Spaniards and the Portuguese, for instance, the North Germans and the South Germans, the English and the Scotch, and so on. I gave this phenomenon the name of the "narcissism of minor differences," a name which does not do much to explain it. We can now see that it is a convenient and relatively harmless satisfaction of the inclination to aggression, by means of which cohesion between the members of the community is made easier.

2. History

Thomas P. Hughes (*American Genesis* [New York: Penguin, 1989]: 184–85) presents the importance of technological systems in transforming modern life.

Since 1870 inventors, scientists, and system builders have been engaged in creating the technological systems of the modern world. Today most of the industrial world lives in a made environment structured by these systems, not in the natural environment of past centuries. . . . Today machines such as the automobile and the airplane are omnipresent. Because they are mechanical and physical, they are not difficult to comprehend. Machines like these, however, are usually merely components in highly organized and controlled technological systems. Such systems are hard to comprehend, because they also include complex components, such as people and organizations, and because they often consist of physical components, such as the chemical and electrical, other than the mechanical. Large systems — energy, production, communication, and transportation — compose the essence of modern technology.

3. Music

Douglas R. Hofstadter (*Gödel, Escher, Bach* [New York: Vintage, 1979]: 8) describes the structure of a musical canon.

The idea of a canon is that one single theme is played against itself. This is done by having "copies" of the theme played by the various participating voices. But there are many ways to do this. The most straightforward of all canons is the round, such as "Three Blind Mice," "Row, Row, Row Your Boat," or "Frere Jacques." Here, the theme enters in the first voice and, after a fixed time-delay, a "copy" of it enters, in precisely the same key. After the same fixed time-delay in the second voice, the third voice enters carrying the theme, and so on. Most themes will not harmonize with themselves in this way. In order for a theme to work as a canon theme, each of its notes must be able to serve a dual (or triple, or quadruple) role: it must firstly be part of a melody, and secondly it must be part of a harmonization of the same melody. When there are three canonical voices, for instance, each note of the theme must act in two distinct harmonic ways, as well as melodically. Thus, each note in a canon has more than one musical meaning; the listener's ear and brain automatically figure out the appropriate meaning, by referring to context.

4. Literary Criticism/Feminist Studies

Gayle Greene and Coppelia Kohn (*Making a Difference* [London: Metheun, 1985]: 1–2) present an overview definition of feminist literary criticism.

Feminist literary criticism is one branch of interdisciplinary enquiry which takes gender as its fundamental organizing category of experience. This enquiry holds two related premises about gender. One is that inequality of the sexes is neither a biological given nor a divine mandate, but a cultural construct, and therefore a proper study for any humanistic discipline. The second is that a male perspective, assumed to be 'universal', has dominated fields of knowledge, shaping their paradigms and methods. Feminist scholarship, then, has two concerns: It revises concepts previously thought universal but now seen as originating in particular cultures and serving particular purposes; and it restores a female perspective by extending knowledge about women's experience and contributions to culture.

5. Sociology/ Cultural Studies

Pierre Bourdieu, a French sociologist, in "How Can One Be a Sports Fan," begins to consider the process by which sports has come to take a large place in the modern world.

It is possible to consider the whole range of sporting activities and entertainments offered to social agents — rugby, football, swimming, athletics, tennis, golf, etc. — as a *supply* intended to meet a *social demand*. If such a model is adopted, two sets of questions arise. First, is there an area of production, endowed with its own logic and history, in which 'sports products' are generated, i.e., the universe of the sporting activities and entertainments socially realized and accepted at a given moment in time? Secondly, what are the social conditions of possibility of the appropriation of the various 'sports products' that are thus produced — playing golf or reading *L'Equipe* [the French equivalent of Sports Illustrated], cross-country skiing or watching the World Cup on TV?

In other words, how is the demand for 'sports products' produced, how do people acquire the 'taste' for sport, and for one sport rather than another, whether as an activity or a spectacle?

6. Politics

James Madison (*The Federalist* #51) comments on how the ambitions of politicians may be controlled.

> But of the great security against a gradual concentration of the several powers in the same department consists in giving to those who administer each department the necessary constitutional means and personal motives to resist encroachments of the others. The provision for defense must in this, as in all other cases, be made commensurate to the danger of attack. Ambition must be made to counteract ambition. The interest of the man must be connected with the constitutional rights of the place. It may be a reflection on human nature that such devices should be necessary to control the abuses of government. But what is government itself but the greatest of all reflections on human nature? If men were angels, no government would be necessary. If angels were to govern men, neither external nor internal controls on government would be necessary. In framing a government which is to be administered by men over men, the great difficulty lies in this: you must first enable the government to control the governed; and in the next place oblige it to control itself. A dependence on the people is, no doubt, the primary control on the government; but experience has taught mankind the necessity of auxiliary precautions.

7. Politics

Alexis de Tocqueville (*Democracy in America,* Book Two, Chapter 26) discusses different ways in which people may enjoy equality and how these ways are different from absolute freedom.

> The principle of equality may be established in civil society, without prevailing in the political world. Equal rights may exist of indulging in the same pleasures, of entering the same professions, of frequenting the same places; in a word, of living in the same manner and seeking wealth by the same means — although all men do not take an equal share in the government. A kind of equality may even be established in the political world, though there should be no political freedom there. A man may be the equal of all his countrymen save one, who is the master of all without distinction, and who selects equally from among them all the agents of his power. Several other combinations might be easily imagined, by which very great equality would be united to

institutions more or less free, or even to institutions wholly without freedom.

Although men cannot become absolutely equal unless they are entirely free; and consequently equality, pushed to its furthest extent, may be confounded with freedom, yet there is good reason for distinguishing the one from the other. The taste which men have for liberty, and that which they feel for equality, are, in fact, two different things; and I am not afraid to add, that, amongst democratic nations, they are two unequal things.

8. Physics

Nigel Calder (*Einstein's Universe* [New York: Penguin, 1980]: 122) describes Einstein's concept of gravity waves.

One of Einstein's most remarkable conclusions was that packets of curved space — tidal ripples, in effect — should travel through empty space, far from the massive objects that created them. Nothing would bring curved space to life better than to sense the curvature changing: to feel a disturbance running though space like an earthquake. That is one reason why the search for "gravity waves" became an obsession of experimentalists in the late 1970s.

Einstein predicted gravity waves in 1916, as a quick by-product of his theory of gravity, in much the same way as James Clark Maxwell had earlier predicted electromagnetic waves as a consequence of his unified theory of electricity and magnetism. The parallel goes further. Electromagnetic waves are created by the jerking or vibration of electric charges. In a radio transmitter, electrons oscillate rapidly to and fro; in an atom, electrons can "jump" into a different orbit, creating visible light in the process; in a hospital x-ray machine, a beam of energetic electrons smashes into a target and the violent arrest of the electrons produces the x-rays. Similarly any vibration or jerking of masses ought to produce gravity waves. And, just as an electromagnetic wave exerts a force at the end of its journey by shaking other electric charges, so a gravity wave can in principle travel through space and shake other masses.

9. Physics

Stephen Hawking (*A Brief History of Time* 135–36) considers the shape and age of the universe, in relation to theories of gravity and geometry.

In the classical theory of gravity, which is based on real space-time, there are only two possible ways the universe can behave: either it has existed for an infinite time, or else it had a beginning at a singularity at some finite time in the past. In the quantum theory of gravity, on the other hand, a third possibility arises. Because one is using Euclidean space-times, in which the time direction is on the same footing as directions in space, it is possible for space-time to be finite in extent and yet to have no singularities that formed a boundary or edge. Space-time would be like the surface of the earth, only with two more dimensions. The surface of the earth is finite in extent but it doesn't have a boundary or edge: if you sail off into the sunset, you don't fall off the edge or run into a singularity.

⌘ Complexity from Multiple Perspectives

To help you develop more complex approaches to your subject, professors may assign readings that don't fit together easily, that contradict each other, or that look at something from different angles. Books of readings in subjects like public policy, history, ethics, or literary studies often include multiple viewpoints. Then in discussion or essays you may be asked to make sense of the complexity.

Consider, for example, the following two passages about the dropping of the atomic bombs in Hiroshima and Nagasaki, which you might examine in a contemporary world history course. The first passage defends the U.S. decision made by President Truman in 1945 on the grounds that the bomb saved many U.S. and Japanese lives that would have been lost had World War II dragged on. The second passage contests that, arguing that the war would likely have ended without nearly as much bloodshed as others predicted.

Japan's defeat was sure, but her leaders were refusing to admit it. They looked determined to take their people into national suicide — together with perhaps hundreds of thousands of Allied lives in a hopeless fight to a finish. . . .

The decision to use the atomic bombs was made on this one overriding consideration: to save countless thousands of Allied lives that were bound to be the price of having to overwhelm the Japanese in their own land. That it would also be bound to prevent the deaths of many more Japanese than died at Hiroshima and Nagasaki was unlikely to have figured much, if at all, in the consideration of military leaders hardened by years of total war. But apart from the battle casualties involving civilians on a huge scale, millions would probably have died from starvation had every yard of Japanese territory been fought and won.

From Stephen Harper, *The Miracle of Deliverance: The Case for the Bombing of Hiroshima and Nagasaki* (London: Sidgwick & Jackson, 1985).

On August 6, 1945, the
American plane Enola
Gay dropped an atomic
bomb on the Japanese
city of Hiroshima.

The conventional justification for the atomic bombing is that
the only alternative capable of securing Japan's surrender was Allied invasion, which would necessarily result in massive U.S. casualties. The most influential text is Truman's 1955 *Memoirs,* which
states that the atomic bomb probably saved a half a million U.S.
lives — anticipated casualties in an Allied invasion of Japan
planned for November. Stimson [Truman's Secretary of War] subsequently talked of saving one million U.S. casualties, and Churchill
of saving one million and half that number of British lives. . . .

Nevertheless, retrospective accounts by Truman, LeMay, Stimson, Churchill, and other U.S. and British leaders claiming that the
atomic bomb saved half a million or more Allied lives are grossly
inflated. Declassified files reveal that U.S. military planners at the
time worked with estimates in the range of 20,000 to 46,000 American lives as the projected cost of landing in Kyushu. Most important, given the destruction of Japan's naval and air power, and the
Soviet decision to enter the war, there is strong reason to believe

that without the atomic bomb, Japan's surrender could have been secured well before the planned invasion.

From Kyoko Selden and Mark Selden, *The Atomic Bomb: Voices from Hiroshima and Nagasaki* (New York: M. E. Sharpe, 1989): xxx–xxxi.

Although we can never know what actually would have happened if the bomb had not been dropped, by examining the reasons for and against the decision we can develop a fuller picture of the situation at the time and the decision-making process that led to the destruction of two Japanese cities, the immediate end to the war with Japan, and the beginning of a nuclear cold war with the Soviet Union. The sample student paper on pages 303–306 examines this subject in greater depth.

Over a period of classes, a course may present a series of different theories and several sets of facts on an issue. The professor may make comparisons or ask you to compare the different approaches you have been studying. Particularly toward the end of the course, you may be asked to compare the different approaches or to see how they might provide different ways of looking at a particular case. Often exams or final papers will involve some comparison, evaluation, choice, or synthesis.

The instructor may also use the perceptions, analysis, or research of members of the class to present complexities. Through class discussions, group activities, or other assignments, you and other students will present the many sides of an issue or subject.

✎ Facing Complexity

If the instructor designs the course to have you confront the complexity of a subject in some way, you are put on a new kind of spot. You are in the position of having to recognize and sort out the complications using all you have learned and your best judgment. Beyond being able to perform well, what is your stake in doing this? After all, seeing complexity is confusing. You may no longer have a simple direct answer or response to various situations. You may no longer know what is right or wrong as you see that people who hold opposite positions have their reasons. You may find you get caught up in tangles of considerations when you feel as if you just want to act.

These are serious issues, for complexity can easily become an excuse for not making choices, for not taking action, or for not participating in important activities. On the other hand, intelligent choice, focused and fair action, and cooperative participation with people of many views is made more likely the more fully you see all the issues and viewpoints at play. Being able to make sense of all the pieces and putting them together in some coherent shape that allows you to evaluate the totality of information can keep you from being overwhelmed. This is true whether you are doing academic research or making business decisions. The purpose of addressing complexity is not to become buried in it, but to be constantly seeing your way through it to informed choice and action.

✍ Two Kinds of Complexity

Let us consider one kind of complexity you may encounter in one of your courses: an event that looks simple but that can be seen as having many dimensions. For example, the old joke goes that only two things are inevitable: death and taxes. We seem fatalistic about them, treat them pretty much as a simple and incontrovertible fact of life. But of course, taxes have a history that is related to the changing forms of rule, the tasks that governments take on that require expenses, the changing structures of economies, and the rights and protections granted to citizens. So there is little that is really inevitable about taxes. Indeed, some people manage to live their lives outside the tax system, and others have no tax system to contend with. Even death, although we all are subject to it, has a history, a sociology, a psychology, and a literature, as well as a biology. Where and when it occurs, with whose involvement, and with what causes and meanings we attribute to it are the kinds of issues that make death far from a simple subject. Indeed, there is little about death that is inevitable other than it will overtake us. And even that many people will deny, resist, or explain away.

Most things you look at, as you look more closely, become more complex. Political parties, popular music, the workings of corporations, and even comic books are no simple matter, each having many varieties or subcomponents, each being the result of complex histories, and each being influenced by many social and economic forces. As Henry Petroski, the writer on engineering history, has noted, even the pencil and the paper clip have complicated stories behind them. This is one kind of complexity, where something that appears massive, incontrovertible, and obvious in its meaning turns out to contain many aspects, variables, and meanings as we look into it.

You will also frequently run into a second kind of complexity, one in which there is no simple answer to a problem or a definite way to understand what is going on. In these cases, the complexity is in the *discussion* that is trying to sort out the issue, rather than in the phenomenon itself. Different people may hold and argue different positions, each for their own reasons. To sort through the discussion, you have to take each of the positions seriously until you have reason to think otherwise. Only once you understand the various positions and examine who is holding which position for which reasons can you begin to evaluate them.

Take, for example, the frequent conflicts that occur when protection of the environment seems to restrict economic development. People on one side or another may have a strong commitment to a single principle such as jobs or the future of the planet, and they may believe that their opponents are either innocent idealists or selfish exploiters. But when one starts to look at the controversies, one finds that there are informed and intelligent people on both sides and that they all have their individual reasons. Working through to some resolution is not simply a matter of picking one side or another on the basis of a simple decision. Coming to an intelligent resolution requires understanding the complexity of the problem and the complexity of the points of view.

Complex conflicts exist not only in the public domain, where people fight over policies that affect their interests. Among researchers and experts there are often major disputes as to which account or description of a phenomenon ought to be accepted. What is the cause of AIDS, and what kind of treatments or potential cures look promising? What is memory? How does photosynthesis work? What are the origin and nature of dreams? What are the meanings and consequences of the violence in our media? The more you look into such questions, you find that there are not only surface differences on the question at hand, but deeper differences in the way researchers approach their subjects and why they take their various approaches.

To help you develop skill in these two kinds of complexity, the remainder of this chapter will present two kinds of assignments: a description of a complex event and an open-question paper. In the first you will start to show the complexity in a seemingly simple event by examining some of its many facets, showing why and how it is interesting and revealing to look at closely. In the second you will look at an issue where people may hold alternative views to figure out what the different positions are, why different people hold them, and how you might evaluate those alternatives. In all cases it is important to not jump to an overall understanding right away, but to use various forms of intermediate writing to work your way through the multiple issues and ideas.

Assignment 1: A Complex Event

For this assignment you will describe some event that depends on many different factors. In an environmental science course you might need to describe a balance or crisis within an ecosystem that depends on the interaction of each of several biological and physical systems, the requirements, contributions, and effects of which need to be described and put into relations to each other. In a history course you might have to describe an event, such as the collapse of apartheid in South Africa, that is the outcome of many individuals or groups interacting politically, economically, and personally. In a sociology course you may be asked to describe a complex social problem, such as violence in schools, that is influenced by many factors, and that affects several groups of people. Or in a cultural studies or communication course you may examine some contemporary cultural phenomenon, such as the rise of TV shopping networks, that grows out of a complex of forces and is viewed differently by different groups of people.

Of course, each of these assignments would require substantial knowledge about the topic, perhaps drawing on material presented in the course or requiring additional research. Seeing complexity depends on knowing a great deal about a subject. So for such assignments it is important to find something you would like to know about in some depth.

Once you have identified a topic of sufficient interest to explore, you then identify its various aspects and dimensions. This process will vary with the nature of the subject, but in any case this is a time for making *lists* — the different people, groups, components, organisms, or processes that might be relevant to the subject and the different ways of looking at each of them. In making lists, you can draw from the professor's lectures and the textbooks. What kinds of pieces and what aspects did they consider relevant in discussing similar subjects? Then for each of the elements you identify how you will find out about them or what information you have at hand (such as from your course and textbook) that will tell you about their role.

After you have gathered information about each of the elements, you start sketching out how the parts fit together or relate to each other. This is a time for *outlines, matrixes, flow charts,* or other devices that help in putting material together. If after juggling the pieces together for a while, no picture becomes clear, you might begin *freewriting* or even do a first draft, in the hope that once you begin to lay the parts out through writing you will begin to grasp the overall picture. As you come up with some kind of big picture, you should try writing a few summary sentences identifying the major parts of the picture and how they fit together — and then suggesting some conclusions.

Once you have written these preliminary pieces, you are ready to start writing a regular draft, using your summary statement or something like it in the opening to help your reader become oriented to the subject. Even though the topic was confusing to you as you were working your way through it, it should *not* be confusing for your reader. All your work in sorting through the subject has its payoff in your being able to explain it clearly to the reader. You should present the vision you have at the end of your work rather than throwing readers into the confusion you had to work through.

✑ Sample Student Essay

The following paper from a sociology course in contemporary urban problems shows how one student moves beyond simplistic views of the Los Angeles riots of 1992 to examine the many factors that contributed to the violent outbreak.

Moira Jimson
The Rodney King Riots: A Case of Complexities

When four Los Angeles police officers were
videotaped using what appeared to be excessive force

against Rodney King, Americans saw excerpts of the tape
on an almost daily basis for more than a year. When the
officers were finally brought to trial in April of 1992,
most people assumed that it would be an open-and-shut
case. And when the jury returned verdicts of not guilty
on almost all counts, the City of Los Angeles erupted
in violent riots that became one of the worst civil
disturbances in our nation's history. But what was behind the violence? Conservative commentators were quick
to judge the riots as a procession of "thugs and hood-
lums" who were "enjoying the opportunity to wreak havoc
on society, without fear of reprisal by law enforcement" (Limbaugh 220-221). But, in retrospect, most social commentators see the riots as a very complex
phenomenon. The initial, widespread shock at the Rodney
King verdict set off a spark, but the explosion was
caused by economic and racial tensions that have been
brewing in Los Angeles — and other large urban centers —
for many years.

        The initial spark that set off the riots came
from people's shock at the not guilty verdicts. This
shock went far beyond mere disappointment; it was something that people could literally not believe or understand. Every American with a television set had seen
countless replays of a videotape that showed the police
beating King relentlessly and repeatedly. For most people, the tape alone proved beyond a shadow of a doubt
that the officers were guilty. A CNN/Time poll taken immediately after the verdict was announced showed that
78% of black respondents and 79% of white respondents
expected a guilty verdict ("The Fire" 22). Many activists were so sure of the evidence that they were already considering the case a victory for the
African-American community — something that showed that
the legal system could sometimes work to protect the
rights of minorities and punish police who abused their
power. June Jordan, in an editorial for _Progressive_
magazine, expressed the sense of betrayal and frustra-
tion that she and many others felt upon hearing the
outcome of the jury's deliberations:

                Because there had been a videotape docu-
                mentary of the police assault on Rodney
                King, I had expected, along with millions
                of other African-Americans, that for once

the guilty would be punished and the victim would be protected by due process under the law. But the visual documentary
evidence of unlawful police violence — evidence that was sickening to watch even at
the remove of a TV set — that evidence did
not carry the day. Racism carried the day.
(Jordan 12)

But the disappointment caused by the verdict
did not cause the riots; it merely triggered them. The
underlying causes are far more complex. In the first
place, the Los Angeles inner-city area had been hit
hard by an economic recession between 1988 and 1992. At
the time of the riots, the countywide unemployment rate
was 10.4% — three and a half points higher than the national average, and the poverty rate for families in
South Central Los Angeles was higher than it was in
1965 — the year of the famous Watts Riots (Lacayo 28).
Not only was the economic situation grim, but it was
disproportionately so for the African-American community. The Rodney King verdict ignited feelings of help-
lessness and rage that had been collecting throughout
the long recession in a community that had been harder
hit in that recession than almost any other in the
country.

But the racial factors involved in the riots go
far beyond these economic factors. The King verdict set
off racial tensions that have been building in Los Angeles — and in America — for many years. Many people saw
the King case as a microcosm of race relations in America. Writing in the wake of the LA riots, political
scientist Roger Wilson argues that the riots were
caused by "widening racial polarization, inequalities,
and tension" between blacks and whites in America. Wilson contends that these tensions have resulted in a
feeling of hopelessness and despair that makes unrest
inevitable:

Many African-Americans, especially young
males, living in inner cities see themselves as becoming worse off in the 1990s.
For black males between the ages of 15 and
34, homicide is the leading cause of
death, one fourth are in prison or on pa-
role or probation, and the unemployment

rate is twice that of young white
men. . . . The notion of a genocide conspir-
acy is growing within African-American
communities, and with such observable social disparities and discrimination,
racial tension is bound to run high.

The Rodney King case, then, became a test case for the
future. Had the jury returned a guilty verdict, people
would have felt that, in the words of one African-
American law student, "we do have rights and you can't
beat us within an inch of our lives and get away with
it" ("The Fire" 22).

Despite what many people think, the Rodney King
Riots were not just an opportunity to loot, kill, and
sow discord in American society. They were the end result of a very complex set of social, political, and
cultural conditions — every one of which contributed in
its own way to the tragedy. Had the verdict been announced at another time, or in another city, it might
have been received with only mild disgust. Had economic
conditions been better, people might not have been
frustrated enough to riot. And had journalists, news
commentators, and politicians been less certain of a
guilty verdict, they might have better prepared us for
the actual decision and prevented the initial shock
that ignited the violence. But the shock of the decision, combined with the social conditions that existed
at the time, set off an explosion that will not be forgotten soon.

Works Cited

"The Fire this Time." _Time_ 11 May 1992: 18-25.

Jordan, June. "The Truth of Rodney King." _Progressive_,
        June 1993: 12-21.

Lacayo, Richard. "Unhealed Wounds." _Time_ 19 April 1993:
        26-31.

Limbaugh, Rush. _The Way Things Ought to Be_. New York:
        Pocket Books, 1993.

Wilson, Roger. "Repairing Race Relations." _Spectrum:
        The Journal of State Government_ 66.3 (Summer
        1993): 8-14.

Thinking About Student Writing

1. What is the event that Moira Jimson tries to explain in this paper? What are the basic facts of that event?

2. What previous event is usually thought of as causing the riots? Why is this event seen as a cause? Why doesn't Moira Jimson see this as adequate explanation?

3. What does Moira see as the underlying causes of the L.A. riots? What does she use to explain and support her reasoning? What conclusion does she come to?

4. What is the overall organization of this essay? How does Moira Jimson gradually lead the reader into the complexity of her subject?

Assignments

DESCRIBING COMPLEXITY

1. Describe a poem, short story, piece of music, video, or work of art that you are familiar with and in which you find several things going on simultaneously. In your description, make clear several kinds of experience or elements the work offers and how the several parts are related to the total experience.

2. Describe an event in your community or college that is the result of complex forces. Present a view of the event that allows us to see all the elements that went into bringing the event together. You may use newspaper and other sources for both facts and the opinions of various people involved in the event.

3. Describe the way a group of your friends relate to each other. Show how this interaction is a result of their different personalities, histories, interests, and goals.

Assignment 2: An Open Question

All fields have open questions — that is, questions on which people hold a variety of positions for good reasons. In your courses your textbooks and instructors may present you with alternative views and theories to show you that several positions are possible and to give you practice in comparing perspectives. As you become more involved in your field, you may be asked to read or write reviews-of-the-literature papers. This kind of paper summarizes current research around open questions in a field to see what conclusions are emerging and what future research is needed.

In writing any such comparison or synthesis, it is important to begin with a careful understanding of each of the texts or statements you are examining, taking it seriously in its own terms. To aid in this process, it is often useful to begin by summarizing each of the articles or texts. In these summaries, identify the reasons for which the authors hold their positions. What kinds of arguments and evidence do they use? What kinds of orientation toward ideas, theories, and problems are unstated but help explain their position? How do their positions relate to their other interests or ideas? Will the position presented in one article help advance some other cause or help solve some problem? You can explore these background questions in informal journal entries or notes after you finish the summary.

After you have summarized and explored the background of each of the statements, then you can compare them, both in what they explicitly state and in their background. Comparison charts, informal journal entries, or visual representations may be helpful in sorting out how the articles relate to each other. First you define exactly what the issue under discussion is. What common issue are all these positions addressing? Then you pinpoint the division or differences among the various statements. They may agree on a number of points and their differences may be focused on a few issues, or they may differ on all counts. Next compare the reasons for which they hold their position — the kinds of arguments and evidence they use — not only to determine who has the better, more complete, or more accurate support, but also to see if they use different kinds of evidence and reasons. Then you consider any underlying reasons for which the writers might hold to their positions.

Once you have sorted out how the positions stand with respect to each other, you explore how you stand with respect to them. How do you evaluate them? Can you reconcile or synthesize the points of view? Do you find one more reasonable or useful than another? Do you find the whole debate misguided? Use an informal journal entry to explore your ideas.

Having worked through the issues and developed your own overview of the discussion and your position with respect to it, you are ready to write a draft. As with the previous paper, write the draft from the perspective you have now developed. Lay out your overview and position right in the opening of the paper. Frame your presentation of each of the writers by relating their positions to your overview and to the other work you are talking about. Then go back to examine where each of the authors stands, what kind of argument they make and the relevant background. That is, don't make the readers do the work you have just done — rather present what you have found so that they can gain by the perspective you have developed. Your instructor will be looking for the kind of perspective you have developed as well as the carefulness and fairness with which you treat each of the positions.

○᳣○   USEFUL CONCEPTS FROM RHETORIC

Stasis, Where Disagreements Meet

Although people may have different points of view, those differences only become focused and possible to discuss when they meet over a specific issue. Without a meeting point people can circle around their beliefs and differences all day without getting anywhere. And unless there is a specific issue at question, there may be no reason to state just how different your views are on one subject or another; it may just get people upset to no purpose. To have a useful conflict that can lead to resolution or at least clarification of the issues, a specific point of opposition needs to be located and the "question joined," as they say in law. You may, for example, have differences with your roommate over politics, but unless you just want to have the fun of comparing thoughts and matching wits there is usually no need for your taking up precious time and building up animosity over a topic you will never agree on. If, however, your roommate decides to make your room the campus headquarters for her advocacy group, you do have an issue to discuss. But the issue is likely not to be the value of her cause, but rather your rights to use the room to study and sleep in.

In classical rhetoric this point of juncture is called the *stasis* (or "standing point"). This is the point where the argument stands still long enough for people to define their disagreements and arguments. In criminal cases, for example, the issue is usually defined by a criminal charge — for example, whether the defendant is guilty of murder. The defense, however, can decide more precisely where the issue should be joined:

1. *Over the facts.*   If it can be established that the defendant was in another city or the deceased died of natural causes, the murder charge goes away.
2. *Over the definition or meaning of the facts.*   The defense can admit all the facts but still argue that the killing was not murder but an act of self-defense. This changes the focus of the argument to motives and perception of threat.
3. *Over the value of the act.*   If one cannot deny the facts or define the act differently, one can still argue that the act was a good thing. Perhaps the murdered person deserved his or her fate because of evil he or she had done to the murderer's family, or perhaps the murder was an act of compassion for a terminally ill comatose patient.
4. *Over procedure.*   If all stronger arguments fail, the defense can try to shift the issue to whether this court has jurisdiction over the case. If the case could be moved to another county or to juvenile court or the events had passed beyond the statute of limitations, perhaps the victim can still get off.

These four kinds of issues are in fact the standard stases in classical rhetorical argument: *fact, definition, value,* and *procedure.*

Sample Student Essay

The following paper from a contemporary world history course combines insights from both sides of the controversial decision to drop the A-bomb. The result is that the essay moves beyond simple oppositions of right and wrong to see how the dropping of the bomb influenced many different aspects of international politics, to which there were no simple answers. Decisions were made on the best estimates and judgments people at the time could come up with, no matter how we may come to judge them at some later date.

Robert Higginson
Dropping the A-Bomb: Conflicting Views
and Complex Realities

On August 6, 1945, the American plane Enola Gay dropped an atomic bomb on the Japanese city of Hiroshima. Two days later, another plane dropped a similar bomb on Nagasaki, and by the time the mushroom clouds cleared, the two bombs had killed more than 110,000 people on impact, with many more deaths to come from fallout and radiation poisoning. President Truman's decision to use nuclear weapons was undoubtedly one of the most fateful decisions of our century, and it has also become one of the most controversial. For some, the decision to drop the atomic bomb was a cruel, racist, unnecessary action that took civilian lives unnecessarily and has caused America to be "branded with the mark of the beast" (Baldwin 107). For others, the atomic bomb was a "miracle of deliverance" (Harper) that shortened the war and saved hundreds of thousands of lives in both America and Japan. Both of these positions, though, represent simplistic reductions of complex historical conditions. The decision to drop the atomic bomb was bound up with two very complicated sets of considerations: the necessity of ending the war with Japan without a costly invasion, and the desire to establish supremacy over the Soviet Union in the postwar era. Both of these are complex considerations that occasioned a great deal of debate among laypeople and scholars of history alike.

The initial justification for using atomic weapons was that they were the quickest way to end the war and save lives. One recent historian who has taken this view is Stephen Harper, whose 1985 book Miracle of Deliverance: The Case for the Bombing of Hiroshima and Nagasaki presents a strong case for the use of the

A-bomb. Harper documents the fact that, before they knew that atomic weapons would be available, the Allies were planning a massive invasion of the Japanese mainland — one that was expected to draw high casualties on both sides. Truman himself, writing in his 1955 Memoirs, put the number of expected American deaths at least half a million (Truman 416), while Henry Stimson, Truman's Secretary of War, projected that, by the end of a prolonged military campaign, the figure could have gone as high as one million (Stimson and Bundy 630). In addition to these American casualties, Americans had every reason to suspect that the Japanese, though hopelessly outnumbered and outgunned, would fight a desperate battle on the homefront. "They looked determined," Harper writes, "to take their people into a national suicide . . . in a hopeless fight to the finish" (205).

However, not all historians share Harper's high estimates of American casualties or his conclusion that Japan would never have surrendered without a costly military invasion. In their book The Atom Bomb: Voices from Hiroshima and Nagasaki, Kyoko and Mark Selden argue against both contentions:

> Declassified files reveal that U.S. military planners at the time worked with estimates in the range of 20,000 to 46,000 American lives as the projected cost of landing in Kyushu. Most important, given the destruction of Japan's naval and air power, and the Soviet decision to enter the war, there is strong reason to believe that without the atomic bomb, Japan's surrender could have been secured well before the planned invasion. (xxxi)

If we accept this evidence, then there are serious reasons to believe that America dropped the atomic bombs unnecessarily. If the Japanese forces were so close to defeat and so demoralized that they would have surrendered before any planned American invasion, then the civilian casualties incurred at Hiroshima and Nagasaki might have been avoided without any great loss of life to either side.

But both authors agree that, despite what press reports said at the time, the American leaders who decided to drop the bombs were thinking of more than just a Japanese surrender. As the Seldens write, "their analysis of planning for the postwar period, from 1942 forward, underscores official designation of the Soviet Union as the primary threat to U.S. supremacy in world affairs" (xxxi). Americans knew that their possession of nuclear weapons would be a decisive advantage in postwar dealings with the Soviet Union, and, before giving the final order to drop the first bomb on Hiroshima, Truman is reported to have said, speaking of the Soviets, "if it explodes like I think it will, I'll certainly have a hammer on those boys" (Norton 827). From the Seldens' perspective, American leaders were acting in bad faith by using Japanese civilians as demonstration models of American superiority.

While Harper admits that the Soviet threat was important in the decision to drop the bomb, he argues that this ultimately worked in favor of the Japanese, since, before the explosions, the Soviets had already declared their intentions to participate in the invasion and annex a portion of Japan as their reward:

> There is little doubt that some American chiefs welcomed the exclusiveness of the power which possession of the atomic bomb gave them to restrain growing Soviet assertiveness. Stalin had steamrollered the West into acceptance of his plans for Poland, the Baltic States, Finland and the rest of Eastern Europe. After that, Western hands were strengthened to resist not only his ambitions in the Bosphorus but also his desire for a share in the occupation and control of Japan — the same desire which was even then causing problems in Germany. (206)

Had the bomb not been used, Harper argues, there is a very good chance that Japan, much like Germany and Korea, would have been carved up among competing Superpowers and never allowed to develop political or economic independence as a whole country.

In human terms, the bombs dropped on Hiroshima and Nagasaki were great tragedies, but so were the purely conventional bombings of Dresden and Tokyo — both of which killed more civilians than either of the atomic bombs that were dropped. However, these atomic

weapons did more than just end one war, they also began
another war — the Cold War. For fifty years, the nuclear
terror that was unleashed on Japan served as a symbol
of the ultimate destruction that always lurked just
around the corner. We can never know for sure what was
going through Truman's head when he gave the ultimate
order to use these weapons, nor can we say with any
certainty what would have happened had he made the opposite decision. However, the factors involved in the
decision, and the myriad of historical forces that it
set in place are much too complex to be reduced to simple absolute statements. In deciding to drop the atomic
bombs, the Americans were neither righteous saviors of
the world nor depraved monsters intent on genocide;
they were ordinary people dealing — sometimes well and
sometimes poorly — with a very complex set of historical
variables that they could only partially control.

Works Cited

Baldwin, Hanson W. <u>Great Mistakes of the War</u>. New York:
      Harper, 1949.
Harper, Stephen. <u>Miracle of Deliverance: The Case for
      the Bombing of Hiroshima and Nagasaki</u>. London:
      Sidgwick & Jackson, 1985.
Norton, Mary Beth, et al. <u>A People and a Nation: A His-
      tory of the United States</u>. 4th ed. Boston:
      Houghton Mifflin, 1994.
Selden, Kyoko and Mark Selden. <u>The Atomic Bomb: Voices
      from Hiroshima and Nagasaki</u>. New York: M. E.
      Sharpe, 1989.
Stimson, Henry L., and McGeorge Bundy. <u>On Active Ser-
      vice in Peace and War</u>. New York: Harper, 1947.
Truman, Harry S. <u>Memoirs: Year of Decisions</u>. Garden
      City: Doubleday, 1955.

Thinking About Student Writing

1. What is the controversy that Robert Higginson examines? What historical event is at the heart of the controversy? What sides to the controversy does the essay present?

2. What facts and ideas lie behind the two positions? Why do the two sides disagree? What is at stake in one side or the other being right?

3. What specific points of disagreement between the two sides does Robert Higginson identify? What points of agreement? To what extent is Robert Higginson able to reconcile or adjudicate the two views? What does he leave unresolved? What conclusions does he come to?

4. How does the structure of the presentation balance the two views? Which paragraphs about one side mirror paragraphs about the other sides? Which paragraphs and sentences bring the two sides together? In what way? Which paragraphs and sentences create a broader view that encompasses both views?

Assignments

WRITING ABOUT OPEN QUESTIONS

1. Choose a recent, controversial issue in your school or community and conduct research into the different points of view. Look at official publications, statements, newspaper articles, speeches, letters to the editor, and any other forum where this issue is discussed. Using the information you gather, write a brief paper summing up the different sides of the controversy.

2. Select an issue in your major field of study where experts disagree with each other. Read at least one major statement (book chapter, article, etc.) from an expert on each side of the issue and then write a brief summary of this disciplinary conflict.

3. Read the following passages on intelligence testing and the way it is applied to individuals and groups. Then write a paper giving an overview on the issues and the various positions people take.

A. Howard Gardner

A young girl spends an hour with an examiner. She is asked a number of questions that probe her store of information (Who discovered America? What does the stomach do?), her vocabulary (What does *nonsense* mean? What does *belfry* mean?), her arithmetic skills (At eight cents each, how much will three

candy bars cost?), her ability to remember a series of numbers (5,1,7,4,2,3,8), her capacity to grasp the similarity between two elements (elbow and knee, mountain and lake). She may also be asked to carry out certain other tasks — for example, solving a maze or arranging a group of pictures in such a way that they relate a complete story. Some time afterward, the examiner scores the responses and comes up with a single number — the girl's intelligence quotient, or IQ. This number (which the little girl may actually be told) is likely to exert appreciable effect upon her future, influencing the way in which her teachers think of her and determining her eligibility for certain privileges. The importance attached to the number is not entirely inappropriate: after all, the score on an intelligence test does predict one's ability to handle school subjects, though it foretells little of success in later life.

The preceding scenario is repeated thousands of times every day, all over the world; and, typically, a good deal of significance is attached to the single score. Of course, different versions of the test are used for various ages and in diverse cultural settings. At times, the test is administered with paper and pencil rather than as an interchange with an examiner. But the broad outlines — an hour's worth of questions yielding one round number — are pretty much the way of intelligence testing the world around.

Many observers are not happy with this state of affairs. There must be more to intelligence than short answers to short questions — answers that predict academic success; and yet, in the absence of a better way of thinking about intelligence, and of better ways to assess an individual's capabilities, this scenario is destined to be repeated universally for the foreseeable future.

But what if one were to let one's imagination wander freely, to consider the wider range of performances that are in fact valued throughout the world? Consider, for example, the twelve-year-old male Puluwat in the Caroline Islands, who has been selected by his elders to learn how to become a master sailor. Under the tutelage of master navigators, he will learn to combine knowledge of sailing, stars, and geography so as to find his way around hundreds of islands. Consider the fifteen-year-old Iranian youth who has committed to heart the entire Koran and mastered the Arabic language. Now he is being sent to a holy city, to work closely for the next several years with an ayatollah, who will prepare him to be a teacher and religious leader. Or, consider the fourteen-year-old adolescent in Paris, who has learned how to program a computer and is beginning to compose works of music with the aid of a synthesizer.

A moment's reflection reveals that each of these individuals is attaining a high level of competence in a challenging field and should, by any reasonable definition of the term, be viewed as exhibiting intelligent behavior. Yet it should be equally clear that current methods of assessing the intellect are not sufficiently well honed to allow assessment of an individual's potentials or achievements in navigating by the stars, mastering a foreign tongue, or composing with a computer. The problem lies less in the technology of testing than in the ways in which we customarily think about the intellect and in our ingrained views of intelligence. Only if we expand and reformulate our view of what counts as human intellect will we be able to devise more appropriate ways of assessing it and more effective ways of educating it. . . .

In what follows, I argue that there is persuasive evidence for the existence of several *relatively autonomous* human intellectual competences, abbreviated hereafter as "human intelligences." These are the "frames of mind" of my title. The exact nature and breadth of each intellectual "frame" has not so far been satisfactorily established, nor has the precise number of intelligences been fixed. But the conviction that there exist at least some intelligences, that these are relatively independent of one another, and that they can be fashioned and combined in a multiplicity of adaptive ways by individuals and cultures, seems to me to be increasingly difficult to deny.

Previous efforts (and there have been many) to establish independent intelligences have been unconvincing, chiefly because they rely on only one or, at the most, two lines of evidence. Separate "minds" or "faculties" have been posited solely on the basis of logical analysis, solely on the history of educational disciplines, solely on the results of intelligence testing, or solely on the insights obtained from brain study. These solitary efforts have rarely yielded the same list of competences and have thereby made a claim for multiple intelligences seem that much less tenable.

My procedure is quite different. In formulating my brief on behalf of multiple intelligences, I have reviewed evidence from a large and hitherto unrelated group of sources: studies of prodigies, gifted individuals, brain-damaged patients, *idiots savants*, normal children, normal adults, experts in different lines of work, and individuals from diverse cultures. A preliminary list of candidate intelligences has been bolstered (and, to my mind, partially validated) by converging evidence from these diverse sources. I have become convinced of the existence of an intelligence to the extent that it can be found in relative isolation in special populations (or absent in isolation in otherwise normal populations); to the extent that it may become highly developed in specific individuals or in specific cultures; and to the extent that psychometricians, experimental researchers, and/or experts in particular disciplines can posit core abilities that, in effect, define the intelligence. Absence of some or all of these indices, of course eliminates a candidate intelligence. In ordinary life, as I will show, these intelligences typically work in harmony, and so their autonomy may be invisible. But when the appropriate observational lenses are donned, the peculiar nature of each intelligence emerges with sufficient (and often surprising) clarity.

From Howard Gardner, *Frames of Mind: The Theory of Multiple Intelligences.* (Basic Books, 1983): 3–4, 8–9.

B. Richard Herrnstein and Charles Murray

Given these different ways of understanding intelligence, you will naturally ask where our sympathies lie and how they shape this book.

We will be drawing most heavily from the classical tradition. That body of scholarship represents an immense and rigorously analyzed body of knowledge. By accepted standards of what constitutes scientific evidence and scientific proof, the classical tradition has in our view given the world a treasure of information that has been largely ignored in trying to understand contemporary policy issues. Moreover, because our topic is the relationship of human abilities to public policy, we will be dealing in relationships that are based on aggregated data, which is where the classical tradition has the most to offer. Perhaps an example will illustrate what we mean.

Suppose that the question at issue regards individuals: "Given two 11 year olds, one with an IQ of 110 and one with an IQ of 90, what can you tell us about the differences between those two children?" The answer must be phrased very tentatively. On many important topics, the answer must be, "We can tell you nothing with any confidence." It is well worth a guidance counselor's time to know what these individual scores are, but only in combination with a variety of other information about the child's personality, talents, and background. The individual's IQ score all by itself is a useful tool but a limited one.

Suppose instead that the question at issue is: "Given two sixth-grade classes, one for which the average IQ is 110 and the other for which it is 90, what can you tell us about the difference between those two classes and their average prospects for the future?" Now there is a great deal to be said, and it can be said with considerable confidence — not about any one person in either class but about average outcomes that are important to the school, educational policy in general, and society writ large. The data accumulated under the classical tradition are extremely rich in this regard, as will become evident in subsequent chapters. . . .

We agree emphatically with Howard Gardner, however, that the concept of intelligence has taken on a much higher place in the pantheon of human virtues than it deserves. One of the most insidious but also widespread errors regarding IQ, especially among people who have high IQs, is the assumption that another person's intelligence can be inferred from casual interactions. Many people conclude that if they see someone who is sensitive, humorous, and talks fluently, the person must surely have an above-average IQ.

This identification of IQ with attractive human qualities in general is unfortunate and wrong. Statistically, there is often a modest correlation with such qualities. But modest correlations are of little use in sizing up other individuals one by one. For example, a person can have a terrific sense of humor without giving you a clue about where he is within thirty points on the IQ scale. Or a plumber with a measured IQ of 100 — only an average IQ — can know a great deal about the functioning of plumbing systems. He may be able to diagnose problems, discuss them articulately, make shrewd decisions about how to fix them, and, while he is working, make some pithy remarks about the president's recent speech.

At the same time, high intelligence has earmarks that correspond to a first approximation to the commonly understood meaning of *smart*. In our experience, people do not use *smart* to mean (necessarily) that a person is prudent or knowledgeable but rather to refer to qualities of mental quickness and complexity that do in fact show up in high test scores. To return to our examples: Many witty people do not have unusually high test scores, but someone who regularly tosses off impromptu complex puns probably does (which does not necessarily mean that such puns are very funny, we hasten to add). If the plumber runs into a problem he has never seen before and diagnoses its source through inferences from what he does know, he probably has an IQ of more than 100 after all. In this, language tends to reflect real differences: In everyday language, people who are called very smart tend to have high IQs.

All of this is another way of making a point so important that we will italicize it now and repeat elsewhere: *Measures of intelligence have reliable statistical relationships with important social phenomena, but they are a limited tool for deciding what to make of any given individual.* Repeat it we must, for one of the problems of writing about intelligence is how to remind readers often enough how little an IQ score tells about whether the human being next to you is someone whom you will admire or cherish. This thing we know as IQ is important but not a synonym for human excellence.

Howard Gardner has also convinced us that the word *intelligence* carries with it undue affect and political baggage. It is still a useful word, but we shall subsequently employ the more neutral term *cognitive ability* as often as possible to refer to the concept that we have hitherto called *intelligence,* just as we will use *IQ* as a generic synonym for *intelligence test score.* Since *cognitive ability* is an uneuphonious phrase, we lapse often so as to make the text readable. But at least we hope that it will help you think of *intelligence* as just a noun, not an accolade.

We have said that we will be drawing most heavily on data from the classical tradition. That implies that we also accept certain conclusions undergirding that tradition. To draw the strands of our perspective together and to set the stage for the rest of the book, let us set them down explicitly. Here are six conclusions regarding tests of cognitive ability, drawn from the classical tradition, that are by now beyond significant technical dispute.

1. There is such a thing as a general factor of cognitive ability on which human beings differ.

2. All standardized tests of academic aptitude or achievement measure this general factor to some degree, but IQ tests expressly designed for that purpose measure it most accurately.

3. IQ scores match, to a first degree, whatever it is that people mean when they use the word *intelligent* or *smart* in ordinary language.

4. IQ scores are stable, although not perfectly so, over much of a person's life.

5. Properly administered IQ tests are not demonstrably biased against social, economic, ethnic, or racial groups.

6. Cognitive ability is substantially heritable, apparently no less than 40 percent and no more than 80 percent.

All six points have an inverse worth noting. For example, some people's scores change a lot; cognitive ability is not synonymous with test scores or with a single general mental factor, and so on. When we say that all are "beyond significant technical dispute," we mean, in effect, that if you gathered the top experts on testing and cognitive ability, drawn from all points of view, to argue over these points, away from television cameras and reporters, it would quickly become apparent that a consensus already exists on all of the points, in some cases amounting to near unanimity. And although dispute would ensue about some of the points, one side — the side represented by the way the points are stated — would have a clear preponderance of evidence favoring it, and those of another viewpoint would be forced to lean heavily on isolated studies showing anomalous results.

From Richard Herrnstein and Charles Murray, *The Bell Curve: Intelligence and Class Structure in American Life*. (Free Press, 1994): 19–21.

C. Richard Nisbett

Murray and Herrnstein have written a book that deals with extraordinarily important issues, many of which have been considered too explosive to discuss in the public arena yet need to be aired. There are, however, three assertions made about race and I.Q. that do not reflect the consensus of scholars.

First, although Murray and Herrnstein do not deny that racism and structural factors play a role in producing some of the I.Q. differences between blacks and whites, they also claim that racial differences in intelligence may be genetically influenced as well. This argument is based in large part on the fact that the races produce different "profiles" of ability patterns, with blacks performing relatively better, for example, on arithmetic and immediate memory and whites scoring higher on spatial and perceptual abilities. The authors note that socioeconomic status could not plausibly account for such profile differences, and imply that this leaves genetics as the most likely explanation.

This is a breathtaking leap. It presumes that the only relevant way groups might differ is in socioeconomic status. But groups differ in all sorts of other ways that might produce ability profile differences. For example, Stanford anthropologist Shirley Brice Heath compared the way working-class whites and blacks in a North Carolina town socialized their children for literacy. White parents regarded it as their job to teach literacy skills in preparation for school, reading to their children from an early age and showing them how to extract information from the printed page. Black parents assumed the school would handle the literacy issues and focused on social matters. They did not read to their children, indeed did not even "teach" them language. (Black babies were, however, bathed in words and verbal play, perhaps explaining in part the new prominence of black novelists, playwrights and poets.) To invoke different patterns of abilities as evidence of a genetic basis for group differences is utterly unfounded.

The claims that cognitive abilities are little modifiable and that the differences between blacks and whites are not likely to be significantly reducible are different. Here Murray and Herrnstein interpret masses of evidence in ways that are eccentric to say the least.

Head Start and similar programs often produce large I.Q. or achievement gains in preschool children, but Murray and Herrnstein call these programs failures, since once children return to their relatively impoverished environments, the gains fade. But if social scientists know anything, it is that the immediate situation is of utmost importance. People are capable of a wide range of behavior depending on their peers, their role models and the reward structure of the world they confront. Malcolm X was the top-ranking child in his Midwestern elementary school (and the only black). He then spent several years in bad company in Boston, and estimates that by the end of this period his effective vocabulary was less than 1,000 words. "Use it or lose it" is the relevant adage for cognitive abilities.

And some preschool programs do produce dramatic and enduring change in I.Q. or other achievement-related attributes, even well after termination of the program, as Murray and Herrnstein admit. They explain away these results on dubious technical grounds that do not accord with the consensus of experts. Intervention has been shown to work at every age level. James Comer of the Yale psychiatry department and others have shown that the academic performance of inner-city elementary school children can be made to exceed national averages. A week's worth of studying will raise scores of high school students on the math portion of the SAT by one-third of a standard deviation (thirty-three points); the renowned teacher Jaime Escalante can do far better with East Los Angeles barrio youths. Experiments at my university and others show that relatively small, inexpensive interventions can improve grades of blacks in particular subjects and can even produce significant improvements in grade point averages.

What has happened to the black-white gap after decades of concerted effort to improve black ability and achievement test scores? Murray and Herrnstein review the evidence and correctly note that the studies range from showing a slight convergence of black and white scores in the past twenty to twenty-five years to indicating that as much as one-half of the difference has been eliminated. The median change reported is somewhere between one-quarter and one-third. Yet they summarily dismiss this extraordinarily hopeful evidence: "too soon to pass judgment."

Such coolness about evidence that contradicts their position together with uncritical warmth shown toward supporting evidence is found throughout the painful sections of the book dealing with race and the modifiability of I.Q. This is not dispassionate scholarship. It is advocacy of views that are not well supported by the evidence, that do not represent the consensus of scholars and that are likely to do substantial harm to individuals and to the social fabric.

From Richard Nisbett, "Blue Genes," *The New Republic* 31 October 1994: 15.

Getting Involved Electronically

Locate an electronic database or Web home-page for some complex issue or event. This database or page should incorporate many different kinds of information and sources or contain links to many other different resources. Discuss the various kinds of information and resources that are considered relevant to the issue or event, why they are all considered relevant, and what they each lend to understanding. If you are examining a Web page, you may also consider how the hyper-text organization of material either helps or hurts our comprehension of the complexity of the issue or event.

14

Writing About Case Problems

AIMS OF THE CHAPTER

Case problems ask you to apply what you have learned to the facts of a specific situation. These problems often appear in practical courses such as management, marketing, teaching, engineering, or writing. This chapter introduces the goals, logic, and process of writing case problems.

KEY POINTS

1. Case problems ask you to analyze a real or hypothetical situation and suggest a solution or course of action.

2. In case studies, you apply all you have learned to practical problems as they appear in real settings. Problem cases help you think about the complexity of real situations and the multiple factors that influence any outcome.

3. In writing about case problems, you formulate the problem, get a sense of the form a solution might take, display all the relevant facts in the most useful way, put the facts together, and develop a plan of action.

4. In writing a case report, you present a problem definition, the criteria for a successful solution, a description of the situation and relevant facts, your analysis and solution, and arguments for the value of your solution. Depending on the situation, an abstract may also be needed.

QUESTIONS TO THINK ABOUT

■ Have you wondered whether what you have learned in your courses will ever actually help you decide how to act in a specific situation?

■ What kinds of professional situations might you be involved in after you graduate?

■ Which courses might you take in which you will have to solve practical problems? What kinds of problems will these courses ask you to address?

Math books present small simplified problems, many already set up in mathematical terms. If you apply the appropriate set of procedures to manipulate the numbers, you come up with the right answer: $(7 + 2 - 3) \times 5 = ?$

Life presents big, complicated problems with no clear terms for thinking about them and no fixed procedures for solving them. Even as you find some way to come to some decisions and work your way through them, you never know whether you have the right answer — you are usually happy if your choices have more positive consequences than negative. Moreover, even if the outcome is good, you often don't know exactly what you did that led to the happy result.

Word problems in math do attempt to connect math with life: 3 apples plus 5 apples; Joe goes to the supermarket with 3 dollars to purchase 6 kumquats at 43 cents each. Such problems actually start helping you as you go to the supermarket and have to compare the money in your wallet to the goods piling up in your basket. So the specific procedures of math do help you make some choices in real-life problems.

But going to the supermarket still remains messy. You are on a diet and your sister loves donuts. You have politically conscious guests coming for the weekend, and they will notice if you serve ecologically wasteful foods. You only have an hour for shopping before you have to leave for class, the parking lot is crowded, and there are long lines at the checkout.

As simple a problem as food shopping involves personal tastes, politics, ecology, nutrition, body image, personal finances, the national economy, and natural disasters in coffee-growing regions. In your shopping you may take into account what you know about nutrition and diet as well as the nutritional information listed on the packets, what news media have said about how political contributions influence legislators, and what your experience tells you about the importance of good family relations. These bits of knowledge complicate your life by making you more aware of the dimensions of any choice; nonetheless, they also provide ways of thinking through the problem and coming to choices. Insofar as you can clearly define each of these problems in relation to the specific knowledge and procedures you have learned, the more certainly and directly you can come to some conclusion. Some problems may be number problems, as in the calories from a nutrient chart, but some clearly are word problems, such as evaluating how tempted you will be if donuts are left around the house, where you can hide them from yourself, and whether you will hear yourself when you tell yourself "No!"

Fortunately, every time you go shopping you don't have to deal with the

Choosing groceries is not always an easy problem.

whole economy, your total psychology of dieting, or your entire history of family relationships. You focus your concerns and make your choices as best you can because you have to. You reduce the complexity to manageable proportions. Practical problems have a way of tying together complexity and then focusing on what is important for making a decision. Some academic subject areas directly prepare you to solve real-world problems: engineering, business, social work, teaching, journalism, and law. There you learn the relevant complexities of the world so you can make intelligent choices about how to run a business, teach a class, develop a piece of software, or write a news story for the morning paper. Problems bring the potentially unending complexity of life together into an intelligible framework.

Even those who study purely academic subjects in the most abstract disciplines, seemingly far removed from the world's mess, still wind up having to address problems — philosophical problems, research problems, and problems of deciding what knowledge is worth knowing. So as you immerse yourself more and more in the complexities of your subject, you are also more and more likely to become focused around the problems that define the work of your specialty or profession. In some majors this happens early — business students are presented with case problems from the first chapter of introductory textbooks — and in other majors it happens later.

One way to learn to deal with complex problems is through studying cases. In fact, case study is one of the main tools in business and legal education. Illustration cases present both problems and the solutions that individuals or groups have come to. The case discusses the factors affecting the situation and evaluates how well the people solved their problem.

Consider the following case from a marketing textbook at the end of a chapter on sales promotion. The case opens with a description of the problem facing the soft drink brand Dr. Pepper in trying to compete with the more popular colas. The case then examines the solution of special promotions, described in detail. The case ends with an analysis of the results to the promotion strategy. The discussion questions that follow in the textbook point toward the main issues raised in the case.

Sales Promotion: Just What the Doctor Ordered.   Dr Pepper was once an also-ran in the race to be the top-selling American soft drink. While Coke and Pepsi battled for the number-one spot, Dr Pepper remained what its commercials told everyone —"so misunderstood." Today many soft drink consumers are looking for cola alternatives. Although the cola giants continue waging market share wars, Dr Pepper has become "just what the Doctor ordered": the number-one-selling noncola soft drink in America. Dr Pepper executives credit the company's strong promotional program with the soft drink's growing popularity and market share.

Underlying Dr Pepper's promotional strategy is one fundamental objective: to increase sales. To accomplish that goal, company executives formulated specific guidelines for creating effective sales promotions. Because the soft drink's unusual taste is a key selling point, sales promotions must reinforce that characteristic. Dr Pepper's marketers always plan sales promotion efforts that target specific channels or packages. If the objective is to increase sales of two-liter bottles, for example, a promotional game will involve that size only. Because the organization's bottling companies and retailers (such as supermarkets and discount stores) offer many sales promotions of their own, Dr Pepper tries to time its sales promotions to complement those of the retailer. Sales promotion techniques must be easy for shoppers to understand, as well as be fun and rewarding for participants. Besides providing an overall strategy for specific promotional campaigns, Dr Pepper's executives believe strongly in couponing. Every promotion features on-pack, cents-off coupons for more Dr Pepper. In one recent year, the company distributed over 74 million coupons.

Dr Pepper's most recent sales promotion gives away trips, vehicles, and, of course, free Dr Pepper products. To drive sales of two-liter bottles of Dr Pepper and Diet Dr Pepper, the company came up with its "American Traveler" promotion, which gives customers a chance to win one-year passes on American Airlines, tickets for one trip anywhere in the United States, or American Express gift certificates simply by checking the back of the Dr Pepper label. "Peel-a-Pepper," also created for the two-liter market, rewards one out of twelve customers with two free two-liter bottles. In the single-drink channel, the "Twist-a-Pepper" promotion gives away free sixteen-ounce, twenty-ounce, or one-liter bottles of Dr Pepper when customers find specially marked twist-off caps. A recent summer promotion targeting convenience store customers combined Dr Pepper and baseball. When buyers of sixteen- and twenty-ounce Dr Pepper bottles found specially marked caps, they won autographed baseballs from Upper Deck or "Pepper Pastime" baseball jerseys. One of the company's newest promotions is a joint operation with Footlocker called "Steppin Out." Soft drink customers who buy specially marked twelve- and twenty-four-packs of Dr Pepper can win Footlocker gift certificates for up to $70, coupons for $10 off a Footlocker purchase, or coupons for 55 cents off their next purchase of Dr Pepper products. In keeping with the company's promotional strategy, all of its games are designed for one specific package or channel and are easy to play. Even though winning the big prizes is a long shot, Dr Pepper drinkers still win lots of the soft drink.

In addition to nationally sponsored promotions, Dr Pepper lovers can usually find local sales promotion. The Dr Pepper bottling company of Canton, Ohio, sponsored a Dr Pepper Night during the Canton Indians baseball game. Three lucky fans won Dr Pepper bicycles and about four thousand people received a free can of Diet Dr Pepper as they left the stadium. In the Louisville, Kentucky, area, McDonald's distributed coupons that customers could redeem for free Dr Pepper on another visit. Returning customers using the coupons were entered in a drawing to win a free pair of Rollerblades. Other local sales promotions gave away free admission tickets to the zoo and free one-year supplies of groceries.

In only four years, Dr Pepper's share of the soft drink market grew by 67 percent. Diet Dr Pepper, America's top-selling diet noncola, is also America's fastest growing soft drink brand of any type, regular or diet. In an industry with a yearly increase in sales of about 3 percent, total Dr Pepper sales were up 14 percent. Dr Pepper's sales promotion efforts continue to build brand awareness, increase total sales volume, and persuade more soft drink consumers to try Dr Pepper. Diet Dr Pepper's slogan, "There's no stopping the taste," can easily be amended to predict the company's future — "There's no stopping Dr Pepper."

Questions for Discussion

1. Identify the major sales promotion methods used by Dr Pepper.
2. Why are Dr Pepper's sales promotion methods focused on either package sizes or channels?
3. Evaluate the overall effectiveness of Dr Pepper's sales promotion efforts.

Court decisions also are forms of problem solutions. From the representations of the two opposing sides, justices must define the problem (that is, determine the issue), evaluate the issue in relation to the relevant facts, rulings, and law, and come to a decision, or "holding." The holding resolves problems of who is in the right, who should be rewarded or punished, and what should be permitted or prohibited. The excerpts of Supreme Court decisions on pages 140–144 provide examples of how problems and solutions are presented in law.

As you gain more skill in a field, more of the responsibility for the problem is yours. You may be given the facts of the case, but it is up to you to define the problem and come up with the solution. Business students in advanced courses are given 20- or 30-page cases filled with extensive detail which they must sort through before they make recommendations. Law students, after they have "briefed," or summarized, many court cases, must write their own arguments. Engineering and architecture students are given increasingly difficult problems of design, usually resulting in a major design project in the senior year. Often the projects are more than classroom exercises, since they are prepared for actual companies where students have worked as interns.

Solving problems draws on all you have learned. As you make sense of the details of a case, you must think about how ideas and models you have learned might apply in the situation, analyze which factors are the most important, and then find a solution that best addresses the factors you have analyzed.

∾ Writing and Problems

In studying how people solve problems, psychologists have found that it helps to externalize your thinking process — to get the thinking outside of your head so you can organize and examine it. Writing allows you to put your thinking on paper, where you can look at the various parts of the problem and your reasoning.

However you solve the problem, you will need to represent your solution to others and convince them that your solution is correct. This is especially true for problems presented in a class context, where the professor is also looking to see how you reason through a problem and how you use the knowledge you have learned to help you think through the problem.

The writing you may do in working through problems and in representing the problem and solution to others may use mathematical or other special symbols, may use drawings and other graphic displays, or may be in more common, everyday prose. The method of representation will depend on the kind of problem and materials you are working with. Computer programs of many sorts can help you in working through, organizing, calculating, and finally presenting the problem. These also will vary in relation to the problem you are working with, and you would be wise to look into the representational and problem-solving practices of the field, as well as the electronic tools currently being used. The courses in your specialties will likely introduce you to the usual way of representing and working through problems.

Psychologists have found some practices important in most problem solving. The following presentation of these techniques emphasizes the way in which forms of writing can help and the kinds of problems that involve ordinary language, resulting in a written report. These problem-solving techniques are also appropriate for nonverbal processes that may be thought about and represented in mathematical, graphical, or physical ways.

⌾⌾ Steps in Solving Problems

Formulating the Problem

Perhaps the most important step in solving a problem is formulating it. The solution you seek depends on how you word the problem, and different wordings may set you on different paths. So it is very important to find a formulation that crystallizes the problem.

Many problems can be seen as a current situation that you would like to see transformed in a certain way. To do this, you have certain constraints and obstacles to overcome and certain resources you can use. Through some series of actions, you wind up with a new and desired situation. Think of the classic puzzle of the farmer, a chicken, a fox, and some grain that need to be transported across a river in one small boat. In the beginning situation, all the creatures and objects are on one side of the river, and the goal is to get them all on the other. The constraints are the size of the boat, the fox's tendency to eat chickens, the chicken's tendency to eat grain, and the grain's tendency to be eaten by passing birds if left untended. The means are to transport the objects one by one and the ways in which the objects can be combined or isolated. The solution would be to specify which ones to carry in what order.

This is not so different in form from many problems in business, where you have a situation that may have some unfortunate consequences and you need to transform it to some happier state, like greater efficiency or harmony or profit. You have only limited means and must take into account all the constraints — so you are looking for opportunities. Similarly, in engineering design problems, you have some capabilities and resources, but you need a component to make the system work. Architectural, social, or political problems can also be defined in similar ways.

If your problem is to transform a situation, you need to specify the current situation, the desired final situation, the possible means of transforming the former to the latter, and the constraints and obstacles that must be overcome.

Another typical kind of problem is a diagnosis, in which you determine how to fix something that is broken or has gone wrong. You must first understand how the system operates and what factors are essential to its success, whether you are concerned with an electric dynamo or a well-functioning family. You then identify those elements that are not as they should be in the particular problem case and present a plan for remedying the difficulties.

A third kind of problem often appears in legal, negotiating, or other adjudicating contexts. In these problems you sort out the claims of disputants and determine a resolution of the dispute. Here are the facts of the case; the principles that guide solutions; the rights and obligations of the participants; the power, interests, and perceptions of the participants; and the consequences of various solutions are all taken into account.

Whatever kind of problem you have, the better you define it in meaningful and useful terms for yourself, the better you can focus your energies in solving it. If an initial formulation is handed to you by the instructor or the textbook, you still need to restate the problem in your own terms. Then it may be useful to chart out the various parts of the problem. A list may be adequate, but a flow chart or other graphic representation may be even more useful.

Once you have the parts of the problem laid out, you may want to think through what is difficult or simple in the problem. Freewriting can help you consider which obstacles seem more difficult than others or raise new questions. It may also tell you whether you may be able to define the desired end state in even more specific terms. Annotating your chart with added comments can also help you see whether there are any hidden assumptions or variables in the starting situation. Any kind of note taking may help you consider parts of your problem formulation more deeply.

Searching for the Form of an Answer

Once you have a sense of the problem, and particularly the goals you want to accomplish, you can probably see fairly clearly what form the solution will take. For example, in the farmer-crossing-a-river problem, you know you will have to establish a sequence for carrying the items across and that that information could be presented in a chronological list. Now consider that your problem is to propose a marketing strategy for a new product. If you know that marketing strategies usually contain an analysis of the demographics of potential consumers, a discussion of the media that reach those consumers, an analysis of what might attract them to the product, a theme for the marketing campaign, and a budget, then you have a pretty good idea what you are looking for. Moreover, if you know that such a plan is usually presented in a standardized format with the specific topics that needed to be covered defined by the standard sections of the report, each section having a standardized presentation, your work is pretty well defined for you. (See the discussion of genre on pages 209–210.)

You may not be able to predict in advance what form the solution of more open-ended problems or more unusual problems might take. Nonetheless, the more you think about the factors that must be fulfilled to solve the problem, the more you will gain a sense of the kind of solution you are looking for.

Becoming Aware of the Facts and Using Them

With a clearer view of what you are looking for, it is easier to identify what facts are relevant and what will help you sort through the problem. If all you know or can know about the problem is given in a case statement in the textbook, then you need to reexamine it to pull out the most important and relevant data. In fact, with your new understanding of the problem, some facts may leap out at you. On the other extreme, if the problem involves a real-world situation, such as from fieldwork or a job-related project, then you need to identify for yourself what information you need and how you can collect it.

You can even think about an ideal shopping list for information. If you could have any information at all about the problem, what would most help you solve the problem? Once you have developed a wish list, you can then think which items you might get or what information might serve as a substitute. You might get that information from a person, existing documents, or your own data collection and measurement, or you might seek the information in a library or a reference source.

It is helpful to make a long shopping list, because in the course of this brainstorming you may realize that one kind of information will open up the whole problem. Then you can eliminate the rest of the list. Any information, if it is relevant, helps a great deal. Discovering some facts can cut through a lot of uncertainty, guessing, and hunches. Paying attention to the facts, although it can't directly tell you what to do, can help you see which choices are more realistic.

From Facts to a Plan

Depending on the problem, there will be great variation in how you put the facts together. Sometimes facts will lead almost directly to a solution. At other times you may have to work to pull everything together. You may need extensive analysis (see Chapter 9) or synthesis of complexity (see Chapter 13). Even with the big picture clear, a solution that addresses all the complex factors may still require some ingenuity.

Whatever method you use to sketch out your solution, it is always useful to rethink the specific details. As your plan becomes more concrete, you may discover that you know better what you need to accomplish, and you may find an even simpler and more direct way to accomplish it. Your solutions may help you know even better what the problem was.

Writing Up the Presentation

Often there are highly standardized formats for presenting problems and solutions in particular disciplines or professions. You should seek out appropriate models and guidelines to follow. The following general principles may help you in many cases, even when you are working with a standardized format.

State the problem clearly near the beginning.   This orients your reader toward what you will accomplish in the paper and provides a way of interpreting and evaluating what you present. Stating the problem clearly also focuses the reader's attention on the importance and interest of your solution. In some cases it may even be useful to explain why the problem is interesting or important, or why the way you formulate the problem is an improvement on usual ways of defining the problem.

Stating the problem near the beginning also helps you structure the paper because it defines the central theme that ties the presentation together.

All the parts of the presentation to follow can be presented in relation to the problem.

Give an idea of the kind of solution that would be adequate for the problem. Identify what a good solution would have to accomplish, what form it would have to take, or what conditions it would have to meet. This statement prepares your readers for the solution you will propose and offers them criteria by which to evaluate that solution. If your solution follows the form and fulfills the criteria you have established, it is likely to appear strong and persuasive.

Elaborate the problem by presenting the relevant detailed facts. Specify the details that define the starting situation, the constraints, the obstacles, the resources, the opportunities, and the puzzles. These details give the readers a clearer idea of the problem and provide the basis for your analysis. Be selective. By presenting some details as relevant, and not others, you are indicating what you think is important to understanding the problem.

Although you have some flexibility in how you present the problem, knowledgeable readers may see the problem in different ways and might wonder why you present some facts and not others. Moreover, your instructor is likely to be evaluating how well you chose your details. If there is any question as to which is the most important information, you might wish to justify your choice by discussing why certain aspects of the situation are more significant than others.

Discuss how the facts fit together to provide clues for the problem's solution. This is your analysis or thinking through of the problem. The purpose here is not to recreate your own thinking process, which may have had many frustrations and false turns, but to present for the reader a clear path to understanding the problem and the value of your solution. You may also wish to discuss some theories, ideas, or models that help put the problem in a perspective that leads to a solution. Again, in an academic setting, where the instructor is evaluating the quality of your analysis and thinking, this section may be of special importance. In certain other situations, however, readers may not be so concerned with the reasoning that led to the solution as much as with the benefits and other consequences of choosing one solution over another.

Describe your solution carefully and clearly. Readers need to know exactly what you propose. Of course, being clear and specific about your solution puts you on the line and makes you accountable for what you propose. Your solution may in fact be wrong. But in an academic setting, a clearly presented, detailed solution is still better than a vague proposal. A teacher may still give you an *A* on your project even while pointing out that the plane you design would never get off the ground.

Argue the value of your solution. It may be appropriate to project the consequences of adopting your solution and to point out the benefits of this solution over others.

Provide an abstract. To tie together a long and complex proposal, it is often useful to put at the front of the presentation a short abstract of the problem and your proposed solution. Depending on the size of a project, this abstract might be from 25 words to a page. This is particularly important in fields where you are following professional models where some kind of executive summary is required, as in engineering, management, and government policy.

✐ Sample Student Problem Solution

The following case problem appears at the end of an education textbook chapter on ethical issues faced by teachers.

> *Case Number Four: Righting Wrongs.*   You expected to encounter a sour apple or two in the teaching profession, but Kingsley is authentically rotten. He is lazy, way out of touch with his field, hostile to students, and totally uncooperative toward his colleagues and the high school's administrators. He has been tenured for twelve years and has been acting this way for about eleven. He flaunts his behavior, occasionally referring to himself as "the Untouchable One." In addition to being mean, he is also smart.
>
> For reasons you can only guess at, Kingsley is carrying on some kind of personal vendetta against Ken, one of the best students in the senior class. Ken's father has been out of work for three years, yet Ken has overcome a great deal in that time. This year, as editor of the school newspaper, he took a dull, sports and soft-gossip paper and made it genuinely interesting, addressing issues of real concern to the entire high school population and doing it in a mature, evenhanded way. In the process, Ken seems to have gotten on Kingsley's wrong side, and Kingsley, his senior-year English teacher, is making him pay. Ken has told you, as his social studies teacher and friend, about what is going on in English. Besides regular ridicule and baiting, Kingsley has given him very low marks on writing assignments and term papers that you frankly think are across-the-board A work. As a result, Ken is running a low C in English, which has been his best subject, and this could mean that he will get no honors at graduation. Worse, it will probably bring his average down just enough so that he will lose the state scholarship he needs to go to college next year.
>
> You have tried to talk with Kingsley about the situation, but after smugly telling you about "a teacher's right and responsibility to give the grade he sees fit," he in effect told you to "butt out." In as professional a manner as possible, you have discussed the matter with the principal, but he has told you that although he sympathizes, his hands are tied. Finally, it dawns on you that there is something you can do. Ken is running a solid B-plus/A-minus in social studies as you enter the last weeks of the school year. If you were to change a few grades upward so he will receive an A-plus, it could compensate for the unjust grade he is receiving from Kingsley. It would also assure Ken of getting the state scholarship. You

would love to see Kingsley's face at graduation, too. What will you do?

Leonard Greenbaum, taking a course on introduction to teaching, was assigned to write a response to the "Righting Wrongs" case after the class had discussed the ethics of standards, expectations, and individualization. This is the paper he wrote.

Leonard Greenbaum
Righting Wrongs: How Far Can a Teacher Go?

Like most other concerned professionals, we as teachers will occasionally face difficult ethical dilemmas. The case described in "Righting Wrongs" presents me with two difficult options: on the one hand, I could give Ken the grade that he has earned and, in doing so, allow him to be victimized by another's injustice; on the other hand, I could raise Ken's grade in my class and possibly rescue his college career. The latter option would certainly appear to be the best thing for Ken. By raising his grade to an A+ I would be helping him to win the chance at higher education that he has legitimately earned. The only problem is that, in doing so, I would also be committing a serious breach of professional ethics — the same kind of breach, in fact, that I suspect Mr. Kingsley of committing. As a teacher I am charged with setting standards of performance for my class and evaluating each of my students consistently within those standards. Failure to uphold this responsibility hurts the school, the other students in the class, and, ultimately, the student who would appear to benefit from the inconsistency.

The central question in this example is this: does one person's unethical action justify another person's equally unethical reaction? I do not believe that it does. Mr. Kingsley has decided to ignore the standards of his profession and give an unfair grade. The grade is unfair, not because it harms a student's chance for college, but because it does not accurately reflect a student's performance. And if I were to give Ken a higher grade than he deserved, I would be making the very same error. The fact that a grade may help or hurt a student has nothing to do with its appropriateness. Teachers must take responsibility for evaluating a student's performance, and any grade that fails to do this — whether it works for or against the student's short-term interests — must be considered unfair.

Unfair grades, whether they help or hurt a student, damage the integrity of the teaching profession and work against all of the students in a class. Teachers have a great deal of leeway in setting grading criteria for their classes, but once these criteria have been set, they constitute an implicit contract with all of the students in the class. When I explain to my class what it takes to get a certain grade, I am promising my students two things: 1) that if they meet these standards, they will get the grade; and 2) that, if they don't, they won't. Every student who fails to make an A in my class has some reason for not doing so. Some of them come from difficult home situations, some have to work to afford college, and some just don't have the effort or the ability to meet my standards. As much as I care for each of my students, I cannot allow my concern to influence my grading. If I make an exception in favor of one student whose extraordinary circumstances have come to my attention, I am, in effect, unfairly punishing all of the students whose circumstances I do not know or have not considered.

But it is not just the other students in the class who are damaged by an unfair grade; ultimately, no student benefits by unearned special treatment. If I were to give Ken a grade that he knew he had not earned, I would teach him that the only way to combat one injustice is with another injustice — and I firmly believe that we should teach our students better than that. Students will remember the values we teach them long after they have forgotten the facts and formulas that they memorize for our tests. If I am honestly concerned about helping Ken get into college, I will gladly use all of the ethical means at my disposal to help him. I will talk to the principal, the superintendent, and the school board on his behalf, and I will even write a letter to his college committee explaining the circumstances. But I will not cheat for him. And I will not teach him that one lie cancels out another.

No matter how much I may wish for their success, it is not my responsibility as a teacher to win scholarships for my students. It is, however, my responsibility to evaluate them fairly and teach them the value of honesty. Ken's college application will contain four years of high school transcripts, his ACT or SAT scores, writing samples, extracurricular activities, and numerous other factors — not just two classes in his senior year.

> The fact that Mr. Kingsley has chosen to ignore
> fair grading should have no bearing on my decision to
> uphold it. In the final analysis, he must answer to his
> conscience about his grading procedures and I must an-
> swer to mine, and the fact that he has acted unethi-
> cally is not an excuse for me to do the same.

Thinking About Student Writing

1. How does Leonard Greenbaum rephrase or summarize the problem posed by the case study? How does his statement compare to the original?

2. What does Leonard Greenbaum state as the central question in this problem? How does the definition of this central question set up the terms for the analysis that follows? Do you agree that this is the central question?

3. What method does the author use to analyze the problem? What elements or factors does he examine in his analysis? What arguments does he use to support his analysis? What conclusions does he come to?

4. How successfully do you think Leonard Greenbaum has analyzed and solved this problem? Are there aspects he ignored or skipped? Does he analyze appropriate aspects of the issue? Are his conclusions appropriately supported?

Assignment

SOLVING CASE PROBLEMS

1. The following three cases are from a chapter on ethical decision making in a textbook on teaching. Read each of the following case problems concerning ethical dilemmas teachers face, and think through what you would do in each case. Then choose one on which you are going to develop a full solution. Use the various writing techniques mentioned in this chapter to think through your solution. Then write up your solution in a case report. You may add any details you feel necessary.

Case Number One: To Strike or Not to Strike

You are a tenured, first-grade teacher who has been teaching in an urban area for five years. Like many of the other teachers, you are frustrated and angry at the city's and the school board's treatment of teachers. You have seen oceans of the taxpayers' money going toward civic projects (a domed athletic stadium, a newly

renovated city hall and downtown area), while teachers' salaries and the conditions in the schools have deteriorated. Like your colleagues, you are desperate to get the attention of the citizens, so you support your professional association's decision to strike.

The teachers walked out three days ago, and gradually you are realizing that the real losers in this strike are your twenty-eight first-graders, many of whom come from disorganized, poverty-ridden homes. You believe that whereas many children in other parts of the city can probably afford to lose the time in school, yours cannot. They are at a critical point in their basic skills development. Also, they have just learned to settle down and really become engaged in their work. You are sure that prolonging the strike will mean disaster for the students. Then, on the strike's fourth day, several of your students' parents approach you, saying that they have secured a church basement and, if you will only come and teach, classes can go on there. However, such action may undermine the strike and will appear to be a betrayal of your coworkers. What do you do?

Case Number Two: A Big Deal or a Little Fudge?

Your community has recently been plagued by drugs, and increasingly they are coming into the schools. You are a sixth-grade teacher and there has only been sporadic evidence of drugs in your building. On the other hand, your principal has been making what seems to you a big deal out of very little in his crusade to stamp out drugs in "his elementary school." He has threatened the student body, first-graders through sixth-graders, in a special assembly about what will happen to them if they are caught with drugs of any kind. Most of your in-service training time this year has been taken up with the subject of drugs. You are concerned about the misuse of drugs in our society. However, you, like most of the other teachers, find the principal's preoccupation with drugs overzealous and slightly laughable, and you are afraid of what will happen to the first offender he catches.

Coming from lunch, you see Alan, one of your sixth-graders, showing two of his friends a plastic bag containing what appear to be three or four marijuana joints. Startled, but unsure that you have actually seen what he has, Alan shoves the bag into his pants pocket. You act as if nothing had happened and usher the boys into class. To gain time to think, you set the students to work on a composition.

Alan is a kid with a spotty record in the school. His family life is rumored to be rather chaotic, but he has behaved himself well in your class. You have never seen the slightest evidence that he has been high in school. Knowing Alan, you guess he got the dope from one of his brothers and brought it to school to impress his friends. On the other hand, you could be wrong, and the situation could be much more serious. One thing you are sure of is that if you report what you saw to the principal, as you are expected to, he will move in on Alan like a SWAT team. As you are mulling all this over, Alan and his friends are nervously watching you and anxiously looking back and forth at one another. Then, suddenly, Alan gets up, comes to your desk, and asks if he can go to the boy's room. What do you do?

Case Number Three: A Tale of Two Students

You enjoy teaching, but not testing. You are proctoring the final exam for your freshman algebra class. You like your students and know they have worked hard, but now they are struggling with and being stumped by your test questions, which you were sure were going to seem easy. It is a little hard, too, to see the students who have coasted all year gliding right through your exam as if it were so much whipped cream. In the midst of your musing, you glance across the room and see Floyd stuffing what looks like a crib sheet up his sleeve. He has been trouble all year. You are certain he copied 90 percent of his homework assignments on the bus; he was mouthy and disruptive in class, and you are fairly sure he cheated on two of the other major tests. Now, finally, you've got the drop on him.

As you move quickly across the room toward Floyd, you see that Judith is copying formulas from a ribbonlike spool of paper. You cannot believe it! Judith is your favorite student, and she recently was elected secretary of next year's sophomore class. She is a very conscientious, diligent girl who gets good grades, but not out of natural brilliance. She gets them the old-fashioned way — through hard work. She has very high standards and puts a good deal of pressure on herself. Although you cannot imagine what has led her to cheat, you suspect that the pressure for good grades she puts on herself is the root cause. You are standing in the middle of the room, trying to decide what to do.

2. The following case in business ethics is from the textbook for a management course. After reading and thinking through the case, write up a case report defining the problem, analyzing the situation, and presenting your solution.

The Scaffold Plank Incident

What had started as a typically slow February day in the lumber business had turned into a moral dilemma. With 12 inches of snow covering the ground, construction (and lumber shipments) had ground to a halt and on the 26th of the month, the company was still $5,000 below break-even point. In the three years since he had been in the business, Bob Hopkins knew that a losing February was nothing unusual, but the country seemed to be headed for a recession, and as usual, housing starts were leading the way into the abyss.

Bob had gone to work for a commercial bank immediately after college but soon found the bureaucracy to be overwhelming and his career progress appeared to be written in stone. At the same time he was considering changing jobs, one of his customers, John White, offered him a job at White Lumber Company. The job was as a "trader," a position that involved both buying and selling lumber. The compensation was incentive-based and there was no cap on how much a trader could earn. White Lumber, although small in size, was one of the bank's best accounts. John White was not only a director of the bank but one of the community's leading citizens.

It was a little after 8:00 A.M. when Bob received a call from Stan Parrish, the lumber buyer at Quality Lumber. Quality was one of White Lumber's best retail dealer accounts, and Bob and Stan had established a good relationship.

"Bob, I need a price and availability on 600 pieces of 3 × 12 Doug fir-rough-sawn — 2 & better grade — 16-feet long," said Stan, after exchanging the usual pleasantries.

"No problem, Stan. We could have those ready for pickup tomorrow and the price would be $470 per thousand board feet."

"The price sounds good, Bob. I'll probably be getting back to you this afternoon with a firm order," Stan replied.

Bob poured a third cup of coffee and mentally congratulated himself. Not bad, he thought — a two-truck order and a price that guaranteed full margin. It was only a half-hour later that Mike Fayerweather, his partner, asked Bob if he had gotten any inquiries on a truck of 16-foot scaffold plank. As Bob said he hadn't, alarm bells began to go off in his brain. While Stan had not said anything about scaffold plank, the similarities between the inquiries seemed to be more than coincidence.

While almost all lumber undergoes some sort of grading, the grading rules on scaffold plank were unusually restrictive. Scaffold planks are the wooden planks that are suspended between metal supports, often many stories above the ground. When you see painters and window-washers six stories in the air, they generally are standing on scaffold plank. The lumber had to be free of most of the natural defects found in ordinary construction lumber and had to have unusually high strength in flexing. Most people would not be able to tell certified scaffold plank from ordinary lumber, but it was covered by its own rules in the grading book, and if you were working ten stories above the ground, you definitely wanted to have certified scaffold plank underneath you. White Lumber did not carry scaffold plank, but its rough 3 × 12s certainly would fool all but the expertly trained eye.

At lunch, Bob discussed his concerns about the inquiry with Mike.

"Look, Bob, I just don't see where we have a problem. Stan didn't specify scaffold plank, and you didn't quote him on scaffold plank," observed Mike. "We aren't even certain that the order is for the same material."

"I know all that, Mike," said Bob, "but we both know that four inquiries with the same tally is just too big a coincidence, and three of those inquiries were for Paragraph 171 scaffold plank. It seems reasonable to assume that Stan's quotation is for the same stuff."

"Well, it's obvious that our construction lumber is a good deal cheaper than the certified plank. If Stan is quoting based on our 2 & better grade and the rest of his competition is quoting on scaffold plank, then he will certainly win the job," Mike said.

"Maybe I should call Stan back and get more information on the specifications of the job. It may turn out that this isn't a scaffold plank job, and all of these problems will just disappear."

The waitress slipped the check between the two lumbermen. "Well, that might not be such a great idea, Bob. First, Stan may be a little ticked off if you were suggesting he might be doing something unethical. It could blow the relations between our companies. Second, suppose he does say that the material is going to be used for scaffolding. We would no longer be able to say we didn't know what it was going to be used for, and our best legal defense is out the window. I'd advise against calling him."

Bob thought about discussing the situation with John White, but White was out of town. Also, White prided himself on giving his traders a great deal of autonomy. Going to White too often for answers to questions was perceived as showing a lack of initiative and responsibility.

Against Mike's earlier warnings, Bob called Stan after lunch and discovered to his dismay that the material was going to be used as scaffold plank.

"Listen, Bob, I've been trying to sell this account for three months and this is the first inquiry that I've had a chance on. This is really important to me personally and to my superiors here at Quality. With this sale, we could land this account."

"But, Stan, we both know that our material doesn't meet the specs for scaffold plank."

"I know, I know," said Stan, "but I'm not selling it to the customer as scaffold plank. It's just regular construction lumber as far as we are both concerned. That's how I've sold it, and that's what will show on the invoices. We're completely protected. Now just between you and me, the foreman on the job kinda winked at me and told me it was going to be scaffolding, but they're interested in keeping their costs down too. Also, they need this lumber by Friday, and there just isn't any scaffold plank in the local market."

"It just doesn't seem right to me," replied Bob.

"Look, I don't particularly like it, either. The actual specifications call for 2-inch thick material, but since it isn't actually scaffold plank, I'm going to order 3-inch planks. That is an extra inch of strength, and we both know that the load factors given in the engineering tables are too conservative to begin with. There's no chance that the material could fail in use. I happen to know that Haney Lumber is quoting a non-scaffold grade in a 2-inch material. If we don't grab this, someone else will and the material will be a lot worse than what we are going to supply."

When Bob continued to express hesitation, Stan said "I won't hear about the status of the order until tomorrow, but we both know that your material will do this job OK — scaffold plank or not. The next year or two in this business are going to be lean for everyone, and our job — yours and mine — is putting lumber on job sites, not debating how many angels can dance on the head of a pin. Now if Quality can't count on you doing your job as a supplier, there are plenty of other wholesalers calling here every day who want our business. You better decide if you are going to be one of the survivors or not! I'll talk to you in the morning, Bob."

The next morning, Bob found a note on his desk telling him to see John White ASAP. Bob entered John's oak-paneled office and described the conversation with Stan yesterday. John slid a company sales order across the desk, and Bob saw it was a sales order for the 3 × 12s to Quality Lumber. In the space for the salesman's name, Bob saw that John had filled in "Bob Hopkins." Barely able to control his anger, Bob said, "I don't want anything to do with this order. I thought White Lumber was an ethical company, and here we are doing the same thing that all the fly-by-nighters do," sputtered Bob in concluding his argument.

John White looked at Bob and calmly puffed on his pipe. "The first thing you better do, Bob, is to calm down and put away your righteous superiority for a moment. You can't make or understand a good decision when you are as lathered up as you are. You are beginning to sound like a religious nut. What makes you think that you have the monopoly on ethical behavior? You've been out of college for four or five years, while I've been making these decisions for forty years. If you go into the industry or the community and compare your reputation with mine, you'll find out that you aren't even in the same league."

Bob knew John White was right. He had, perhaps, overstated his case, and in doing so, sounded like a zealot. When he relaxed and felt as though he was once again capable of rational thought, he said, "We both know that this lumber is going to be used for a purpose for which it is probably not suitable. Granted, there is only a very small chance that it will fail, but I don't see how we can take that chance."

"Look, Bob, I've been in this business for a long time, and I've seen practices that would curl your hair. Undershipping (shipping 290 pieces when the order calls for 300), shipping material a grade below what was ordered, bribing building inspectors and receiving clerks, and so on. We don't do those things at my company."

"Don't we have a responsibility to our customers, though?" asked Bob.

"Of course we do, Bob, but we aren't policemen, either. Our job is to sell lumber that is up to specification. I can't and won't be responsible for how the lumber is used after it leaves our yard. Between the forest and final user, lumber may pass through a dozen transactions before it reaches the ultimate user. If we are to assume responsibility for every one of those transactions, we would probably have time to sell about four boards a year. We have to assume, just like every other business, that our suppliers and our customers are knowledgeable and will also act ethically. But whether they do or don't, it is not possible for us to be their keepers."

Bob interjected, "But we have reason to believe that this material will be used as scaffolding. I think we have an obligation to follow up on that information."

"Hold on, just a second, Bob. I told you once we are not the police. We don't even know who the final user is, so how are we going to follow up on this? If Stan is jerking us around, he certainly won't tell us. And even if we did know, what would we do? If we are going to do this consistently, that means we would have to ask every customer who the final end user is. Most of our customers would interpret that as us trying to bypass them in the distribution channel. They won't tell us, and I can't blame them. If we carry your argument to its final conclusion, we'll have to start taking depositions on every invoice we sell.

"In the Quality Lumber instance, we are selling material to the customer as specified by the customer, Stan at Quality Lumber. The invoice will be marked, 'This material is not suitable for use as scaffold plank.' Although I'm not a lawyer, I believe that we have fulfilled our legal obligation. We have a signed purchase order and are supplying lumber that meets the specifications. I know we have followed the practices that are customary in the industry. Finally, I believe that our material will be better than anything else that could conceivably go on the job. Right now, there is no 2-inch dense 171 scaffold plank in this market, so it is not as though a better grade could be supplied in the time allotted. I would argue that we are ethically obligated to supply this lumber. If anyone is ethically at fault, it is probably the purchasing agent who specified a material that is not available."

When Bob still appeared to be unconvinced, John White asked him, "What about the other people here at the company? You're acting as though you are the only person who has a stake in this. It may be easy for you to turn this order down — you've got a college degree and a lot of career options. But I have to worry about all of the people at this company. Steve out there on the forklift never finished high school. He's worked here thirty years and if he loses this job, he'll probably never find another one. Janet over in bookkeeping has a disabled husband. While I can't afford to pay her very much, our health insurance plan keeps their family together. With the bills her husband accumulates in a year, she could never get him on another group insurance plan if she lost this job.

"Bob, I'm not saying that we should do anything and then try to justify it, but business ethics in the real world is not the same thing you studied in the classroom. There it is easy to say, 'Oh, there is an ethical problem here. We better not do that.' In the classroom, you have nothing to lose by taking the morally superior ground. Out here, companies close, people lose their jobs, lives can be destroyed. To always say, 'No, we won't do that' is no better than having no ethics at all. Ethics involves making tough choices, weighing costs and benefits. There are no hard-and-fast answers in these cases. We just have to approach each situation individually."

As Bob left John's office, he was more confused than ever. When he first entered his office, he had every intention of quitting in moral indignation, but John's arguments had made a lot of sense to him, and he both trusted and respected John. After all, John White had a great deal more experience than he did and was highly respected in both the community and the lumber industry. Yet he was still uncomfortable with the decision. Was selling lumber to Quality merely a necessary adjustment of his ivory tower ethics to the real world of business? Or was it the first fork in the road to a destination he did not want to reach?

This case was prepared by Stewart C. Malone and Brad Brown, University of Virginia. This case was prepared as a basis for class discussion rather than to illustrate either effective or ineffective handling of administrative situations.

3. The following discussion and case is from a textbook used in courses on law and society, *The Legal Enforcement of Morality,* by Thomas Grey (New York: Knopf, 1983). Read the material and follow the instructions.

All societies of which there is any record have had customs concerning the treatment of the bodies of the dead. In some cases these customs have been central to basic values and symbols of a culture; for example, the burial customs of ancient Egypt have left to us the pyramids, the mummies, and the Book of the Dead. A basic document of Western civilization is Sophocles' *Antigone,* in which the center of the drama is the heroine's refusal to obey the king's command that her brother's body be left unburied. Such a command could not be lawful, she says; it would violate "the gods' unwritten and unfailing laws."

Our own culture has its own rules about the treatment of human remains, and many of these rules are enforced by law. The law governing the treatment of human remains rests on widespread horror at corpse desecration. Are these restrictions different in kind from the prohibitions of the culturally deviant sexual practices that have traditionally been called perverted and unnatural? Lord Devlin argued that sexual prohibitions have had and need no better justification than that they are supported by widespread "indignation, intolerance and disgust" and the prohibited acts. His critics have urged that irrational emotion, however intense, cannot support coercive law. Do the contemporary and historical restrictions on the use of cadavers that follow depend upon a Devlinite justification?

A.
The Law of Cadavers: Introduction and Historical Background

After reading this report, imagine that you work for Congressman Moss and try to state why this use of cadavers is morally offensive, while using them for dissection in anatomy classes is not.

The Department of Transportation has issued a stop-work order putting all work with the cadaver population into suspended animation.

The Department has been prompted to this exercise of its powers by Congressman John E. Moss of California. During the recent debate on air bags, Moss learned that dead bodies had been used to assess the protection afforded by the devices to passengers in car crashes.

He wrote to the Secretary of Transportation saying, in effect, that the Department had better have good reason for its use of cadavers because many would find such research morally offensive. Moss is chairman of the House sub-committee on oversight and investigations, and his opinions are of interest to the Department of Transportation.

Department officials soon ascertained that Moss himself was among those who found such research morally offensive. It was explained to Moss that almost all the cadavers so used come from the "willed body program," and that family permission is secured whenever possible. Crash testing requires an insignificant number of bodies compared with other uses, such as in medical schools. The information gained from cadavers is regarded as critical to the design of better dummies, and the present research program will be completed by 1980.

In full understanding of all these reasons, Moss replied to Secretary Brock Adams on 6 January, he nevertheless adhered to the view "that the use of human cadavers for vehicle safety research crudely violates fundamental notions of morality and human dignity, and must therefore permanently be stopped."

The Department issued 90-day stop-work orders to its six contractors in mid-November, and the ban is being continued by mutual agreement until 1 July, when a review of policy will have been completed. Some observers believe the Department may just be trying to wait Moss out — he has announced that he is retiring at the end of this session — but others say that Joan Claybrook, the new head of the National Highway Traffic Safety Administration, is interested in a serious review. The issue is not likely to become a political bandwagon: most congressmen seem interested in keeping as far away from it as they can.

One research contractor is at Wayne State University. Asked what he will use instead of cadavers in crash tests, chairman Albert I. King says "Living volunteers — but at lower g's." Wayne State uses about 10 to 20 cadavers a year in its crash test program.

Moss's inquiries elicited from the Department of Transportation the following official account of how cadaver crash testing came into being. Originally, it seems, crash studies were performed on "a dummy representing a 50th percentile male." Unfortunately a court "found the dummy insufficiently objective as a test device." After further test and development, "the Hybrid II dummy was adopted . . . as the official measuring instrument." One feature lacked by the Hybrid II dummy was the characteristic known as "bio-fidelity." It behaved well in frontal crashes but failed to mimic human kinematics in side and rear crashes as well as in pedestrian impacts.

The search began for an advanced dummy. But design of a better dummy required comparison with the real thing. "Of all available surrogates for the human body, the cadaver possesses by far the greatest mechanical and geometrical similarity with the living person," the Department of Transportation explained to Moss. True, cadavers were of different shapes and sizes, but "the variability of the cadaver population accurately reflects the variability of the population of living humans which the safety standards are designed to protect." Not that cadavers are perfect: "It is generally recognized that a number of limitations surround using the cadaver as a surrogate for a living human being." Nonetheless, a prohibition of cadaver use for trauma research would set back progress toward these important ends many years into the future, the Department of Transportation concluded.

Moss read this document, but was not persuaded to the opposite view.

4. The following case is from a writing textbook, *Casebook Rhetoric*, by David Tedlock and Paul Jarvie (New York: Holt, Rinehart and Winston, 1981). Read the material and write one of the suggested assignments.

Marcia Johnson

Marcia Johnson sat alone in her room overlooking Commonwealth Avenue. She watched the traffic snarls, the buses coming and going, and the students rushing back and forth to the dorm. She was trying to review her situation and decide on her next move.

Marcia had just come from a meeting with Peter Wallace, instructor in biology and premedical advisor. Wallace's news had not been good. Marcia's grades did not seem strong enough, he said, to allow much hope that she would be accepted by a medical school. Her grade-point average was fair, but 60 percent of her freshman and sophomore grades were C's, and in that 60 percent were clustered most of her important premed courses.

"It's only the second semester of your sophomore year," Wallace had said. "Your record here at the university is not bad. You can easily change your major and do very well after you leave here in two years."

Wallace added that it was his definite opinion that Marcia should get out of premed now.

The Johnson Family

Marcia was the oldest of the three children of Dr. Samuel Johnson, a prominent surgeon. Dr. Johnson, chief of surgery at City Hospital and professor of surgery at the medical school, was the son of a heavy machinery operator. He had worked hard to get through his four years as an undergraduate and his four years at a major medical school, from which he graduated with distinction. He had once run the Boston Marathon (26 miles) in under three hours, at age 47. He prided himself on having brought his children up to believe that there was no such thing as failure.

It was no secret to Marcia's family and friends that her father wanted her to go to medical school. He had given several parties for her after her graduation from high school and at one had had the guests toast her as "the next Dr. Johnson." He was liberal in his financial and moral support and had tried to convince his daughter of the need to make her own decisions. Generally, he and Marcia got along well, and she considered him an even-tempered and reasonable father.

Marcia's Career

For Marcia, the news from her advisor was not unexpected. She felt that she was a dutiful daughter, and she had been working hard in her studies. She'd always assumed she was going to become an M.D., but lately her view of herself had begun to change. For example, she had received high praise for a biomedical engineering paper she'd written this year (she'd taken the course as an elective), and more than one of her instructors had pointed out that math and physics were her strong points. In fact, most of the A's and B's she had received at her university were in these subjects. Also, she had found it easier to concentrate on math, physics, and engineering courses. All in all, although she was a little scared at the change in her attitude, she was pleased to think that she was getting a clearer idea of what she wanted to do with her life.

Last week Marcia had written to Susan Wilson, her closest high school friend and a premed student at a different university, outlining her feelings:

> I really think I have more ability as an engineer or physicist than as a doctor or biologist — and besides, I like working with machines and numbers a lot better than I ever thought I would. But I'm not sure that getting out of

premed is the best thing to do because you know Dad's going to be mad as hell — did I tell you he got me a summer job at the hospital??? — and I don't have any idea how to tell him so he'll understand.

Suggested Discussion Questions

1. What is the problem in this case?

2. What should Marcia do? Why?

3. How will Marcia's father react to what she tells him?

4. How much does Marcia's father know about how she is doing?

Suggested Assignments

1. You are Marcia Johnson. Write your father a letter in which you explain your situation, but first:

   a. Write out answers to the general questions you should ask yourself about any reader.

   b. What special characteristics, as a reader, does Dr. Johnson have? (List each characteristic separately.)

   c. For each characteristic you can identify, state how that trait is relevant to your writing situation.

   d. List the questions you believe your father (Dr. Johnson) will have in mind as he reads your letter.

2. Select a writing situation in which you have to tell your reader something unexpected (your parents about your sudden marriage, your roommate that you are moving out, your boyfriend, girlfriend, lover, or spouse that you aren't going to see him or her anymore).

   a. Identify your reader.

   b. Write out answers to the general questions you should ask yourself about any reader.

   c. List your reader's characteristics.

   d. State whether and how these characteristics are relevant to your writing situation.

   e. List the questions you believe your readers will have in mind as they read your letter.

3. Assume you are Susan Wilson, Marcia's friend. Complete an audience analysis for Marcia and write her a letter telling her what you think she should do.

4. Write an essay to any student who has read about the Marcia Johnson case. State what you think Marcia should do, and why. Complete an audience analysis for a general, unknown reader.

5. Analyze the factors that should (or, in reality, *do*) go into a student's choice of a major. Don't restrict yourself to your own decision: "I chose art education because I've always liked to draw . . ." Make your analysis useful to readers of the brochure provided for those interested in attending your college or university.

6. Write an essay suitable for a family magazine. Discuss the parents' role in decisions such as a student's choice of college, major, future occupation, and so forth.

5. Using the principles presented in this book, write a case report describing the writing problem presented in another course, your analysis of the situation, and your plan for a solution.

6. Using concepts and principles from a class in sociology, psychology, political science, business, or some other appropriate subject, write a case report about a problem in some school, community, business, political, or government organization with which you are familiar. Describe the problem, analyze the situation, and present your solution.

7. Through interviews and readings, identify the kinds of problems that typically have to be solved in a profession or career you are thinking of pursuing. Then write an essay describing the kinds of challenges people in that profession or career must regularly address, how they address these challenges, the resources that they use, and the form in which their solution or response is typically presented. This essay will be a general description of the problem-solving practices of that profession.

Getting Involved Electronically

Many areas of study and practical work have simulation programs that use the computer environment to create real-seeming situations for you to respond to. These programs range from simulations of the stock market's response to various economic factors to simulations of climate change due to atmospheric pollution. Locate a problem simulation program for some area that interests you and work with it for a while. Then write a description of the kinds of problems it poses for you to solve and the kinds of thinking you need to do to solve those problems.

15

Arguing Your Case

AIMS OF THE CHAPTER

As you learn to synthesize facts and ideas, analyze problems, do research, and think through problems and cases, you will become involved with the issues you examine and more committed to your conclusions. This chapter provides guidance on how to support your conclusions through argument. Argument helps everyone come to a better understanding, even when some disagreement remains after all sides have been heard.

KEY POINTS

1. Often people who think much about the subjects they study disagree with each other. Argument helps them compare and evaluate their conflicting views.

2. In academic argument you present all the reasons and evidence that support your view while still respecting alternative views.

3. In developing an argument paper, you decide what kind of argument you want to make, how your view differs from those your readers might hold, how you can move the readers from their position to yours, and the resources you have available to help them see the value of your position.

4. In presenting your argument, you assert your own position and your reasons clearly, but in a way that both acknowledges and connects with your opponents' views.

QUESTIONS TO THINK ABOUT

■ Have you ever avoided stating your opinion because you felt that you couldn't make yourself understood or couldn't develop a strong enough argument to make the other person accept your position?

- Have you ever gotten into a disagreement with a classmate or an instructor? What did you learn from the disagreement? Did you feel you were able to express your ideas well enough so that others could understand what you were saying and why, so that they took your argument seriously? To what extent did you feel that your arguments influenced them?

- On the other hand, did the disagreement simply come to a dead end, with neither side learning from the other or fully understanding the other's position? Why do you think that happened? How could the interaction have been changed to have a more satisfying outcome?

- When have you been persuaded by another's argument? What do you think caused you to see the validity of the other person's position?

- What ideas have you been developing that might put you at odds with some of your classmates, teachers, or members of your community? Who would you like to convince of your new ideas? Why?

✆✍ Plenty to Say

In the previous chapters of this book we have been working on many kinds of statements that allow you to participate in academic life:

- The kinds of statements that allow you to deploy the material taught in lectures and textbooks (Chapters 5 and 6).

- The kinds of statements that bring in your own experiences and thoughts in relation to the concerns of the course (Chapter 4).

- The kinds of statements that enable you to apply what you are learning to real situations in the world and analyze them (Chapters 7, 8, and 9).

- The kinds of statements that allow you to report the results of your own investigations back into the class (Chapters 10, 11, and 12).

- The kinds of statements that embody your own way of putting complex ideas together (Chapter 13).

- The kinds of statements that present your solutions to problems (Chapter 14).

As you gain skill and confidence in these kinds of statements, you will find that you have much to say. You will have your own way of seeing and talking about things that are important and real to you, as well as many substantial ways of contributing to discussions in the classroom, in discussion groups, and in cafeterias.

Of course, skill in the kinds of statements we have worked on in the book should have a direct effect on your grades — after all, you should be rewarded for being able to produce the kinds of writing instructors assign. However, as you are able to speak with clarity and confidence about things you know and think and perceive, you will feel the power of a more substantial reward — being able to share knowledge, explorations, and thinking with other people who are learning, exploring, and thinking.

As you enter into these conversations, you will be building ideas, images, visions, and plans in your areas of interest and concern. Finding that other people understand what you are working on and thinking about will give your thinking energy and confidence. Even more, finding people who have been thinking along lines similar to you will confirm to you that something important is to be found in the direction you are going. The conversation becomes even more pleasurable when you discover that others are influenced by your comments.

✺ Complexity of Beliefs

Unfortunately, as you get caught up in your own new ideas and want to share them, you will find that many other people are doing the same. They draw on different experiences and skills, put together different pieces of information, investigate different areas, and develop different concepts.

These other people, busy at looking at what interests them, won't see what you see. They may not even be aware of the kind of thing you are trying to show them. The more alive the learning environment is at your college — the more students bring richer resources to bear on the problems and issues of the classroom — the more different ideas and perspectives people will develop. Moreover, the more people have ideas and information of their own, the more likely they are to resist what you say, for they will have a stake in their own ideas. They will have a standpoint from which to evaluate, criticize, and counter yours.

Professionals in any field often do not see eye to eye on crucial issues, even in areas where there are agreed-upon principles, limited facts, and specific procedures. Even though mathematicians may agree on many things, they hardly think alike — each has picked a personal set of problems to work on, and each has his or her own way of trying to solve them. Mathematicians do not find it easy to convince other mathematicians of a new proof for a theorem. Other mathematicians work very hard from all their perspectives to find flaws, and each has powerful tools for finding them.

Of course, some truths are accepted as part of agreed-upon knowledge and principles. On many standard issues and problems, almost all professionals agree. But such problems are not worth discussing because the answer is obvious: Give the patient penicillin and send them home; file the deed with the county and collect your fee. Those things that are worth discussing are open problems that people are trying to solve, new ways of looking at something, or a confusing turn of events. In trying to come to terms with the uncertain, people will see different things, apply different tools, and

Calvin and Hobbes   by Bill Watterson

work in different directions. When issues are interesting, people tend to disagree.

In order to be heard in this world of strong and conflicting ideas, you need to present your thoughts clearly and forcefully. To participate in the discussion, you need to know how to argue for your ideas.

∽∾ USEFUL CONCEPTS FROM RHETORIC

Logos, Ethos, and Pathos

Aristotle, in his *Rhetoric,* identifies three aspects of making an argument:

■ *Reasoning, logic, and evidence presented in the text.* For such appeals to the reason, we use the Greek term *logos.* Much of academic argument relies on logos, and much of this book has been devoted to developing the ability to present and analyze facts in extended statements.

■ *The character and trustworthiness of the speaker.* The more we see a speaker as knowledgeable, careful, honest, well-intentioned, and intelligent, the more we are likely to accept what the speaker says, whereas we may be more quick to criticize, find flaws, or otherwise discount the words of someone we suspect isn't knowledgeable, careful, reliable, or truthful or who may be ill-willed and hostile to our interests. The Greek term for the trustworthiness of the speaker is *ethos,* from which we get our terms *ethics* and *ethical.* Academic argument cannot totally depend on ethos, for people on all sides of an issue may be intelligent, careful, knowledgeable, and honest; nonetheless, a failure of ethos is likely to make it hard for people to take seriously the logos of your argument. If you are not careful with the facts, make errors of reasoning, or show an aggressive hostility to opposing opinions, readers may doubt your trustworthiness and may be predisposed to treat the logic of your argument with skepticism.

■ *The feelings of the audience.* This emotional part of the argument is called in Greek *pathos.* We often associate emotion with advertising and political movements, for we often think that emotions cloud reason and judgment and therefore are the enemy of reasonable argument. However, many emotions are perfectly consistent with reason — such as a passion for truth, a distaste for unsupported opinions, and professional pride — and reasonable arguments could not be carried out without them. Any argument that asks people to give up their professional pride, their commitment to detailed evidence, or their loyalty to specific sets of ideas developed over the history of their discipline is likely to have rough going. The more we can draw on the strong attachment professionals have for certain kinds of reasoning and investigation, the more likely they are to take our arguments seriously.

EXAMINING ACADEMIC ARGUMENTS

In a subject area of interest to you, identify a recent area of controversy. Locate several articles presenting serious arguments on various sides of the issue. Examine how each article defines the point at issue, identify the position taken in the article, and explain how that position relates to the arguments made by others. What kinds of arguments does each article make for its own position and against alternatives? What kinds of evidence or support are used? What is the attitude or tone taken toward alternative views? What are the standards of mutual respect and decorum? Which kinds of arguments seem to be most effective and persuasive?

From your examination of these examples, describe in several pages what you find about how controversy is conducted in your field. Compare your findings in a discussion with classmates who have been looking at other examples from either your subject area or other areas.

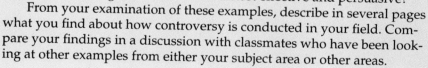

 ## Arguing for Ideas

Arguing for one's ideas in an academic context means presenting your ideas clearly and completely, presenting the most persuasive reasoning and evidence that could lead to your conclusions, and showing the advantage of your view over others'. It does not mean trying to blow opponents away, disregarding their ideas, and dismissing their evidence.

Respect for the ideas of others is not just a matter of politeness. If you are to influence others who have spent time, energy, and serious work developing their own views, it will help you to take those views seriously. Most obviously, you need to understand those views because you need to help them see how your ideas fit or clash with theirs, and then move them from their position to yours. Another reason is that they may have seen something you haven't. Doctors working together in trying to determine a diagnosis may each be convinced of their own view, but each would do well to listen carefully to what the others have to say.

This is where academic and professional argument may differ from other kinds of argument, such as in the political sphere or in commercial advertising. In the political sphere (as opposed to policy discussion, which under the best circumstances may be more like academic and professional argument), you may be looking for a quick win — getting someone's vote for the election just a few days away or getting someone to write a contribution check on the spot. Even if you want voters to develop a long-term belief and commitment to your position, you may wish to work more on their emotions, interests, and self-identity rather than on a careful consideration of the alternative views.

In advertising you want to get consumers to purchase your product or just to remember its name. What consumers believe may not be nearly so important as that they purchase a product or that they wind up carrying a name and a feeling around in their head. Persuading others doesn't necessarily mean respecting or taking them seriously. At times, being less than serious is the right way to go. How else should one sell perfumes and colognes except through fantasies and desires, and might not life be a little more fun for the romantic world evoked?

But academic and professional argument is a way to carry on a serious discussion to come to the best understanding of a phenomenon or the wisest policy or the best bridge design. To do this everyone needs to make his or her wisdom as clear and forceful as possible, identifying all the reasons and evidence that support that wisdom. This cannot be done at the expense of the seriousness of everyone else's proposal.

IDENTIFYING POINTS FOR ARGUMENTS

Review the papers you have written for this term. On a sheet of paper list all the claims you have made (or controversial conclusions you have reached) in those papers. Of all those claims, select the three that might appear most controversial to your classmates, members of your family, one of your former high school teachers, one of your current professors, or some other audience. For each of those three, write a brief informal paragraph explaining who would disagree with you and why.

USEFUL CONCEPTS FROM RHETORIC

Identification

The American rhetorician Kenneth Burke pointed out that one of the deepest tools we have to influence others is not to oppose their arguments, but to get others to identify themselves with us and our arguments. In the most basic sense, rhetorical identification occurs whenever a rhetor (a speaker or writer) identifies his or her interests with those of a reader. Identification encourages audiences to move beyond existing points of agreement to accept new ideas that are made to seem part of the same identity. If, for example, a speaker is talking to a liberal, feminist group about the dangers of pornography, she might identify the spread of pornographic images with rape, sexual abuse, and the exploitation of women. However, the same speaker speaking to a Fundamentalist Christian audience might emphasize the immorality and spiritual degradation that pornography causes and compare it to the evils of Sodom and Gomorrah. In each case, the speaker would be trying to influence others by identifying their interests with her own agenda.

Advertisers regularly engage in this kind of identification. When a potato chip company uses a popular athlete to endorse its product, it is attempting to create an identification between a product and a popular personality. This strategy relies on the fact that we already identify with the sports and entertainment figure because of the emotions we feel as we watch that figure perform.

For Kenneth Burke, however, identification means more than just using someone else's concerns or feelings as a rhetorical ploy. This, Burke insists, is "false identification." True identification occurs when people find areas where their values and perceptions honestly intersect, and then use those areas as the basis for genuine cooperation and compromise. Human interaction for Burke consists of a series of *identifications* (areas of common interest) and a series of *divisions* (areas of conflicting interest). In fact, the two exist on the same ground. Where there are no common interests or assumptions at all, then neither division nor identification can take place, since even disagreeing with someone requires that we have enough common ground upon which to argue.

As an example of the division/identification phenomenon, consider the question of a hypothetical tax increase. On one side, you may have administrators and legislators insisting that an increase in income taxes would sharply decrease disposable incomes and would therefore slow down the economy and lead us into a recession. On the other hand, there may be those who argue that, unless taxes are raised to eliminate the national debt, our debt payments will take up an increasing amount of our money and the economy will suffer. From one perspective, this represents a sharp *division* between opposing sides. From another perspective, though, both sides acknowledge the value of a strong economy and the necessity of government action to ensure economic growth. All of the parties will have to agree on these points, or there will be no sense in having the argument. The very grounds of disagreement supply a strong *identification* between the two sides. If the opposing sides work with these areas of identification, they may be able to arrive at a working compromise that allows them to cooperate toward the goals they share.

The epigraph of Burke's *Grammar of Motives* reads, in Latin, *ad bellum purificandum*, or "toward the purification of war." This motto reflects Burke's belief that we can never eliminate conflict and division from human interaction. We can, however, "purify" conflict by using rhetoric, instead of violence, to carry out our battles, and we can recognize that, while conflict is inherent in human relationships, identification is inherent in human conflict. The key to the purification of war, so central to Burke's twentieth-century rhetoric, is to recognize that disagreement creates the possibility for agreement and that every division that creates conflict between people also presupposes a common ground upon which we can mediate our differences and begin to cooperate and coexist.

Kenneth Burke, *A Grammar of Motives*, University of California at Berkeley Press, 1969. Kenneth Burke, *A Rhetoric of Motives*, New York, Prentice Hall, 1952.

❧ Building an Idea into an Argument

Assuming you have developed a way of viewing things that you want to share with others, how can you build an argument that presents your ideas in the clearest and strongest light? You begin by thinking through some underlying issues.

1. *State what you want others to see.*   As you develop your argument, you may refocus, develop, expand, or otherwise modify the claim that you want to make, but knowing from the beginning what you want others to see will keep you on track. State that claim in a single sentence. Such a sentence can form the core of your argument, with the rest of your essay expanding outward from it but always connecting back to it.

Early in the writing process you can jot down some brief notes to yourself or keep a discovery journal as you start to put your thoughts together. Then as you start to define what your position is, you become more precise about the nature of your claim, how it adds to or is different from the position of others, and what you might have to do to help them see things your way. The following considerations will help you define your task further.

2. *Identify what kind of argument or claim you want to make.*   Each kind of argument requires its own kind of support and elaboration. The following are typical kinds of argument:

a. *Arguments over definition.*   Often whether an event fits the definition of one category or another is important: Was Smith's action a crime or not a crime? Was it murder or manslaughter? But even in cases where terms do not identify distinct categories into which everything must be pigeonholed, as in law, it is often important to know what something is, how it should be identified and described. Is the change in prices a random fluctuation or an indicator of an economic downturn? In this kind of argument you establish what categories might be possible ways to describe the event or phenomenon you are trying to define and what criteria would help you select among categories or support identification for a particular category. Then you show how the event or phenomenon fits the definitional criteria.

b. *Argument over cause.*   In this kind of argument you show how one situation is transformed into another. Moreover, you may need to isolate a specific factor, force, or sequence of events as being responsible for bringing about the change. The most effective way to make such an argument is by explaining a mechanism that could bring about the change and then providing evidence that that was indeed the mechanism. One of the most persuasive findings in the history of neurobiology occurred when the specific chemical mechanism by which an opiate binds to a nerve was identified and chemical evidence was presented to show that this was the process that indeed occurred.

A less forceful method of demonstrating causality is to show a regular pattern of association where event A always seems to lead to situation B. This is a weaker form of argument, because the association could be based on an entirely different third factor. For example, in economics increasing unemployment is often associated with increased inflation; with this belief in mind government policies often slow down inflation if unemployment increases. However, this association is far from a direct cause. High employment may tend to increase spending, and that spending may increase inflation. Or the security of low unemployment may alleviate the anxieties that cause people to save, and that decrease in saving may make less capital available, thereby driving up interest rates and increasing inflation. If either of those is the case, one might adopt policies to hold spending down and keep savings up, even under conditions of low unemployment. Or both high employment and inflation may be caused by a third factor, such as the introduction of new kinds of products that spark demand.

Weakest of all is an argument by analogy. If we agree on the cause of one simpler, less controversial event, we can by analogy make a causal association in a more complex and less certain set of events. But such analogies are only suggestive and may not accurately tell you what is going on in the new situation. For example, it is now widely recognized that the total centralization of policymaking in Soviet Russia led to great inefficiency and lack of motivation at the local level. Is it accurate, however, to argue by analogy that every centralized policy in the United States inevitably leads to inefficiency and lack of motivation, and that all decisions should be made only locally?

   c. *Argument over evaluation.*   Whether something is to be considered good or bad depends on what you are evaluating it for. One car may be comfortable on long highway trips but may not handle well in poor weather. So evaluative arguments always address the purpose of the evaluation. They ask, "Good or bad — for what?" Then you establish the criteria that will help you determine whether it is good or bad. Finally, you provide the evidence that indicates how well the object matches the criteria. All three of these stages of the argument — the purposes of evaluation, the criteria, and the evidence matching the criteria — are open to dispute and so must be presented persuasively.

   d. *Argument over policy.*   In this kind of argument you are trying to establish the wisest course of action. First you establish that there is a need for some action or change. This usually requires some statement of the current situation that reveals some problem or threat that needs to be addressed. Then you identify the goal any solution or action must achieve to be considered successful. This sets the stage for your plan and its justification. In justifying your plan, you usually provide evidence of the plan's likely effectiveness; a projection of the cost in time, money, or trouble; and a comparison to alternative solutions. Only if your audience accepts the need you identify and then accepts that your proposal meets the need better than alternatives and is not more trouble and expense than it is worth will they be likely to pursue your line of action.

   3. *Think about the situation* that brought you to your insight and the situation that makes you want to address your readers. Sometimes these may be the same. For example, in political science, your professor may assign all the students to predict the party alignment of American voters over the next ten years; the student papers would then be discussed in class. Here your thoughts come to you as part of the discussion in which you will have to argue for your ideas.

   On the other hand, your ideas about party politics may have developed through your work on campaigns outside of class. This background may or may not be relevant if you are asked to write a paper for the class. You may need to take a stance of a disengaged political scientist not caught up in pressing power struggles, or your hands-on experience may give you the credibility of someone who knows politics from the inside. (See the discussion of rhetorical situation on pages 42–43.)

4. Define *what others might think and what questions they might raise* so that you know what issues and points of view you need to address as well as what aspects of their beliefs and knowledge you can use to help make your own point. Think about *those points where your positions meet with or conflict with other views.* (See the discussion of the meeting point or stasis of an argument on page 302.)

In identifying those specific points where you suspect that people may question your argument and where some of your audience may directly oppose you, you can identify those issues you need to address to satisfy those who might have doubts and to counter strong arguments. For example, if in a communications class you are arguing that a recent series of television advertisements is employing a new visual technique, and if you know that your professor has been pointing out all term how most "new" techniques are usually adaptations of prior techniques, you will have to work hard to distinguish your technique from all similar techniques.

On the other hand, identifying points of *agreement* with your likely audience allows you to focus your attention on real points of contention. Even more, you can use points of agreement as foundations on which to build the more controversial parts of your argument. If your communications professor, despite her skepticism about novelty, has presented advertising as the sector of television most responsive to social change, you might be able to show how the technique you are examining is a creative response to recent social changes. (See the discussion of identification on pages 349–350).

5. Identify those *texts* you have all read or the lectures you have all heard that can serve as reference points in the argument. Those reference points present knowledge and ideas you can use because they are already part of the course discussion. Thus, if your psychology textbook examines in detail patterns and causes of human aggression, you can use its ideas and information as you build your own argument on why youth act more aggressively in some situations than in others. (See the discussion of intertextuality on pages 231–232.)

6. Identify those *resources, ideas, and methods* that make your thinking different from other people's. By identifying what has led you to see things differently from others, you will understand better what makes your argument different; moreover, you will have a better sense of what you might have to show readers so they can start to see things your way. For example, if your detailed knowledge about the history of the black baseball leagues gives you a different perspective on the way sports have been related to American politics, perhaps it may be useful to describe relevant moments in that history that will help others see the relationship between sports and politics that you perceive.

7. Identify *what in the readers' minds will have to be added to, changed, reversed, or otherwise modified* for them to accept your view. This is another way to think about the differences raised in the previous points. If you really want to change other people's minds, you have to understand how they think about things now and *what would have to change* for them to think about something in your terms. Then you can start to develop some strategy for moving their minds from one place to another. So if you want to argue that a plan to cut back on school breakfast programs might have unfortunate consequences that may not be immediately evident in dollars and cents, you may have to convince some of your readers that all interests and consequences are not directly expressed in economic terms. People who believe that the marketplace is the only useful way of working out conflicting interests may not see the point of your argument on school breakfasts until they first see that economic exchange may not be the full and adequate expression of social values. By examining what you will have to change, you will also locate the places in the thinking or commitments of your audience that you will have to touch. (See the discussion of common places below.)

8. Consider why it would *benefit* your readers to adopt your position or vision rather than stay with their own. Think about the *consequences* to the readers of accepting or not accepting your view. What do you hope would happen if your argument were persuasive? Are you attempting to resolve a long-standing problem or only adding a new bit of evidence? Are you attempting to overthrow a major theory or only suggesting that certain elements of that theory be expanded or reconsidered? Are you trying to open a new question up to discussion or are you trying to close off discussion?

9. Think about how you might want to *qualify your claims*. Are there any points about which you do not have certain arguments or where there are plausible alternative accounts? Is there good evidence or reason for some aspects of opposing points of view? The more you identify and honestly present the value of alternative views and the limitations of your own claims, the more precise and credible your argument becomes.

These considerations can be explored in notes or journals or by talking with other students. Not every point will be as useful for each case, but if you think about them you will have a much better view of what the discussion is about, what you need to accomplish, and what resources and obstacles you have in presenting your view.

✺✺ USEFUL CONCEPTS FROM RHETORIC

Common Places

Where do you look to find persuasive reasons to support your position? The reasons you find need to be recognizable and important to the people you hope to persuade. Your arguments need to touch the beliefs, knowledge, and commitments in their minds. They need to go literally to some *place* in their minds. Those persuasive mental places shared by many people are called the *common places* — the places of arguments that we share in common. They are also called *topics*, following the Greek word for place, *topus*.

We can understand how mental common places work by thinking about real places that people consider important. For example, if someone running for office promises to lower their taxes, she is in a sense taking the argument to the voters' bank accounts. If, however, her opponent states that tax cuts will make city life unbearable not just for the homeless and poor but for all people, she is taking the argument into the city streets. In a sense, then, the voters must balance their gain in one place against their loss in the other. The candidates may then also visit and argue in the opponent's place of argument, one claiming that tax cuts are the only path to the prosperity that will revive cities, and the other claiming that we will never have prosperity unless we make the city livable for all people.

Common places can also be more totally mental, identifying general mental strategies that might apply in any circumstance. These are places in logic, reasoning, or imagination, such as definition, comparison and contrast, analogy, or classification. Thus, in looking for arguments to support a candidate, you might look to see whether comparing your candidate with the other yields some strong points.

Strong arguments can also be found in the values, beliefs, and ideals of a community, in what is sometimes called *ideology*. Thus, if your audience comes from a community that values strong family cohesion, you might explain how your candidate or proposal will strengthen families and reward those people who maintain traditional families. If your audience values education and free inquiry, you might explain how your candidate or proposal will rely on and strengthen our systems of education and research.

Each area of activity also has special arguments that are regularly useful. In arguing for political candidates there are standard qualifications and criteria that people usually consider and that most campaigns address. The common places of political campaigns include such things as the candidate's honesty, experience in office, roots in the community, lack of obligation to special interests, toughness on crime, and leadership. Often campaigns will wind up going down one of these paths.

Disciplines and professional activities, too, have their special common places. In history, the strongest place to go with your argument is into a previously unexamined archive that provides documents that demonstrate your point. In literary studies, arguments frequently go to the details of the text you are discussing. In experimental psychology, arguments always lead to the laboratory. In contemporary medicine, few decisions are made without first visiting test results. In corporate life, people regularly look at the "bottom line" to clinch their arguments.

If you listen to the arguments people make in your field, you may be able to develop a fairly reliable and specific list of typical places where arguments in your field go. What issues and criteria are always invoked in support of an idea or proposal? If one person wants to counter an opposing view, what points of weakness will be attacked? Such a list of common places will give you a starting place to think about where you might take your arguments. The concept of common places helps you think about how your words tie in to many aspects of life — the interests people have, the beliefs they hold, the way their minds work, their professional commitments, and the ways in which they carry out their work.

✑ Writing the Essay of Argument

Arguments are carried on in very different ways in different disciplines and professions. Different kinds of claims are made to solve different kinds of questions or establish different kinds of knowledge. Arguing that a particular wing design is best for certain tasks is very different from claiming that the spread of the printing press had several consequences for intellectual life in sixteenth-century Europe. Both are different from arguing that one has identified the structure of a neuron. And even more different is an argument that a certain defendant be declared not guilty.

Each claim does a different kind of work, and each would be supported by different kinds of evidence, reasoning, and argument. The audiences for each kind of argument would have different concerns, know different things, and use different criteria. Each claim would be inserted into different universes of competing claims and consequences. So the best guide as you enter the world of claims is to pay attention to other arguments in the field. Look for examples and models that can help you see how arguments are framed in your field.

Remember that an argument is always addressed to specific people you hope to convince, so you must think about what questions and considerations they will raise, what issues they need to see addressed before they will be willing to go along with you, what alternatives they might entertain, and what criteria and knowledge they have. In academic and disciplinary arguments these considerations and criteria are often revealed in the journals, books, and reports that people in the field read and write for each other. People in a discipline are trained in a certain way of gathering evidence and thinking, and they hold themselves and others accountable to these disciplinary and professional practices. A lawyer who tries to convince other lawyers but refuses to pay attention to the standards of legal argument will have a hard time of it. So it is not surprising that a lawyer's argument will sound like it came from a lawyer. (See the discussion of topics on pages 354–356.)

No matter what professional standards, patterns, and practices your argument needs to follow, a few pieces of general advice can assist you in writing an effective argument.

1. *Define the point you want to make early in the essay.* Both your own energies and the energies of your reader are focused if they are directed to well-identified issues.

2. *Identify the importance of the argument.* If readers know what is at stake in your argument, they will be more likely to take it seriously. Readers may wonder why you are spending so much energy arguing over whether a fossil bone belongs to one species or another. But if the bone identification would place a species on a continent where it had not been observed before, or place it a hundred million years earlier than it had been observed, readers may start to see more at stake than haggling over a few bones. The stakes will increase further if you make clear that the evolutionary picture will change significantly if your identification is correct.

3. *Show how your claim fits in with other things that are known and believed in the field.* This demonstrates that you are competent and well informed in your area and that your argument will add to the shared wisdom of the field.

4. *Take the arguments of other people seriously.* This may mean specifically mentioning and addressing opposing points of view. If parts of your opponents' arguments make sense or are irrefutable to you, admit that, but then carefully identify your points of difference and offer reasons for your position.

5. *Use the kind of evidence accepted in the field, but whenever possible offer substantial evidence.* In every field there are many interesting and exciting ideas, often in conflict with each other. And there are many clever and even brilliant ways of elaborating those ideas. Nonetheless, although ideas by themselves may excite people, they do not in themselves offer good reasons why they and not the alternative exciting idea ought to be accepted. Most fields work on the principle that specific evidence, gathered in ways and according to standards appropriate to the field, are the best way to sort out competing ideas. It pays to do the necessary work to develop persuasive evidence. Your argument will be stronger for your going to the laboratory, doing a survey, or digging more deeply in the library archive.

6. *Make clear what new resources you bring to the discussion.* Arguments are more likely to be decided not by clever words, but by a totally new piece of the picture that makes everyone see the issue differently. A new theory, a new kind of telescope that makes more stars visible, a new experimental technique, or a newly discovered letter where a philosopher explains exactly what an idea means — these are the kinds of resources that make people change their minds. If you can make clear exactly what new thing you are adding to the discussion and how that new resource changes the picture, you may help people move beyond their current ways of seeing things.

7. *At the end explain the consequences of accepting your argument.* If others come to agree with you, what might they see and do as a result? What kinds of positions might they support? What kinds of other ideas gain strength or interest in relation to the ideas argued in your essay? What kinds of research might follow on your claims? This kind of discussion indicates the benefits and value of your view and also directs people to-

ward the kinds of actions that will help carry out your ideas. Ideas thrive only when people continue to use them.

♔✄ Sample Student Essay

The following essay is based on the selections in Chapter 13 on pages 307–315. The student, after viewing the complexity of the issue of intelligence testing, came to her own conclusions about the value of testing in education. Having come to this conclusion in the course of her analysis of the complex issue, she then wanted to argue her position in a more direct way. The following paper is the result.

Shana O'Malley
IQ Obsession Distorts Education

Throughout the 20th century, standardized IQ tests have become an important part of America's educational system. Intelligence tests are regularly used to counsel students in school and career choices, to give teachers a profile of their student bodies, and to place students with high IQs in special "gifted and talented" classes where they receive extra attention. Some scientists, such as Richard Herrnstein and Charles Murray in their 1994 bestseller The Bell Curve, believe that IQ scores actually do give an accurate picture of a person's "cognitive ability" (22) and should therefore be used by scientists and educators as an accurate measurement of intellectual ability. However, many more scientists, such as Harvard biologist Stephen Jay Gould, reject this view entirely and see the IQ score as nothing more than "the mismeasure of man." However, even if we do accept the view that IQ tests accurately measure some abstract quantity of intelligence, we should still be cautious about the importance they have been given in our nation's schools. Our society has made a commitment to attempt to provide a quality education for all of its citizens, and a person's testable cognitive ability should have no bearing whatsoever on this commitment.

The overriding danger of using IQ tests as the basis for any educational policy is that doing so creates a small class of students whose academic abilities are validated and encouraged, while creating an even larger class of students whose special talents are ig-

nored. Most psychologists agree that the IQ test measures <u>something</u>. At the very least, students who perform well on IQ tests are better under test conditions
at answering word-association questions and figuring out
cognitive puzzles than other students. However, there
is no reason to believe that, in an enlightened democracy, these abilities should be valued any higher than
other abilities. Many students who score average or low
on traditional IQ tests display enormous talents in
other areas, such as speech, music, art, mechanics, and
spatial relations. Schools should encourage all students in their respective talents, not just the few who
demonstrate the ability to solve abstract cognitive
problems in a standardized test.

One of the traditional justifications for using
IQ tests in elementary and secondary schools is that
they allow teachers and administrators to identify "ex-
ceptional" children and segregate them accordingly into
gifted and talented classes. Despite the fact that all
children have their own individual gifts and talents,
children are often assigned to these special classes
solely on the basis of their IQ score. Thus, students
who perform well on timed word-association tests qualify for special attention and extra funding, while all
other students who are equally but differently talented
do not. Such a practice violates the democratic principles of our society, since it uses taxpayer dollars to
encourage one small group of children who are labeled
"gifted" while doing nothing to encourage other students whose gifts cannot be measured by an IQ score.

But even when schools do not segregate students
on the basis of IQ, they do them a disservice by using
the tests as a basis for counseling and evaluation. In
the first place, students often learn their IQ scores
and use them as a basis for comparing themselves with
other students. Even more often, teachers and counselors, upon learning a student's intelligence quotient, treat students differently and allow this
abstract score to color their perception of the student's intelligence or potential for success. While
teachers do have the right and the responsibility to
evaluate students based on their concrete performance,
there is no justification for evaluating them on their
abstract reasoning capacity unless the course material
requires such skills. Standardized intelligence tests

create unnecessary categories that label some students as "superior" and others as "inferior" without any reference to effort, concrete ability, or actual performance.

In the preface to his ground-breaking book Frames of Mind, Howard Gardner writes that our current intelligence testing practices are "not sufficiently well honed to allow assessment of an individual's potentials or achievements in navigating the stars, mastering a foreign tongue, or composing with a computer" (4). The problem, he asserts, lies in the way that we think about intelligence. For Gardner, human intelligence is a broad spectrum that includes a number of different complex talents. It is this perspective, I believe, that our schools need to adopt. For nearly a century, we have valued a specific, narrowly defined cognitive ability as the true mark of intelligence, and this belief has led us to segregate our schoolchildren unfairly on the basis of a single test score.

Works Cited

Gardner, Howard. Frames of Mind. New York: Basic Books, 1983.
Gould, Stephen J. The Mismeasure of Man. New York: Norton, 1981.
Herrnstein, Richard, and Charles Murray. The Bell Curve. New York: Free Press, 1994.

Thinking About Student Writing

1. What is the issue that Shana O'Malley addresses in this essay? How does she use opposing views of other authors to frame the issue? How does the position she takes differ from the positions of the authors she refers to? How does the position she argues for reframe the issue from that argued by the other authors? Why does she reframe the issue in the way she does? How does the reframing help make her argument more credible?

2. What arguments does Shana O'Malley offer in support of her position? How does she elaborate her arguments?

3. How do Shana O'Malley's arguments join specifically with the views and motives of those who hold the opposite view? In what ways does she show she understands and respects those arguments? In what ways does she oppose them?

4. In the course of her argument, where does Shana O'Malley point out how people use IQ tests? Why does she think these are inappropriate uses? What kinds of tests would she allow and for what purposes? What arguments does she give for those tests? Why does she bring in those allowable tests as part of this argument?

5. What overall conclusions does Shana O'Malley come to? How well are these conclusions justified by her argument?

6. What is the overall structure of the argument in the essay? How does one point relate to the next? How do the levels of argument transform? How does the conclusion grow out of what has come before?

 **ssignments**

ARGUMENTATION

1. Choose one claim, statement, or conclusion you developed in response to one of the writing assignments this term which you think is controversial. In an essay, argue the value of this conclusion in order to convince those who might argue against you.

2. Consider the various statements you have heard or read this year in college, from instructors, from other students, or in textbooks. Choose the one statement with which you most disagree. Write an essay arguing either directly against this statement or in support of an opposite statement to convince either the person who made the statement or your classmates to adopt your view.

3. Read the following two statements that take different positions on the question of congressional term limitations. After class discussion, develop your own position on this controversial subject and argue for your position in an essay.

The simple, essential reason for congressional term limits is to unrig a rigged system, end automatic reelection, and make Congress mortal again.

    Many Americans cling to the now lost idea of the citizen-legislator. Term limits can't completely recreate this extinct creature. But it will take us a couple of places backward and away from the professional congressman-for-life. It will also allow more citizens to serve in Congress, and it could reduce some of the advantages of incumbency, even during the 12-year term.

    Predicting the inner workings of Congress is highly speculative, but, at the least, the seniority system will be truncated and weakened by term limits. At best, it may yield to another system

that could provide more equal opportunities for leadership for all members and less entrenched regionalism.

From Bill Frenzel, "Term Limits and the Immortal Congress," *The Brookings Review* Spring 1992: 18.

Would term limits increase the competitiveness of congressional elections? If more competitiveness means lower reelection rates for incumbents, the answer is clearly no. A term limit would very likely turn into a floor, with would-be candidates deferring their challenge and awaiting the involuntary retirement of the incumbent. If a norm of deference to the term-limited incumbent took root, elections would be contested only in open seats, and then only those not safe for one political party.

Indeed, there is little reason to think that congressional term limits would produce anything approaching a surge in high-quality, well-financed challengers, which is essential for increased competitiveness. More targeted interventions are required to produce that result.

From Thomas E. Mann, "The Wrong Medicine," *The Brookings Review* Spring 1992: 23.

4. Read the following two statements that take different positions on environmental protection. After class discussion, write an essay arguing your view on how far we should go in protecting the environment.

We have taken over this planet as if we owned it, and we call it progress because we think we are making it better, but in fact we are regressing. Species are dying and we seem not to realize that our life depends on theirs. Peter Raven, director of the Missouri Botanical Gardens in St. Louis, says that the destruction of species is more critical for the world than the greenhouse effect and ozone depletion, because it is moving faster and is inevitable. He predicts that over the next thirty years human beings will cause the extinction of a hundred species per day. For fifteen years, I traveled the world warning people about the medical and ecological consequences of nuclear war, not aware that life was already dying quietly and unobtrusively from man's ongoing activities. Now I see that the threat of species extinction is as serious as the threat of nuclear war.

From Helen Caldicott, "Species Extinction," in *If You Love This Planet* (New York: Norton, 1992): 95.

The view that the loss of a single species can have disastrous consequences represents a misguided notion about the significance of individual animal or plant categories. The Endangered Species Act assumes that preserving one species has enormous value or benefit. But this assumption is not warranted.

Suppose we lost a species. How devastating would that be? "Mass extinctions have been recorded since the dawn of paleontology," writes Harvard paleontologist Stephen Gould. These evolutionary disruptions delineated the major boundaries of geologic time. . . . There is a general agreement among scientists that today's species represent a small proportion of all those that have ever existed — probably less than one percent. This means that over 99 percent of all species ever living have become extinct.

From Michael Copeland, "No Red Squirrels? Mother Nature May Be Better Off," *Wall Street Journal* 7 June 1990: A1.

Getting Involved Electronically

For a controversial or political issue of interest to you, locate a World Wide Web home-page of some relevant organization or advocacy group. Examine how the page and associated materials make a case for one side of an issue. Then locate a home-page for an organization or advocacy group presenting an opposite view. Compare the argumentative strategy of the two sides.

Text Credits

Page 56: From W. Russel Neumann, Marion R. Just, and Ann N. Crigler, *Common Knowledge: News and the Construction of Political Meaning*, pp. 60–72. Reprinted by permission of the publisher. The University of Chicago Press.

Page 83: From *Hunger of Memory* by Richard Rodriguez. Reprinted by permission of David R. Godine, Publisher, Inc. Copyright © 1982 by Richard Rodriguez.

Page 85: Reprinted with permission of The Free Press, a division of Simon & Schuster from *Lives on the Boundary: The Struggles and Achievements of America's Underprepared* by Mike Rose. Copyright © 1989 by Mike Rose.

Page 87: Excerpt pp. 53–56 from *Dust Tracks on a Road* by Zora Neale Hurston. Copyright 1942 by Zora Neale Hurston. Copyright renewed 1970 by John C. Hurston. Reprinted by permission of HarperCollins Publishers, Inc.

Page 118: From Sydney Head and Christopher Sterling, *Broadcasting in America*, 7/e. Copyright © 1994 by Houghton Mifflin Company. Used by permission.

Page 128: From Dan O'Hair and Gustav Friedrich, *Strategic Communication*. Copyright © 1992 by Houghton Mifflin Company. Used by permission.

Page 197: "Take this Fish and Look at It," by Samuel H. Scudder from *The Critical Eye: Thematic Readings for Writings* by Sally T. Taylor, copyright © 1990 by Holt, Rinehart and Winston, Inc. Reprinted by permission of the publisher.

Page 270: From Raymond S. Nickerson and Marilyn Jager Adams, *Cognitive Psychology*, vol. 11, 1979. Copyright © 1979. Used by permission of Academic Press, Inc.

Page 310: Reprinted with the permission of The Free Press, a division of Simon & Schuster from *The Bellcurve: Intelligence and Class Structure in American Life* by Richard J. Herrnstein and Charles Murray. Copyright © 1994 by Richard J. Herrnstein and Charles Murray.

Page 313: Reprinted by permission of *The New Republic*, © 1994, The New Republic, Inc.

Page 319: From William Price and O.C. Ferrell, *Marketing*, 9/e. Copyright © 1995 by Houghton Mifflin Company. Used by permission.

Page 326: From Kevin Ryan and James Cooper, *Those Who Can, Teach*, 7/e. Copyright © 1995 by Houghton Mifflin Company. Used by permission.

Page 337: Reprinted with permission from N. Wade, "The Quick, The Dead, and the Cadaver Population," *Science*, 199:1420-1421, March 1978. Copyright © 1978 American Association for the Advancement of Science.

Page 339: Excerpts from *Casebook Rhetoric: A Problem-Solving Approach to Composition* by David Tedlock and Paul Jarvie, copyright © 1981 by Holt, Rinehart and Winston, Inc. Reprinted by permission of the publisher.

Photo and Cartoon Credits

Page 5: The Granger Collection

Page 8: Bettmann Archive

Page 10: Reuters/Corbis-Bettmann

Page 12: CALVIN AND HOBBES © 1996 Watterson. Dist. by Universal Press Syndicate. Reprinted with permission. All rights reserved.

Page 21: CALVIN AND HOBBES © 1996 Watterson. Dist. by Universal Press Syndicate. Reprinted with permission. All rights reserved.

Page 30: J. Langevin/Sygma

Page 36: Beringer/Dratch/The Image Works

Page 41: CALVIN AND HOBBES © 1996 Watterson. Dist. by Universal Press Syndicate. Reprinted with permission. All rights reserved.

Page 46: PEANUTS reprinted by permission of United Features Syndicate, Inc.

Page 59: Brad Markel/Gamma-Liaison

Page 75: DILBERT reprinted by permission of United Features Syndicate, Inc.

Page 77: Corbis/Bettmann

Page 87: The Granger Collection

Page 96: Reprinted from the Collections of the Library of Congress

Page 104: CLOSE TO HOME © 1994 John McPherson. Reprinted with permission of Universal Press Syndicate. All rights reserved.

Page 134: Ulf Andersen/Gamma-Liaison

Page 144: UPI/Corbis-Bettmann

Page 155: CALVIN AND HOBBES © 1996 Watterson. Dist. by Universal Press Syndicate. Reprinted with permission. All rights reserved.

READINGS INDEX